ENEMIES AMONG US

ENEMIES AMONG US

THE RELOCATION, INTERNMENT,
AND REPATRIATION OF GERMAN, ITALIAN,
AND JAPANESE AMERICANS
DURING THE SECOND WORLD WAR

JOHN E. SCHMITZ

University of Nebraska Press
LINCOLN

© 2021 by the Board of Regents of the University of Nebraska

All rights reserved

The University of Nebraska Press is part of a land-grant institution with campuses and programs on the past, present, and future homelands of the Pawnee, Ponca, Otoe-Missouria, Omaha, Dakota, Lakota, Kaw, Cheyenne, and Arapaho Peoples, as well as those of the relocated Ho-Chunk, Sac and Fox, and Iowa Peoples.

First Nebraska paperback printing: 2024

Library of Congress Cataloging-in-Publication Data
Names: Schmitz, John E., author.
Title: Enemies among us: the relocation, internment, and repatriation of German, Italian, and Japanese Americans during the Second World War / John E. Schmitz.
Other titles: Relocation, internment, and repatriation of German, Italian, and Japanese Americans during the Second World War
Description: Lincoln: University of Nebraska Press, [2021] | Includes bibliographical references and index.
Identifiers: LCCN 2020051335
ISBN 9781496224149 (hardback)
ISBN 9781496238870 (paperback)
ISBN 9781496227553 (epub)
ISBN 9781496227577 (pdf)
Subjects: LCSH: German Americans—Evacuation and relocation, 1941–1948. | Italian Americans—Evacuation and relocation, 1942. | Japanese Americans—Evacuation and relocation, 1942–1945. | Aliens—United States—History—20th century. | World War, 1939–1945—Evacuation of civilians—United States—Historiography. | World War, 1939–1945—Prisoners and prisons, American. | World War, 1939–1945—Concentration camps—United States. | World War, 1939–1945—Forced repatriation. | United States—Ethnic relations—History—20th century.
Classification: LCC D769.8.F7 G488 2021 | DDC 940.53/1773—dc23
LC record available at https://lccn.loc.gov/2020051335

Set in Minion Pro by Laura Buis.

"A welcome addition to literature on the treatment of enemy aliens in World War II."
—Fred L. Borch, *Journal of Military History*

"Highly recommended to anyone interested in the history of U.S. experience with civilian internees."
—Jean-Michel Turcotte, *H-War*

"Schmitz's in-depth study is a useful and much-needed beginning for a new direction in this period of America's wartime history."
—Steph Hinnershitz, *Southwestern Historical Quarterly*

"The breadth of *Enemies among Us* makes it well suited for inclusion in undergrad and graduate school courses in history, American studies, war studies, and international relations."
—Alan Rosenfeld, *Michigan War Studies Review*

"An indispensable resource for those seeking to comprehend how, during World War II, it came to be that 'Americans created, castigated, and then incarcerated alleged enemies; all this, despite lack of evidence, or worse, evidence to the contrary.'"
—William Issel, *California History*

"Schmitz's account does much to offer the well-demonstrated and lucid ground to demand that repeating this history would be a tragedy that leaves no one unscathed."
—Tyler Correia, *H-Socialisms*

"Schmitz's work untangles the psychological, political, social, and, yes, racial forces that culminated in a sad historical episode."
—Mark G. Brennan, *Chronicles Magazine*

"John Schmitz makes astute use of previously unused documents to weave together the internment and relocation story, the military situation abroad, and the machinations of American politicians struggling to master it all. *Enemies among Us* is a unique and important addition to our understanding of this sad episode."
—Stephen Fox, author of *Fear Itself: Inside the FBI Roundup of German Americans during World War II*

"This book sheds important light on little-remembered but undeniably significant episodes in twentieth-century history. By expanding our understanding of American detention, internment, and repatriation during World War II, John Schmitz exposes the dynamics that can lead to the mass violation of civil rights, even by otherwise well-intentioned policy makers and law enforcement officials. As much as a historical text, this work presents an important warning for our world today."
—**Bradley W. Hart**, author of *Hitler's American Friends: The Third Reich's Supporters in the United States*

"John Schmitz has accomplished something no other scholar has attempted: a comprehensive, thoroughly researched investigation of the wartime treatment of all three major national groups treated as 'enemy aliens' in the United States during World War II: Germans, Italians, and Japanese. The interpretive arguments are provocative [and] important."
—**Max Paul Friedman**, author of *Rethinking Anti-Americanism: The History of an Exceptional Concept in American Foreign Relations*

For my father, John A. Schmitz (1936–2020)

CONTENTS

List of Illustrations. ix
Preface xi
Acknowledgments. xiii
List of Abbreviations xv
Chronology of U.S. Relocation and Internment xvii

Introduction 1
1. Pejoratives, Precedents, and Prejudice. 13
2. Fifth-Column Fears and Foreign Challenges 36
3. Dire Preparations 64
4. The Fifth-Column Threat. 84
5. Pearl Harbor and the Home Front. 114
6. Defeats, Rumors, and Reactions 129
7. Dual-Coast Relocation and Nationwide Internment. . . . 167
8. Internment, Repatriation, and Exchange 206
9. Internment Camps and Relocation Centers 248
Conclusion. 289

Notes 293
Bibliography 347
Index 361

ILLUSTRATIONS

Following page 128

1. Fingerprinting a German American, 1917
2. Germans interned at Fort Douglas, Utah, ca. 1918
3. Australia registration of aliens notice, 1917
4. Adolf Max Schmitz's alien registration card, 1942
5. World War II poster warning of enemy agents, 1940–41
6. United States relocation centers and select internment camps map
7. War Relocation Authority centers map, 1942
8. War and Justice Departments internment camps map
9. Aerial view of Crystal City internment camp, ca. 1945–46
10. Drawing of Crystal City internment camp, 1945
11. Drawing of Fort Lincoln internment camp, ca. 1944
12. Crystal City musicians, ca. 1945
13. Crystal City band members, ca. 1945
14. German school students and teacher, ca. 1945
15. Crystal City classroom, ca. 1945
16. Crystal City, German school, ca. 1945

PREFACE

Growing up in Raleigh, North Carolina, I often told neighborhood kids about my father's internment, which I learned about by listening to his recollections of Camp Crystal City, Texas. He spent three years there, from age seven to ten, going to school, swimming, playing in the nearby orchards, and having many experiences typical of a child—minus the barbed wired, guard towers, and lack of freedom, which, thankfully, younger children are not able to comprehend fully. My father viewed the camp in a mainly positive light, although that changed over time. I remember my grandfather as being often sullen and bitter—it took me many years to understand why. My grandfather was thirty-five when he along with his wife and three children (a fourth child, Christa, would later be born in the camp's hospital) were interned, and he understood fully what the experience meant. Not only did he lose three years of freedom, his job, and many of his possessions, but he, and others, were warned by authorities to keep their wartime experience to themselves, lest their lives be made more "difficult." As I went to high school and then college, I wanted to know more about what happened to my father and his family, and why. This book reveals a great deal about what the American people, elected officials, and military did to those they feared and distrusted. As I write this, the country is again in crisis—once again innocent families are being ripped apart, children are forcibly put in cages, and countless numbers of people are being treated as less than human in part because of names and labels, many created and repeated by those with influential voices, including, sadly, the forty-fifth president. This book tells a still neglected tale, but it also reminds us of what can happen when fear leads to calling some among us enemies, or worse. It remains unknown how our nation will continue to act toward those whom it fears and labels as enemies among us. Often we hear that the past is prologue, that history repeats itself unless we learn its lessons—perhaps this is true, but until we start valuing all people equally and learn to temper our own insecurities, we are likely to perpetuate this vicious cycle. It was once said we should love our enemies, for where is the profit in loving only those who love us. Wise words.

ACKNOWLEDGMENTS

To write a book is neither an easy nor a solitary task. I am indebted to my mentors at American University, particularly Allan Lichtman, Peter Kuznick, and Robert Griffith, who urged me to broaden my previous work dealing with German American internment to include the experiences of Italian and Japanese Americans. The result was a far richer and more comprehensive study. I am indebted to Art Jacobs, a child internee at Crystal City who shared many dozens of primary sources and made me realize how many sources were as yet undiscovered. I am indebted to so many others, including the board of directors of the German American Internee Coalition and its current president, Karen Ebel (herself the daughter of an internee), who created the GAIC website, an online space where internees and their families can share their stories and increase awareness of internment. I would also like to thank the many archivists and scholars at the National Archives, the Library of Congress, and other repositories. I also wish to thank the editors at the University of Nebraska Press—Bridget Barry, Heather Stauffer, and Emily Wendell—who patiently and successfully guided me through many eddies en route to the copyediting phase. Finally, I wish to thank the countless teachers and other educators who encouraged me, from Mrs. Shepard, my kindergarten teacher, to my current colleagues at Northern Virginia Community College, Annandale Campus. While so many people helped me craft this book, the responsibility for any errors or shortcomings remain mine.

This book is dedicated to my father, John A. Schmitz, who, along with my grandparents Adolf and Margaret, Uncle Bill, and

Aunts Louise and Christa, endured internment at Camp Crystal City, Texas, from July 1943 to July 1946 (Christa was born in the camp hospital in September 1944). My father's family story was the impetus for my initial investigation into this subject, and it remains to this day a cautionary tale about the dangers of fear and intolerance in a democracy under stress, as well as the triumphs of ordinary people in extraordinary times.

ABBREVIATIONS

AECU   Alien Enemy Control Unit
CAD   Civil Affairs Division
CDI   Custodial Detention Index
CPD   Emergency Advisory Committee for Political Defense
CWRIC Commission on Wartime Internment and Relocation of Civilians
EDC   Eastern Defense Command
HUAC   House Un-American Activities Committee
INS   Immigration and Naturalization Service
MID   Military Intelligence Division (Army G-2)
ONI   Office of Naval Intelligence
OSS   Office of Strategic Services
OWI   Office of War Information
PMG   Provost Marshal General
SDU   Special Defense Unit
SWPD   Special War Problems Division
SWPU   Special War Policies Unit
WCCA   Wartime Civil Control Administration
WDC   Western Defense Command
WRA   War Relocation Authority

CHRONOLOGY OF U.S. RELOCATION AND INTERNMENT

1930

May — House Resolution 220 creates a special committee to investigate domestic communist activities and propaganda.

1933

January–May — Hitler and FDR come to power, Japan leaves the League of Nations, and Goebbels heads his newly created Propaganda Ministry (PROMI).

September — PROMI issues a master plan for propaganda in the Western Hemisphere.

October — Germany leaves the League of Nations while continuing to foster global German unity.

1934

January 3 — Representative Samuel Dickstein introduces House Resolution 198 to investigate Nazi propaganda activities.

February — Auslandsorganisation is established to promote Nazism worldwide.

March 20 — Passage of HR 198 creates the McCormack-Dickstein Committee, named for its chair and vice chair, John W. McCormack and Samuel Dickstein. The committee investigates the

	Friends of New Germany, Nazi propaganda, and German activities.
May 8	J. Edgar Hoover's bureau (officially named the FBI in March 1935) secretly begins investigating American Nazis.
1935	
February 2	The U.S. becomes one of the key targets of the German secret service's worldwide operations.
February 15	The McCormack-Dickstein Committee's report fuels suspicion of German Americans and strains relations between Germany and the United States.
1936	
March 7	Germany denounces the Locarno Treaty and reoccupies the Rhineland.
April	Fritz Kuhn's Bund declares the Third Reich the true Germany.
July 18	Spanish Civil War begins. The term *fifth column* originates.
August 28	Hoover creates a "suspect list," later the Custodial Detention Index (CDI), which includes Germans, Italians, and Japanese, many of whom the FBI arrests once the nation goes to war.
1937	
January	Senator Dickstein seeks approval for a new investigation of American Nazism.
June	Representative Martin Dies Jr. requests $100,000 to investigate subversive influences.
October 5	FDR's "Quarantine Speech" notes the "epidemic of world lawlessness."
1938	
March 11–12	Germany annexes Austria.

May	New investigations of Americans begin as House Resolution 282 officially establishes the House Un-American Activities Committee (HUAC), formerly the McCormack-Dickstein Committee, also known as the Dies Committee.
September 6	The Foreign Agents Registration Act is passed, ensuring that the public and lawmakers know the source of information (propaganda) intended to sway public opinion, policy, and laws.
November	Japan declares its objective of establishing a "new order in East Asia."

1939

March–May	Germany invades and annexes Czechoslovakia and establishes a military and political alliance with Italy.
June 26	FDR secretly creates the Interdepartmental Intelligence Committee. The Military Intelligence Division, the Office of Naval Intelligence, and other agencies forward information about espionage, counterespionage, or sabotage to the FBI.
September 1	Germany invades Poland. The State Department's Special Division is created.
September 2	Hoover orders reports on alien and citizen subversives to go in the CDI.
September 6	FDR secretly directs the FBI to handle investigations of all subversive activities.
December 6	Hoover expands inclusion criteria for aliens and citizens in the CDI.

1940

April	The Justice Department creates the Neutrality Laws Unit (NLU) to review the FBI's detention list (CDI) and gives it power to authorize

	arrests for and prosecute cases dealing with violations of neutrality laws, foreign enlistment, espionage, sabotage, treason, and sedition.
May 10	Germany attacks France and Belgium and overruns Holland.
May 16	FDR addresses Congress, condemning Germany's "treacherous use of the fifth column."
May 26	In a fireside chat, FDR warns how the fifth column betrays an unprepared nation and states that "spies, saboteurs, and traitors are all actors in the new strategy."
June 14	German troops enter Paris. The Immigration and Naturalization Service (INS) administers laws regarding aliens and investigates alleged violations of those laws.
June 22	France surrenders to Germany.
June 28	The Alien Registration Act (Smith Act), the first modern peacetime anti-sedition statute, requires the registration and fingerprint identification of all aliens.
July	Facing the threat of invasion, Britain interns 82,000 enemy aliens, including 60,000 after June as thousands fled the continent, but frees the vast majority quickly. The Justice and War Departments discuss detaining all aliens of enemy nations if the U.S. goes to war.
August 21–27	Hoover requests authorization to direct activities and prepare records of the names of aliens as well as naturalized and native-born citizens for internment. Secretary of War Henry Stimson suggests coordinated investigations of the alien enemy problem. The INS begins

	registering all aliens, and by year's end nearly five million comply.
September 16	U.S. officials confer to determine the nature of alien enemy hearings and locations for detention facilities.
September 27	Germany, Italy, and Japan sign the Tripartite (Axis) Pact.
October 14	Congress's Nationality (Naturalization) Act is used to target Bundists and naturalized citizens who sympathize with Germany or criticize U.S. policies.
October 17	The Voorhis Anti-Propaganda Act becomes law and the Justice Department intensifies investigations of subversive activities, including espionage, propaganda, and military training.
October 26	Hoover discusses permanent internment facilities to handle suspects; by December a rough outline for handling alien enemies exists.
December 29	Roosevelt's "Arsenal of Democracy" speech asks for "the same resolution . . . sense of urgency . . . spirit of patriotism and sacrifice . . . were we at war."
1941	
January 10	The INS begins examining potential detention facilities for "emergency use."
late January	Fort Stanton, New Mexico, the first U.S. internment camp, begins receiving the first of three groups that total over 400 German sailors. Most will be interned for the war's duration.
February 5	The FBI's suspect list is to include German, Russian, Italian, and Japanese aliens and naturalized citizens as well as any native-born citizens.

March	The Justice Department's Special Defense Unit (formerly the NLU) is created to help develop and manage the alien enemy program.
April 30	Hoover clarifies and consolidates custodial detention instructions as 2,000 German and Italian sailors will go from Ellis Island to Fort Stanton.
May 9	Fort Missoula, Montana, internment facility receives 125 Italian sailors.
May 17	The Special Division expresses concern about imperiled Americans abroad: 51,000 in Europe, 6,700 in China, 15,300 in Japan, and thousands more throughout Asia.
May 20	Executive Order 8757 creates the Office of Civilian Defense.
May 21–27	FDR permits wiretapping and other measures against spies and aliens and announces that the U.S. can be attacked from anywhere in this "war for world domination." An "unlimited national emergency" now exists.
May 30	Fort Lincoln, North Dakota, receives several hundred German sailors for internment.
July 18	The Justice and War Departments cooperate; the INS detains aliens and interns women, and the Army holds male internees.
September 11	FDR, in another fireside chat, warns the nation that "Hitler's advance guards" are preparing "footholds in the New World" with their "intrigues . . . plots . . . machinations . . . sabotage."
December 7	Pearl Harbor is attacked. The FBI steps up its arrests of German, Italian, and Japanese aliens and citizens. Under Presidential Proclamation 2525, all citizens and subjects of the hostile

	nation of Japan can be arrested and removed as alien enemies.
December 8	The U.S. declares war on Japan. Proclamations 2526 and 2527 apply the same conditions and restrictions to German and Italian aliens as Proclamation 2525 applied to Japanese aliens.
December 9	The FBI has arrested 620 Germans, 98 Italians, and 1,212 Japanese aliens.
December 11	Germany and Italy declare war on the United States; the U.S. reciprocates.
December 13	Negotiations for the exchange of U.S. and Japanese nationals begin.
December 15	The Alien Enemy Control Unit is established to oversee arrests, detention, and other forms of control over alien enemies including forbidden articles, travel restrictions, registration, and forbidden and restricted areas. Secretary of the Navy Frank Knox states that the most effective fifth-column work of the war was done in Hawaii.
December 22	Japan launches a major attack on the Philippines.
December 25	The U.S. Navy sinks a Japanese submarine off the California coast.
1942	
January 2–5	General DeWitt advocates a vigorous enemy alien control program as demands for evacuation of West Coast Japanese Americans begin.
January 14	Proclamation 2537 classifies all citizens and subjects of Germany, Italy, and Japan as "alien enemies" who must get certificates of identification.

January 15	The Committee for Political Defense coordinates hemispheric security, deporting dangerous Axis nationals to the U.S. in exchange for their own nationals.
January 18	Demands escalate for Japanese American evacuation.
January 25	The Roberts Commission concludes that Pearl Harbor was due largely to Japan's fifth columnists.
January 28	The *Santa Lucia* arrives in New York with German and Italian Latin Americans for internment, repatriation, and exchange.
January 29	The Department of Justice orders all enemy aliens to vacate West Coast prohibited areas by February 24; California Attorney General Earl Warren warns of another Pearl Harbor.
February 1	Attorney General Francis Biddle announces a new personal identification program for all aliens. Those over age fourteen must apply for a certificate of identification by month's end.
February 2–5	All enemy aliens must register with the Western Defense Command and abide by travel, curfew, and conduct regulations in the Army's twelve restricted areas. The FBI begins spot searches of enemy alien residences.
February 11	Stimson recommends mass evacuation of West Coast Japanese to FDR, who defers to military necessity.
February 13	A West Coast congressional delegation urges removal of all Japanese from strategic areas. Demands for Japanese American evacuation reach their height.
February 18	Japanese submarines begin attacks on U.S. vessels and shore targets.

February 19	Roosevelt signs Executive Order 9066, authorizing the secretary of war to establish military areas from which any person may be excluded. No particular ethnic or racial group or location on either coast or the nation's interior is specified.
February 20	Stimson puts DeWitt in charge of carrying out EO 9066. The War rather than Justice Department will handle the Japanese problem.
February 21	The Tolan Committee opens its hearings in San Francisco concerning the removal of enemy aliens and citizens, mainly Japanese Americans, from the West Coast.
February 23	In a fireside chat, FDR stresses the new global war as a Japanese submarine shells oil-storage tanks near Santa Barbara. After a series of Japanese military victories throughout the Pacific, *Time* warns that the nation's fate hangs in the balance.
March 2	DeWitt's Proclamation No. 1 designates Washington, Oregon, California, and Arizona as military areas. Enemy aliens and those of Japanese ancestry now face restrictions, relocation, and incarceration.
March 11	The Wartime Civil Control Administration is established to directly supervise the evacuation program. The WCCA ran seventeen assembly centers.
March 18	Executive Order 9102 establishes the War Relocation Authority, which runs ten relocation centers for Japanese Americans.
March 19	The Tolan Committee supports Executive Order 9066 and calls evacuation a military matter. A War Resettlement Board will handle

	enemy aliens, and hearing boards will issue certificates to Italian and German aliens.
March 20	Executive Order 9106 eases restrictions on most German and Italian aliens.
March 21–23	Public Law 503 penalizes anyone who violates military-area orders. The first Japanese evacuees, some 1,000 "volunteers" from Los Angeles, are moved to Manzanar.
March 24	Exclusion Order No. 1 affects few Japanese but portends the forced evacuation of German and Italian Americans and all West Coast Japanese.
March 27	DeWitt's Proclamation No. 3 extends curfews, limits travel, and regulates the lives of all enemy aliens and persons of Japanese ancestry.
March 29	The voluntary movement of Japanese Americans from strategic West Coast military areas ends and their forced evacuation begins.
March 30–31	Proclamation No. 4 forbids Japanese from voluntarily leaving Military Area No. 1, and civilian exclusion orders are posted in prominent public locations.
April–August	West Coast Japanese move from homes to assembly centers.
April 22–30	General Hugh Drum applies Executive Order 9066 for the Eastern Defense Command and announces the creation of military areas along East and Gulf Coast seaboards and inland, but Stimson announces that there will be no mass evacuation.
May–November	Japanese Americans are moved from assembly centers to relocation centers.
May 7	First wartime civilian exchange begins between the U.S. and Germany.

May 16	Drum's Proclamation No. 1 notes the millions of loyal citizens and aliens whose economic life should be undisturbed. Alien enemy violators can be expelled, interned, or prosecuted and citizens expelled or prosecuted.
May 19	Executive Order 9165 protects essential facilities from sabotage and other acts.
June 7	DeWitt announces that the removal of 100,000 West Coast Japanese is complete.
July 28	Roughly 934,000 ID cards are issued to Axis aliens per FDR's proclamation.
August–December	U.S. exchange policy shifts to repatriating harmless Axis nationals.
September 10	Drum announces an exclusion program for sixteen states along the Eastern Military Area seaboard. Anyone deemed dangerous can be removed.

1943

January 2	HUAC publishes its *Special Report on Subversive Activities*.
May	The Justice Department assumes responsibility for all internees.
July 16	Biddle ends dangerousness-based custodial detention. Hoover creates a new Security Index.
September	Exchanges resume with Japan, reflecting the U.S. repatriation shift.

1944

February	Exchanges resume with Germany, reflecting the U.S. repatriation shift.
December 18	The U.S. Supreme Court upholds Executive Order 9066 in *Korematsu v. United States*.

1945

January 2	The War Department lifts West Coast exclusion orders.

June 4	Truman issues Executive Order 9562, which terminates the Office of Civilian Defense on June 30.
September 2	Japan formally surrenders, and World War II ends.
September 4	The Western Defense Command lifts all restrictions against Japanese.

1946

March 20	All relocation centers are empty, but some 1,000 Japanese are still in INS camps, while 1,000 Germans are interned at Crystal City and Ellis Island.
May	U.S. camps hold 1,125 Japanese, 497 Germans, and 2 listed as "other."
June 30	The War Relocation Authority closes.

1947

March	Crystal City holds 106 Germans.
May	Ellis Island holds 160 Germans.

1948

August	The U.S. holds 174 German alien enemies under removal orders.

1949

April	The U.S. holds 36 Germans (still referred to as alien enemies) whose cases are pending in a number of district and appellate courts.
June	There are no longer any Germans interned in the United States.

ENEMIES AMONG US

Introduction

> What things are called is incomparably more important than what they are.
>
> —FRIEDRICH NIETZSCHE, *THE GAY SCIENCE*

It often began with a simple knock on the door as FBI agents advised, "You had better pack some things, take at least a toothbrush, but don't take any clothes; well, maybe a few clothes, but you won't be gone long." In the early hours of December 8, 1941, in an ongoing national effort, the FBI arrested several thousand aliens, including Peter Theberath.[1] At 2:30 a.m., agents entered his Milwaukee home and split up the family for reasons that remain unexplained. They took Peter and his wife, Marie, into custody and left their three children to fend for themselves. After two months Marie was released, but she found the children gone and the home robbed. She herself was now on the street while Peter remained in prison for two more months, after which he spent the next few years in three different internment camps. By April 1944, nearly two and a half years after the FBI suggested Peter and Maria would not be gone long, he was still pleading with officials through the Swiss Legation while she had lost custody of the children, since she could not, in the judgment of presiding officials, adequately care for them. Fear of an enemy within led to thousands more such tragedies over the next few months and years.[2]

Civilians throughout the world endured hardships on an unprecedented scale during World War II. Even in the United States, a nation largely unscathed by the war, the government expected civilians to do their part to win the war. For most Americans this meant coping with relatively minor inconveniences such as rationing, curfews, blackouts, and censorship. Others fared much worse. Accounts of the indignities Japanese Americans suffered as the nation mobilized for total war in the aftermath of Pearl Harbor are well known, but there is a great deal more to this story of why the United States dealt as it did with those whom officials believed were enemies among us.

Few know about the relocation, internment, and repatriation of German Americans and Italian Americans or that they were interned in greater numbers than Japanese Americans. During the war, in order to ensure the safe return of Americans overseas as well as to rid the Western Hemisphere of dangerous or unwanted enemy nationals, the United States acted on behalf of many nations; it received, interned, and then arranged for the exchange of thousands of civilians, including many women and children. Ultimately, it orchestrated the deportation, internment, and repatriation of more than six thousand "dangerous" aliens, most of them Germans, from Latin America and aided in the expulsion of thousands more directly from Latin America to Europe and Asia.

This book examines the causes, conditions, and consequences of America's selective relocation and internment of its own citizens and enemy aliens. It explains relocation and internment policies, and it examines the experiences of all three major groups of relocatees and internees: German Americans, Italian Americans, and Japanese Americans. It places internment in an international context, discusses the United States' leading role in the repatriation and exchange of thousands of internees during and after the war, and describes the effects of internment by those who experienced it.

Focusing on both relocation and internment and on German and Italian Americans as well as Japanese Americans reveals remarkable similarities in the U.S. government's dealings with perceived domestic and hemispheric threats. Many factors influenced the formulation and implementation of policymaking at the highest levels of government. There was a dual-coast relocation of German, Italian, and Japanese Americans based on perceived German and Japanese military threats along with predicted economic consequences; there was also a selective, nationwide internment of America's enemy aliens and citizens based upon political, social, and diplomatic considerations. Underlying both relocation and internment, including actions taken by the United States in Latin America, was a widespread belief in and a deep fear of a fifth-column or subversive threat, especially of Japanese Americans along the West Coast and Germans throughout the hemisphere. Countless predictions of destruction circulated, adding to fears that made the fifth-column menace a real and present danger. The public demanded action, and the nation's military and government complied. Finally, a pattern of precedents, especially during World War I, laid the groundwork for later events. Relocation and internment were much more than viable options in a democracy under stress; for most Americans, such measures had become necessary expedients to deal with those officially categorized as, and commonly referred to by the public as, enemies among us.

Differences between relocation and internment are important. Relocation, authorized on February 19, 1942, by Roosevelt's Executive Order 9066, meant removing enemy aliens and citizens (including Germans and Italians) under the War Relocation Authority (WRA) from restricted military areas along the Pacific Coast. These orders affected 112,700 Japanese American citizens and aliens and some 10,000–20,000 German and Italian Americans—overwhelmingly aliens but some citizens too. The government forcibly relocated another 10,000–20,000 Germans and Italians from East Coast exclusion areas. The relocation center's primary purpose was to help evacuees relocate and continue with their lives. Yet most evacuees spent many months or even years in WRA facilities. Internment, by contrast, meant repatriating and exchanging enemy aliens and citizens when conditions permitted for Americans interned in camps throughout Nazi-occupied Europe and the Japanese Empire. Internment lasted many months, several years, or the duration of the war and beyond. The Department of Justice eventually ran all internment camps. Such differences are critical to understanding how the government's policy toward German, Italian, and Japanese Americans evolved during the war.

Scholarly and popular histories of relocation and internment have traditionally focused solely on Japanese Americans. The literature consists of more than a thousand works and over one hundred manuscript collections. Nearly all of these—from those that emerged during the war itself to the government's own *Personal Justice Denied* (1982) to Allan Winkler's *Home Front U.S.A.* (2000)—argue that racism drove the U.S. government's relocation and internment policies. Historians and former Japanese American relocatees or internees cited racism as the sole or determining factor of their wartime plight. This view, which dominated the literature for some fifty years, changed recently as a few historians learned of the relocation and internment of German and Italian Americans. Some studying the Japanese American experience have also begun to reexamine government policies and rethink the long-held notion that racism was largely or solely responsible for the indignities enemy aliens and citizens suffered in the United States and throughout the Western Hemisphere.

Despite recent scholarly efforts, myths and misperceptions still pervade the literature, and Japanese Americans still occupy center stage in this important national and international story. Even current works on relocation and internment, the home front, and broader historical surveys reflect these errors and typically neglect or distort the German and Italian American experience. It is as if only Japanese Americans endured the mental, physical, and monetary consequences of relocation and internment. This was simply not the case. German and Italian Americans often lived for months or years with their Japanese counterparts in many of the same camps. Yet some texts allege that only Japanese Americans suffered and state emphatically that German and Italian Americans were neither mistreated nor interned. Surprisingly, too, the Museum of American History's recent exhibit on World War II internment was curiously silent about the plight of German and Italian Americans, making no mention at all of their wartime experiences.

The first works on internment established analytical, interpretive, and contextual precedents that dominated the literature for several decades. Of the early studies, Morton Grodzins's *Americans Betrayed* (1949) was the most important. Grodzins accessed a wide variety of sources and a wealth of information and concluded that racism determined the fate of Japanese Americans. His well-researched work raised a number of provocative moral, legal, and ethical issues. Jacobus tenBroek, Edward Barnhart, and Floyd Matson's *Prejudice, War, and the Constitution* (1954), Charles Allen's *Concentration Camp, U.S.A.* (1966), and Audrie Girdner and Anne Loftis's *The Great Betrayal* (1969) continued the academic focus on Japanese Americans and cited racism as the primary motivation for their relocation and internment.

By the late 1960s, studies examining the American home front and internment increased dramatically. Research yielded many important books published throughout the 1970s. Scholars became more critical of the nation's wartime policies, and the subject of internment found its way into more mainstream texts and popular journals. Personal accounts and memoirs also emerged, yet German and Italian Americans remained largely invisible. The few texts that mentioned them did so only in passing, and the authors generally failed to differentiate between the government's separate but related policies of relocation and internment. Scholars failed or neglected to note that German and Italian Americans also endured internment, and had not examined relocation or internment within a broader chronological, hemispheric, or global context.

The 1980s witnessed a significant increase in the number and diversity of home-front literature, including Studs Terkel's *The Good War* (1984) and Paul Fussell's *Wartime* (1989). Others added to the large corpus of Japanese American internment literature, including Peter Irons's *Justice at War* (1983), Thomas James's *Exile Within* (1987), Mike Masaoka's *They Call Me Moses Masaoka* (1987), and John Armor and Peter Wright's *Manzanar* (1988). Most authors still argued that racism drove the nation's relocation and internment policies, and they left German and Italian American internees out of their narratives. Yet these investigations led to new discoveries, and by the end of the decade a few scholars began challenging the entrenched internment paradigm.

Some writers and historians began challenging the long-held notion that racism had driven internment policies and programs as scholarly interest in previously marginalized or ignored topics led to several innovative works that broke new interpretive and analytical ground. These included Lillian Baker's *American and Japanese Relocation in World War II* (1990), Stephen Fox's *The Unknown Internment* (1990), the author's master's thesis, "Democracy under Stress" (1993), Page Smith's *Democracy on Trial* (1995), Timothy Holian's *The German-Americans and World War II* (1996), Arnold Krammer's *Undue Process* (1997), Fox's *America's Invisible Gulag* (2000), Max Paul Friedman's *Nazis and Good Neighbors* (2003), and the author's dissertation, "Enemies among Us" (2007). Including German and Italian Americans in the scholarly discourse complicates the question of how racism and ethnicity affected policymaking.

Recent scholarship, including Eric Muller's *American Inquisition* (2007), John Howard's *Concentration Camps on the Home Front* (2008), Carlos Meissner's *A Resilient Elite: German Costa Ricans and the Second World War* (2010), Jay Feldman's *Manufacturing Hysteria* (2011), Jan Jarboe Russell's *The Train to Crystal City* (2015), Mary Chopas's *Searching for Subversives* (2017), and Roger Lotchin's *Japanese American Relocation in World War II* (2018), has added a great deal to what has largely been a political, economic, racial, and military focus on just one major enemy group (still primarily Japanese Americans). This book is the first to address comparatively all three major alien enemy and citizen groups, fully examine their repatriation and exchange, and place relocation, internment, and repatriation in a broader chronological and international context. It presents a multi-causal approach to events and, relying heavily on previously overlooked archival sources, offers a new interpretation of the relocation, internment, and repatriation of German, Italian, and Japanese Americans.

Enemies among Us contributes to our understanding of the United States' treatment of its enemy aliens and citizens in three important ways. First, including the experiences of German and Italian Americans provides fresh insight into the reasons for internment. Second, it reveals consistencies in the government's treatment of all its enemy aliens and citizens, regardless of race. Third, it offers a comprehensive analysis and proposes a fresh interpretation of American internment during World War II.

As the first comprehensive work on this subject, this book is necessarily revisionist in its analysis and comparative in its narrative: it reveals errors with relocation and internment histories that deal only with Japanese Americans, and it demonstrates consistencies in both relocation and internment policymaking regarding German, Italian, and Japanese Americans. Examining the experiences of all relocatees and internees yields a more complete, intelligible, and accurate story of the United States' wartime policies. Old theories maintaining that racism guided policymakers' decisions give way to more convincing arguments and reasons for relocation or internment. In short, the government based its wartime decision to relocate and intern enemy nationals neither upon race nor upon public fears alone—racism and fear there was, but other factors mattered too.

As conflict erupted in the Far East and Europe in the 1930s, pragmatic assessments of relevant political, economic, geographic, diplomatic, national-security, and military considerations guided relocation and internment policymaking. Officials in Washington realized that there could be no mass evacuation of Italian and German Americans from either coast, because their numbers reached into the millions. Similarly, there was no mass relocation or internment of Hawaii's Issei and Nisei, who comprised nearly 40 percent of the population. Yet the government interned more German and Italian Americans than Japanese Americans, arrested them in greater numbers, and relocated members of all three enemy groups. During these turbulent times, Roosevelt issued a number of secret directives that led to subsequent policies. These orders reflected the worsening political conditions abroad and the personal convictions of key individuals responsible for national security, such as J. Edgar Hoover, director of the Federal Bureau of Investigation, and General John DeWitt, head of the Western

Defense Command. Initial national-security measures designed to identify and detain potential internal enemies (fascists, communists, spies, saboteurs) evolved into an elaborate plan to intern thousands if necessary.

Precautionary measures against suspected internal enemies intensified as war spread in Europe and Asia and the nation's entry into it seemed ever more likely. Hoover's FBI compiled an extensive list of subversives and potential troublemakers in the agency's secret Custodial Detention Index. The Special Defense Unit of the Department of Justice, led by Lawrence M. C. Smith, created its own list of suspects. Such efforts proved effective as FBI agents apprehended hundreds of aliens just hours before the Pearl Harbor attack and then arrested or interned thousands more in the following weeks.

The United States now had internees it could exchange for its citizens interned abroad. By early 1942 the first exchanges took place. Internment made exchange possible. Over time, the government modified its relocation and internment policies when national and international circumstances warranted, but there was never a racially based master plan geared toward depriving Japanese Americans of their civil liberties. Rather, the U.S. government acted and reacted to changing internal and external pressures. Policymakers applied their relocation and internment plans, preparations, policies, and practices in an even, albeit heavy-handed manner to all perceived enemies.

There were three primary reasons for the relocation and internment of America's enemy aliens and citizens. First, fear, racism, and a general public mood of intolerance provided the political, ideological, and social climate that made the removal and incarceration of enemy civilians seemingly necessary, prudent, and just. Second, for personal and public-relations reasons, and above all for the sake of national security, the federal government, through the FBI and other agencies, categorized, identified, located, apprehended, and interned "dangerous" and "potentially dangerous" aliens and citizens. A burgeoning though powerful belief in a seditious fifth-column threat, reinforced by an ingrained and culturally pervasive fear of "outsiders" along with the stunning and seemingly inexplicable string of Axis military victories—from the German conquest of western Europe to the Japanese attack upon Pearl Harbor—powerfully reinforced these beliefs. As a result, the U.S. Army managed the removal of thousands of Germans and Italians from both coasts along with over one hundred thousand Japanese Americans from the West Coast, and the WRA handled the incarceration of West Coast Japanese American evacuees. Roosevelt was by no means alone in his conviction that the nation faced a credible domestic threat and needed to respond accordingly. A consensus had been developing among top military officials and policymakers and their subordinates in the State and War Departments, FBI, Office of Naval Intelligence, and Army G-2 that potential subversives and disloyals threatened the nation's security. Once the fifth-column threat was clearly articulated and formally accepted, few challenged the government's responses.

Third, and perhaps most importantly, the process of selective internment rested upon the government's need to ensure the safety of its own citizens trapped in Nazi-occupied Europe and the Japanese Empire. The Justice Department interned German, Italian, and Japanese Americans residing throughout the hemisphere in order to exchange them for Americans and Allied nationals interned abroad. Simply put, internment meant exchange; inextricably linked, the processes were two sides of the same coin. The series of exchanges that took place thus ensured a benevolent reciprocity, meaning that the Axis and Allied powers mutually benefited by getting their own citizens back while expelling dangerous persons, troublemakers, or those some officials called "bottom of the barrel." Because Germany, Italy, and Japan as well as the United States held thousands of enemy civilians, the implicit threat or the mere possibility of mistreatment remained low, especially as exchanges proved successful, demonstrating the good faith of all nations. In short, the United States' selective internment of thousands of German, Italian, and Japanese Americans proved to be practical and advantageous—except, of course, to the internees.

Once we understand the reasons for relocation and internment, the next step is determining why the government selected particular individuals and groups. Internees and relocatees found their lives disrupted at best and torn apart at worst. Authorities sometimes released aliens brought in for questioning within a few hours, while others, after enduring months or years of confinement, committed suicide. For most, relocation and internment meant loss of property, including homes, and forced incarceration behind barbed wire hundreds if not thousands of miles away from where they once lived, typically for many months or even several years.

Only the war's end slowed the government's removal of undesirables. By late 1946 the United States had successfully repatriated nearly all Japanese internee renunciants and had released all Japanese internees. Yet even to the summer of 1948 and the spring of 1949, the government doggedly persisted in its efforts to repatriate forcibly the last of its internees, German Americans, many of whom adamantly resisted. It was not until June 1949 that the U.S. no longer had internees. These last few, all Germans, ended a process that had begun fifteen years earlier with investigations of American Nazis and their sympathizers.

Few accounts of the Japanese American experience mention the relocation or internment of German or Italian Americans, much less the experiences of interned German, Italian, and Japanese nationals from Latin America. Reframing relocation and internment by considering a broader chronological perspective, examining all three major relocatee and internee groups, and looking at policies in Hawaii, the continental United States, and the Western Hemisphere reveals a new set of conclusions as to why the U.S. relocated, interned, and repatriated aliens and citizens who were categorized as enemies.

What emerges, then, is more than just a story of internee experiences. Indeed, those German, Italian, and Japanese Americans who experienced relocation or internment personified the deeper social and cultural rifts of a democracy under stress. Their stories are those of individual versus national rights, personal versus group identity, and fallacies versus facts. This book will, I hope, serve as a cautionary tale reminding us of what can happen when complex social, economic, political, and military circumstances combine to create a fearful atmosphere in which individuals are stereotyped and suspected of wrongdoing solely because of their race or ethnicity. Americans came to see arresting, relocating, interning, and repatriating their fellow aliens and citizens as just. How might we treat our fellow Americans and resident aliens, human beings all, in future times of stress? A suggestion from long ago offers some guidance: "When an alien resides with you in your land, you shall not oppress the alien. The alien who resides with you shall be to you as the citizen among you; you shall love the alien as yourself" (Leviticus 19.33–34).

1

Pejoratives, Precedents, and Prejudice

> We can have no "fifty-fifty" allegiance in this country. Either a man is an American and nothing else, or he is not an American at all!
> —THEODORE ROOSEVELT, 1917

The United States struggled with growing diversity at the dawn of the twentieth century. Waves of immigrants from eastern and southern Europe and from East Asia significantly added to the nation's cultural mix. The society was varied—too much for those frightened by rapidly changing sociocultural demographics. America proclaimed itself a land of freedom, toleration, and inclusion yet fostered racial segregation, allowed hostility toward immigrants to go largely unchecked, and excluded those it did not want: an oft-repeated immigrant slogan ran, "America beckons, but Americans repel."[1]

By the 1920s, rather than appreciating the newly arrived immigrants' difficulties, many Americans equated diversity with domestic woes and believed the newcomers personified change and instability and represented sinister designs exported from afar. Anti-immigrant sentiment coalesced under the weight of numerous, dire warnings of the massive "invasion" of "beaten men from beaten races." In 1924 came the most enduring and effective anti-immigrant legislation. The Immigration Restriction Act limited the annual immigration of any given nationality to only 2 percent of its 1890 resident population and excluded Japanese immigrants. This landmark legislation emerged amid numerous reports decrying the fitness of the newcomers to assimilate into American life.[2]

At the height of the new immigration, more than a million immigrants were arriving annually. Most Italians, over 4.5 million, came between 1880 and 1925, as 3.1 million new Germans doubled the German American population during the same period. The number of Japanese immigrants, while quite low (only 24,000 in 1900—excluding the Hawaiian Islands), elicited a response well out of proportion to their numbers. The *San Francisco Chronicle*, on February 23, 1905, for example, warned of the "Japanese Invasion: The Problem of the Hour" and asserted that 100,000 "little brown men" were menacing the country. A few months later, after Japan's stunning naval victory at Tsushima, anxiety over the Japanese "menace" increased dramatically as they arrived for the first time in significant numbers. The following year, headlines in William Randolph Hearst's rival San Francisco paper, the *Examiner*, along with others in his chain, occasionally warned of a Japanese military threat, but by December Hearst's *Examiner* went much farther and proclaimed "Japan Sounds Our Coasts: Brown Men Have Maps and Could Land Easily!" Despite efforts to limit immigration in the late 1800s and again in the 1920s, by 1930 foreign-born nationals constituted 15 percent of the U.S. population of 123 million, while roughly one-third were either first- or second-generation Americans. Adding those whose ancestors were foreign-born in 1890, then nearly half the population and more than half the whites were of immigrant stock. The two largest immigrant groups were the Germans and the Italians: the former was by far the biggest, and the latter had the most foreign-born. Defining an "American," never an easy task, would become far more pressing when millions were later redefined as enemies. As Friedrich Nietzsche noted: "What things are called is incomparably more important than what they are."[3]

Asian Immigration and American Reactions

Nineteenth-century Asian immigrants, like others, were seen by many established Americans as a threat to their wealth and way of life—including a challenge to firmly cherished notions of racial integrity and superior social status. Coming primarily to eke out a better living, Asians found work readily provided by entrepreneurs who exploited them as an abundant source of cheap labor. Yet many white Anglo-Saxon Americans viewed them as "inferior races" and often said so. Anti-Asian sentiment ran the gamut from subtle forms of prejudice to mob violence that sometimes resulted in the destruction of property and death.[4]

Workers feared losing their jobs, while labor unions feared economic competition. Third-party movements, including progressive or workingmen's parties, sought political gain. Conservatives feared subversion and the intermingling of races, viewing Japanese men as spies bent on destroying the nation and raping white women. Nativists of various stripes, for their racist reasons, believed American mores were at stake. Populists, Republicans and Democrats, labor leaders, and many others vilified Japanese immigrants, influenced public opinion, and halted the influx of Asians. Not surprisingly, Asians faced discrimination, often open and wanton, by those agitating to limit or eliminate the entry of foreigners or expel those already in the country. What had begun as an anti-Chinese movement expanded to include, over time, "the passage of the alien land acts, the exclusion of Japanese, and the incarceration of persons of Japanese ancestry."[5]

The anti-Japanese movement began in earnest in 1888. The San Francisco labor movement was the initial driving force against the Japanese immigration "menace." Agitators found numerous supporters. Dennis Kearney, the Workingmen's Party leader, changed his rallying cry from "The Chinese Must Go!" to "The Japs Must Go!" Dozens of politicians embraced Kearney's racist sentiments. When former San Francisco mayor and then California senator James Phelan ran for reelection in 1920, he used the popular campaign slogan "Keep California White." Under a drawing of Uncle Sam's hand stopping a Japanese grab of the state, the caption read: "HOLD . . . And let him finish the work he now has under way to stop the SILENT INVASION." Politicians and nativists along with growing numbers of West Coast residents coupled earlier anti-Chinese sentiment with the new Japanese threat. They were, as Phelan put it, starting what "we thought we had checked twenty years ago. . . . The Chinese and Japanese are not bona fide citizens. They are not the stuff of which American citizens can be made."[6]

Following planters' claims in 1920 that a workers' strike on Oahu was a Japanese attempt to control the sugar industry and more broadly "a dark conspiracy to Japanize" the territory, a secret federal investigation began. The Labor Department's report concluded that "national defense and the necessity to curtail the domination of the alien Japanese in every phase of the Hawaiian life is more important than all the other problems combined." Military intelligence and the Bureau of Investigation (forerunner of the FBI) supported the conclusions. The military, therefore, "planned and prepared for the coming war with Japan at least as early as 1921, when the secretary of war approved a plan that included the internment of enemy aliens." In 1923, Colonel John DeWitt argued for "the establishment of complete military control over the Hawaiian Islands, including its people, supplies, material, etc." should Japan and the United States go to war.[7]

Anti-Japanese Sentiment and Legislation

Federal anti-Asian legislation began with the Naturalization Act of 1870, which separated Asians from others eligible for naturalization. In 1882 Congress passed the Chinese Exclusion Act, effectively halting Chinese immigration. This act was the first federal law to discriminate against any immigrant group, and it set a precedent for later anti-immigrant legislation, including literacy tests. The Bureau of Immigration, created by Congress in 1891, supported such exclusionist policies. Under Terrence Powderly's leadership, the bureau institutionalized exclusionist regulations, as "mob violence and a sustained political drive had successively carried local, state, and the federal government, and secured a sharp drop in the new arrivals and a gradual reduction in the Chinese population in the United States as a whole." No sooner had Chinese immigration ended than a wave of Japanese immigration began. Few welcomed the newcomers. Racist sentiment compounded the perceived threat Japanese immigrants posed as politicians worried about Japan's emergence onto the world stage. Many highly influential and inflammatory news articles in early 1905 stirred nativists, politicians, and others who disliked immigrants generally or Asians particularly to join forces to remedy the Japanese "problem." The conservative *San Francisco Chronicle*, California and the Pacific Coast's most influential paper, warned of the "Japanese Invasion," decried the rise of "crime and poverty" that went "hand in hand with Asiatic labor," and cautioned that the "Yellow Peril" would soon "Crowd Out the White Race."[8]

In 1905 the Russo-Japanese War marked Japan's emergence as a world power. Although tensions between Japan and the United States declined somewhat with the 1907–8 Gentlemen's Agreement, anti-Japanese sentiment surged amid renewed controversy over landownership issues in California—leading to the state's first alien land law in 1913. Homer Lea's *The Valor of Ignorance* (1909) called Japan's emigrants "a military vanguard" and warned that Japan in "three months could land on the Pacific Coast four hundred thousand troops" seizing major cities with no real opposition.[9] Enmities resurfaced with even greater ferocity and breadth after World War I, especially along the West Coast. The Oriental Exclusion League, an assemblage of nativist groups that formed in 1919, along with California's Alien Land Act of 1920, typified the renewed hostility toward Asians, especially Japanese. Military intelligence reports along with the Bureau of Investigation concluded in 1921 that "Japan's program for world supremacy," if unimpeded, would reach California, drive "the white race, in no long space of time" from the state, turning it and, in time, the Pacific Coast region into a "province of Japan." Such regional ambitions, the bureau report noted, were part of Japan's goal to "amalgamate the entire colored races of the world against the Nordic or white race, with Japan at the head of the coalition, for the purpose of wrestling away the supremacy of the white race and placing such supremacy in the colored peoples under the dominion of Japan."[10]

The Bureau of Investigation reported Japan's quest for global domination as the War Department developed contingency plans to intern Hawaii's enemy aliens in case of war. Senators and representatives from a dozen western states declared:

> The process of invasion has been aptly termed "peaceful penetration." The invasion is by an alien people. They are a people unassimilable by marriage. They are a race unto themselves, and by

virtue of that very fact ever will be a race and a nation unto themselves, it matters not what may be the land of their birth.

Economically we are not able to compete with them and maintain the American standard of living; racially we cannot assimilate them. Hence, we must exclude them from our shores and prohibit them from owning land. Those already here will be protected in their enjoyment of life, liberty, and legally acquired property.

The alternative [to exclusion] is that the richest section of the United States will gradually come into the complete control of an alien race. A careful study of the subject will convince anyone... that the attitude of California and other states is not only justifiable but essential to the national welfare.[11]

German American Numbers, Status, and Loyalty

German Americans were not immune to nativist invective or public concern. Although they had assimilated fairly well into mainstream society by the turn of the century, that all changed with World War I as anti-German sentiment reached its zenith and latent tensions erupted. No longer the pope's loyal minions, they had become enemy agents, the kaiser's dutiful toadies. Arguably the most esteemed immigrant group before the war, German Americans became the most estranged. Princeton professor Robert McElroy, educational director of the National Security League (NSL), said "the melting pot has not melted. In the bottom lie heaps of unfused metal," while the *Saturday Evening Post* demanded the wholesale removal of the melting pot "scum."[12]

Approximately five of the eight million Germans who immigrated to the United States did so during the nineteenth century. Some 2.1 million arrived between 1880 and 1921, and roughly 430,000 more came between 1922 and 1933. In 1930 Germans were by far the largest foreign stock population, with nearly seven million; the Italians followed with four and a half million. By 1940 another 160,000 Germans had arrived—bringing the interwar immigrant total to nearly 600,000, the German-born population to 1.6 million, and the number of German Americans to over seven million. Only the Italians exceeded the Germans as either foreign-born or unnaturalized. Many more claimed Italian and

German ancestry. In March 1935 the Special Committee on Un-American Activities reported twenty million Americans of German birth or descent.[13]

German Americans, those of German ancestry, were the nation's largest ethnic group, comprising one-quarter of the U.S. population. Roosevelt, his key advisers, and top military officials knew this, and German and Italian American numbers clearly worked to their advantage, as did their high degree of social and cultural assimilation. Conversely, the Japanese, apart from those on the Hawaiian Islands, were not nearly as numerous or influential. If taking out first papers or speaking English was any indication of loyalty or a desire to embrace the American culture, then "the German-born in the United States continued to show a conspicuous tendency toward naturalization. By 1910, more than 90 percent of the German-born had taken out first papers."[14]

Initial European Internment Practices and United States Precedents

Investigating, arresting, relocating, or even interning and repatriating those considered dangerous were hardly unique practices. The wartime treatment of resident aliens has varied according to specific national policies within the evolving Western nation-state system. Even up to the late 1700s, few citizens crossed their nation's borders. As travel and trade increased over the next two centuries, the treatment of citizens abroad became an issue. Statesman and jurist Hugo Grotius, whose writings mark the beginnings of international law, said nothing explicit about their protection. By 1758, however, when Emerich von Vattel published his classic *The Law of Nations*, the issue of travelers' rights had become consequential. It was also a point of good faith, Vattel argued, for a belligerent not to detain enemy subjects, since there was an implied promise of being able to leave safely. Prior to World War I, international law dealt with aliens leniently.[15]

World War I marked a new chapter in enemy aliens' treatment. To ensure their own survival, states now took extraordinary measures against citizens and aliens. National needs outweighed individual rights should a critical choice be required. Given conflicts between the treatment of aliens and international law, states adhered to decisions of the community of states. With no specific source of international agreement, however, "the relations between belligerent states and enemy nationals in the territories of the former, as distinct from occupied territories, are chiefly governed by municipal law, that is, the rules underlying the principle of sovereignty. Thus, civilians of enemy nationality may be interned or subjected to other restrictions in the interest of public policy, and their property may be sequestrated."[16] Self-preservation allowed nations great latitude in dealing with aliens or disloyal citizens, especially in time of war. Citizens generally supported the temporary sacrifice of aliens' rights as nations cracked down on enemy aliens and survival of the state became paramount. Governments adopted sterner measures to combat domestic enemies in an age of total war.

Although aliens had traditionally enjoyed the same civil rights as subjects or citizens of nation-states—protection of life and property, access to the courts—World War I changed their customary treatment. Belligerent nations now rounded up and interned large numbers of enemy nationals, taking all necessary measures to safeguard the state. For example, at first "only suspects were arrested and interned in the United Kingdom," but by May 1915, "in consequence of mob outbreaks and a widespread popular demand, practically the entire enemy population, as well as the majority of naturalized British subjects of enemy origin, were interned in concentration camps."[17] Britain interned 46,000 aliens, of whom 32,000 were civilians while 14,000 were naval and military men. France interned some 45,000 enemy aliens, while Germany adopted similar measures and interned some 4,300 British and 2,000 French men from a total of 15,000 British and French residents in Germany when war broke out. Even nations far removed from European battlefields acted. Australia interned 7,000 German Australians, of whom 700 were naturalized British subjects; the United States arrested more than 6,000 and interned another 6,300 alien enemies (4,000 German sailors and 2,300 civilians), nearly all of them German Americans.[18]

Governments justified internment on a territorial basis of jurisdiction—that is, nations have jurisdiction over all persons within their territory but none over their nationals in another state's territory. Nations did, however, aid and protect their own through international treaties, agreements of mutual humane treatment, and the implied threat of reciprocity. Barring gross inhumane treatment—physical or moral coercion and policies of extermination, pillage, and collective punishment—states treated aliens as they saw fit. By World War II interning enemy aliens had become commonplace among belligerents. Allied as well as Axis nations constructed camps or used whatever facilities were at hand to detain or incarcerate thousands of aliens, who often lost their property and land and sometimes found themselves separated from family and friends for months or years. Governments explained that such actions ensured not only the nation's safety but also protected the aliens themselves from mob violence.

The United States, like other nations, took responsibility for its citizens abroad and jurisdiction over all persons, citizen or alien, within its territorial boundaries. The legal basis for the internment of German, Italian, and Japanese American aliens rested on the Alien and Sedition Acts of 1798, which Congress passed in a wave of patriotic war fever. The Alien Act empowered the president to expel "dangerous" aliens. The Sedition Act defined as a high misdemeanor "any combination or conspiracy against legal measures of the government, including interference with federal officers and insurrection or riot." In addition, "the law forbade writing, publishing, or speaking anything of 'a false, scandalous and malicious' nature against the government or any of its officers."[19] Authorities accused and acted against persons who exercised their constitutional rights of speech, assembly, and press. Then there was the powerful Alien Enemy Act, which empowered the president during war to detain, imprison, or expel enemy aliens. It formed the statutory basis for the internment and deportation of civilians. It also defined an alien enemy as an alien, denizen, citizen, or subject of a nation at war with the United States. "Alien enemy" does not mean an enemy who happens to be an alien, but an alien who happens to have enemy nationality. If threatened by invasion or the imminent prospect of war, the president could arrest, incarcerate, or deport alien enemies—persons whose country was or might soon be at war with the United States. The earliest cases disclosed the whim of authorities, scandalous lies and misrepresentations, paranoia, and misapplication of the law, resulting in the punishment of innocents—including Federalists indicting their Republican opponents. The first case resulted in one unfortunate being fined $100 for wishing aloud that the "wad of a salute cannon might hit President Adams in his rear."[20]

World War I Parallels

Numerous and significant parallels exist between the United States' treatment of German Americans during World War I and the treatment they, along with Japanese and Italian Americans, later received. Although the U.S. and Japan were political allies during World War I, most Americans viewed Japanese Americans as social and cultural enemies during the late nineteenth and early twentieth centuries. Moreover, the United States and Germany, aside from a brief but amicable relationship during the 1920s, were political and military adversaries, while the public viewed German Americans during both wars as potentially disloyal at best and as outright enemies engaged in sabotage at worst. Historian Susan Canedy notes:

> While their harsh treatment during the war drove most to rapid assimilation, a segment would desperately cling to their ethnicity and attempt to remain as culturally pure as possible for as long as possible. This group would endure the interwar years and all its conflicts as a separate entity. It is not surprising, then, to find this strand of German Americans dressed in the uniforms of the Third Reich some eighteen years later. German American Bundists stand not as Germans nor as Americans, but as a people caught in the limbo of assimilation.[21]

In its report, *Personal Justice Denied*, the Commission on Wartime Relocation and Internment of Civilians (CWRIC) noted that common misperceptions of Germans stemmed from "rumors in the press of sabotage and espionage, use of a stereotype of the German as an unassimilable and rapacious Hun, followed by an effort to suppress those institutions—the language, the press and the churches—that were most palpably foreign and perceived as the seedbed of Kaiserism." The CWRIC found "numerous examples of official and quasi-governmental harassment and fruitless investigation of German Americans and resident German aliens." The lack of centralized responsibility for alien enemies resulted in careless and overzealous acts. Marshall Dimock of the Justice Department noted:

> During the 1917 war, arrests were made by the Federal [sic] Bureau of Investigation and other law-enforcement agencies; the alien was then brought before a United States Attorney who reported to a Washington office; the alien was incarcerated in a Federal prison in the custody of a United States Marshal until a decision in the case had been made in Washington. Such a method is complicated and fails to make any one unit of Government responsible for the results achieved.

Yet after the war there was hope. By the end of the 1920s, German Americans had well assimilated themselves into American culture. "No two major powers were on better terms with each other than Germany and the United States before 1933, and the destruction of that relationship must be considered one of the signal events of the 1930s." Wartime abuses perpetuated against German Americans foreshadowed later injustices.[22]

The Home Front and German Americans

Officials in Washington initially had acted cautiously when World War I began in August 1914. Eight to ten million recent immigrants had been born in Germany or were first-generation German Americans. As involvement in Europe's war became increasingly likely, Woodrow Wilson faced the difficult task of mobilizing the minds of the American people. After the United States entered the war in April 1917, the administration banned German newspapers. Public schools no longer offered courses in German. In communities throughout the nation, German American families Americanized their surnames while sauerkraut and frankfurters became "liberty cabbage" and "hot dogs." Not even the hamburger was safe as it morphed into "Salisbury steak." Many stopped reading German authors or listening to Wagner or Beethoven. Many thousands lost their jobs, and thousands more spent days, weeks, or months languishing in prisons or internment camps, often without any charges or a chance to challenge their accusers.

George Creel, who chaired Wilson's Committee on Public Information (CPI), published a daily *Official Bulletin*. The CPI utilized thousands of talented writers, professors, politicians, and artists to convince citizens to fight for freedom and democracy. The results were dramatic. Numerous spy scares and attempts to ferret out disloyal citizens, coupled with government propaganda and public fear, led to a modern witch hunt. Americans caught war fever and had their pick of organizations to join—many government endorsed. Attorney General Thomas Gregory, for example, openly worked with the Chicago-based American Protective League, which had over 200,000 amateur detectives searching for saboteurs and spies.

President Wilson restricted the activities and movements of German aliens from the war's start. The Black Tom explosion on July 30, 1916, certainly did not help matters. Once the United States was in the war, events at home accelerated. On June 14, 1917, Flag Day, Wilson warned that the kaiser had sent spies and conspirators to "spread sedition among us." These German agents, he added, were seeking to "undermine the government with false professions of loyalty to its principles."[23] Creel's CPI promptly created and distributed more than seven million copies of the speech. By the fall, all German aliens fourteen or older had to register with the government. German Americans were barred from strategic areas or places of military importance—including, among others, harbors, canals, and dams, and transportation and communication centers such as railroad depots and wharves. They were forbidden to travel anywhere by water (except on public ferries), were forced to leave Washington DC, and their property was subject to search and seizure.

Individual states also took action. Kansas and Nebraska, which had allowed unnaturalized aliens to vote in order to attract immigrant settlers, now reversed course, fearing the Germans' use of the ballot. Other states made it a misdemeanor to possess or display an enemy flag. Iowa made it a crime to "incite or abet" any form of hostility or opposition to the state or federal government. At the local level, stories told of German teachers, "Herr Professors," whipping children who spoke English in German schools, neglecting the national anthem while singing "Deutschland über Alles," and replacing portraits of Washington and Lincoln with the kaiser's. By war's end, rumors of unidentified aircraft flying over cities, influenza outbreaks, and unexplained industrial accidents abounded. Some citizens thought it prudent and just to incarcerate or expel Germans, and thousands asserted that if the government failed to act, mob violence would result. By 1918 a spirit of intolerance epitomized the nation's mood.[24]

Assimilation and Assaults

World War I forced German Americans to assimilate into mainstream culture. Organizations such as Creel's CPI, the American Protective League, Four-Minute Men, and 100 Percenters fostered and perpetuated xenophobia, anti-radicalism, and nativist tendencies. Wilson, Creel, and others invoked idealistic rhetoric and religious imagery affirming a people's war and requiring patriotic conformity and consensus. This, in turn, further drove German American assimilation. Popular publications such as *Everybody's Magazine*, *Life*, *New Republic*, and *Atlantic Monthly* only increased public suspicion. In June 1918 *Life* printed a German American version of "My Country, 'Tis of Thee," which went as follows: "My country over sea, Deutschland, is sweet to me; To thee I cling. For thee my honor died, for thee I spied and lied, so that from every side Kultur might ring." The singing cartoon character is an older, obese man with a thick mustache and spectacles, dress jacket, and the words "plans of forts" on a document protruding from a pocket next to his burning cigar.[25]

As vandalism and violence—German Americans were publicly tarred and feathered, flogged, and lynched—peaked in the spring of 1918, widespread anglicization of German names took place. Whether out of fear, patriotism, or a long-term process of Americanization, German Americans gave up key aspects of their ethnicity—including speaking and writing in German, reflected by the marked decline in German newspapers and publications.

Numerous efforts furthered their assimilation and conformity and promoted patriotism, compelled consensus, and mobilized the minds of America's citizenry, including the massive numbers of recent immigrants. Liberty loan campaigners often intimidated (by threat or force) recalcitrants, including the pacifist Mennonite sect, for refusing to do "their part." Several states, including Nebraska, South Dakota, Iowa, and Indiana, prohibited German instruction in public schools—although the U.S. Supreme Court overturned such state laws in 1923. In June 1917 the Espionage Act suppressed antiwar sentiment, while the Alien and Sedition Acts of 1918 severely curtailed aliens' rights and free speech. In addition, the NSL pushed for the militarization of society, including universal military training. The NSL published anti-German propaganda, including Earl Sperry's pamphlet *The Tentacles of the German Octopus in America*, in which he declared that there was "overwhelming proof" that "large numbers of German-Americans are disloyal citizens." The NSL also promoted "patriotic education and national sentiment and service among the people of the United States."[26]

The National Education Association, the NSL's Committee on Patriotism through Education, and the National Board for Historical Service promoted "correct" thinking in the nation's classrooms. These pedagogical trends, begun during the war, remained prevalent throughout the 1920s. Additionally, the German American Alliance came under increasing criticism. It was founded in 1901 (granted a congressional charter in 1907) for the purpose of educating German Americans about their ethnicity and promoting cultural well-being, but politicians thought the organization too dangerous, and Congress disbanded the alliance in 1918. Yet the alliance's purpose was to "defend the traditions of the Fatherland regarding alcoholic beverages." The German government did not subsidize the alliance, as alleged, but the association of American brewers did as a profession battling against prohibition. In fact, "the beer keg provided a far stronger rallying point for Germans in America than the Pan-German cries of the German Kaiser and the Prussian officer class."[27] Nevertheless, Congress and the public were not taking chances.

These pervasive but typically groundless fears were startling when one considers that "the war had so enhanced the distance between the German and the American that no hyphen could stretch from the one to the other. The German Americans, disowned and derided by the Germans of Germany, had no further reason for clinging to their Deutschtum [Germanness] at such great sacrifices to themselves."[28] Yet Hitler's racial purity and pan-Germanic ravings similarly encouraged suspicions about domestic enemies.

Often overlooked were German American attitudes and acts that expressed both loyalty to the nation and fidelity to its government. The lack of disloyal rhetoric and subversive activities mattered little as media "evidence" pointed to German American misdeeds and their suspicious nature. They were, rumor had it, poisoning food, tainting medical supplies, and undermining the war effort. The Senate's probe of the German American Alliance in 1918, among other investigations, reaffirmed nativist fears, while its foregone conclusions dissolved the alliance. Soon afterward, German clubs, lodges, and associations of almost every description at the national, state, city, and community level simply disbanded. An impressionable public, receptive to simplistic stereotypes and swayed by propaganda and committee reports, was mobilized to fight a maniacal foe that fought both on European battlefields and in American cities and towns.[29]

The government realized, as did the media, that the war was about winning hearts and minds. Swaying public sentiment proved invaluable. By World War II, Washington officials established and sustained a firm, symbiotic relationship between themselves and the public through the creation of agencies such as the Office of Facts and Figures, which disseminated politically sanctioned propaganda. In the meantime, though, the Red Scare, the Johnson-Reed Act, growing anti-Semitism, and other nativist acts built upon wartime nationalism and xenophobia. This made the later typecasting of German, Italian, and Japanese aliens easy and effective. The foundation for creating and sustaining the illusion of an internal enemy, later called fifth columnists, had been laid.

There was tremendous pressure on all immigrants to conform and demonstrate their unqualified loyalty. The CPI, through its

"Loyalty Leagues," and signs such as one on New York's Fifth Avenue that demanded in bright, flashing lights "Absolute and Unqualified Loyalty to Our Country," created an Orwellian environment. A notorious case exemplifying nativist intolerance and public jingoism involved the lynching of Robert Prager. In April 1918, as anti-German passions peaked, fearful and suspicious Americans acted, destroying property such as immigrant-owned shops and, resorting to vigilantism and mob violence, harmed and occasionally took life, including Prager's. The media often condoned such actions. The *Washington Post*, among others, supported such "patriotic murders." John Ratham, editor of Rhode Island's *Providence Journal*, thundered, "German and Austrian aliens should be considered spies unless proved otherwise." Few dared openly question government decrees or attempt to stop mob violence. Superpatriotism was king, and it would remain so in the early postwar era.[30]

German Americans in the 1920s

After World War I, intolerance and suspicion of perceived domestic enemies abounded as anti-radical, nationalist, and conformist attitudes endured. The Red Scare, immigration restrictions, anti-Semitism, court cases such as *Sacco-Vanzetti* and *Schenck v. United States* (the 1919 Supreme Court case demonstrating Justice Holmes's view of a "clear and present danger," thus justifying the Espionage Act), and attacks on the Industrial Workers of the World are but a few examples. In foreign affairs, America's repudiation of the League of Nations presaged the political conservatism of the 1920s. Americans yearned for what Warren G. Harding referred to as "normalcy."

Continuing pressures on ethnic groups—especially former domestic enemies, and notably German Americans and their associations—to conform to so-called American values and social and cultural norms led to varied responses. The Steuben Society was founded in May 1919 to expedite the Americanization of German Americans and prove that they, "far from being 'mongrels with a divided allegiance . . . hyphenates . . . linked to treachery,' were and always had been loyal Americans." The society's mission included inculcating in German Americans a sense of pride and loyalty to the United States. The society also dabbled in politics as it fostered German American respectability and pride. The slightly older German American Citizens League, established in June 1918, also revived Germanic culture. Disunity, dissension, ambiguous goals, mistrust, and diversity of interests meant, however, that neither group amounted to much. Such was the inauspicious and inoffensive beginning of reactionary elements of the German American community that would create new and more militant Germanic associations to fill the sociocultural void.[31]

As a few German American organizations sought to establish themselves, numerous associations that promoted nationalist values arose or gained strength. The American Legion, organized in 1919, sought 100 percent Americanism and fought any group that advocated otherwise. Nativism assumed several guises: anti-radical, anti-immigrant, anti-Catholic, anti-Semitic, and anti-black in the case of the Ku Klux Klan. Nativists gained strength during the early 1920s amid widespread intolerance. New or resuscitated nativist organizations, stimulated by World War I, enjoyed broad popularity. And while most German Americans accepted the changes produced by war, some harbored resentment and waited to reassert themselves and celebrate their heritage. Still others established the first major German American political clubs or associations.

In October 1924, Fritz and Peter Gissibl helped found the National Socialist Teutonia Association. It laid the foundation for subsequent Bund organizations, including the Gau-USA, Friends of the New Germany, and the German American Bund. Even though the newly organized National Socialist German Worker's Party (NSDAP), which Hitler joined in 1920, never officially recognized Teutonia, its rough American counterpart functioned as a shadow movement of Germany's NSDAP. Most German Americans, while not political zealots, were hardly apathetic. Overwhelmingly they voted Republican or for third-party candidates, including Warren G. Harding and Eugene Debs in 1920 and Robert La Follette in 1924. Nearly all of them blamed Democrats for America's entry into World War I and the programs and policies that effectively eliminated many of their legal rights and extinguished their cultural institutions. German American voters looked to any candidate (preferably non-Democrat) who might forget the past and leave them alone.

As a whole, the 1920s was a period of rebuilding and reorganization for German Americans. Most simply wanted to put the past behind them and move on as "thoroughly Americanized" citizens. The interwar period became a "sort of cultural amnesia" that "characterized the new generation of persons of German antecedents" who grew up during this time.[32] While the German American community sought to reestablish and redefine itself, so, too, did American society.

Wilson and FDR

Despite German Americans' repeated affirmations of their patriotism before World War I and demonstrations of their loyalty during it, President Wilson remained deeply suspicious. Colonel Edward House, Wilson's close friend and trusted adviser, warned Wilson as early as August 1915 that German agents were likely to "blow up waterworks, electric light and gas plants, subways and bridges in cities like New York." Wilson often spoke out against "hyphenates" and made clear that if one was not for America, one could only be against it—and it was high time that "the nation should call [them] to reckoning."[33] Wilson told Congress much the same in his State of the Union of December 7, 1915:

> There are citizens of the United States, I blush to admit, born under other flags but welcomed under our generous naturalization laws to the full freedom and opportunity of America, who have poured the poison of disloyalty into the very arteries of our national life; who have sought to bring the authority and good name of our Government into contempt, to destroy our industries wherever they thought it effective for their vindictive purposes to strike at them, and to debase our politics to the uses of foreign intrigue. Such creatures of passion, disloyalty, and anarchy must be crushed out. The hand of our power should close over them at once.

When asked by the House members to be more specific in his charges, Wilson claimed that divulging specifics would "seriously interfere with the ends of justice."[34]

By March 1917, many of Wilson's advisers believed the nation was swarming with spies and saboteurs. Census data confirmed large numbers of potential disloyals—aliens, "hyphenates," naturalized citizens, refugees—many of whom officials would label as fifth columnists twenty years later. The 1910 census revealed that "one of every three Americans in that year had either been born abroad or had at least one parent born abroad. Of those 32 million persons from families with close foreign ties, more than ten million derived from the Central Powers." Attorney General Thomas Gregory, who had earlier opposed surveilling German aliens, now felt it necessary to investigate "a very large number of German citizens" because the government "must expect trouble of a sinister sort."[35]

In December 1919, a year after the war's end, Franklin Roosevelt, then involved in intelligence work as assistant secretary of the navy, received an alarming intelligence report:

> A Nation-wide Terrorists' campaign is being hatched on the Pacific and Atlantic Coasts by Germans, Russian and Mexican Terrorists. The main planning is being done in Mexico City by old-time German anarchists who escaped from Chicago during the Haymarket Riots. No definite date has yet been set. The Terror will surpass anything that ever happened in this country and the brains of the plot are already on the Pacific Coast, the real directing is being done from Mexico City.[36]

The report, however erroneous, undoubtedly influenced the future president, whose keen interest in covert operations and fascination with spy novels led him to believe he had been the intended target of German assassins: "The Secret Service found in the safe of the German Consul in New York, a document headed: 'To be eliminated.' Mine was the second followed by eight or ten others. The Secret Service asked us to carry revolvers as we habitually walked to and from our offices. I was given the revolver and the shoulder holster." Roosevelt recalled that German secret agents and subversives had engaged in acts of sabotage, including Black Tom. Government investigations found German aliens guilty of inciting labor disputes in East Coast munitions factories and shipyards. As Roosevelt worked closely with the Office of Naval Intelligence (ONI) he frequently passed along numerous and "disturbing reports" about German Americans from sources he considered reliable. The ONI claimed that subversives worked at Brooklyn's Krantz Manufacturing Company: "The employees are almost German to a man. Every official has a German appearance and pro-German influence is very strong. The German officials keep their business activities very quiet and always converse in German." If this was not damning enough, another ONI report asserted that the Philadelphia firm of Schutte and Koerting had been "installing defective apparatus in the U.S. Navy." The reason none were found was that the "defects" had been "carefully concealed."[37]

Perceived German and Japanese Encroachments

On March 1, 1917, newspapers published the Zimmerman telegram. The note proposed an alliance whereby Germany would help Mexico reclaim its lost territories if it attacked the United States and also suggested a German-Japanese alliance so Japan might grab chunks of the American West in return for switching sides. Wilson released the note to the press. News of the German offer inflamed public opinion, particularly among those living along the Pacific Coast, and a month later, during which time German U-boats sank several American merchant ships, Germany and the United States were at war with one other. It mattered little that Japan had been at war against Germany since August 1914 and had taken many of Germany's Far East colonial possessions. Nor did many realize that the successful implementation of such a grandiose operation was all but impossible given the technological limitations, great distances, and logistical problems. More importantly, the enthusiasm, willingness, and risk required for such a venture on Mexico's part simply did not exist.[38] The nation's postwar distrust of German Americans and the emerging fear of a Japanese invasion of the West Coast, dramatically reinforced by movies and popular magazines, did, however, exist, and in fact grew over time.

In retrospect, it is remarkable that the Bureau of Investigation arrested only 6,300 aliens during World War I—nearly all German

Americans. Aside from the 4,000 alien enemy sailors interned for the war's duration, 2,300 civilian enemy aliens likewise endured internment until the end of the war or beyond in Fort Oglethorpe, Georgia, or Fort Douglas, Utah—two of the War Department's four major internment camps.[39] Others endured privation differently. Thousands bore the stigma of arrest or interrogation, while thousands more spent weeks or months languishing in overcrowded prisons before their release.

The early interwar era saw the persistence of nativists' assaults and racists' passions along with the continuation of wartime fears. Popular magazines and newspapers ran stories of German American intrigues, while political cartoons lampooned German Americans. Fascinating tales of espionage and sabotage activities fueled and reinforced such stereotypes. Columnists accused German Americans of fostering a pan-Germanic state while cartoonists depicted them as stooges willing to fight and die, if necessary, for the kaiser. Reports accused these disloyals of hiding under the very banner of freedom they sought to eradicate. Other signs of intolerance included scientific ethnocentrism, which had become common. Sixteen states passed sterilization laws. The Immigration Restriction League attracted eminent reformers. Even the liberal *New Republic* told readers to doubt "our power of assimilation" and the ability of newly arriving immigrants to "put off their national characters and become good Americans."[40]

Widespread racist attitudes focused on Japanese Americans, whom even some progressives referred to as the "yellow peril," a concept that H. G. Wells had popularized in *The War in the Air* (1908). In the novel, the Japanese and Chinese engage the white powers in an internecine struggle that nearly destroys humanity itself. The moral: "The Yellow Peril was a peril after all." Meanwhile, the ONI focused on the possibility of war with Japan and worried about Japanese Americans living near naval bases, key industrial centers, munitions plants and utility companies, and vital transportation arteries such as subways, bridges, and railroads along the West Coast, Alaska, and Hawaii.

Assimilation and Loyalty

Woodrow Wilson and others labeled as disloyal members or associates of the Bund or pro-German organizations. Japanese Americans became a "yellow peril," while Italian Americans aroused some suspicions too. All three groups, many felt, harbored secret agents, spies, and saboteurs who would provide logistical aid, information, and ammunition and would spearhead an invasion. Acceptance of Germans and Italians came more easily than acceptance of the Japanese, yet both European groups faced hostility and stereotyping, and only the hardships borne by German Americans along with their abandonment of old-world ties allowed them to fare better later. In short, as historian La Vern Rippley concluded: "World War I was the catalyst that jelled the Americanization of the German population."[41] The war's effects accelerated their assimilation, while many still found ways to embrace elements of their former culture and others joined the Bund in its various guises between 1924 and 1941. The Bund's antics, coupled with a massive propaganda campaign waged against its members, led millions to believe that such miscreants represented the vanguard of Hitler's army. Italian immigrants occasionally faced widespread hostility too; they were considered a "nightmare of the American dream," with "Chianti, Catholicism, and Crime" as their "indelible stigma."[42]

Many immigrants clung to cultural elements that set them apart. Some chose not to become citizens. Political apathy, economic mobility, social status, fond memories of their homeland and faraway relatives, and a nostalgic respect for their customs and heritage kept 25 percent of Germans and 43 percent of Italians from obtaining citizenship by 1940. Yet by 1910 more than 90 percent of the German-born had taken out first papers, and naturalized Germans remained at 75 percent during the early 1900s—higher than the naturalized English (67 percent). Naturalized Italians doubled from only 28 percent in 1920 to 57 percent by 1940.[43] Historian Stephen Fox concludes that for Italian Americans residing in California:

If the correct measure of assimilation is whether the aliens learned English and spoke it with their children, became citizens, and moved out of ethnic ghettos, then Italians of California were not assimilated before the war. They first thought of themselves as Italian, then American. On the other hand, if assimilation is judged by the number of aliens who occupied key economic positions or planned never to return to their homeland, or believed that merely living in America made them "American," then many of California's immigrant Italians were assimilated by 1942. Each of the aliens met one or more of the criteria of both assimilation and nonassimilation. The Italian aliens believed they were Americans, but Americans who had deliberately retained some of their old-world traditions.[44]

Regardless, all three enemy alien and citizen groups served as scapegoats, what Geoffrey Perrett referred to as "the ritual sacrifice," as the United States again went to war.[45]

2

Fifth-Column Fears and Foreign Challenges

> The Bureau desires to obtain from all possible sources information concerning subversive activities conducted in the United States.... Immediately transmit any information on the part of any individual or organization, regardless of the source.
>
> —J. EDGAR HOOVER TO SPECIAL AGENTS IN CHARGE, SEPTEMBER 5, 1936

As early as 1927, some self-professed patriotic Americans, including Dr. Charles Fama, were able to see fascism's darker side. In 1929, Fama, an ardent anti-fascist, became the president of the Defenders of the Constitution. Active and outspoken, he was given police protection due to constant death threats. Nevertheless, Fama spoke at anti-fascist rallies and petitioned all who would listen and heed fascism's dangers. He wrote to anyone who might help, from Herbert Hoover and later Franklin Roosevelt to State Department and local officials. His *Beware of the Menace of Fascism in America* warned citizens of a real and present danger. "I am enclosing a pamphlet written by me," Dr. Fama wrote, "in order to open the eyes of the American public that she might not fall for the propaganda of this new 'ism.' In my opinion, there is no room in this country of ours [for] any 'ism' but Americanism." He provided examples of the "fraudulent purposes of Fascism," its aims and activities, and pleaded with his fellow Americans to "awake from lethargy and rally once more to our Constitution":

> Fascism is slowly and surely spreading its dark tentacles, like a huge spider, around Italians in America, attempting to make Mus-

> solini Black Shirts of them. Fascism—more subtle, more dangerous, more insidious than Bolshevism, is conducting its widespread anti-American propaganda in the Italian press, ninety per cent of which is either owned or has been bribed by Mussolini. Fascism is making dupes of hundreds of Italians in this country, who are unaware of the vicious character of this Black Shirt organization. The Italian Press here recently published the news that Fascisti Popular Universities have just been established in New York City and Chicago advertising the teaching of such subjects as Philosophy of Fascism, Fascist Literature, Fascist Law, History of Fascism, etc.[1]

Convincing politicians and the public that fascism was an evil even worse than Bolshevism was going to be a tough sell. Secretary of State Charles Evans Hughes congratulated Mussolini on his rise to power. Ambassador George Harvey, for his part, cabled from his London post that fascism would be the "death knell of Bolshevism" and advised Ambassador Richard Child, who "extolled the merits of Fascism and spoke of the dictator in tones of adulation," to "manifest a spirit of somewhat notable friendliness and hopefulness" toward Mussolini and the new regime.[2]

America's Flirtation with Italian Fascism

An Italian fascist movement, while overshadowed by Communists, the Bund, and Nazi Party activities, was well under way in the United States during the 1920s. In Italy, dissident socialists joined syndicalists, radical democrats, and the nationalist right in creating nascent fascist organizations. The National Fascist Party's coup, the March on Rome, and Mussolini's seizure of power in October 1922 marked the beginning of a twenty-two-year era. It also began a cooperative time between Il Duce's Italy and the 160,000 members of the Order of the Sons of Italy, viewed as the official representative of Italian emigrants. Until 1935, the symbiotic relationship worked well.[3]

Fascism's allure and Mussolini's charm proved ephemeral, as Italy's war in Ethiopia, from October 1935 to May 1936, strained diplomatic relations, soured media contacts, and quickly turned American public opinion against fascism and Il Duce. The war marked the end of Washington's brief flirtation with fascism and the beginning of anti-fascist policies. When asked, "What foreign country do you feel least friendly toward?," Americans in the fall of 1935 ranked Italy third, behind Germany (first) and Japan (second) but ahead of Russia (ranked fourth—despite the Red Scare and anti-communist sentiment).[4] Such attitudes, though, were virtually nonexistent during Italian fascism's rise due to favorable press coverage. Nevertheless, those few who best understood the aims of Mussolini's regime fought doggedly and passionately until anti-fascist sentiment began to crystallize. Even so, America's anti-fascist struggle required great effort from its passionate organizers along with years of unwavering determination.

The First Challenges to Fascism

In the spring of 1930 a House of Representatives special committee investigating communist activities was identifying potential troublemakers. In January 1931 Congressman Hamilton Fish proposed legislation authorizing the Bureau of Investigation to study "Communist and revolutionary activity." At the time, J. Edgar Hoover opposed it. He told Fish that it would be better to enact a criminal statute and not expand the bureau's power beyond criminal investigation, especially since the agency had "never been established by legislation" and operated "solely on an appropriation bill." Yet within a few years, both military and civilian organizations joined the hunt for subversives and disloyals, especially Hoover's Bureau of Investigation.[5] The federal government, however, tempered its private investigations as State Department officials sought to maintain a mutually beneficial relationship with Italy and Germany.

In January 1932, Undersecretary of State William Castle Jr. wrote his superiors, including Secretary of State Henry Stimson, about a recent conversation with the Italian ambassador, Giacomo De Martino, who was perturbed by Fish's resolution to investigate fascist and anti-fascist activities. The ambassador argued that the fascists had "no organization" and, "in any case, were urging Italian Americans to live up to the laws of their adopted country." Still, even after talking with Stimson, De Martino was "evidently very much exercised over the possibility of an investigation," to which the undersecretary tried to assure him that, given "the amount of work Congress had to do, it would not waste much time over an investigation of this sort."[6]

Congress was then far more concerned about communists. Fish's special committee spent six months investigating communists and revolutionary activity while ignoring fascism. Only by late 1933 and early 1934, after Hitler's seizure of power, did Congress, the president, the FBI, and the American public begin to take the fascist threat seriously. Still, a few citizens continually raised their voices as Congress, for its part, accepted the media's increasingly negative portrayal of fascist ideology, groups, clubs, associations, and organizations. On March 1, 1931, Herbert Goddard, a self-proclaimed "American Citizen," had had enough and wrote President Hoover:

> As an American Citizen, I with many hundreds of thousands of others am absolutely against Fascist propaganda going on as it does continually in the United States. It is high time to drive from our shores those whose sole purpose in being here is to spread Fascism, Communism, and Bolshevism throughout our country and to attempt to tear down the principles of American freedom and our great Constitution. How much longer must we submit to these insults without taking strenuous action to free our beloved America of these foreign undesirables? . . . There is no time to lose—great caution is necessary.[7]

Many others agreed and wrote their elected officials, including the president. Laura Austin emphatically stated, "We do *not* want *Fascism* in *America*." Elizabeth Hoffmann succinctly wrote, "We are against fascist propaganda in the U.S.A.," while Paul Kast added, "I hereby desire to respectfully register my protest of the existing propaganda work in this country in behalf of Fascism." William Hartmann put it simply, "I protest against the fascist movement in this country." The Bentz family, writing President Hoover and "those in authority," was "in favor of peace," but not "at any price."[8]

Gradually an increasing number of Italian Americans objected to the presence of fascists and fascist groups. Girolamo Valenti, managing editor of *La Stampa Libera*, "the paper read by intelligent Italians," outspokenly criticized the Order of the Sons of Italy and the Lictor Federation, another prominent Italian fascist organization. Proud of his paper's masthead—"The Only Italian Labor Daily in the United States"—Valenti, in correspondence in the summer and fall of 1932, alerted Stimson and others of fascist activities, including a planned disruption of an anti-fascist Fourth of July celebration, which, Valenti noted, happened also to be the birth date of Giuseppe Garibaldi, renowned Italian general and patriot who was instrumental in his nation's unification.

Writing of the July 4, 1932, riots on Staten Island, Valenti emphasized that the fascists sought conflict and noted that some Italian officials actually participated in the disorders. Valenti described the crowd of two to three thousand, riots, fighting on trains, and the shooting death of Salvatore Arena—a fascist accidentally slain by one of his own. He expressed outrage over the involvement of two vice-consuls as well as the Italian consul general, Emanuel Grazzi, who sought the provocations. He warned of "officials of the Italian government engaging in political activities" and requested an investigation of all fascist agitators. A State Department legal adviser thought it best that local authorities handle things, while Fish informed Stimson of the events. Valenti, undeterred, used his *La Stampa Libera* as a bully pulpit, warning of trouble ahead. Unfortunately, his warnings, along with those of other prominent anti-fascists, went largely unheeded.[9]

Another raising the cry against fascism was historian and social reformer Gaetano Salvemini. Born and raised in Italy, Salvemini became a first-rate scholar and untiring political activist. He aimed to "develop an active and unrelenting propaganda campaign designed to inform world opinion about the true nature of Fascism, to expose the brutal, corrupt, and suppressive nature of the dictatorship, and to shatter the false image built on lies that Mussolini's propaganda agents were spreading throughout Europe and America."[10] Through speeches, lectures, debates, and publications—including *The Fascist Dictatorship in Italy* (1927), *Mussolini Diplomate* (1932), and *Under the Axe of Fascism* (1936)—Salvemini rebuked Mussolini and decried the dictator's programs and policies. Heeding such activists, Congress in January 1934 finally resolved to investigate Nazi and subversive propaganda, and while surveillance of Hawaii's Japanese population had begun during World War I, officials now searched for spies among mainland Japanese.

Evolving Reactions to the Fascist Challenge

By 1933, in several important respects, the "fascist challenge" was already well under way. While few realized Hitler's potential, the Teutonia Association (1924–32) and the Gau-USA (1931–33), which connected itself to the Nazi Party, began America's Nazi movement. Just after Hitler's accession to power came the German Nazi Party–inspired Friends of Germany (1933–34) along with a domestic umbrella group, the Friends of the New Germany (1933–36), consisting of dozens of disparate and loosely organized Nazi factions. All, including the Friends of the New Germany, were forerunners of the influential German American Bund (1936–41), led by Fritz Julius Kuhn.[11]

As the decade progressed, the public began to see any anti-American group as part of a unified, subversive, and anti-democratic front. Although fascism may not have appealed to most Americans, the Great Depression's ravages coupled with Mussolini's and Hitler's alluring promises caused some to question democracy and wonder if fascism might cure the world's ills.[12] Hitler and his advisers knew that the Western Hemisphere had a substantial German population. In May 1933, Joseph Goebbels began concentrating all foreign propaganda activities under his newly created Propaganda Ministry, or PROMI, while Hitler sought to coordinate the activities of Germans abroad and emphasize the dual doctrines of race and space. Meanwhile, Roosevelt and others became increasingly suspicious of Japan's military motives and distrustful of Japanese Americans. A massive fifteen-volume Army Intelligence report, *Estimate of the Situation—Japanese Population in Hawaii*, portrayed Japanese Hawaiians as disloyal, even dangerous.

Reports of discrimination against Jews, attacks upon the Church, interference with academia, and Germany's exit from the League of Nations in 1933 together with its concurrent military buildup demonstrated a new course for German domestic and foreign policies. At home, the German American Bund's antics only exacerbated matters. "We are," Kuhn stated in October 1936, "first of all, Germans by race, in blood, in language. We belong to the great commonwealth of all German peoples on this earth. We remain what we are: Germans in America, American-Germans, because we did not become Americans." Efforts to foster National Socialism in the United States along with loyalty to Hitler and the fatherland aroused suspicion and distrust. The belief of an enemy within, a "fifth column," was reborn and soon provided the driving force behind relocation and internment. All the while Roosevelt battled the Depression, readied the nation for war, and worried about the destabilization of Latin American nations, whose alliance with America was tenuous and opposition to Germany dubious. The Bund's antics, Nazi actions, and Hitler's policy pronouncements soon led to a breaking point. In short, the 1930s saw a remarkable deterioration in German-American relations.[13]

Germany Acts

In the spring of 1933, Goebbels's PROMI issued a master propaganda plan, Germany left the League of Nations, and Rudolf Hess, Hitler's number two man, established the Volksdeutsche Mittelstelle (Coordination Center for Ethnic Germans) to coordinate activities of Germans abroad and create a sense of global Germandom. The American media frequently ran stories of Nazi brutalities and excesses in addition to aliens and organizations professing loyalty or sympathy to Hitler and Deutschtum (Germanness). Headlines such as "Deportation Urged for Hitlerites Here" soon appeared in major U.S. newspapers, including the *New York Times*. Popular films likewise fed the nation's appetite about the "insidious, treacherous activities of Nazi agents masquerading as American citizens." By trying to build a pan-Germania, however, Hitler disaffected the very German Americans he sought to direct.[14]

Goebbels's Press Department of the Foreign Ministry, since May 1933 under the auspices of the PROMI, issued and sent a significant directive that September to the German Consulate in New York City, a hotbed for National Socialism. Historian Alton Frye concluded that the instructions constituted nothing less than a master plan for German propaganda in the Americas. A major and explicit premise was that public opinion in both North and South America was especially susceptible to a carefully executed campaign. Goebbels also took note of the generally greater importance of public opinion among the American democracies than in Europe, and pointed to the dependence of American governments on popular support. Viewing the hostile environment into which the New Germany had been born, Goebbels proposed to cultivate a favorable attitude toward Germany among the masses in the Western Hemisphere, hoping thereby to exert a corresponding pressure on American governments.[15]

While Western sources paid the directive scant attention, concerned political activists sought to stymie perceived Nazi encroachments while, in December 1933, Hitler chose Rear Admiral Wilhelm Franz Canaris to head the Abwehr, Germany's secret service. "What I want," Hitler told Canaris, "is something like the British Secret Service—an Order, doing its work with passion." Hitler's new spymaster was not about to fail the führer. And by the time Roosevelt had given the FBI both the designated authority and virtual autonomy to combat subversive elements, Nazi agents had stolen countless government, industrial, and defense-related secrets in what was, in historian William Breuer's words, the "most massive espionage penetration of a major power that history had known."[16]

Americans React

The American Protestant Defense League, based in Yonkers, New York, urged their fellow citizens to stop, read, think, and act. "Your God and country call you to prayer, service and action," because "Bolshevism, Atheism and Political Romanism, as well as other foreign-minded enemies and repealers of the Constitution are working day and night, and believe that the day is not far distant when they will seize the government." Ministers Elmo Bateman, William Nichol, and Thomas Little warned, "Foreign dictators are rising up all over Europe threatening democracy and preparing the way for a reign of terror not only in those countries but in the rest of the world."[17] Fear of foreign, especially Nazi, encroachments—of "enemies within"—was taking root.

In October 1933, Inspector George MacDowell, having investigated Nazi propaganda activities for months, described Nazi activities in New York to Colonel MacCormack, commissioner general of the Immigration and Naturalization Service (INS). His findings supported a confidential INS report that had outlined the American Nazi Party's origins, tracing them to Fritz Gissibl's Teutonia, founded in Detroit on October 12, 1924. The report noted the movement's dissolution when the "official representative of Hitler in the United States, Captain Luedecke, had reported to his German masters that it would be dangerous to have official groups organize in this country under the Nazi leadership."[18] There seemed reason to fear a widespread underground movement led by Nazi agents.

Numerous reports warned of disturbing developments abroad and their potential ramifications at home. In October 1933 the American Consulate in Trieste, Italy, cabled:

> It appears that pressure is brought by Italian fascists upon naturalized American citizens of Italian birth to induce them to become members of the Fascist party and to take the Fascist oath of allegiance and that Italian officials endeavor to control the actions, in the United States, of naturalized Americans of Italian birth. The Fascist oath may be translated as follows: "In the name of God and of Italy, I swear to obey the orders of the Duce and to serve with all my strength and, if it is necessary with my blood, the cause of the Fascist Revolution."[19]

The following month the American Consulate in Stuttgart cabled Secretary of State Cordell Hull. Disturbing news in the *Chicago Daily Tribune* and the *New York Herald* (Paris editions) prompted Leon Dominian, American consul general in charge, to write:

> Press reports have come to my notice regarding alleged Nazi agitation in the United States, and I wish to invite the Department's attention to the insufficiency . . . to prevent issuance of visas to members of Fascist organizations whose purpose is . . . the inten-

tion of undertaking propaganda, which would be destructive to free institutions and the rights of individuals guaranteed by the Constitution.

In Germany . . . religious persecution has been directed against every religion in the country. Jews have been assaulted and have died as a result of brutal treatment. Roman Catholic priests have been attacked and jailed. Protestant ministers have been confined in concentration camps. Harmless religious sects . . . have been dissolved. In Italy, similar religious persecution was carried out by the Fascist regime.

Attempts are being made to spread National Socialist doctrines in the United States. German agitation in foreign countries is far more serious than Italian because Germans are more energetic, more active, and organize their efforts efficiently than Italians. . . . One of the aims of the German National Socialist party is to create favorable world opinion. . . . It seems probable that action will be taken through National Socialist agents. The application of government measures to prevent National Socialist agitation is required.[20]

Nazi Propaganda and German Americans

In October 1933, Congressman Samuel Dickstein began investigating several hundred "Nazi agents" who he believed were in the United States under the guise of diplomatic or consulate attachés. Dickstein had begun "an unofficial study of the charges that have been made against aliens who entered this country from Germany for the purpose not only of forming here a brand of Hitler's government and Hitler's newspapers but to establish here racial and religious hatred and bigotry." Reasons for the inquiry centered on the activities of Heinz Spanknoebel, the former leader of Detroit's Nazi group and current leader of the Friends of the New Germany. The committee learned from a "Mr. X" that "the Hitler government desired to build up Nazi organizations in the United States to the end that the government of the United States may come under Nazi control."[21] The Friends sought to unify German Americans across the nation and work to achieve Hitler's doctrine of racial purity and the related goal of lebensraum within which German peoples everywhere could prosper. They linked German foreign-policy actions, including an increased rearmament program and use of force, with belligerent Bund decrees. With public demands for action against the perceived threat rising, Congress obliged.

On January 3, 1934, Dickstein introduced House Resolution 198, which Congress passed on March 20. The resolution created the so-called McCormack-Dickstein Committee, named for its chair and vice chair, Massachusetts's John W. McCormack and New York's Samuel Dickstein. The investigation of Nazi propaganda included that of the Friends of the New Germany and Silver Shirts. After complimenting the "twenty-odd-million Americans of German birth or descent, who have refused to participate in the Nazi movement and propaganda in this country," the committee revealed worrisome "evidence showing the strenuous efforts made to enlist these twenty-odd-million persons" and claimed it had "unearthed evidence showing that an effort to spread the theory of the National Socialist German Labor Party, commonly referred to as the Nazi philosophy, had been under way in the United States for several years." Believing that it had "evidence to show the wiles and blandishments" employed by the German government to dupe erstwhile Germans along with unwitting German American citizens "into the Nazi program," the committee's hunt for subversives was on.[22]

In April the McCormack-Dickstein Committee began its inquiry into fascist activities, investigating the Silver Shirt Legion and the Khaki Shirts of America, among others, but focusing on the Friends of the New Germany because it echoed Hitler's call for a global National Socialist revolution, the German people's mission expressed in *Mein Kampf*. The Friends responded enthusiastically to the Reich's repeated declaration that ties of blood and race united all Germans, including the thirty million living outside Germany. Statements made by German Americans at rallies, including Sylvester Viereck's at Madison Square Garden in May 1934, illustrate why Congress investigated the Friends:

> We shall not remain silent. We shall no longer submit to intolerable insult. We are being forced into battle. When Adolph Hitler freed the German soul, he freed not only the Germans within the Reich

but one hundred million Germans throughout the world. Cowed by years of abuse, crucified by their enemies, Americans of German descent, like their co-racials across the ocean, had developed a sense of inferiority. Relieved at last from this burden, the German Americans are better able now than at any time in all their history to collaborate with the forces of reconstruction in American life.

Clearly, such public pronouncements did not help the cause of German Americans:

> The committee conducted public and executive hearings intermittently between April 26 and December 29, 1934, in Washington, DC; New York; Chicago; Los Angeles; Newark; and Asheville, NC, examining hundreds of witnesses and accumulating more than 4,300 pages of testimony. The committee accumulated evidence regarding individuals and organizations who worked to establish in the United States policies followed by the Nazis in Germany, the Fascists in Italy, and the Communists in Russia. The committee gave particular attention to the organization and activities of Friends of New Germany and Silver Shirts of America. The committee submitted its report on February 15, 1935.[23]

Danger at Home and Abroad

Reports in August 1934 warned Roosevelt and others of the imminent danger posed by Japanese agents in virtually every major city throughout the country and all along the West Coast. Thousands of spies and saboteurs, allegedly acting as farmers, fishermen, and common laborers, stood ready to attack. The perceived threat alarmed the Office of Naval Intelligence. The following October its headquarters received a report stating "through the subversion and exploitation of American navy personnel with the inducement of prostitutes and drugs," a Japanese espionage ring operating in Seattle and Portland along with naval officers attached to the Japanese Embassy was "secretly compiling information on strategic areas along the West Coast." The ONI then warned the White House of suspicious activities near Pearl Harbor as Japanese residents interacted with the crews of Japanese merchant ships headed to or from the West Coast and Japan. Roosevelt then wrote the chief of naval operations in August 1936: "One obvious thought occurs to me—that every Japanese citizen or non-citizen on the island of Oahu who meets these Japanese ships or has any connection with their officers or men should be secretly but definitely identified and his or her name placed on a special list of those who would be the first to be placed in a concentration camp in the event of trouble."[24]

Roosevelt worried about the loyalty of Japanese American communities in Hawaii and on the West Coast and wondered what diplomats, spies, saboteurs, and German Americans might do as international relations worsened. Another concern was the safety of Americans residing abroad—particularly in the Far East and Europe. In 1936 the State Department sent its first instructions to diplomatic missions and consular establishments for returning Americans in an emergency. It repeated the instructions in 1938, 1939, and 1941 and also issued warnings in Europe in May 1940 and later that year in China, Japan, Hong Kong, and French Indochina. Efforts to return Americans safely and expeditiously from so-called danger zones were effective. In August 1939 the State and Navy Departments and the Maritime Commission began considering how best to evacuate large numbers of Americans in harm's way, which the State Department estimated at 80,000 in Europe and 17,000 in the Far East. In September alone, thanks to cooperation with Britain and other European nations as well as several shipping and freight companies, the State Department estimated that some "50,000 passengers arrived at our Atlantic ports on United States and foreign vessels" and noted that even more returned home "by way of Canadian ports."[25]

Worsening Conditions and Mass Communicating

Throughout the 1930s, hundreds of articles appeared in scholarly as well as popular journals about enemy intrigues. Berlin, Rome, and Tokyo looked covetously at Southeast Asia, China, and South and Central America. Stories focused on the Nazi regime's brutalities and those professing loyalty to Hitler and Deutschtum. After Italy's declaration of war against France in June 1940, concern about Italian American loyalties to Mussolini and fascist Italy grew. Although the media focused on Berlin and Rome, occasional stories warned of dangers from Tokyo and Moscow. Communists as well as fascists, Americans learned, were undermining the nation's cherished ideological principles and sacred institutions. As the 1930s ended, however, international circumstances changed radically, as did views of Russians and Japanese. After Germany invaded the Soviet Union in June 1941 the government and the media quickly adjusted course. *Life*, for example, declared the Russians "one hell of a people" who "look like Americans, dress like Americans and think like Americans." The Japanese now appeared clothed in new ideological mufti—ubiquitously typecast as nasty, dwarfish animals.[26]

Roosevelt convincingly warned his fellow Americans of the fifth-column menace. On October 5, 1937, his Quarantine Speech dispelled the illusion that the nation and the hemisphere were impervious to enemy attack. It was "unfortunately true," FDR proclaimed, that the "epidemic of world lawlessness is spreading." That said, when an epidemic spreads, "the community approves and joins in a quarantine of the patients in order to protect the health of the community against the spread of the disease." Because "war is a contagion, whether it be declared or undeclared," the international community must quarantine diseased or aggressor nations. Despite Roosevelt's assurances to the contrary, the speech not only heralded the nation's willingness to involve itself on the world stage but also indicated his personal desire to be more active in global affairs. Representatives, for example, tried to resolve the Sino-Japanese War that had begun in July 1937, while the *Panay* incident in December, when Japanese aircraft sank the U.S. gunboat in Chinese waters, suggested the difficulties of neutrality.[27]

FDR used radio, as did other prominent orators of the time, including foreign and domestic nemeses Hitler and the anti-Semitic Father Charles Coughlin, who appealed to racists and many of the Christian Right. Roosevelt's famous "fireside chats" effectively galvanized public support for a war he knew was coming, perhaps to America's very shores. On May 16, 1940, Roosevelt addressed to a joint session of Congress and denounced Germany's "treacherous use of the Fifth Column by which persons supposed to peaceful visitors were actually a part of an enemy unit of occupation."[28] A "Trojan Horse," he and top advisers mused, would aid a future invasion.

An external attack aided by internal traitors was still a far-fetched idea for many. Thought problematic at best and fictional at worst, the scenario soon became plausible. The specter of what subversives and spies could do manifested in the spring of 1940. Using Germany's military successes and tales of fifth-column activities for maximum political effect, Roosevelt astutely coaxed public support for a "just cause" or "good war" fought against an enemy bent on insurrection and destruction. Germany would use any means necessary, including Nazi agents posing as civilian tourists or students, to defeat its foes. It was time for a special fireside chat. On May 26, amid a rapid succession of German victories in western Europe (resulting in the Dunkirk evacuation), FDR warned millions that "today's threat to our national security is not a matter of military weapons alone. We know of new methods of attack, the Trojan horse, the Fifth Column that betrays a nation unprepared for treachery. Spies, saboteurs, and traitors are all actors in the new strategy. With all that we must and will deal vigorously." In later fireside chats, Roosevelt invoked the fifth-column specter and emphasized that Americans could no longer rely upon the "broad oceans" to serve "as our protection from attack."[29]

Movies, too, created indelible images of the enemy and their sinister plotting. The Marx Brothers' *Duck Soup* (1933) lampooned blundering dictatorial leaders, fascism, and authoritarian regimes. Despite its brilliant satire, audiences, taken aback by the film's disrespect of government, its sheer buffoonery, and callous cynicism at a time of political and economic crisis, failed to see much humor. Moviegoers especially detested Groucho's memorable quote: "And remember while you're out there risking life and limb through shot and shell, we'll be in here thinking what a sucker you are." Still, it was impactful, as Mussolini banned *Duck Soup* in Italy.

News of Germany's actions abroad and the Bund's activities at home led to a severe backlash against the Bund, German Americans, and Germany. The repercussions along with the McCormack-Dickstein Committee's report in February 1935 prompted Germany to sever its ties with the Friends of the New Germany. On October 11, 1935, the German Foreign Ministry and the Auslandsorganisation (AO, or Foreign Organization) formally ordered all German nationals, including those with first papers, to resign from the Friends. Failure to comply would mean loss of German citizenship. Nevertheless, ardent American National Socialists refused defeat. The following April, Kuhn's Bund emerged from the Friends' chrysalis. The media alleged links between European events and the Bund's activities. As relations between Germany and the United States soured and the situation in Europe worsened, media coverage intensified. Stories of Nazi intrigues, both abroad and at home, and tyrannical plots, supported by legions of un-American minions, your next-door neighbors, captivated the public. As early as 1933, warnings of fascist dangers frequently appeared in leading papers and magazines.

Ultimately, Goebbels's Propaganda Ministry's attempts to influence or subvert the American media proved fruitless. Likewise, attempts to establish German-run papers and propaganda centers within the borders of the United States typically ended in failure. Unable to win the hearts and minds of mainstream America, increasingly attacked by an unsympathetic press, and ostracized by the German government from which they claimed their legitimacy, Nazi propagandists eventually turned their attention to Central and South America, where they fared better and achieved a limited degree of success.

The Bund was often its own worst enemy. The media frequently exposed the ugly side of National Socialism that Kuhn and Bundists tried to hide. The negative imagery, beginning in the spring of 1933, helped end America's Nazi movement before it could gather real political strength or cultural appeal. Yet the intensity and duration of the media blitz—along with the official investigations of German Americans, especially aliens—was so constant and the vilification so convincing that by decade's end few Americans doubted that some of their neighbors were loyal to Hitler's Germany.

In March 1933 the *New York Times* offered the following headline: "Nazi Units in United States List 1,000 Aliens; Admit Their Aim Is to Spread Propaganda." In September the *Times* warned that a "new element has made its appearance, sent here for the express purpose of spreading Nazi propaganda under the direct auspices of the present German Government, whose aim it is to inject into the American system the deplorable theories of Hitlerism." Sensational headlines such as "Nazis' Hand Seen in Activities Here" and "Hitler Men Said to Be Ready to Send Report of 'Sabotage' to Reich Authorities" captured readers' attention. Though headlines were sometimes misleading, since the context of "Hitler Men" clarified that "Nazi agents had threatened dissenting officers of a local German organization with denunciation to authorities in Germany as 'saboteurs,'" many readers undoubtedly saw Nazi agents as insidious foes hard at work.[30]

Given such widespread perceptions of Nazi intentions, officials wasted little time investigating Nazi activities after HR 198 was passed in March 1934. Meanwhile, members of the League for the Defense of Jewish Rights petitioned for the deportation of Nazi propagandists. The *New Republic* also expressed alarm over militaristic German attitudes. While it acknowledged that Germany had withdrawn its newest official high school and university textbook, Professor Ewald Banse's *The Science of Arms*, it maintained that "there is no doubt that Professor Banse's book accurately represented the attitude of Germany's rulers." Other books, the article noted, upholding similar ideas but achieving less notoriety, were still in use in Germany. After citing Banse's mantra, "War is constructive. It builds up what it destroys. War is therefore a perpetual rejuvenator and it is wrong to see destructive tendencies in it," the *New Republic* noted German factories directly charged with producing arms and war equipment and concluded:

> With effective opposition to war within Germany totally destroyed, with industry organized into a vast war machine, with both pacifists and revolutionists killed, imprisoned or forced into hiding or flight, with the government in complete control of the church and press, with strikes forbidden and, finally, with education reduced to little more than propaganda for war, the Nazis are certainly in a splendid position to assure the world of their peaceful intentions, but hardly in a position to be offended if the world refuses to believe them.

In November and December 1933 the *New York Times* ran a series of articles detailing the activities of alleged Nazi agents, plots, and plans for German Day celebrations.[31]

Novelists, too, sounded the tocsin. Sinclair Lewis's chilling 1935 best-seller, *It Can't Happen Here*, demonstrated that it could. The novel portrayed future revolutionary and master orator Berzelius Windrip's fascist coup d'état. Buzz Windrip, an amalgam of Louisiana "Kingfish" politician Huey Long and "Kansas Hitler" right-wing evangelist Gerald Winrod, stormed the White House on the shoulders of the common man, helped by his brutal private army, the Minutemen. The lesson: America could succumb to demagogues, its own native-born Hitlers.[32] Ernest Hemingway's popular 1940 novel turned box-office smash, *For Whom the Bell Tolls*, revealed that liberty's loss anywhere in the world signaled its potential loss everywhere as the protagonist, American professor Robert Jordan (played by Gary Cooper), fought alongside Spanish loyalists against the fascists. Hemingway had dealt with turbulent stories of life and love before; his play *The Fifth Column* (1938) lent credence to and reinforced the veracity of such activities. George Britt's *The Fifth Column Is Here* (1940) followed Hemingway's story of a besieged Madrid. Britt warned that internal enemies were not only active on the Iberian Peninsula or in the Old World but also throughout the United States and the New World.

Artists canvassed social and political issues too. Some, critics charged, were mere propagandists. William Gropper's *Legislative Paunch*, a widely reproduced painting, depicted grotesque politicians with swollen bellies, while one of Peter Blume's most important works, *Eternal City*, revealed a surreal Rome ruled by an ugly, ignoble Mussolini. Many academicians joined the anti-fascist crusade in the 1930s. Although some teachers had praised Italy's extraordinary educational renaissance and other scholars had spoken or written sympathetically about Mussolini's accomplishments, many, even in the mid-1920s, were skeptical of both Mussolini and fascism and began to say so. A small but determined anti-fascist cry grew into a chorus. Newspapers, magazines, novels, films, and radio broadcasts alerted the public to the fascist threat generally and Nazi designs and Bundist activities particularly. The media and the government symbiosis intensified and formalized later as the emerging global conflagration would be articulated as a battle between good and evil.

Roosevelt, Hoover, and National Security

On May 8, 1934 Roosevelt privately, by a secret directive, authorized J. Edgar Hoover to investigate the Nazi movement and its associates. Initial investigations were limited due to lack of personnel and funding, secrecy issues and related legal concerns, and the FBI's focus on capturing high-profile criminals. The next few years witnessed an abrupt shift of focus, a tremendous increase in agents and funding, and a heightened sense of secrecy coupled with an often-wanton disregard for constitutional rights much less legal niceties. With Italy's Ethiopian invasion and then Germany's Locarno Treaty denunciation and Rhineland occupation, Secretary of War George Dern warned Attorney General Homer Cummings that certain domestic organizations would "probably attempt to cripple our war effort through sabotage." Dern recommended creating a civilian counter-espionage service "to prevent foreign espionage [and] to collect information so that in case of an emergency any persons intending to cripple our war effort by means of espionage or sabotage may be taken into custody."[33] Meanwhile, a War Department study and Army war planners envisaged a Nazi-dominated Latin America and lamented America's lack of military preparedness.

Reacting to worsening conditions in Europe, in August 1936 the State Department began a confidential program that Foreign Service officers would implement if civil strife endangered Americans, and Roosevelt secretly directed the FBI to investigate subversive activities. Hoover's already impressive investigative powers increased, and he used the ambiguous directive to begin compiling a secret list of all individuals who might pose a security risk in the event of war. Francis Biddle, who served as attorney general throughout World War II, later described such steps this way: "A new expression, *fifth column*, was on everyone's lips. Something must be done. Fifth columnists in the popular mind came from the alien population—the very word *alien* suggested those who had been estranged and excluded. And in a tide of enthusiastic energy the beginning of a witch hunt was on."

In May 1924, when Hoover accepted Attorney General Harlan Fiske Stone's offer to become temporary director of the Bureau of Investigation, he made it on the condition that "the Bureau must be divorced from politics and . . . responsible only to the Attorney General." Stone replied, "I wouldn't give it to you under any other conditions." This event proved critical, and Hoover's dogged persistence ferreting out supposed domestic enemies, whether communists, radicals, or fascists, was instrumental. He shaped policies and directed processes that resulted in the internment of more than thirty thousand resident aliens and citizens from the United States and Latin America. Yet it was Roosevelt's verbal orders that sanctioned Hoover's peacetime pursuit of so-called fifth columnists.[34]

With the threat of war growing, FDR focused his attention largely on matters abroad while Hoover concerned himself with domestic security. Both took great personal and political risks marshaling resources to counter potential internal and external threats. As events unfolded—from Japanese incursions in the Far East to conflict in Europe—Roosevelt empowered Hoover to act against subversives within the nation and throughout the hemisphere. Hoover's obsessions reflected a deep distrust of foreigners and his hostility toward anything un-American, however ambiguously defined. In July 1917, shortly after Congress had declared war against imperial Germany, Hoover joined the Justice Department's Enemy Alien Bureau. The anti-radical fervor of the times profoundly influenced him. Caught up in the maelstrom, he enthusiastically joined the hunt for radicals and revolutionaries of all stripes. Thus began Hoover's penchant for collecting information and creating lists of potential subversives, which by the 1930s included suspected communists, fascists, anarchists, socialists, pacifists, and others.

While Roosevelt's policy deliberations with his close advisers remain something of a mystery, we do know that he, Hoover, and Stimson, among others, were clearly worried about fifth columnists. By the mid-1930s, Stimson believed that fascists were planning to attack the nation from within and without warning, Hoover believed right-wing pro-Nazi and German American groups posed a real threat, and FDR directed the military and FBI to prepare lists of potential internees.³⁵

Initial FBI Investigations

The FBI began investigating American fascism immediately after a White House meeting on May 8, 1934—less than two months after passage of HR 198. In addition to Roosevelt and Hoover, attendees included Attorney General Homer Cummings, Treasury Secretary Henry Morgenthau, Labor Secretary Frances Perkins, and W. H. Moran, chief of the Secret Service. Concern over the growing Nazi movement led to a secret directive authorizing the FBI's limited investigations of America's Nazis and possible sympathizers. According to Hoover, FDR requested the FBI, in conjunction with the Secret Service and the INS, to conduct "very careful and searching" investigations of Nazi and fascist organizations and to find "any possible connection with official representatives of the German government in the United States." Roosevelt's need for secrecy allowed Hoover to go well beyond the investigative efforts FDR had in mind. Working confidentially, Hoover maintained separate filing systems. Documents "pertaining to 'sensitive,' 'illegal,' or 'embarrassing' activities were filed separately and not serialized; they could be destroyed, as many were, without a retrievable record." In many cases there were no written records.³⁶

On August 24, 1936, Roosevelt summoned Hoover to the White House for a private meeting. The following day both met with Cordell Hull. Three days later, as historian Athan Theoharis found, Hoover directed his agents to institute a far more extensive surveillance program:

> Bureau officials instituted a broad surveillance and indexing program involving the extensive use of informers, daily reports on "major developments in every field" of subversive activities, and an elaborate filing system containing indexes and dossiers on "persons whose names appear prominently at the present time in the subversive circles." To compile these files, the FBI went beyond its agents and informers and acquired an extensive library of radical pamphlets, newspapers, and periodicals as well as quietly devel-

oping relations with conservative patriotic organizations, such as the American Legion.

So eager was Hoover to exercise his new powers that on September 5 he sent a personal and confidential letter to his special agents in charge (SACs), directing them as follows:

> The Bureau desires to obtain from all possible sources information concerning subversive activities conducted in the United States by Communists, Fascisti, and representatives or advocates of other organizations or groups advocating the overthrow or replacement of the Government of the United States. No investigation should be initiated into cases of this kind in the absence of specific authorization from the Bureau, but you should immediately transmit to the Bureau any information relating to subversive activities on the part of any individual or organization, regardless of the source from which this information is received.[37]

Significantly, the White House meetings confidentially authorized the FBI to investigate "subversive activities and related matters." FDR desired a broad picture of domestic communist and fascist movements and wanted to know if they were foreign-directed. Secretary of State Hull was more direct, telling Hoover to "go ahead and investigate the hell out of those cocksuckers." Roosevelt's verbal order and subsequent directives served as justification for greatly expanding the FBI's authority. Hoover also used Roosevelt's preoccupation with secrecy to avoid congressional and judicial scrutiny. Finally, Hoover enhanced his own image and the agency's prominence.[38]

Hoover had long been struggling to amalgamate power and ensure his place as the FBI's undisputed head; he was also competing against other law-enforcement and national-security organizations. He usually won contentious turf battles with other investigative agencies, such as the Secret Service, and thwarted the investigative endeavors of his political adversaries in the House and Senate. These included Kenneth McKellar, chair of the Senate Appropriations Committee; Justin Miller, chair of the attorney general's Advisory Committee on Crime; and Secret Service operative G. L.

Boatwright. The intelligence gathering enabled him to learn about and then monitor the plans of executive branch adversaries too.[39] Such covert actions even included collecting illegally obtained correspondences between the American Youth Congress and Eleanor Roosevelt. Not surprisingly, Hoover never told FDR.

Hoover closely observed and managed day-to-day FBI operations. Each of his SACs submitted a daily report, and Hoover always seemed able to review them. With the help of trusted assistants and some reorganization of bureau methods and functions, he began monitoring communist and fascist organizations and individuals, aided by other agencies and groups such as the National Republic Organization. The FBI expanded rapidly in the 1930s, growing from three hundred agents in 1932 to over six hundred in 1936 (by war's end it had five thousand personnel). Through SAC reports and elaborate filing systems, the FBI increased its investigative scope and stayed aloof from public and private scrutiny.[40]

Investigations and Nazi Intrigues

The State Department became increasingly concerned about AO activities during the mid- to late 1930s. After Hitler's seizure of power, in January 1933, most Americans began to take the fascist threat seriously too. In March 1934 the McCormack-Dickstein Committee began its exploration of domestic Nazi propaganda and German activities while largely ignoring Italian fascism, much to the dismay of Italian anti-fascists. The nation was directing its energies against its greatest perceived domestic threat—the Friends of the New Germany, which soon withered and died only to reemerge as the German American Bund.

In February 1935 the committee reported its findings, focusing on the history of American Nazism. Conceding that most of the nation's twenty million German Americans were undoubtedly loyal, the report nevertheless argued a direct connection between the Nazi Party and German proxy groups abroad, galvanized members of the Friends of the New Germany, fueled suspicion of German Americans, and strained relations between Germany and the United States. By late 1936, overseas reports warned Hull and others of the AO's relative autonomy and its connection with Hitler's Germany; they linked "German National Socialist activities probably taking place on our soil" with Germany's "Foreign Organization." Such activities, one State Department official noted, "are legitimately viewed as undesirable by American citizens, are unwelcome to the government, and are of technical concern to the Department." In June 1937, Texas representative Martin Dies requested funds to investigate the Bund and un-American activities as thousands of citizens and many in Congress wrote the FBI and the State Department asking about or offering to prove links between German aliens and "the Nazi military training camps being established in this country."[41]

In May 1938, Congress approved new investigations of subversive Americans as HR 282 officially established HUAC. The new committee, morphed largely out of the old and now headed by Martin Dies and Samuel Dickstein, continued investigating un-American activities. In 1940, Dies announced:

> The experience of this generation, more than that of any other, has demonstrated that the enemies within a country constitute a peril as great as any foe. Treason from within, aided by invasion from without, has been responsible for the speed with which modern governments have collapsed in the face of totalitarian assaults. Stalin and Hitler have pushed their Trojan Horse tactics to the point of perfection.... Indeed, the Trojan Horse, as we have seen, has been drawn into labor organizations, political parties, peace societies, educational institutions, civic clubs, and even into the government itself.[42]

The resurgence of the German American Bund from the ashes of the Friends of the New Germany stimulated new, albeit highly exaggerated, fears of American Nazism. For example, even as the Bund struggled to exist and Kuhn tried to improve his image, Helen Vooros, a former youth group Bundist, cited Germany's objectives in her Dies Committee testimony: "Nazi Germany would get back all the territory lost in the World War. Then it would take over Scandinavia. After that it would capture the United States because of the large content of German blood among its citizens."[43]

In 1938, notables including James Byrnes, Felix Frankfurter, Senator Claude Pepper, and Henry Stimson compiled Nazi documents, speeches, and decrees into *The German Reich and Americans of German Origin*, and issued a clear warning: "The problem of the 8,000,000 Germans within our borders is one of great and growing importance. The intensification of the campaign of Pan-German propaganda will result in the creation of a large group of inhabitants of the United States whose primary allegiance would be to the ruler of a foreign power. The result would be friction between this group and the rest of the American people." The book's preface warned, "National Socialism is now attempting to unify all persons of German birth or ancestry, regardless of their present citizenship." It continued:

> Nazi groups outside Germany are now consolidated under the official direction of the Foreign Division of the National Socialist Party. . . . This organization and a number of others have been coordinated into the League for Germanism Abroad, which reaches out to all so-called "Volksgenossen," or racial comrades. Recently, there has been a marked intensification of this campaign of propaganda on the American continent . . . all directed toward one goal: to instill in the American citizen of German descent a consciousness of the German "race" and a feeling of allegiance toward the Reich.
>
> A person of German descent is always a German and belongs to Germany. If this foreign propaganda . . . continues unchecked, it cannot fail to create a cyst in the body politic of the American people. It will result in setting apart a large group of inhabitants whose duty it would be to render primary allegiance to the ruler of a foreign power. Friction might result in unrest and possible bloodshed.[44]

Contents include Hitler's July 1934 Reichstag Speech, laws against the formation of parties, and instructions to German educators going abroad. The second section, "The Reich and Germans Abroad," reveals German foreign-policy designs and notes that "in their totality all Germans inside and outside [the Reich] are a community of blood, art, and language." Gauleiter Ernst Bohle's speeches to the NSDAP/AO have similar ideas: "Loyalty, discipline, and blind obedience are the foundation pillars of every branch of the National Socialist movement [and] absolutely necessary for victory in the struggle for Germans living abroad.... We believe in the eternal values of race and blood." German youth, having sacrificed for America, had become "fertilizer for the culture of that country." Instead, German Americans must "bring the Germans in the United States . . . back to the great community of blood and fate of all Germans [and] thus prepared shall then be used under our leadership in the coming struggle with Communism and Jewry in the reconstruction of America." Excerpts from the German American Volksbund *Yearbook* of 1937 and 1938 herald the Reich's global ascendancy, assert the importance of being German first and foremost, glorify the Bund's undertakings and achievements, and remind its disciples of the movement's "highest and most distinguished goal: unification."[45]

The Bund under Siege

Reacting to the fifth column and Bundist threat, the Dies Committee urged citizens to quash these conspiratorial elements for their own safety and well-being. Its 1938 hearings set precedents for aliens during the war. Dies, for example, permitted witnesses to make "unsupported charges of the most fantastic character, and rarely accorded the accused the right to reply." Alabama senator John Bankhead called for "concentration camps for those trying to spread un-American propaganda." California senator Sheridan Downey, however, articulated what was quickly becoming a minority view. He defended any group's "right to hold a meeting so long as it is authorized," though by far the prevalent opinion, *Time* magazine reported in March, was that

> if a nationwide vote were taken to discover the most despised politico-social organization currently extant, the Amerikadeutscher Volksbund (German-American Bund) would stand at least a fair chance of winning. A group of some 125,000 U.S. citizens of German blood and clubby tendencies, it is hated in the U.S. as an offspring of Nazism . . . functioning under the leadership of a sleek, pompous, garrulous ex-chemist named Fritz Kuhn whose offices in Manhattan are decorated by portraits of Franklin Roosevelt and Adolf Hitler.

Many newspapers ran headlines similar to the *Brooklyn Daily Eagle*'s front page: "U.S. Citizens Drilled by Bund in 28 Camps: Nazis on the March in Intensive Training Used in Hitler's Rise." Little wonder many feared the "legions of men in uniform goose-stepping throughout the country in company with a virulent campaign of propaganda."[46]

Fritz Kuhn tried to defend himself and the Bund, but failed. In August 1937 he gave an impassioned speech and circulated a document articulating his and the Bund's concerns. Kuhn called Dickstein a liar, declared all the charges "barefaced lies, invented for the purpose of misleading American public opinion and turning neighbor against neighbor," and demanded the "unsupported, wholly fantastic, defamatory campaign cease, or that [Dickstein] be compelled to prove his charges." Most listeners, however, considered Kuhn's admission of friendship with the "New Germany" treasonous and dismissed his countercharges against Dickstein as maniacal ravings.[47]

The nation's media and investigative agencies characteristically overestimated the Bund's membership and the fifth-column threat. *Time*'s mention of the Bund's 125,000 members in March 1938 was similar to HUAC's later report on subversive activities in January 1943. Although five years had passed since the *Time* article, and the possibility of an attack was virtually nonexistent, HUAC authoritatively, but inaccurately, described a "dangerous condition existing and threatening to become increasingly worse."[48]

Because HUAC, the FBI, and other agencies greatly exaggerated fifth-column and Bund threats, fear of subversives would remain high throughout the war. Dies's report noted "subversive activities aimed at destroying our form of government":

> We must guard, as never before in any wars of the past, our internal safety against the machinations of fifth columns.
>
> This global war is unique in the use by our totalitarian foes of saboteurs whose work is to spread both physical and spiritual destruction within our borders. This systematic sowing of rumors, the calculated whispers of defeatism, and the treacherous campaigns to create internal disunity by un-American hatreds may be as dangerous as the saboteur's bomb and flame.

In 1938, the German-American Bund had many posts throughout the nation and boasted 100,000 members. The committee's files and records on subversive activities fill 135 file cabinets. The index to these files contains over 1,000,000 cards. All of these cards are based upon documentary evidence and are readily available to any government agency desiring it.

From the time Hitler marched into the lowlands, we were shocked into the realization that there was a fifth column in America; the files of this committee have served as a veritable fountainhead of information for the various agencies of government charged with the internal safety of the United States.[49]

Reality was quite different. Kuhn himself placed the Bund's membership at 8,299 in April 1939, while the Justice Department found only 6,617 members, the majority of whom, 4,529 by its count, were in New York City. And although Kuhn testified in August before the Dies Committee that there were 20,000 Bund members with several times that number of sympathizers, the *New York Times* put the number at 10,000 in 1937, a year after Kuhn became the Bund's president. Nevertheless, Hans Dieckhoff, who became Germany's ambassador to the United States in May 1937, worried that the Bund was hurting diplomatic relations. After complaining about the "stupid and noisy activities of a handful of German Americans," Dieckhoff studied the German American population, investigated the Bund, and discovered that of the twelve to fifteen million German Americans, less than one-third could read or speak German and far fewer had any fascist leanings. Even in large cities with many German Americans, few were trying to maintain their Deutschtum, and even fewer were Bundists; of Chicago's 700,000 German Americans, only 40,000 belonged to any German American group, and just 450 were Bund members.[50]

3

Dire Preparations

> A new expression, fifth column, was on everyone's lips.
> Something must be done. Fifth columnists in the popular mind
> came from the alien population—those who had been estranged
> and excluded. And in a tide of enthusiastic energy the
> beginning of a witch hunt was on.
>
> —ATTORNEY GENERAL FRANCIS BIDDLE, *IN BRIEF AUTHORITY*

Hostility toward outsiders took new and surprising forms as the nation readied for war. A range of conduct—from nasty invectives, racial slurs, and violence to discriminatory legislation, arbitrary arrests, and incarceration—revealed that German, Italian, and Japanese Americans were viewed with suspicion. Japanese were acutely vulnerable—easily identifiable, culturally isolated, numerically weak, politically impotent, and with few influential advocates. Even before U.S. entry into the war, some states were treating aliens like criminals, requiring them to register with and periodically report to authorities. Several states passed laws barring aliens from working in defense industries and state programs. Pennsylvania forbade aliens to obtain hunting and fishing licenses or even own dogs as other states adopted similar legislation. Congress, too, was active. In May 1939, Representative Sam Hobbs of Alabama pushed through a bill (it passed 289 to 6) legalizing detaining aliens who awaited deportation.[1] By summer, prospects for peace diminished rapidly and internment preparations began in earnest. Aliens were under the FBI's auspices. In June, FDR authorized Hoover's FBI to act as the central clearinghouse for all espionage, counterintelligence, and sabotage matters. Immediately after Germany's invasion of Poland, Roosevelt expanded Hoover's investigative authority even further.

By March 1940, Congress was reviewing over seventy bills aimed at aliens. German, Italian, and Japanese Americans ceased to be a local, state, or regional problem and became a federal concern on June 14, 1940, when Roosevelt transferred the INS from the Labor Department to the Justice Department. The next day, Hoover's Custodial Detention Index (CDI) received its official designation while a massive propaganda campaign vilified German, Italian, and Japanese Americans.[2] Yet no politician could risk losing the support of millions of German and Italian voters and thereby the social cohesion and economic stability necessary to wage and win a war. Few cared much about the Japanese, numerically significant only on Hawaii, where officials essentially left them alone.

Roosevelt had a difficult job—appeasing overzealous officials who advocated incarcerating thousands or even millions of aliens and citizens while reassuring the public that they were safe. Prudence demanded not antagonizing millions of loyal German, Italian, and Japanese Americans, lest they be driven into the enemy's arms, yet pragmatism required measured actions against perceived enemies. Throughout the war, citizens and enemy aliens lived as best they could while politicians and those defending the nation tried to find a balance between national security and civil liberties. In the end, FDR and Hoover pursued a course of minimum candor.[3]

Federal authorities had sometimes deferred to state and local government as well as private initiatives in dealing with subversive threats. Believing in the fifth column and the urgent need to counter it, FDR, steadily though quietly, granted Hoover the power both deemed necessary. Yet only when the nation was at war did the president and others openly take charge of enemy aliens and citizens—further organizing, streamlining, and formalizing processes already well under way.

War and the Fifth-Column Threat

On September 1, 1939, as Hoover's General Intelligence Division continued gathering information and creating lists of individuals and organizations possibly engaged in subversive or anti-American activities, Germany invaded Poland. On September 6, Roosevelt, acting on the 1909 Penal Code, World War I Espionage and Sedition Acts, and Hoover's assurances, announced that all citizens and foreign nationals who might not "conduct themselves to the premises" of the proclamation would "do so at their own peril" and could "in no way obtain any protection against the consequences of their misconduct." Roosevelt proclaimed that the following acts were forbidden, under severe penalties, within the territory and jurisdiction of the United States: serving with the armed forces of belligerent nations, hiring a person to do the same, giving military aid, and aiding a belligerent nation in any way. A person could not knowingly give money for, or take part in, any military act "against the territory or dominion of a belligerent." No member of the armed forces of a belligerent "who [had] been interned . . . or [found] leaving or attempting to leave the limits of internment . . . without the permission from the proper official of the United States in charge, or willfully overstaying a leave of absence granted by such an official" could leave the country. One could not aid or entice an internee to escape. These last stipulations referred to military internees. Nevertheless, Hoover and others felt that war would necessitate interning civilians; this, in turn, required planning and preparation.[4] The FBI and other agencies, therefore, had great leeway with forthcoming internment orders. Individuals lost constitutional rights such as freedom of speech; many lost their property. Citizens and resident aliens had little recourse.

Meanwhile, anti-alien legislation was making its way through the courts, a New Jersey judge told German nationals that he would deny them citizenship if they were Bund members, and many local officials soon closed German and Italian bars (alcohol would adversely affect America's fighting ability). Schools that had language courses in German or Italian, or history courses about Germany or Italy, either stopped offering the classes or found their doors closed. Aliens could not travel more than five miles from their home or place of work unless they obtained a government travel permit.

State governments acted too. In August 1940, state delegates met in Washington to discuss sabotage and explosives. The "Law Enforcement and Problems of National Defense" conference spurred numerous anti-subversive and anti-sabotage laws. In 1941 and 1942, nineteen states adopted legislation to deal with fifth columnists. Federal arsenals supplied new state guards charged with enforcing the new laws and keeping order. Delaware's Guardsmen could cross the state line in "pursuit of insurrectionists, saboteurs and enemies or enemy forces," while Virginia's Protective Force could suppress disorders, civil disturbances, and the activities of "Fifth Columnists and paratroops." Texas had the largest state reserve force in the nation, some fifteen thousand strong, and even boasted a women's auxiliary. Although state guard units were typically ill equipped and poorly trained, they still provided a force of one hundred thousand to counter and suppress expected fifth-column activities. FDR created the Office of Civilian Defense in May 1941, and by November all states and nearly six thousand towns had set up defense councils. By January 1942 over 5.6 million Americans were in civil defense programs as auxiliary police, air-raid wardens, and medical personnel, among others.[5]

The British Example

The United States learned from Britain's Home Office as it devised policies and laid the groundwork for internment in the mid-1930s, and both nations drew from World War I precedents. In that war, the British interned 30,000 foreigners. Canada, too, interned 8,500 enemy aliens. The United States, by comparison, interned 6,300 enemy aliens, overwhelmingly German, including 4,000 sailors and 2,300 civilians. When war began in Europe in 1939, Britain avoided interning German and Austrian aliens en masse, as it had done twenty years earlier, and for a time it worked. The fall of France, however, forced Britain to rethink its policies as thousands crossed the English Channel.[6]

Britain's internment preparations started in earnest in 1939 when it began reviewing the status of German and Austrian aliens, including 55,000 recently arrived refugees from Czechoslovakia, Austria, and Germany, most having fled after Kristallnacht. High-level policy planning had actually begun in 1923, when the Committee for Imperial Defense reviewed wartime lessons and decided that simply expelling enemy aliens was best. While it was neither practical nor possible to do so fully, the Home Office at the same time charged the War Office with preparing facilities to house 5,500 internees. When Hitler came to power, some of those who felt they were in immediate danger, including Jews, political opponents, intellectuals, artists, writers, and journalists, fled the Reich; others were not so fortunate. By the end of 1933 some 65,000 Germans had managed to leave (40 percent went to France), but 27,000 political prisoners were in concentration camps.[7]

The Home Office began considering ways to deal with the two thousand German racial and political refugees who had come to Britain. Meanwhile, contingency planning for dealing with internees continued over the next five years. By September 1938, Britain's ability to house internees had increased from the 5,500 anticipated in 1923 to 18,000, as some 30,000 refugees had arrived despite stricter immigration quotas and temporary residence permits. Britain's Home Office sent the following message to chief constables: "In the event of a war emergency it is hoped that as many aliens as possible would leave the country." The message to immigration officers was more vigorous: "It will be the policy of HM Government to encourage aliens to leave the country, and aliens who desire to do so should be permitted to embark." Anticipating a worsening situation, the War Office decided upon a "hospital, a Scottish castle, several country houses, four race courses, and the Olympia exhibition hall" for housing.[8]

Menaced by the possibility of invasion, government and civilian agencies coordinated home-front defense efforts. However serious the intent, anti-subversion drills could be comical. *Life* magazine had a picture of a "Nazi fifth columnist" disguised as a nanny pushing a baby stroller "firing on" a Home Guard sentry who had unwittingly asked for identification. The "fatal" mistake, readers learned, was that the enemy could be anybody—even an elderly nanny. Home-front preparations were not so humorous. Thousands of civilians, many never having held a gun, drilled in the countryside, shooting at clay pigeons (Nazi parachutists) with antiquated weapons (some dating back to 1900). Injuries and even death sometimes occurred as the trainees fired straight up into the air and the bullets returned to earth. The training did, however, boost morale and gave participants some sense of empowerment. For a time, home-front drills were "Britain's most popular activity."[9]

Britain temporarily held 82,000 persons, picking up 60,000 after June 1940 as refugees crossed the Channel while France collapsed. Officials soon freed nearly all, realizing that most were opponents of the Nazi regime and that interning 19,000 individuals, scattered throughout Britain, was problematic. This reaction was largely based on Britain's recent experience following Germany's invasion of Poland in September 1939, when the Home Office devised and implemented internment policies; over one hundred tribunals were tasked with ferreting out potential subversives. Working quickly, the tribunals began in early October, had considered 35,000 cases by late November, and interned 348 enemy aliens. By March 1940, internee numbers reached 569 out of 71,600 cases (the final was 73,353 cases of 75,000 Germans and Austrians living in Britain and 64,254 were allowed to remain at liberty, known as "Category 'C'" which included 55,460 refugees). The low percentage of internees (less than 1 percent) reflected a pragmatic restraint. Britain had changed its policies as military circumstances warranted, public fears of anticipated fifth-column activities subsided, and politicians realized that interning 70,000 or more persons was impractical. Moreover, most Britons, after getting past the shock of Germany's occupation of the Low Countries and its swift defeat of France, understood that most resident aliens and recent immigrants were loyal to Britain or else were victims or enemies of Nazi Germany. Still, by July 1940, Britain had interned 27,200 men and women, mainly German and Austrian aliens—mostly refugees, including thousands of Jews, from Nazi Germany. Despite British actions, Roosevelt at a press conference the previous month had cautioned that spies, including Jews, were among those refugees making their way to other nations, including those in the Western Hemisphere, in order to launch attacks.[10]

Members of the Justice Department's Special Defense Unit (SDU), formed in March 1941, met in April with managers of Britain's internment program. Notes from the meeting reveal that Britain initially held many thousands, but they do not mention the quick release of nearly all once the threat was understood as largely nonexistent. Yet American officials believed the fifth-column threat and applied many of Britain's premises and standards:

> The English have interned approximately 82,000. These figures reflect the fear of invasion and public opinion. The fear that Fifth Columnists and Quislings were among these caused British authorities to act promptly and summarily.
>
> Arrests are summary and resorted to where there is a doubt concerning an individual suspected of being disloyal. All the traditional forms to preserve civil liberties are reversed in the case of alien enemies. Any doubt is resolved against the alien enemy. He is not privileged to know the nature of the charges brought against him. He is not allowed counsel when arraigned.
>
> The alien enemy is locked up pending a hearing. The alien enemy is not privileged to hear the statement against him. He has no counsel. He makes a statement, however, regarding his life, his associations and occupation, and he is permitted to have friends speak for him. The tribunal asks questions.
>
> Any alien enemy who is pro-German and against whom there is any suspicious evidence, such as living without visible means of support, making frequent trips to Germany, purchasing German securities, etc., should be arrested at least and further investigation made.... As to enemy organizations... arrest leaders and organizers only... members of these organizations, such as the Fascist party, were members merely for business reasons. In these cases also, if any doubt existed however, he would arrest and find out the facts later.
>
> Civilian supervision far excels military.... The ideal set-up for a civilian internment camp would be a combination supervision, requiring... military guards... and internal supervision as to food, clothes, recreations, welfare, etc., by civilians altogether.[11]

Internment Preparations

Internment preparations accelerated during the summer of 1939. On June 26 a secret presidential directive established the Interdepartmental Intelligence Committee (IIC). A unified coordinating committee now included the FBI, the War Department's Military Intelligence Division (MID), or (G-2), and the Office of Naval Intelligence. Roosevelt's order allowed the IIC to oversee all "matters involving actually or potentially any espionage, counterespionage, or sabotage." The agencies forwarded suspects' names to the Justice Department's Neutrality Laws Unit (NLU). Established in April 1940, the NLU was subsequently designated the SDU and then renamed the Special War Policies Unit (SWPU) in May 1942. Lawrence Smith took charge of the SDU and kept track of the master list, later known as the "ABC list." Contributing agencies had lists of persons deemed, as in the FBI's case, "dangerous" or "potentially dangerous," and all federal investigative agency heads were to provide Hoover's FBI "any data, information, or material that may come to their notice bearing directly or indirectly on espionage, counter-espionage, or sabotage." Although FDR did not appoint anybody to head the IIC, he kept track of important security updates from Assistant Secretary of State George Messersmith and his successor, Adolf Berle Jr. While the FBI, MID, and ONI may have been equal partners in theory, FDR instructed federal investigative agency heads to report all security matters to Hoover. Roosevelt neither mentioned subversive activities nor envisaged or empowered the FBI to investigate them, yet almost overnight his directive changed Hoover's FBI from a super police force that fought crime to a secret police force dedicated to eliminating the "Fifth Column of destruction."[12]

During the latter half of 1939 and throughout 1940 the FBI received an ever-increasing volume of memos and letters identifying dangerous aliens and citizens. Some suspects reportedly received or distributed propaganda, others were rumored to be sending information to Germany, and still more were overheard denouncing Americans. Christel van Elden of Sunbury, Pennsylvania, was investigated for saying that Rev. Toadvine of St. Andrew's Church, was an "anti-Nazi spy and goes to Germany every year and on his return spreads the filthiest lies."[13] Hoover investigated van Elden and countless others. The FBI, under Hoover's aegis, expanded its capabilities and extended its authority and often relied on oral or secret presidential directives. Strict secrecy and clear authority were necessary, Hoover believed, as the FBI became the central clearinghouse for all espionage, counterintelligence, sabotage, and antiradical matters.

On September 6, 1939, Hoover publicly announced that the FBI was "to take charge of investigative work in matters relating to espionage, sabotage, and violations of neutrality regulations." As the task must be "conducted in a comprehensive and effective manner on a national basis," Hoover continued, Americans "should cooperate" and "all police officers, sheriffs, and other law enforcement officers in the United States must promptly turn over to the nearest representative of the FBI any information . . . relating to cases in the above classifications."[14] Attorney General Frank Murphy added:

> Foreign agents and those engaged in espionage will no longer find this country a happy hunting ground for their activities. There will be no repetition of the confusion and laxity and indifference of twenty years ago. We have opened many new FBI offices throughout the land. Our men are well prepared and well trained. At the same time, if you want this work done in a reasonable and responsible way it must not turn into a witch hunt. We must do no wrong to any man.[15]

By November, Congress repealed its arms embargo and munitions began flowing to Britain and France, albeit by "cash and carry." Despite Roosevelt's public calls for neutrality, privately he readied the nation for war; at home, this meant greatly increasing the FBI's investigative functions. Hoover ordered all special agents to prepare reports on subversives for inclusion into a "suspect list," later the Custodial Detention Index. The CDI included the names of thousands of aliens and citizens based on information indicating that they might be dangerous to the public or the government.[16]

Concerned about internal security and eager to boost the Bureau's involvement, Hoover sent a personal and confidential memo to all SACs on December 6:

> The Bureau is at the present time preparing a list of individuals, both aliens and citizens of the United States, on whom there is informa-

tion to indicate that their presence at liberty in this country in time of war or national emergency would be dangerous to the public peace and the safety of the United States government. . . . Obtain additional information relative to the affiliations, business interests, activities, present address, age, and citizenship status of each.

The Bureau will, therefore, in the near future commence . . . requesting an appropriate confidential investigation to develop from confidential sources and in a discreet manner the necessary information to enable rendering of a decision as to the action to be taken . . . in the event of the outbreak of hostilities.

Initiate the appropriate investigation immediately upon receipt of the letters referred to, and issue appropriate instructions to the employees assigned to your Field Division to make certain that the fact that the Bureau is making such investigations does not become known to individuals outside of the Bureau.

It will be necessary, in all instances, to determine whether the individual . . . is a citizen. . . . if an alien, it should be determined, if possible, whether he has taken out his first papers. . . . This information is essential in each case because in time of war alien enemies are placed in a status differing entirely from that of citizens, and the cases would be handled differently.

The names of suspected groups and individuals went into the newly created and highly secretive CDI, and because it and the preventive detention program lacked statutory authority, Hoover added:

The purpose should be entirely confidential and handled [to determine] if the individual has violated the Foreign Agents Registration Act or is engaged in subversive activities. . . . The Registration Act [requires] agents of foreign principals to register with the State Department. The classification "Registration Act" still exists and investigations conducted under that classification should not be confused with those conducted under the classification "Internal Security."

Most of the information necessary about each individual may be obtained from sources already known to the Bureau, such as public and private records, confidential sources of information, confidential informants, newspaper morgues, public libraries, employment records, school records, etc. . . . but in cases where these sources are unavailing, the investigation must be complete but confidential. . . . Make certain that complete information is obtained . . . a decision cannot be rendered . . . unless full and complete information . . . is made available.

You should ascertain the present home and business address of the subject and all information which would indicate the advisability of including him on the list referred to, such as current or past activities, affiliation with organizations engaged in activities in behalf of a foreign nation, participation in dangerous subversive movements, advocacy of the overthrow of Government by force and violence et cetera.[17]

Congress's Foreign Agents Registration Act of 1938 in no way allowed such practices. Yet Hoover used the act to justify the FBI's first arrests in mid-December 1939.

The president's September 6 directive, which prohibited exporting or attempting to export arms, ammunition, or implements of war, allowed the FBI and other agencies to investigate those who owned radios, bought questionable reading material, were members of suspect organizations or included on mailing lists (such as the German Library of Information). Then came FDR's September 8 national emergency decree: "A national emergency exists," he stated, "for the proper enforcing of the neutrality of the United States and the strengthening of our national defense within the limits of peacetime authorizations." Strengthening the nation's defense, for Hoover, meant conducting extralegal covert activities already under way (formally initiated September 2). Hoover's CDI included persons of German and Italian background and those with "communist sympathies." He had publicly alluded to a detention program during congressional testimony in 1939 and 1940 but implied that the FBI had merely developed contingency plans, thereby masking a far-reaching and distinctly political effort.[18]

First Arrests and America's First Internees

In December 1939, the summer of 1940, and the spring of 1941 the FBI arrested Italian and German sailors. Officials charged some with violating the 1924 Immigration Act by remaining in the United States after their ships had sailed, while others faced sabotage and attempted sabotage charges after they damaged or attempted to destroy their ships docked in U.S. ports. The INS handled the first internees, German sailors seeking neutral ports to avoid seizure by the Royal Navy. On December 19, 1939, the crew of the merchant ship SS *Columbus* scuttled their ship off Cape May, New Jersey, in an attempt to avoid capture by a British destroyer. An American cruiser picked up the survivors, who found themselves incarcerated the next day on Ellis Island, recently converted into an alien (later enemy alien and citizen) detention camp. Officials operating under the Espionage and Dangerous Cargo Acts seized numerous merchant ships flying Axis colors and detained the crews. The Italian liner *Conte Biancamano*, for example, homeward bound from Valparaíso, found itself in the Panama Canal Zone at the outbreak of war. The U.S. neutrality patrol impounded the ship and confined its crew of 483 for the next eleven months before finally transferring the sailors to Ellis Island in May 1941. The Italians joined a large group of German mariners, including the *Columbus* crew, as well as a group of Italian Pavilion employees from the 1939 New York World's Fair. The crews of the *Arauca*, *Pietro Campanella*, and others, including American Standard Oil tankers, ended up detained at Forts Stanton, Lincoln, and Missoula. The U.S. Maritime Commission took charge of most of the ships and later turned them over to the War Shipping Administration for operation by the U.S. Navy.

As for the *Columbus*'s crew, they left New York for Angel Island, just north of Alcatraz in San Francisco Bay. They did not receive a warm welcome. San Franciscans learned that several crewmembers had escaped during transit, and authorities regularly permitted the alleged dangerous German sailors to come ashore during their yearlong detention. Newspaper accounts reveal that the city's residents clearly did not want the sailors there. The Justice Department consequently sought more remote locales, but it lacked facilities for the growing number of German and Italian sailors. In December 1940, officials settled on Fort Stanton, New Mexico, a frontier post established in 1855 to contain Apaches and later a

Civilian Conservation Corps camp. From January to March 1941, 410 of the *Columbus*'s crew of 435 distressed seamen, including Captain Wilhelm Daehne and his senior staff, arrived at Fort Stanton, where they would remain for the war's duration.[19]

In late March 1941, British and American intelligence agents learned of Mussolini's plan to sabotage or scuttle Italian merchant ships docked at U.S. ports in order to prevent their capture. Tipped off by agent Amy Thorpe, the FBI rounded up nearly all of the Italian and German merchant crews in New York and interned them on Ellis Island. On March 30, U.S. Coast Guard boarding parties seized two German and twenty-eight Italian vessels, mainly freighters and tankers, as well as thirty-five Danish freighters, in sixteen harbors and ports, but not before the sailors damaged most of their ships. The Coast Guard took 850 Italian and 63 German sailors into custody while authorities seized 67 Axis vessels until Roosevelt's Executive Order 8771 of June 6, 1941, authorized the Maritime Commission to acquire ships "lying idle" in order to "assist in the national defense."[20]

Ellis Island's internee population swelled that winter to more than two thousand, exceeding its capacity. Internees then went to remote locations; in addition to the 410 men at Fort Stanton, another 735 German and Italian sailors went to Fort Missoula, Montana, and Fort Lincoln, North Dakota, in May 1941. By December the detainees included 279 Japanese, 248 Germans, and 81 Italians, all removed from the East Coast. Thereafter several hundred persons, mostly German and Italian nationals, arrived at Ellis Island monthly. Most were transferred or released within months, but some remained for years. By May 1942 over one thousand aliens were in its congested facilities. Hundreds left for distant camps, others were forcibly repatriated, and a few gained their freedom. As late as May 31, 1946, Ellis Island still held 264 Germans.[21]

Fort Stanton, then, was the United States' first internment camp. Captain Wilhelm Daehne and nearly 1,700 Axis noncombatants, crews of German and Italian ships, remained there or at other facilities until the end of the war or beyond in a country not at war. Yet on December 29, 1940, FDR had asked his fellow Americans to show "the same resolution, the same sense of urgency, the same spirit of patriotism and sacrifice as we would show were we at war" in what became known as his "Arsenal of Democracy" speech. In many ways, the nation was at war—at home and abroad. Only after Germany's surrender in May 1945 did the *Columbus*'s crew and hundreds of other German merchant sailors get to go home. The last of the German sailors left Fort Stanton on August 27, 1945.[22]

Accelerating Preparations

Many shared Hoover's national-security concerns but were unwilling to support Roosevelt's cautious lead in foreign affairs. Even after Germany invaded Poland, polls showed that 90 percent of Americans favored neutrality, although 80 percent wanted an Allied victory. By the summer of 1940, however, everything changed. Germany occupied Norway and Denmark, overran Belgium and Holland in days, and on June 22 France surrendered, just a week after German troops had entered Paris. Everyone, it seemed, wanted to help ready the nation for war. Isolationism and pacifism sharply declined as polls showed that those who just months before opposed conscription and intervention now favored both. Congress passed a National Defense Tax Bill and the Selective Service Act, the nation's first peacetime draft, and approved not only FDR's considerable request of five billion dollars for defense in 1939, but also a record seventeen billion dollars in 1940.[23]

The specter of war helped Democrats, allowing Roosevelt to win the 1940 election but with far fewer (55 percent) popular votes than before. The greatest decline came from German and Irish Americans, who resented aid to and support of Britain, and from Italian Americans, who disliked FDR's speech in Charlottesville, Virginia, on June 10. One Connecticut representative reported "a wave of sentiment in New England . . . against Italians," while the assistant attorney general found "some sections of the population hysterical" along with "the wholesale denunciation of all aliens" and in some cases "mob violence."[24] In New York, New Jersey, Pennsylvania, Ohio, and Missouri, states with large German and Italian communities, Roosevelt won by the slimmest of margins. He had risked winning an unprecedented third term by endorsing two controversial policies—Lend-Lease and the draft. At issue was the nation's neutrality and Britain's survival.

That summer, the Justice Department's Alien Registration Division began a nationwide effort to register and fingerprint all aliens. A staff of twenty lawyers began working on what Attorney General Robert Jackson called "a phase of our national defense program." Jackson and Solicitor General Francis Biddle prudently had the registration and fingerprinting done at post offices rather than police stations as originally intended. Biddle, who succeeded Jackson as attorney general on September 5, 1941, and served until June 30, 1945, realized that the Alien Registration Act, also known as the Smith Act, could backfire. Jackson's public pronouncement notwithstanding, both men recognized it as a "neurotic reflection of congressional fears which could easily create irreparable harm by alienating the large segment of foreign-born residents who were not citizens." Nevertheless, it was just the beginning. The Nationality Act, or Naturalization Act, passed in October 1940, allowed the revocation of a naturalized American's citizenship if there was evidence of allegiance to a foreign power or deception at the time of naturalization. Resident aliens were fearful, equating registration with deportation, so the government used news releases, pamphlets, radio broadcasts, and speeches by foreign-born celebrities to make its preemptive measures look harmless and convince aliens that by registering they would not endanger themselves. To this end, Biddle hired lawyer Earl G. Harrison. Biddle and Harrison assured the public that nearly all aliens were loyal yet tried not to estrange America's aliens as officials learned much more about them—just in case.[25]

The efforts of the INS were impressive. Five million aliens registered within a period of four months beginning in August 1940. Under the nation's first modern peacetime anti-sedition act, every alien answered under oath fifteen primary and twenty-seven secondary questions. Violations were punishable by a fine of $1,000, imprisonment for six months, or both. Rather remarkably, there were only 1,061 prosecutions for willful failure of compliance. Hoover's FBI, meanwhile, was cracking down on subversives, adding names of both aliens and citizens to his CDI. And while Robert

Jackson had seemingly cared little about the FBI's modus operandi, his successor was different. Biddle, as we will see, criticized Hoover openly, albeit belatedly, and ultimately concluded that the CDI served no useful purpose.[26]

Hoover, despite several prewar admonitions from Biddle, proceeded carefully with extralegal agency practices by not filing self-incriminating information in the FBI's central records and using his own memo book, which he could modify or destroy. Biddle allowed wiretaps of some espionage and subversive activities, because Roosevelt had authorized these and other clandestine methods against spies and aliens in May 1940 and Jackson had also permitted them. While Hoover authorized and continued taps, Biddle limited some investigations by requiring his permission or Hoover's written request, and hoped to stop others when or if the Supreme Court ruled such actions illegal. Hoover, in typical fashion, used his superiors' concerns for secrecy and avoided written records.[27]

Hoover's FBI Takes Charge

They had planned to "knock off about a dozen Congressmen . . . blow up the goddam Police Department!" Hoover charged seventeen miscreants with conspiring to overthrow the federal government. The case was as sensational as it was preposterous. How could a few men establish a fascist dictatorship here in America? The answer: "It only took twenty-three men to overthrow Russia." The plot began in January 1940 and ended a few months later with no convictions and one suicide, but it heralded alien abuse. On June 15, Hoover dispatched the following message to all SACs: "Furnish Bureau as soon as possible a list of the names and addresses of those persons in your district who should be considered for custodial detention pending investigation in the event of a national emergency. Indicate whether the individual is or is not a United States citizen. Information should indicate whether these persons possess Communistic, Fascist, Nazi or other nationalistic background." Hoover desperately sought information about disloyal or dangerous aliens and citizens and cared little about accuracy or sources. Denunciations by acquaintances, employers, co-workers, friends, neighbors, or family were enough to arouse suspicion and warrant investigation. Many were falsely accused with little basis and the flimsiest evidence.[28]

On August 21, 1940, Hoover wrote to Matthew McGuire, assistant to the attorney general, requesting legislation for the FBI to step up investigations of citizens and aliens in preparation for internment. Hoover reminded McGuire that during the last war various activities justified enemy internment on presidential warrant. He added that FDR had designated the FBI as a clearinghouse in national defense and general intelligence matters. Hoover also got Assistant Director Edward Tamm involved in high-level discussions of the alien enemy problem. Tamm had worked closely with Hoover since 1936 monitoring domestic political radicals, gathering information about communist and fascist organizations, and creating lists of members or associates of "organizations or groups advocating the overthrow of the U.S. government." Internment processes accelerated as worldwide threats increased when Germany, Italy, and Japan signed the Tripartite Pact on September 27. As Japan expanded militarily, strained relations worsened (in July 1939 the United States had refused to renew the 1911 Treaty of Commerce and Navigation) and its militarist government, greatly dependent on U.S. exports, felt threatened. While Japan discussed a co-prosperity sphere, its troops occupied northern French Indochina. Hoover's speech to the FBI's National Academy in October echoed America's concerns: "That there is a Fifth Column that has already started to march is an acknowledged reality. That it menaces America is an established fact. That it must be met is the common resolve of every red-blooded citizen. A Fifth Column of destruction, following in the wake of confusion, weakening the sinews and paralyzing it with fear can be met only by the nationwide offensive of all law enforcement."[29] Fearing that the "postponing of activity" would "result in rough shod tactics," Lawrence Smith's Neutrality Laws Unit (later the Justice Department's Special Defense Unit) likewise concluded:

> As many steps as possible should be taken now. . . . The investigation and preparation for formal action should be completed in

as many cases as possible.... initiating steps in the case of aliens and naturalized citizens considered dangerous persons, developing the possibilities of deportation and denaturalization. Review the suspect list to determine if any action other than prosecution may be taken to eliminate the threat of persons of such types.... Consider the establishment of forbidden areas and provide additional controls over those dangerous persons who are United States citizens or naturalized citizens as well as aliens and natives of neutral nations.[30]

The War Department also took the fifth-column threat seriously. In July 1940, Brigadier General Sherman Miles, G-2, produced the memo "Counter-Fifth Column." Approved by the chief of staff, it defined the threat, outlined military decisions already made to counter it, and proposed further actions. Throughout the summer, Hoover wrote Roosevelt's newly appointed secretary of war, Henry Stimson, to begin coordinating the handling of what they now called the "alien enemy problem."[31]

Hoover, meanwhile, broadened the FBI's investigative authority, increased funding, and effectively bolstered relations with patriotic citizens groups—most notably the American Legion—to learn more about subversives. By August 1941 the FBI had contacted 813 American Legion department and district officers and 8,847 Legion post commanders and local officers. These Legion officers in turn identified 46,864 potential informers, of whom FBI agents eventually interviewed 32,918. The FBI recruited some 43,000 informers from 11,700 posts nationwide, but Hoover, wanting more, had agents contact overlooked Legion posts, so by 1943 the FBI had recruited approximately 60,000 Legionnaires. The FBI also had contact programs with the American Bar Association, B'nai B'rith, Boy Scouts, Daughters of the American Revolution, Kiwanis International, Knights of Columbus, Optimists International, Rotary International, U.S. Chamber of Commerce, and Veterans of Foreign Wars. Publicly, Hoover eagerly repeated his vague but frightening message of subversive threats. Privately, a flurry of memos establishing procedures for interning alien enemies were exchanged among the FBI, the War and State Departments, and the attorney general. On June 26, 1941, Hoover finally asked Biddle if he could issue arrest warrants for those on the FBI's "suspect list."[32]

The Special Division

The State Department's Special Division helped develop and implement internment policies and processes. Established on September 1, 1939, and renamed the Special War Problems Division (SWPD) in 1943, it had several important, unique, and specific duties. Because of the deteriorating conditions overseas, the Special Division handled all matters pertaining to Americans abroad, including their evacuation and repatriation and offers of financial assistance. It acted as a liaison between the American Red Cross and the Relief Control Board for coordinating operations between private and government agencies. The Special Division represented government dealings with third (neutral) powers and supervised third-power representation of enemy nation interests. Finally, it oversaw the exchange of official and non-official American and Axis personnel, including civilian internees and prisoners of war. To help ensure their proper treatment, division officials accompanied representatives of protecting powers on civilian and prisoner of war camp inspections and investigated allegations of chemical or biological warfare.

Roosevelt asked longtime friend Breckinridge Long to head the Special Division at its inception. The Special Division helped to repatriate thousands of American citizens and created an Internee Branch under Albert Clattenburg's direction to handle Geneva Convention related matters for prisoners of war and civilian internees. Lamentably, it also barred thousands seeking refuge from Nazi Germany. Shortly after Germany invaded France, Assistant Secretary of State George Messersmith asked Long not to admit refugees; German spies, he warned, were already in Mexico—undoubtedly the same was true in the United States. The FBI and the Office of Strategic Services (OSS) agreed: aliens and refugees were a threat.[33]

Long feared infiltrators and interpreted America's willingness to admit thousands of refugee children, particularly British, as a sign of the public's "enormous psychosis" and attributed it to "repressed emotion [and] the chance finally to do something, however wrongheaded it may be." By June 1940, Long, like many of his contemporaries, coupled anti-refugee sentiment with the belief that German spies and saboteurs had arrived in advance of Axis military forces, aiding in the rapid collapse of western Europe. These "nests" of spies and saboteurs were a proven military asset that threatened the nation.

To be sure, others, including Eleanor Roosevelt, correctly believed the fifth-column threat grossly exaggerated and the plight of refugees genuine. What she and like-minded members of the President's Advisory Committee did not know was that Long had sent a secret memo to fellow State Department officials Adolf Berle and James Dunn informing them of his proposal to "delay and effectively stop" immigration. The goal, he knew, was to win over the president. Long's ally, Undersecretary of State Sumner Welles, arranged for him to meet FDR a week before Eleanor's view could be argued. It worked. Meeting with FDR on October 3, Long recounted fearsome stories demonstrating that many of the refugees Eleanor and others wanted to admit were in fact German agents who would take advantage of America's hospitality for their own sinister purposes. Roosevelt vividly recalled German intrigues and plots against himself and the nation during the Great War. Afterwards, Long wrote: "I found that he was 100% in accord with my ideas. . . . He was wholeheartedly in support of the policy which would resolve in favor of the United States any doubts about admissibility of any individual."[34] In the end, fears of a fifth column overcame Roosevelt's sense of compassion and distorted his judgment. Allowing a few wolves in with the sheep was simply too great a risk.

4

The Fifth-Column Threat

> The Nazi masters of Germany... intend to enslave Europe and
> then dominate the world. Their secret emissaries are active in our
> own and in neighboring countries. American citizens are aiding
> and abetting the work of these agents. For us this
> is an emergency as serious as war itself.
>
> —FRANKLIN D. ROOSEVELT, FIRESIDE CHAT, DECEMBER 29, 1940

By the summer of 1940, German spies had arrived, as headlines in *Life* ("These Are Signs of Nazi Fifth Columns Everywhere"), *Newsweek* ("Trojan Horses"; "The Bunders' Resume"; "Fifth Column Dossier"; "Nazi Pipeline"), and the *Nation* ("The Fifth Column") warned. An article in *Harper's* surely made the point: "Every home with a foreign-born head is believed to be the nucleus of a fifth column, and a hue and cry is aroused about the alien which is amounting to proportions unheard of since World War One." Not surprisingly, 90 percent of Americans believed in the fifth-column threat while 80 percent believed it menaced the entire hemisphere. Axis encroachments, it was thought, were under way. A July 1940 *Fortune* survey concluded it was "clear that the U.S. is fearful of the outcome of the European war, is willing . . . to throw its resources (but not its men) into the scales to help the Allies win, and meanwhile is grimly determined to prepare for the worst by arming. . . . The opinions of the people, indeed, are running neck and neck with, if not ahead of, the policy declarations of their leaders." A June 1940 poll had revealed that 78 percent thought that if Germany took Europe, then South America was next, and "nowhere in the country . . . are there as many as 10 percent who disbelieve that a Fifth Column is being established here." In addition, 63 percent thought Germany would try to seize territory on "our side of the ocean," while 45 percent felt Hitler would "actually attack us on our own territory as soon as possible" and 43 percent thought Germany and Japan would join forces "to dominate the world."[1]

Crafting the Fifth-Column Threat—Europe

Fifth-column rhetoric and the term itself had first appeared during the Spanish Civil War. Now, in the spring of 1940, rumors about and fears of subversive activities intensified with Germany's victory over Norway as Major Vidkun Quisling aided the Nazis. "Quisling" became synonymous with "traitor" when France collapsed and thousands of tourists, refugees, exchange students, and citizens of German background greeted the Wehrmacht. British officials panicked.[2] Britain's media sounded the alarm. The *Yorkshire Post* on April 16 warned in language that was soon commonplace: "There is no doubt that help from a 'Fifth Column' in Norway figured in Hitler's invasion plans." The editorial continued:

> Before attacking a country, Hitler always tries to undermine it from within. How does he enlist his sympathizers, ready to work for him when the hour strikes? Partly by a long-continued policy of threats, which compels the chosen country to allow the organization of the Nazi Party, raised around a nucleus of German nationals in its midst. Partly by spreading fears of invasion, which tempt the unscrupulous and the timorous to ensure their good standing with the invaders in advance. Local adventurers and ne'er-do-wells are attracted by the promise of fat jobs when the Nazis arrive.[3]

Germany's "secret weapon" was legions of disguised loyal minions ready to aid and join the Reich. *Newsweek*, *Life*, *Time*, *Reader's Digest*, and *Fortune*, the more conservative *Saturday Evening Post*, and leading liberal journals such as the *New Republic* and *Nation* also sounded the tocsin. They revealed links between Reich directives and Nazi methods by "means of terrorizing or otherwise inducing practically all Germans to become spies and agents."[4]

These periodicals rarely ran an issue without an exposé of subversion and efforts to combat spies and saboteurs.

In September 1940, *Newsweek* reported that for nearly two years the Princeton Listening Center had been eavesdropping on Axis short-wave broadcasts. The article, titled "Crescendo of Nazi Propaganda Charted in Princeton Analysis," revealed "German propaganda barrages usually heralded Nazi political and military offenses." The center's charts revealed the "increasing intensity of the Nazi short-wave blasts leading up to the invasion of Scandinavia and the Low Countries" and showed "Germany's radio attempts to influence American opinion to stimulate 'a psychological civil war.'" Germany had used the "same propaganda pattern against Austria, Czech-Slovakia, and Poland." The article then noted a change:

> The Low Countries' invasion saw a departure from the method. Germany for weeks hinted at action in the Balkans . . . only to drop sharply at the moment Britain was considering the Cabinet shake-up that made Churchill Prime Minister May 10, the day Holland was invaded. This sudden switch from German regularity causes the Center to ask . . . "Could it have been that Berlin, fearing the inauguration of a more vigorous British policy in the west, changed its Balkan plans and moved instead against the Low Countries, with no time to redirect its radio 'barrage'?"[5]

Details seemed unimportant. Significantly, the Nazis had demonstrated a pattern of radio propaganda that "blazed up" before a "typical invasion." German successes resulted, and Hitler now directed a "psychological civil war" against America. His forces could strike at any time, without warning—aided by insiders and a large, sympathetic base.

Even one's own spouse might help subversives achieve their sinister ends. An Englishwoman using the pseudonym "Margaret Schmidt" told her story to *Reader's Digest* in March 1940. "I Married a Nazi" was a cautionary tale. A Nazi could dupe anybody. Her husband might be "splendidly educated, a generous and devoted father [with] no hatred of Jews [or] foreigners," and her world "frosted, pretty, beautifully built," but "everything non-German" was "blandly ignored . . . the world outside . . . lost."[6]

Creating the Fifth-Column Consensus—United States

During the mid-to late 1930s, top State and War Department, FBI, ONI, and Army G-2 personnel believed the nation faced an imminent threat from its own citizens and resident aliens, some of whom had been in the country for decades. Through sheer repetition of wildly exaggerated and false tales of sinister activities, few questioned the fifth column's existence. Those of German, Italian, and Japanese descent—viewed as fifth columnists and so labeled—proved ideal, convenient, and acceptable scapegoats for Axis successes. The equation was, as one historian put it, "We lose, they pay."[7]

Because many in the White House, Congress, the military, the intelligence community, investigative agencies, law enforcement, and citizens organizations had long considered Germany and Japan viable external threats—Germany during World War I and Japan even earlier—doubts existed about the assimilation and loyalty of German and Japanese Americans. While the Trojan Horse concept (Roosevelt and others used the term) dates back to antiquity, Americans had for many decades readily embraced the ancient idea. Fear, racism, and nativism created the ideal political, ideological, and social climate that made relocation and internment seemingly necessary, prudent, and just. Once the nation was at war, everything was at stake, emotions ran high, tempers ran short, and tolerance for anything un-American was sorely lacking.[8]

Roosevelt believed in the fifth-column menace, as did Vice President Henry Wallace, an ardent anti-fascist; Harry Hopkins, perhaps FDR's most trusted adviser; and William Bullitt, another close friend of the president's and ambassador to France. There were also J. Edgar Hoover, Secretary of the Interior Harold Ickes, William Donovan (who would head the Office of Strategic Services), Treasury Secretary Henry Morgenthau, Secretary of State Cordell Hull, and Secretary of War Henry Stimson. Still others included Assistant Secretary of State Adolf Berle, Undersecretary of State Sumner Welles, Secretary of the Navy Frank Knox, the Western Defense Command's General John L. DeWitt, and the Special War Problems Division's Breckinridge Long. Besides state and local

West Coast politicians, many others, from New York City mayor Fiorello LaGuardia to San Antonio mayor Maury Maverick, worried about subversives. (To stop fifth columnists from crossing the Mexican border, Maverick claimed he had armed the city's police force with submachine guns while the Immigration Department doubled the number of border guards.)[9] Well before going to war, FDR and key personnel had created a fifth-column consensus.

Extensive media coverage and reports from Europe coupled with their own preconceived notions led policymakers, including FDR, to exaggerate internal threats. Roosevelt was not being hyperbolic when he spoke of the "epidemic of world lawlessness" in his October 1937 "Quarantine Speech." Yet obsessed officials frequently confused the most banal events as intricately choreographed sinister actions. Ignorance, misunderstanding, stereotypes, misinformation, anxiety, and prejudice influenced decision making.

Latin America and the Fifth Column

Roosevelt envisaged fifth columnists operating throughout the hemisphere. Coups in Brazil in 1938, Argentina and Chile in 1939, Uruguay in 1940, and Bolivia and Colombia in 1941 were thought to be inspired, directed, and supported by the Nazis. By the late 1930s, Bullitt, Berle, and many diplomats had become concerned about possible fifth-column activities, Hitler's rhetoric, and Nazi intrigues. Hitler had long been considering expanding the Reich into the Western Hemisphere. In conversations with conservative revolutionary Hermann Rauschning from 1932 to 1934, he had stated, "We shall create a new Germany there. . . . We shall find everything we need there."[10]

In July 1940, at Frank Knox's urging, Roosevelt asked William Donovan to study Britain's fifth-column policies. The Home Office eagerly shared remarkable documents, and Britain's relocation and internment experiences served as a blueprint for subsequent U.S. efforts.[11] National-security personnel increasingly had FDR's support. By April 1941, when Hoover's monitoring of "subversive activities" had gone too far in Attorney General Robert Jackson's eyes, Hoover wrote Jackson:

> I am convinced from the Bureau's study [that] the collapse in France ... was brought about by ... the French Government failing to be alert or aware of the growth and influence of the subversive groups. ... Nazi and Communist agents have deliberately endeavored to attach their tentacles to the labor groups in Britain, the United States, Mexico, and in many countries of South America. Recognizing the tremendous force for evil that may be exercised through domination of the labor organizations, the agents of the totalitarian powers have attached themselves to legitimate labor like barnacles attaching themselves to a ship. It is consequently highly important that the FBI be unhampered in its authority to conduct investigations into situations involving potential danger to the Government of the United States.[12]

Believing that German fifth columnists were on the move in Europe, American military analysts and officials feared their potential worldwide reach. Word of subversive threats from anxious politicians and popular newspapers, journals, and magazines, along with Roosevelt's fireside chats, reached millions of Americans.

Frederick Sondern warned *Reader's Digest* followers that the Nazi propaganda blitz was masking the regime's far more sinister and destructive intentions. Sondern's "Hitler Looks to South America" exposed Nazi designs throughout the hemisphere and revealed the creation of a social and political climate suitable for further encroachments, all part of Hitler's plans for global conquest. The August 1940 article noted the U.S. cruiser *Quincy* was en route to Montevideo because "Herr Fuhrmann, Hitler's deputy in Uruguay, was plotting to seize the mouth of the Rio Plata as a base for a revolution of the 2,500,000 Germans in Argentina and southern Brazil." A "high official" predicted that French West Africa would soon be in Nazi hands, followed by its conversion into a German-Italian base. Sondern's inside source explained that Hitler would then focus on Brazil, "a hotbed of Nazi activity." Sondern asked, "Do you seriously expect an invasion?" to which the "tired-looking official shook his head. 'Not now,' he answered. 'For the present they are just stirring up a war of nerves to keep us running between fires in Uruguay, Mexico, Brazil, Chile.'" "Can't those countries take care of themselves?" Sondern pressed. His source smiled, "'They're ripe for Hitler's sowing. It's going to take lots of cruisers from now on—and much wisdom.'" Uruguay was now "permeated with Nazi activity," while in Brazil it was "common knowledge" that Nazi formations were "being trained by German officers." The Rio Plata would serve as an "ideal harbor for landing 'volunteers' from Europe." The anonymous official concluded: "We know what we've got to do, and we're doing it." Sondern dourly responded: "The country certainly hopes so."[13]

Arsenal of Democracy

At a June 1940 press conference the president had stated, "There are at the present time . . . about forty or fifty factories in this country where somebody in the factory has tried to destroy tools." Rather than admit employees' dissatisfactions, Roosevelt affirmed: "That is the fifth column. Those are perfectly known cases." The fact that no evidence of sabotage had been found in more than 20,000 FBI investigations didn't matter; what did matter were spectacular examples of "enemy activities." When a suitcase bomb exploded in the British Pavilion at the New York World's Fair on July 4, killing the two detectives sent to disarm it, an anxious public suspected aliens and enemy agents. The culprits, never arrested, would surely bide their time and strike again.[14] On December 29, Roosevelt delivered a fireside chat, later known as the "Arsenal of Democracy" speech. There could be no peace with Germany, Italy, or Japan, he said. "No man can tame a tiger into a kitten by stroking it. . . . There can be no appeasement with ruthlessness":

> Never before has our American civilization been in such danger. The Nazi masters have made it clear that they intend not only to dominate all life and thought in their own country, but to enslave the whole of Europe and then dominate the world. The vast resources and wealth of this hemisphere constitute the most tempting loot in all the world.
>
> The evil forces that have crushed, undermined, and corrupted so many others are within our own gates. Your government knows much about them and is ferreting them out. Their secret emissar-

ies are active here and in neighboring countries. They seek to stir up suspicion, dissension, and internal strife . . . to divide our people, destroy our unity, and shatter our will to defend ourselves.

There are American citizens who, unwittingly, are aiding and abetting the work of these agents. They say that we can and should become the friends and even the partners of the Axis powers. Some of them even suggest that we should imitate the methods of the dictatorships. . . . We must be the great arsenal of democracy. For us this is an emergency as serious as war itself. We must apply ourselves to our task with the same resolution, the same sense of urgency, the same spirit of patriotism and sacrifice as we would show were we at war.[15]

In the spring of 1941, Roosevelt received ominous reports about Germans and Japanese from the FBI and U.S. military intelligence, British Security Coordination (headed by William Stephenson), and his own informal intelligence unit under John Franklin Carter. In November, Carter's final report warned of "Japanese in the United States who will tie dynamite around their waist and make a human bomb out of themselves" and that "dams, bridges, harbors, power stations" and the like along the West Coast but also throughout the nation were "wholly unguarded everywhere."[16]

On May 27 FDR delivered another fireside chat. More than sixty-five million, a new record for radio, listened. Think of attacks in a new way, the president urged. Normally "we are not attacked until bombs actually drop in the streets of New York or San Francisco or New Orleans or Chicago." Such views, FDR argued, were part of a bygone era. The unity of the American republics was of "supreme importance," because "what started as a European war" has become a "war for world domination." The lesson: "We must learn from the fate of every nation the Nazis have conquered. The attack on Czechoslovakia began with the conquest of Austria. The attack on Norway began with the occupation of Denmark . . . and the attack on the United States can begin with the domination of any base which menaces our security. . . . But we know enough by now to realize that it would be suicide to wait until they are in our front yard." Finally, after reasserting hemispheric solidarity, FDR declared: "I have tonight issued a proclamation that an unlimited national emergency exists and requires the strengthening of our defense to the extreme limit of our national power and authority."[17]

By the fall, after Germany invaded the Soviet Union and Japan ventured into Southeast Asia, and as Washington and London exchanged warnings about spies and saboteurs, Roosevelt shared some sensitive information with a nation still reluctant to prepare for war. If Germany were victorious in Europe, Hitler would then eye the Western Hemisphere—attacking the United States aided by Nazi spies and sympathizers. On September 11, Roosevelt again warned Americans of impending Nazi intrigues, plots, machinations, and sabotage. Once more he raised the specter of fifth-column activities and asserted that enemy agents were operating in communities throughout the nation and in countries throughout the hemisphere. As he had in previous fireside chats, Roosevelt told millions of listeners that "Hitler's advance guards" were busy readying "footholds" and "bridgeheads" in the New World, "to be used as soon as he has gained control of the oceans." Evidence of this existed, Roosevelt claimed, in the jungles of Colombia, where we were now aware of "secret air landing fields, within easy range of the Panama Canal."[18]

Listeners, if *Reader's Digest* fans, might have recalled Sondern's "Hitler Looks to South America." Sketching a "shrewd and methodical" pattern of Nazi intrigues throughout Latin America, his warnings sounded like Roosevelt's: Lufthansa using dozens of South American airfields, many suited for long-range bombers, and Berlin's establishing "a Fifth Column in every flying field and hangar on the continent," resonated with FDR's disclosure of Colombian airfields. Headlines such as "Nazi Fifth Column and Communist Allies Are Active in Mexico," "Pan-America vs. the Nazis," "Nazi Spy Activity in Mexico Charged," "Wings for the Trojan Horse: German and Italian Airplanes over South America," and "Swastika over Mexico" reinforced claims of German plots south of the border, while "The Nazis Are Here," "Financing the Fifth Column," "Hitler's 'Fifth Columns,'" "These Are Signs of Nazi Fifth Columns Everywhere," and "The War of Nerves: U.S. Front, Nazi Agents in U.S." highlighted Nazi scheming closer to home.[19]

Roosevelt had often referred to the Nazi fifth-column threat generally, and as early as April 1939 he had mentioned an aerial threat specifically. German planes could cross the ocean, FDR stated, in "three hops . . . Cape Verde, Brazil, Yucatan and Tampico." Fearing Germany's use of Brazil's strategically vulnerable northeastern "bulge" as a springboard to further hemispheric encroachments, Roosevelt on May 25, 1940, authorized an emergency deployment of 100,000 troops to Brazil if needed. On January 16, 1941, after meeting with Secretaries Hull, Stimson, and Knox along with General George Marshall and Admiral Harold Stark, the president had issued a verbal directive that provided forces to assist "in backing up friendly Latin American governments against Nazi-inspired fifth column movements." In a Navy Day speech on October 27, FDR again announced the discovery of subversive plots—this time a map (later proved spurious) illustrating Germany's plan to conquer Latin America.[20]

By March 1942, during the height of relocation and internment, the FBI suitably distributed another map showing vast areas of South America beneath ten large and easily recognizable Axis symbols—five Nazi swastikas, three Japanese rising suns, and two Italian flags. Axis domination or influence, as the images suggested, meant access to strategic war materials, control over vital waterways, and bases from which to attack the United States itself. Many such maps turned out to be phony at best or intentional fabrications at worst. Although such fears were wildly disproportionate to the actual threat, they were certainly not feigned. Axis military victories, culminating in the Japanese attack upon Pearl Harbor, demonstrated the enemy's resolve and reach. Those who remained skeptical of enemy designs beyond Europe, unconvinced of a fifth-column menace in the United States and the New World, found themselves diminishing in number and increasingly marginalized as FDR readied the nation for total war.[21]

Carter's Report and Allied Intelligence

In February 1941, Roosevelt selected John Carter, a New Dealer and close adviser, to create and head a White House covert intelligence network tasked with uncovering Nazi influences in the Americas as well as determining the "Japanese situation" in Hawaii and the West Coast. Carter immediately went to work, and by October his evidence reinforced FDR's belief in the risk posed by Axis forces and their supporters. Carter's report included information from Curtis Munson, who in turn relied heavily on the findings of Lieutenant Commander Kenneth Ringle of the ONI, who knew West Coast Japanese American communities well. At least 75 percent of Japanese Americans, Ringle noted, were loyal, with "surprisingly few differences between them and their American contemporaries." Whether the "younger and succeeding generations" of Japanese were "truly American in thought, word, deed, and sentiment," he added, would largely depend on how they "are treated now, and on how they are helped to meet the test of war." Despite these findings, FDR and others focused on Munson's warnings and then Carter's report, which stressed the dangers posed by Japanese Americans and fifth columnists.[22]

Key passages of Carter's summary of Munson's report included the following:

> 1) There are still Japanese in the United States who will tie dynamite around their waist and make a human bomb out of themselves. 2) There will undoubtedly be some sabotage financed by Japan and executed largely by imported agents. There will be the odd case of fanatical sabotage by some Japanese crackpot. 3) Their espionage . . . would be very effective as far as movement of supplies, troops, and ships. 4) For the most part the local Japanese are loyal or, at worst, hope that by remaining quiet they can avoid concentration camps or irresponsible mobs. 5) Dams, bridges, harbors, power stations, etc. are wholly unguarded everywhere. The harbor at San Pedro could be razed by fire completely by four men with grenades and a little study in one night. Dams could be blown and half of lower California might actually die of thirst. One railway bridge at the exit from the mountains in some cases could tie up three or four main railroads.[23]

FDR promptly ordered Stimson to investigate the "guarding of key points," despite Munson and Ringle's warning against overreacting. Ringle had suggested that "stressing the differences between Japanese Americans and Caucasian Americans" was simply "wrong," yet nearly all of Roosevelt's advisers and British intelligence sources exaggerated the threat or, worse, lied to the president. In the spring of 1940, William Stephenson, head of the New York station of the British Secret Intelligence Service (SIS or MI6), tried to impress Roosevelt with forged Nazi documents. If there was a fifth column that "interfered in the political process, suborned news media, sabotaged the campaigns of some congressmen and supported covertly others, and spread false information," journalist Norman Moss suggests, "it was run by British Intelligence, from the British passport control office in downtown New York." Stephenson wanted to aid Britain and get the United States into the war.[24]

All the while, British intelligence sent their War Cabinet alarming reports as Germany overran France and the Low Countries. After the Dutch surrendered on May 15, the British envoy in The Hague cabled: "Every German or Austrian servant, however superficially charming and devoted, is a real and grave menace." Moreover, there was "a Fifth Column waiting in Britain for the order to embark on a massive sabotage campaign." Donovan's and Britain's own alarmist reports reinforced Roosevelt's personal distrust of German Americans that began during World War I. Fantastic "worst case" scenarios prompted FDR and jittery officials to overreact and see saboteurs and subversives behind military debacles, political coups, social unrest, industrial accidents, crop failures, labor strikes, business failures, and the like.[25]

Frustrated at Hoover's apparent inattention to foreign threats, Congressman Dies delivered a nationwide radio address in May 1940 claiming that HUAC had "a wealth of information on alien agents, including plans, names, and their headquarters." Senator Robert Reynolds of North Carolina announced to his colleagues that the FBI was receiving over two hundred reports of sabotage daily. Every American, Reynolds said, should be fingerprinted: "Alien enemies, members of the 'fifth column,' are coming from across the Atlantic. They are entering the United States from across the Canadian border; they are coming north across the Rio Grande . . . and the 'fifth column' are already here by the hundreds of thousands. The 'fifth column' is here and the Trojan

Horses in great herds are grazing upon the green, tender grasses of the pastures of America."[26]

A year later HUAC learned that Nazi infiltrators posing as political refugees had arrived in the United States. Richard Krebs, alias Jan Valtin, a former Nazi prisoner, described to HUAC, and then readers in his best-seller *Out of the Night* (1941), Nazi propaganda, espionage, and hemispheric sabotage activities. Krebs told Dies and HUAC how, after years in a labor camp, he had deceived the Nazis and gained his release. Many German businesses, he warned, were a Gestapo facade. Pro-Nazi cartels, Krebs testified, employed enemy agents and German Americans masquerading as mechanics, engineers, reporters, and teachers. Employing spies and maintaining a close partnership with the Reich enabled IG Farben to "obtain information about our security program and to produce choke points, or to sabotage our war efforts," Krebs added. The Nazi regime could pressure anyone who had family in Germany into becoming a collaborator. Even more, "anyone released from a Nazi concentration camp must pledge to work for the Gestapo." Krebs's testimony helped prompt the first arrests and subsequent internment of German and Italian merchantmen, influenced HUAC, and, through *Out of the Night*, provided millions of readers with a powerful, cautionary tale of political fanaticism and fifth-column danger.[27]

Newspapers headlined the arrests and detention of hundreds of "Nazi sailors." The *New York Times* reported the "spectacular" arrests of aliens in conjunction with the sabotage of several dozen Axis vessels docked in U.S. ports. A few civil libertarians, including Hugh De Lacy, head of the American Committee for the Protection of Foreign Born, argued that the arrests and detention of aliens were a prelude for a congressional "concentration camp bill." To reassure millions of Italian and German immigrants, Robert Jackson delivered a nationwide radio address in which he stated emphatically that the government did not intend a general roundup of aliens. Yet *Time* reported a widespread roundup and deportation of Axis aliens, including dozens of Italian waiters who, having worked at the 1939 World's Fair in New York, overstayed the pavilion's closing in October 1940. Jackson, *Newsweek* added, asserted that "the secret weapon of the Nazis has been the failure of nation after nation to recognize and deal with... nonmilitary invasion."[28]

Dingell's Report and Internment Issues

Foreign nationals became bartering chips as tensions mounted and the soon-to-be belligerents demanded reciprocal treatment of the other's citizens. And it was not just Dies, Reynolds, and other demagogues in Congress who expressed their apprehension of and called for action against spies, saboteurs, aliens, and even enemy citizens. On August 18, 1941, Congressman John Dingell (a normally responsible New Dealer) advised Roosevelt:

> Japan has barred the departure of one hundred American citizens and... the detention is in reprisal for the freezing of Japanese assets.
>
> If it is Japan's intention to enter into a reprisal contest, we remind Nippon that unless assurances are received that Japan will facilitate and permit the voluntary departure of this group of one hundred Americans... the U.S. Government will cause the forceful detention or imprisonment into a concentration camp of ten thousand alien Japanese in Hawaii; the ratio of Japanese hostages held by America being one hundred for every American detained by the Mikado's Government.
>
> Remind Japan that there are 150,000 additional alien Japanese in the U.S. who will be held in a reprisal reserve whose status will depend upon Japan's next aggressive move. The U.S. is in an ideal position to accept Japan's challenge.[29]

Dingell's suggestion resonated, as threats with global implications were made throughout the war. The *San Francisco Chronicle* reported that after the FBI arrested German correspondents hours after the Pearl Harbor attack, the Nazis put American journalists in Germany under house arrest, promising that "whatever might be done as reprisal [will] be done 'in the noblest form.'" Sumner Welles, replying to letters written by concerned citizens, affirmed that "the treatment of Japanese prisoners of war and other Japanese nationals in the United States will naturally be influenced by the treatment accorded American prisoners of war and other American nationals under Japanese control."[30]

As the FBI was also arresting those considered national security threats, nearly all of them German and Japanese rather than Italian aliens, now enemy aliens with the United States at war, Roosevelt faced difficult decisions. And on December 11, Biddle met with Roosevelt who expressed his concern about enemy nationals. When asked how many Germans were in the country, Biddle (perhaps recalling the number of Italians) told the president there were about 600,000. "And you're going to intern all of them," FDR continued. "Well, not quite all," Biddle replied. To which Roosevelt added, "I don't care so much about the Italians. They are a lot of opera singers, but the Germans are different; they may be dangerous." Stimson and Hull and others at the highest levels of government repeated their concerns for Americans interned by the Axis throughout the war, and Knox, for example, told Roosevelt that Germany might use Americans as "hostages for captured Germans." Knox and Long, among others, fretted about repatriates aiding the enemy and knew that Japanese Hawaiians could reveal military secrets. Reciprocity and internment were two sides of the same coin; repatriation and exchange were seen in a military and national-security context.[31]

Military and ONI Fears

By the late 1930s, the Western Defense Command (WDC) had become increasingly worried about Japanese American loyalty. In July 1937 its analysts believed that the full-scale though undeclared war between Japan and China had politicized established social Japanese organizations while newer militant groups were more openly pro-Japanese. The WDC's Research Branch noted:

> It was not safe to assume that these societies or groups continued their earlier pattern. . . . The Japanese used similar techniques to those used by the Germans and Italians; every effort was made to take over already existing organizations and mold them to the "New Order." . . . There is ample evidence that this technique produced excellent results. Hundreds and hundreds of the older orga-

nizations acquired the new nationalistic pattern as then emanating from Japan. Although this technique was highly successful . . . it was also found either necessary or desirable to form many new organizations which were patriotic in character.[32]

Concurrently, the ONI developed an increasing interest in Japanese fishing and industries operating in Los Angeles, the Columbia River, and Puget Sound. In March 1941, discovery of the Tachibana spy ring prompted intensified FBI and ONI investigations of Japanese aliens, organizations, foreign contacts, and activities.[33] In May the ONI reported:

> The activities of Japanese individuals, groups, and associations in this country . . . stem directly from the Imperial Government in Japan. The Japanese military and naval espionage system is organized into more than one independent decentralized machine and may be classified as professional, commercial, domestic, and political.
>
> Undoubtedly there are . . . many agents operating independently whose trail will never be picked up or proven to be anything but irresponsible individuals operating without pay, authority, or direction. The latter class, estimated in the thousands, presents by far the greatest menace, and is generally overlooked by our counter espionage service.
>
> Communist, Nazi, and Fascist elements . . . have the territory in this country divided into sections, districts, states, etc., for the express purpose of exercising direct political control over subversive units. . . . Japanese . . . individuals or small groups . . . function separately . . . and principally in the field of military and naval espionage.
>
> Every Japanese commercial organization or business firm is . . . an actively functioning information unit . . . [and the] . . . activities of these concerns are nation-wide and practically endless. . . . The Japanese Government exercises direct control over these individuals and firms through the Imperial Government Embassy and the Consulates in the United States.[34]

Subversives included diplomats, businessmen, and spies. Sixty companies stood ready to collect information or disseminate propaganda, including the Japan Tourist Bureau, Japan Institute, Japanese Chamber of Commerce, and Tokyo Commercial and Industrial Museum. The report found Axis members "exploring all possible avenues by which they can achieve mutual benefit" and revealed Japanese government instructions: "In view of the Tripartite Treaty, please make every effort to maintain close contact with the officials of Italy and Germany in order that we may reap the fullest benefits in the way of exchanging information, etc. Please encourage friendships between Japanese subjects residing abroad and Italian and German citizens." The ONI stressed Japanese operational methods and attack points; Japanese American collaboration with spies made the West Coast especially vulnerable:

> Under the head of direct spy activity, we may include the lengthy study of the entire Western Coast line of North America by Japanese fishermen. Similar studies . . . include the Western Mountain area. Every conceivable objective has been included in these studies—railroads, highways, industries, and military terrain features.
>
> The Japanese are aiming at a very thorough knowledge of the terrain of the Western United States in the event that this area becomes a theatre of operations.
>
> Japanese propaganda is disseminated through commercial and business firms and through sympathetic articles and comments by individuals . . . [of] the Japanese Government. There are 56 individuals and organizations registered with the State Department carrying on propaganda work for the Japanese Government in this country.
>
> Similar efforts are being made through Japanese language newspapers and publications. This is particularly true along the West Coast where the Japanese population is concentrated. There is every indication that military and naval installations throughout the country, but especially on the West Coast, and all naval yards, bases, etc., are receiving very close attention from Japanese agents[35]

Japan was, the ONI believed, working closely with Germany and Italy to procure "military, naval, and commercial information, with special emphasis on the West Coast, the Panama Canal, and

Hawaiian areas" and directly controlling and dominating domestic Japanese elements. "There can be no question of a spontaneous movement," stated the ONI, "apart from official Japanese inspiration which in turn is collaborating with Nazi and Fascist elements looking forward to the establishment of a New World Order." The ONI detailed the extensive use and dissemination of propaganda, chiefly by the Japanese Foreign Office, through radio, newspapers, subsidized speakers, and underworld organizations, as well as "130 known Japanese associations, societies, clubs, federations, bureaus, etc.," some of which had "as many as 80 branches." Japan's government had been grooming local sympathizers too, including businessmen, teachers, newspapermen, and others, by sponsoring all-expenses-paid "good will trips" to Japan. The ONI added:

> Pro-Japanese propaganda among negroes in the United States is a phase of the Japanese "Holy War" in China and her Pan-Asiatic anti-white race movement. It is extended to the United States in the form of Japanese sponsored organizations of negroes, East Indians, and other colored races. The theme of these activities is a "Japanese policy of a new epic in history by leading the darker majority of mankind to a new life founded on international justice and the emancipation of the dark races from the white."

Japan's military representatives were promoting and controlling espionage activities with the help of Japanese Americans who, the ONI believed, were "decidedly loyal to Japan" and had an "agent in every Japanese community." The Naval Attaché's Office served as an intelligence and propaganda coordinating center, and the "actual purpose" of the Naval Inspector's Office was to "provide an efficient intelligence bureau to observe and procure the latest technical developments." The ONI warned:

> They [Japanese Naval Reservists] are in close contact with thousands of Japanese civilians in this country. . . . After a study of their extensive intelligence system, it can logically be assumed that a large number of their "civilians" are actually members of the organized reserves. It is known that officers of their merchant

marine keep in close contact with intelligence officers when their ships touch U.S. ports.

All able-bodied males who have lived in Japan until age 20 have received military or naval training.... A large number of naval reservists are residing in the country, most certainly used in intelligence work. Various Military and Patriotic Japanese Clubs exist openly in the large Japanese communities on the West Coast and are assuredly reservist organizations. The primary reason for posting a language officer in San Francisco or Los Angeles is to maintain close liaison with these reservists.

A heavy traffic of telegrams, radios, and cables is noted between the Japanese Ministry of Marine, Tokyo, and the various Naval Attachés and Inspectors in the United States, Canada, Mexico, and Europe.

Japanese language schools (248 in California and 234 in Hawaii) employed teachers who were "dangerous suspect" aliens instructing from Japanese government textbooks and were "by reason of superior mentality, education, and strategic location an ideal group for espionage work." Moreover, hundreds of Buddhist and Shintoist priests, fishermen and businessmen, diplomatic and consular agents, editors and publishers, along with over a hundred thousand resident Japanese aliens and citizens, lived and worked in areas vital to national security. The ONI concluded:

> The greater part of the Japanese on the West Coast reside in the Los Angeles-San Francisco Bay-Puget Sound Areas... our main naval strategic areas. There is *not* a commercial town, seaport, or strategic point in the United States... that does not have Japanese representation. The Japanese Intelligence Service in this country has at its service a reservoir of actual or potential agents that it can call upon to furnish information.... That a *large number* of Japanese civilians aid the Japanese Intelligence Service is beyond doubt. That certain Japanese civilians are closely connected with the Japanese Intelligence Service is absolutely positive.

The report found that "prominent manufacturers, technical designers, exporters, writers, editors, inventors, college professors," and government officials maintained relations with the Japanese Inspector's Office. Admittedly, "many Americans are friendly with the Naval Inspectors because *they can get something out of them* in the form of orders and contracts." Some Americans would "sell the Japanese anything," the ONI noted, "regardless of the fact that our own national defense might be prejudiced in the transaction. The Japanese know this quite well and use it to their advantage."[36]

The FBI at War

On March 31, 1941, Joseph Prendergast, special assistant to the attorney general, Special Defense Unit, recorded developments about those classed "Communist, Fascist, Nazi, or Japanese" per Director Hoover's strictly confidential instructions. Some had been under investigation for years, others after Germany invaded Poland. Prendergast now received large daily batches of copies of FBI master index (custodial detention) cards.[37]

FBI agents, working discreetly, sent copies of the cards to be "filed immediately, maintained under lock and key at all times, and accessible only to the Special Agent in Charge." Prendergast's office analyzed them according to the person's status (naturalized or native-born), address, political sympathy, employment, and membership in suspect organizations such as the "German-American Bund, Communist Society, Sons of Herman, singing societies, etc." Agents considered indications of "engaging in or preparing sabotage, espionage, a propagandist or engaged in other subversive activities, an organizer or trouble-maker." Special facts—German military service, relations to leaders or persons in Germany (family or friends), and hobbies like amateur flying, photography, and traveling—were also assessed. Classifications included A, the most dangerous subject to custodial detention during war; B, those subject to conditional release or limited control; and C, those who needed no control:

> The index cards may show . . . objectionable characters in regions close to army camps, national industries, and other vital points. . . . Employment file may show objectionable characters in key positions in national defense industries, public utilities, and elsewhere. . . .

> There should be studies and methods of handling [problems] by non-prosecutive means and preventive action. . . . As far as possible, they should be solved under the laws today. However, new legislation may be necessary.
>
> Definite recommendations: a) All aliens on the list should be checked for the legality of their entry and presence here. b) All naturalized citizens checked to see that they were properly naturalized. c) Any undue concentration of suspects in vital areas of our national defense is to be studied. d) Any organization officered by or having large numbers of the suspect list should be investigated from the Voorhis Act.[38]

Under the 1940 Voorhis Act, the Justice Department intensified its investigations of subversive activities, including "espionage, propaganda, contribution of money to Axis causes, Fascist indoctrination of their youth, and military training." Federal authorities soon had "considerable information on 3,700 suspected associations, of which approximately 350 (with 1,500 branches) had pro-Axis tendencies." The prospect of selective internment led to the INS surveying abandoned Civilian Conservation Corps camps, antiquated federal labor camps, forts, and prisons. In February 1941, Jackson told Hoover to divide the "list of persons against whom proceedings are recommended" into aliens, naturalized citizens, and native-born citizens, and to further divide the first two groups into Germans, Russians, Italians, and Japanese. Jackson wanted planning to include the immediate arrests of suspects and placing others "on bond, parole, or limitations as to travel etc." Hoover had agents "clarify, consolidate, and supplement instructions" for those being considered "for custodial detention pending investigation in the event of a national emergency."[39]

Targets included the Third Communist International, the Young Communist League, the German-American Bund, the Knights of the White Camellia, and the Silver Shirt Legion. FBI agents reported any member of a suspect group who attempted to further the aims or purposes of that organization by engaging in any the following:

> Candidacy for political office of any such organization or any of its fronts; distribution of organization propaganda or literature; speak-

ing at rallies, demonstrations, meetings, conventions; attending meetings where revolutionary or subversive principles are taught or advocated; writing books, articles, pamphlets, etc.; promulgating or advocating . . . revolutionary or subversive principles; acting as organizer, agitator, or propagandist for any such organization; participating in riots, demonstrations, or meetings accompanied by violence or breaches of the peace; holding a strategic or key position, such as employment in an aircraft, munitions, or defense plant, or any other position of potential influence or importance. There are, of course, countless other ways in which members of such organizations can attempt to advance the purposes of the organizations.

Hoover wanted Bundists and others considered for custodial detention who were "pronouncedly pro-German, Japanese, Italian, or disloyal or hostile to the United States, or loyal or sympathetic to any foreign country and aliens whose continuance at liberty during an emergency might constitute a danger to the internal security or the national defense (and) any other individuals."[40]

Beyond the basics—name (and aliases), address, occupation, citizenship status, criminal or military record, relatives, friends, and associates—agents considered loyalty, membership in subversive organizations, and access to confidential information. Hoover asked for ONI and MID help with suspects serving in the U.S. armed forces. Donald Perry, assistant commissioner for Alien Registration, INS, later concluded that "the government now knew more about the aliens in its midst than it did about anyone else." Registration, he noted, helped "temper intolerance by showing that an overwhelming number of aliens were loyal and law abiding; there was no fifth column menace—period."[41] Yet neither FDR nor the FBI was willing to take risks with national security.

Changing Times

Concerned over Hoover's power grab and FBI abuses, in 1934 Senator Kenneth McKellar of Tennessee had wanted information about dubious FBI activities released (the two had first had words in 1931 at an Appropriations subcommittee hearing). When told that such a disclosure would be "unwise," the senator replied, "I think the idea of a Cheka in this country is something that ought not to exist." In 1935, meeting once more at the Appropriations subcommittee hearings, McKellar warned:

> We are getting to have a tremendous secret service organization.... [Such] are frequently used as a means of doing great wrong, and I have my doubts about secret service systems in a republican form of government like ours. I have been astounded at the tremendous growth and the use of large sums of money for the "secret service," as it is called, of the Department of Justice.

By May 1940, Senator George Norris of Nebraska had had enough. Calling Hoover the "greatest publicity hound on the American continent," Norris cautioned,

> there will be a spy behind every stump and a detective in every closet in our land. Unless we do something to stop this furor of adulation and praise as being omnipotent . . . the FBI—which, instead of protecting our people from the civil acts of criminals—will itself in the end direct the government by tyrannical force, as the history of the world shows has always been the case when secret police and secret detectives have been snooping around the homes of honest men.[42]

A few politicians echoed these concerns, but events overseas along with the much-publicized fifth-column threat allowed for the increasing scope of FBI activities and justified overlooking its secret and illegal investigations. Roosevelt and Congress accelerated America's preparedness efforts. Jerre Mangione, a Justice Department official acting as the government's liaison with relocatees and internees, recalled:

> For the first time since the advent of Hitler as Germany's Führer, Congress expressed alarm over the events in Europe. Moved to a point of hysteria by the rapid conquests of the Nazi armies in their westward drive, and suddenly fearful that a "Fifth Column" might be forming in the United States to take over the government, Congress hurriedly passed the Smith Bill (eventually known

as the Alien Registration Act), which in the late summer of 1940 made it mandatory for all aliens in the United States to be registered and fingerprinted.[43]

Nearly five million aliens had complied by year's end. The Justice Department posted registration requirements at local post offices nationwide. All aliens had to carry at all times identity cards with their picture, thumbprint, and biographical information. The INS, under the Justice Department since June 1940, managed alien admission or exclusion along with naturalization or deportation laws and planned to build internment camps as the FBI added names of potential subversives to its list. The hunt was on.[44]

The classification scheme was simple. "A" stood for officers or leaders of American fascist or similar types of organizations; "B" was for members of such groups; and "C" indicated potential sympathizers. As James Rowe, an assistant to Francis Biddle, later recalled,

> At the Department of Justice, a war planning committee . . . had been operating for about a year . . . on the theory we might get into a war . . . [and] that our enemies would be the Japanese, Germans, and Italians. They were trying to make a selection of German, Italian, and Japanese aliens, enemy aliens, thought dangerous. There was a planning committee; Charles Fahy, the Solicitor General was on it; Frank Jay, a distinguished Assistant Attorney General was on it; and Edward Ennis was on it.
>
> If there is a hero . . . his name is Edward Ennis. They classified enemy aliens, and the way they did it. . . . they would, for instance, take a dangerous German and if the evidence showed he was very dangerous he was an "A." If the evidence was good, he was an "A-1." If it was poor, [he] was an "A-4."[45]

Aside from the FBI's investigative work, FDR asked William Donovan to gather information. Donovan, who later headed the OSS, and Edgar Mowrer, a journalist, issued a pamphlet "Fifth Column Lessons for America." Created from their own syndicated articles, it warned that a "colony" of millions of German Americans stood ready to aid Hitler's Reich. Believing fifth columnists helped Germany to victory in Europe, Roosevelt wanted to know how Britain was handling its enemies within. He dispatched Donovan to meet with Churchill, King George VI, and Stewart Menzies, chief of Britain's Secret Intelligence Service. The meetings marked the beginning of joint intelligence collaboration.[46]

State, War, and Justice Departments

After the passage of the Alien Registration Act on June 28, 1940, but before its implementation on August 27, War and Justice Department officials began discussing how to deal with alien enemies. The day before registration was to begin, Stimson (who became secretary of war on July 10) suggested coordinating activities and studying those on Hoover's suspect list. On July 18, 1941, given the expected need to intern thousands of aliens, War and Justice Department representatives reached a tentative agreement as to which of them should be responsible for the custody of enemy aliens. The Army, having explored the "alien enemy problem" for a year, would take the lead, mainly because it had the facilities. In October, during a budding turf battle, the War Department confidentially requested the State Department for support in its disputes with the Justice Department.[47]

Welles and Hull agreed, for the moment, that the State Department should "remain aloof." Yet they suggested an "interdepartmental board upon which the Secretaries of State and War and the attorney general should be represented." While the Justice Department could not yet adequately house and care for very many internees, the War Department would likely treat them too harshly. Seeking a speedy resolution, State Department consultants ensured camps started off properly in order to avoid difficulties abroad. Hull expressed the State Department's ongoing interest in ensuring the well-being of American internees held by Germany and Japan:

> The treatment rendered alien enemies in this country will largely determine the treatment to be afforded to American[s] . . . interned in other countries. If we do not afford quarters, sanitary facilities, food and clothing adequate in every respect to the human requirements of the respective localities . . . then we may expect our own citizens to be treated infinitely worse.

> The Justice Department is not equipped to intern except in jails. That . . . is not admissible. The treatment accorded American citizens in Germany and Italy would then be indescribable. The War Department's proposal to put them in tents during the severe weather of winter is equally unacceptable. The State Department must have voice in the character and quality of the equipment, accommodations, food, and clothing of the internment camps here.
>
> The State Department ought to be consulted . . . in order that we may plan in advance that the conditions . . . will . . . satisfy the requirements of humanity which we expect to be offered to our citizens abroad.[48]

Canadian officials aided their American counterparts by sharing lessons learned. First, Canada and England had initially interned too many, including numerous anti-Nazi refugees. Second, both had experience handling prisoners of war, civilian internees, and anti-Nazi refugees. U.S. officials welcomed Canada's help, but problems persisted well into the war—too few facilities for too many internees (plus later relocating over 100,000 West Coast Japanese). As a result, the Army quartered male internees from July 1941 to May 1943 when the INS, then in charge of female internees, took charge of all internees.[49]

The INS, like the State Department, worried that anti-alien measures would have a negative impact on Americans abroad. Lawrence Smith's SDU, anticipating the need to solve legal, logistical, housing, and other difficulties, began reviewing the matter. At the end of 1940, SDU attorneys developed "plans to handle the problem," and by January 1941 the INS had responded to the SDU's review of detention facilities for emergency use. By April, Justice and War Department personnel worked jointly with the SDU. Those urging cooperation convinced Jackson and Acting Secretary of War Robert Patterson that appointing a committee of two representatives from both departments along with three civilians should commence "without delay." Hoover had the FBI direct activities, prepare records, and coordinate efforts to create records of those who would be interned. Jackson and his successor, Francis Biddle (who took over in September 1941), agreed and proposed that the INS assume responsibility of the "alien enemy problem." The FBI turned over 4,500 names, 1,800 tentatively classified as aliens, from its suspect list to the INS.[50]

The War and Justice Departments and the FBI had been working, albeit sporadically, to intern aliens and citizens, and by the summer of 1941 they had a general agreement for handling the "alien enemy problem." The INS put forth the most persuasive case, having moved from the Labor to the Justice Department a year earlier after what FDR called a "startling sequence of international events." It had also been a year since the passage of the Alien Registration Act. As events accelerated, Axis military victories, secretive investigations and detention preparations of suspect aliens based on well-established precedents, widespread public fear of fifth columnists, and a consensus among top policymakers all but ensured internment once the nation was at war. Policymakers envisioned and subsequently used the related policy of relocation as an instrument of national defense against a widely perceived but largely nonexistent internal enemy. Few questioned the means that justified winning the war. The issues remaining were how to accomplish the task, the number of relocatees and internees, and which department—War, Justice, or State—would run the show.[51]

Searching for a Solution

Some within the INS, including former assistant secretary of labor Marshall Dimock, suggested they run the entire enemy alien program, and in June 1941 they submitted a plan to Jackson. Dimock informed Jackson that in the fall of 1940 he and other INS officials had begun discussing "war plans relating to the arrest, detention, and parole of alien enemies." Several conferences followed in April and May 1941 between INS and War Department officials. Dimock relied on the FBI's work and secret CDI along with the legal right and physical ability to detain thousands of aliens and citizens.

Dimock believed that the INS was the best equipped to take charge. Highlighting key INS "peculiar contributions," he submitted a report in June to the attorney general:

> The INS ... is peculiarly adapted to the investigation, arrest, detention, and parole of aliens when the need arises. This Service has ... considerably more informational data on aliens. ... Considering its already trained and experienced personnel, its records, and its facilities for immediate detention, this Service appears to be the logical unit that should primarily decide what aliens are included within the term "dangerous enemy alien," arresting those deemed dangerous, and detaining those who should be removed from society during war.
>
> The objective ... should be to arrest and place in detention only those who are a danger to the country and not cause mass arrests and detentions of all aliens. The result of mass arrests and detentions would undoubtedly be more injurious to the country ... [and] would unquestionably cause resentment among aliens, which would likely create a real menace in time of war. The INS has 500 offices in 22 districts. It has 3,500 men trained and experienced in the interrogation and arrest of aliens. ... "Build upon what you have."[52]

Several SDU attorneys, including Patricia Collins, questioned the proposal, noting that the INS would be overseeing "the arrest, hearing, parole and detention as well as a portion of the investigation of all persons who would be classed as alien enemies" by presidential proclamation. It would be too much, and Collins offered several reasons why. First, the INS (much less the SDU) was incapable of handling all aspects of the developing program. Second, others were far better at investigating and incarcerating alien enemies. Third, the proposed plan entailed a decentralization of control, including district hearing boards, that was antithetical to interdepartmental integration and cooperation. District boards, she argued, offered a disjointed approach to a national problem, whereas "our own experience, as well as the British, to which this Unit has given considerable study, demonstrates that centralization of control is essential." Alien enemies, said Collins, "are important more because they may constitute a dangerous element and ... might engage in subversive activities involving the national defense, than because they are of an alien population who may be in this country in violation of immigration laws or admission quotas. . . . The preservation of secrecy of information is often of utmost importance, and centralized control alone accomplishes that purpose." Collins emphasized that while the INS was "traditionally best suited to deal with the alien aspects of the problem. . . . If the Immigration Service should cut across the functions of all agencies . . . the President's directive, which assigned the control of investigations regarding subversive activities, would have to be interpreted as applying to citizens and naturalized citizens only."[53]

Smith urged the use of INS "proffered facilities" and advised the FBI to investigate all subversive activities per FDR's September 6, 1939, secret directive. The INS, Smith felt, could fit in at the investigative stage by submitting information to the FBI. It could help at the arrest stage as needed and its officers would be available to attorneys in a consultative capacity and for interrogating aliens at the hearing stage. INS officers could be responsible for alien enemy parolees. Finally, given adequate facilities, the INS could permanently detain enemy aliens. Smith stressed using the INS to "the fullest extent possible" and advocated the "need for the continuation of centralized authority to determine policy decisions within the Unit."[54]

Authorities received their first internees—over four hundred German sailors from the *Columbus*—at Fort Stanton, New Mexico, in January 1941, after the crew had endured a year's incarceration, first at Ellis and then Angel Island. As internee numbers rose sharply, two more facilities were readied. On May 9, Fort Missoula, Montana, got its first internees, as did Fort Lincoln, North Dakota, by month's end. Nearly two thousand German and Italian sailors found themselves in INS camps. Fort Missoula's population swelled from one hundred to one thousand Italian aliens as preparations to house twenty-five hundred proceeded. Construction at Fort Lincoln allowed for an increase from two hundred German aliens to an anticipated two thousand (a fourth camp, Crystal City, opened in December 1942). The INS created seven "regular immigration stations" at Ellis Island; Boston, Massachusetts; Gloucester City, New Jersey; Detroit, Michigan; Seattle, Washington; and San Francisco and San Pedro, California. These held some 1,000 persons as the INS prepared the ten facilities to hold

7,000 internees—roughly 2,500 at the immigration stations plus 4,500 at Forts Lincoln, Missoula, and Stanton.[55]

Lemuel Schofield, special assistant to the attorney general, estimated that the INS would soon have ten thousand detainees. He informed Biddle of the projected costs of personnel, facilities, construction, equipment, and other necessities (especially food). Schofield also raised the problem of the "large number of Japanese fishermen located on Terminal Island, San Pedro, in the midst of the many defense activities," as well as "merchants located up and down the West Coast." He added that the "alien registration program has progressed to a point where very shortly we will know accurately how many Japanese are on the West Coast, where they are, and how many admit that they are here illegally." Schofield hoped to compel aliens to establish their continuous residence prior to the 1924 Immigration Act. If not, then "deportation warrants could probably be issued in many cases."[56] While his plan was not implemented, Schofield wanted to deal preemptively with the perceived disloyalty of hyphenated Americans—despite no proof of any wrongdoing.

As word spread of the internment of German and Italian sailors, Biddle worried that aliens might become anxious. On November 5, 1941, he had asked Stimson to keep news about camps and internees restricted. When Stimson replied on February 1, 1942, the United States had been at war for two months, and everything had changed:

> It is important at this time to let it be known that detention camps are a fact and that the government is in a position to deal with legitimate cases. Furthermore, as civilian internees and prisoners of war are received in increasing numbers, the need for carefully conceived and well-timed publicity cannot be overemphasized, particularly from the viewpoint that lack of such publicity may have a serious effect on American nationals in enemy hands.
>
> I am accordingly rescinding previous instructions on the subject to the Corps Area Commanders and others concerned, and advising them of the need, from now on, of carefully conceived and well-timed publicity on the subject of alien enemies and detention camps within their respective jurisdictions.[57]

5

Pearl Harbor and the Home Front

> This is war; death and destruction may come
> from the skies at any moment.
>
> —GENERAL JOHN L. DEWITT, DECEMBER 11, 1941

The morning of December 7, 1941, forever changed America. Shortly after the attack came the first indelible images of the devastation wrought by Japanese military forces. The surprise of the attack coupled with its tremendous success led to a rapid series of decisions and responses. Foremost was a massive mobilization effort—a daunting task as the country still struggled with the Great Depression's ravages. Despite suffering its worst military disaster, the United States had a tremendous psychological advantage. Because Japan had struck first, all but a handful of the most fervent isolationists and pacifists joined mainstream society in what soon became an unparalleled demonstration of patriotism, unity, and resolve. "Remember Pearl Harbor," the oft-repeated slogan expressing the nation's outrage over Japan's "sneak attack," sustained the people's determination over four long years to avenge the disaster and humiliation suffered that Sunday morning. The adjective "treacherous," more than any other single word in the nation's vernacular, became the descriptive that characterized the Japanese people for the war's duration. There existed a widespread sense of outrage and accompanying thirst for revenge in the aftermath of Pearl Harbor.[1]

Pearl Harbor

In 1921, those charged with Hawaii's defense began considering aliens as threats. The War Department accordingly developed contingency plans to intern Hawaii's aliens in the event of war. Two years later, Colonel John DeWitt called for the "establishment of complete military control over the Hawaiian Islands, including its people, supplies, material, etc.," if the United States went to war with Japan.[2] Over the years, surprisingly few resources and little effort were put into decrypting Japanese naval codes and cipher systems, yet considerable resources and a sustained effort from FBI, ONI, MID, and OSS personnel went into studying and countering the fifth-column threat. Key State and War Department officials and military intelligence analysts were well acquainted with rumors, circulating since January 1940, of Japanese plans to attack Pearl Harbor. Submarines reconnoitered Hawaiian waters as Japanese agents gathered detailed information about U.S. defenses along the West Coast, the Hawaiian Islands, and the Panama Canal. By September 1940 the Hawaiian Defense Project had concluded that enemy submarine or sabotage was the most likely form of attack. The War Department concurred, and the military planned accordingly. Yet FDR and Churchill believed that the "little yellow men," as Churchill sometimes called the Japanese, lacked the strength and willpower, much less the imagination and intelligence, to pose a threat.

America's political and military leaders never took the Japanese military too seriously. General Marshall believed that a few dozen bombers and a hundred or so fighter aircraft made an attack against Oahu or the Pacific Fleet impracticable. In May 1941 he told FDR that "in point of sequence, sabotage is first to be expected." Despite occasional warnings to the contrary, including a Honolulu paper's November 30 headline "Japanese May Strike over Weekend," military intelligence and top brass feared fifth columnists far more than Japan's navy. The undue emphasis on the largely nonexistent internal threat, meanwhile, disrupted or destroyed the lives of thousands along the West Coast. Germans, Italians, and the far more numerous Japanese living on the Hawaiian Islands were subject to martial law and endured numerous restrictions.

The shock waves generated by the Pearl Harbor attack reverberated, affecting thousands of Germans and Italians living along both coasts and thousands more who lived far from either shore.[3]

The surprise attack led to several critical assumptions that were widely believed at the time. One was that fifth columnists had played a key role in Japan's military success at Pearl Harbor, just as they had in Germany's successes throughout western Europe. Polls indicated that most Americans, influenced by media reports, government declarations, and their own prejudices and fears, believed not only that another attack and an invasion of the West Coast was imminent but also that throngs of Axis sympathizers would rise up in support, revealing their true loyalty and wreaking havoc. On November 5, 1941, Mrs. Roosevelt had written Biddle asking about the "possibility of loyal Japanese aliens of many years' good standing becoming naturalized citizens." Biddle answered that Japanese aliens could not enjoy the "privilege of naturalization." But, he continued, they "should be reassured by the knowledge that their alien status will not prejudice them in anywise or deprive them of scrupulously fair and just treatment, so long as they remain loyal." Pearl Harbor changed everything. Within a few months, FDR and top policymakers took steps against aliens that the attorney general had assured the First Lady the government would not. Americans soon demanded action—primarily against the Japanese. A March 1942 national public-opinion poll showed "93 percent in favor of evacuating alien Japanese. While 59 percent wanted to evacuate U.S. citizens of Japanese origin, only 25 percent disapproved."[4]

Nobody knew where or when the enemy might strike next. On December 8, as wild rumors circulated and reports indicated that San Francisco and Los Angeles were likely targets for another Japanese strike, Eleanor Roosevelt and Mayor Fiorello LaGuardia headed to California to reassure the public. Before leaving, LaGuardia unreassuringly told his fellow New Yorkers: "We who live on the Atlantic coast are just as much in danger of being bombed as our countrymen who were bombed last night in Honolulu." En route to Los Angeles their pilot stated that San Francisco was under attack by Japanese aircraft; although it was a false report, rumors spread quickly and officials were jittery.[5]

Pearl Harbor led to an all-out effort to engage the enemy—including enemy aliens and those citizens believed by their neighbors to be disloyal. Responding to Biddle's request for cooperation with local and state officials in carrying out federal policies regarding enemy aliens, some, including LaGuardia, appealed for calm, seeking to avoid "discrimination or abuse." New York's mayor sought "justice and decency" that the "overwhelming majority of loyal aliens" should expect, and hoped that "we may be sparing American citizens stranded in enemy countries any unjust retaliation." At the Conference of Mayors on December 20, LaGuardia noted: "The Department of Justice knows that the majority of non-citizens in our country are peaceful, law-abiding, and in complete sympathy with our form of government."[6] Yet non-citizens could prove their loyalty via relocation and internment. The sacrifice of captivity ought to be a welcomed way to serve the nation and do one's duty.

Most Americans, already believing in the inherent inferiority of Asians, heard that Germany had planned the Pearl Harbor attack and had convinced Japan to carry it out. LaGuardia, having spent most of Sunday issuing orders to protect city bridges, factories, and tunnels, held a late-afternoon press conference. Broadcast over city station WNYC, the mayor accused "Nazi thugs and gangsters" of "masterminding" the attack and warned his fellow New Yorkers to expect the unexpected there too. Listening to their radios in unprecedented numbers for any news from Hawaii, millions believed such sensational revelations. Two months later, more than two-thirds of those polled suspected Germany was behind the attack—Japan was technologically and intellectually incapable of planning and executing such a feat. Equally bemused were many of FDR's top advisers and military officers. Adolf Berle smelled an Italian rat, while Henry Stimson wrongly informed FDR: "We know from the intercepts and other evidence that Germany pushed Japan into this." Just hours after Pearl Harbor, when General Douglas MacArthur learned that Japanese aircraft had destroyed his own in the Philippines, he "insisted that the pilots must have been white mercenaries." British soldiers defending Hong Kong, experiencing similar losses from Japanese air attacks, "firmly believed . . . that Germans must be leading the sorties."[7]

Notwithstanding the false assumptions regarding the events of December 7, the attack itself, along with many coordinated strikes elsewhere in the Pacific, created an indelible wartime image of the Japanese as a treacherous and diabolical foe. The public's search for scapegoats instantly commenced along with the government's concurrent resolve to safeguard the nation by removing, and then punishing by way of interning, those previously deemed and now openly declared to be enemies among us.

Demographics, Old and New Enemies, and Opinion Polls

By 1940 the U.S. population was 131 million. Of those foreign-born in the United States, 42 percent of the Italians, 25 percent of the Germans, and 37 percent of the Japanese population were not citizens. The foreign-born white population was 11.4 million, of which Germans were 1.2 million and Italians 1.6 million (both roughly 1 percent of the total population). If one included the immediate descendants of Germans and Italians, their numbers were substantial—some 7.2 million Germans and 4.5 million Italians. Such numbers, almost 9 percent of the total population, worried those in charge of the nation's defense. Given the rapid collapse of western Europe and the surprise attack on Pearl Harbor, further calamities, including those supported by fifth-column activities in the hemisphere, were anticipated.[8]

When America went to war in December 1941, it did so against one recent enemy—Germany—and two new ones—Italy and Japan. Unknown was whether Germany or Japan was the greater threat and whether German or Japanese Americans posed the greater danger. Few questioned the probability of an invasion or the reality of a fifth column. As late as June 1943, half of those polled about a Japanese invasion of the West Coast still expected it. Even at war's end, military and civilian officials warned of wonder weapons and desperate measures, including traitors, to strike a final, parting blow. It boiled down to loyalty: the nation's right to test it, and aliens' and citizens' need to prove it.[9]

Despite the official Germany-first strategy decided by FDR and Churchill in March 1941, more U.S. forces went to fight the Japanese than the Germans until 1944. This was due to demands from Pacific allies, the U.S. Navy, and MacArthur to halt the string of Japanese victories and avenge Pearl Harbor. The threat to England had also lessened considerably after the Battle of Britain and Hitler's invasion of Russia. Americans clearly favored the Japan-first approach. Polls taken in late February and early March 1942 revealed that nearly two-thirds of Americans wanted to fight Japan first, believing it was the primary enemy. Meanwhile, calls for action against enemy aliens and citizens reached a crescendo as demands for evacuation peaked. While many wanted all enemy aliens and disloyal citizens removed from the West Coast and others asked for the same along the East Coast, attention remained fixed upon West Coast Japanese Americans. By late June 1942, with significant Allied naval victories in the Pacific, the public slightly favored fighting Germany first. Throughout 1943, however, most still felt that Japan was the chief enemy, and many still feared an invasion. National goals and objectives informed strategy, but so did fears and the desire to punish Japan for its "unprovoked and dastardly attack."[10]

Enemies were malleable. Asked in January 1939 which side, the Soviet Union or Germany, they would like to win if war broke out between the two, 83 percent wanted a Soviet victory, despite the recent Red Scare. A few months later, when asked which country they liked least, 58 percent said Germany. In 1942 the Daughters of the American Revolution praised Stalin as a "man of great studies . . . who, when he sees a great mistake, admits it and corrects it." After Pearl Harbor, a *Fortune* magazine poll asked whether Germany or Japan posed the greater danger. The results: 47.5 percent said Germany, 32.3 replied an equal danger, and 10.2 percent chose Japan. Over 57 percent of West Coast residents believed Germany was the greater danger. The results reflected beliefs of Japanese technological inferiority, German military prowess, and perceived external threats. Emotionally, though, even before Pearl Harbor the public hated Japanese far more than Germans, and archetypical images of apes and vermin strongly reinforced the pejorative rhetoric that typecast Japanese and by extension Japanese Americans.[11]

Following Pearl Harbor, a considerable government, military, and media effort vilified the enemy. The propaganda campaign against "Nazis" and "Japs" included not only distant soldiers and diplomats but also resident aliens and unwelcome citizens. The enemy could be a suspicious stranger, a friendly neighbor, or even one's beloved spouse. Fear gripped the public mind. Proof of disloyalty, past and present, abounded, it seemed. There was German treachery during the Great War, the garrulous antics of the Bund, warnings of the "yellow peril," official reports of "Japan's program for world supremacy," and ethnic Italian enclaves unwilling to denounce Mussolini. Enemies, Americans readily believed, were living among them. While the German blitz offered proof of enemy deceit, the Japanese bore the brunt of America's hatred due to the treachery associated with the "date which will live in infamy." Such ire remained for the war's duration as nearly all the fighting, along with the resultant casualties during those first few months, was in the Pacific, and because racial differences apparently made Japanese Americans unassimilable.[12]

Decision Making

Related fears of a West Coast invasion and subversive activities led to the relocation of West Coast Japanese Americans and the internment of German, Italian, and Japanese Americans. Roosevelt often spoke of vulnerabilities and facilitated the widespread belief in subversives through his policies and speeches. In a February 17, 1942, press conference he stated that "enemy ships could swoop in and shell New York. . . . Enemy planes could drop bombs on war plants in Detroit. . . . Enemy troops could attack Alaska." Six days later, FDR reached a record sixty million listeners during a fireside chat, his first national address since Pearl Harbor. As he was explaining a "new kind of war" in which the vast oceans would no longer protect the nation, a Japanese submarine fired thirteen rounds on a Santa Barbara petroleum complex before disappearing. The damage was minor, the audacity impressive, and the psychological impact so great that the following night a stray weather balloon over Los Angeles prompted jittery anti-aircraft crews to fire fourteen hundred shells into the dark. Falling explosive fragments injured dozens, and a few died either from heart attacks or from being trampled in a "stampede in the streets" during the chaotic "Battle of Los Angeles." No enemy aircraft was responsible, though the Western Defense Command for months insisted there had been an attack, telling the public the same, and refusing to admit its mistake. The denial was costly. Fears dramatically escalated, and just two days later came the first large-scale evacuation of Japanese from Terminal Island, Los Angeles Harbor. With the Pacific Fleet largely in ruins, General DeWitt and others knew that the West Coast was vulnerable to Japanese attack.[13]

Time asked if Americans were "Smug, Slothful, Asleep?" Politicians, including FDR, worried about complacency and, acknowledging a morale problem, decided to wage a psychological battle against America's enemies, including fifth columnists. The vitriolic campaign against the Japanese was highly successful. Although the nation's official policy as declared and reaffirmed before and after Pearl Harbor was to hold Japan in check until Germany could be defeated, Admiral Ernest King, among others, called for a military focus on Japan and an overarching Pacific-first strategy. Besides strategic military reasons, King's view was that "Australia—and New Zealand—are 'white man's countries' which it is essential that we shall not allow to be overrun by the Japanese because of the repercussions among the non-white races of the world."[14]

The exigencies of warfare, stresses on those charged with the nation's defense, and a crescendo of voices, amplified by the media, demanding action all affected relocation and internment decisions. Besides interning those thought dangerous through a screening process that involved hearing boards, the federal government in conjunction with the military decided to remove wholesale persons whose loyalty it could not discern or prove. After Pearl Harbor, DeWitt and others became convinced they could not "weed the disloyal out of the loyal and lock them up if necessary." The initial impulse to remove all aliens was followed by the more pragmatic removal of all Japanese from the West Coast and thousands of Germans and Italian aliens from both coasts. It emerged from many factors—domestic and international. Similar factors and reasoning led ultimately to leaving alone the large Japanese population in Hawaii and many millions of Germans and Italians, citizens and aliens, living far from designated "sensitive areas." Despite greater hatred toward and fear of the Japanese, the United States vowed to prosecute the war against Germany first, judging Hitler's regime the greater threat and Europe the decisive theater. In reality, however, until 1944 most forces went to the Pacific to counter Japanese offensives and satisfy Allied pleas for help and public demands for vengeance. Officials considered Japanese Americans a greater threat than German Americans and deemed both far worse than Italian Americans. Pearl Harbor and Japan's ability to strike or support a West Coast invasion kept the nation's focus on Japan and Japanese Americans.[15]

Widespread panic ensued across the nation in the months after Pearl Harbor. Air-raid sirens shrieked in West Coast cities and as far away as Smithville, Georgia. Hastily strung barbed wire stretched along beaches from Mexico to Canada. Women in coastal areas learned from *Life* magazine "How to Kill a Jap" in case they waded ashore. Birmingham, Alabama, residents conducted antiparachutist exercises, tagging would-be saboteurs on a country club golf course. Cities as inland as Boise, Idaho, began practicing blackouts as rumors of Japanese carrier operations near the mouth of the Columbia River circulated.[16] Believing that thousands of fifth columnists stood ready to act, and unwilling to risk another catastrophe, General DeWitt wanted all enemy aliens, Germans and Italians too, removed from the West Coast en masse.

Carefully weighing the pros and cons, all with the ultimate aim of winning the war, Roosevelt removed West Coast Japanese Americans en masse, and applying the same considerations, removed lesser numbers of German and Italian Americans from the West Coast and thousands more on a selective basis from the East and Gulf Coasts. Biddle later summarized the president's thinking:

> Roosevelt... was never theoretical about things. What must be done to defend the country must be done. The decision was for his Secretary of War... whose judgment as to the appropriateness of defense measures he greatly respected. The military might be wrong. But they were fighting the war. Public opinion was on their side, so that there was no question of any substantial opposition, which might tend toward the disunity that at all costs he must avoid. Nor do I think that the constitutional difficulty plagued him—the Constitution has never

greatly bothered any wartime President. That was a question of law, which ultimately the Supreme Court must decide. And meanwhile—probably a long meanwhile—we must get on with the war.[17]

In Hawaii, despite the threat Japanese Americans posed, their sheer numbers kept authorities from overreacting and removing them wholesale. Actions taken against enemy aliens and citizens were consistently pragmatic and even-handed, albeit harsh and irrational in hindsight. By December 9 the FBI had taken into custody 93 German, 13 Italian, and 391 Japanese aliens in Hawaii out of 620 German, 98 Italian, and 1,212 Japanese aliens nationally. By January 12, 1942, it was 79 German, 11 Italian, and 389 Japanese aliens in Hawaii out of 1,301 German, 243 Italian, and 1,566 Japanese aliens nationally. Meanwhile, the U.S. Army interned 482 Japanese, Germans, and Italians.[18]

Only 1,875 of 157,905 Japanese Hawaiians went to relocation or internment camps. Mass evacuation, Chief of Staff George Marshall and Admiral King informed FDR, was "not feasible." Assistant Secretary of State Breckinridge Long told Assistant Chief of Staff George Strong that the "token number of Japanese" sent to mainland camps would be repatriated "in exchange for American nationals from Manchuria and Korea." Japanese Hawaiians became part of a series of wartime exchanges. They, along with other Japanese Americans, were exchanged for Americans held by Japan. According to Long, the policy was "particularly desirable in order that the Japanese government will have no hesitancy in including on the next exchange vessel the remainder of the Americans from remote areas under Japanese control." Several factors kept nearly 99 percent of Hawaii's Japanese free. First, they were an indispensable part of the Hawaiian economy. Second, evacuating and interning 37 percent of the population was impossible. Third, almost 80 percent, or roughly 120,000, were citizens. Nevertheless, all Hawaiian Germans, Italians, and Japanese faced restrictions under martial law.[19]

In addition to the relocation of 112,704 Japanese Americans, an estimated 10,000 Italian and German Americans were evacuated from restricted West Coast areas in February and March 1942.[20] Guiding every evacuation, relocation, or internment decision was a calculated weighing of pros and cons. Military and civilian officials never seriously questioned their conclusion that there were enemies among us. Nor did they question their decision, reached years earlier, to relocate and intern enemy aliens or even citizens, if necessary. But deciding which individuals or groups, the size and location of the exclusion zones, how many to evacuate, where they should go, when to order an evacuation, and how to accomplish such tasks successfully while fighting a war were weighty issues demanding prudence and compromise. Roosevelt and others made all major decisions with the aim to win the war.

There were 85,000 German and Italian aliens in the three Pacific Coast states. Their average age was sixty, and their average length of residence was twenty-four years. Relocating families would add another 145,000 persons. A dual-coast evacuation of 300,000 German and 675,000 Italian aliens plus the follow-up prospect of moving 923,000 naturalized Germans and 929,000 naturalized Italians would become "an even more unmanageable proposal." Including children, this meant "approximately 7,000,000 persons in families of whom at least one parent was born in Germany or Italy." There was safety in numbers. The same applied to Japanese Americans in Hawaii, but not to those along the West Coast. Japanese Americans here were too few relative to the overall population, too dangerous a threat, well concentrated and not so well assimilated, and there was little reason to stop a powerful momentum.[21]

As with the Japanese Americans in Hawaii, German and Italian Americans were far too numerous to relocate en masse. The Tolan Committee (named after Representative John Tolan of California), acknowledging a "nation of alien peoples," concluded after a series of West Coast hearings in February and March that "uprooting fifty trustworthy persons to remove one dangerous individual" was simply impossible. Nevertheless, Germans and Italians also served as scapegoats. In all cases, authorities tempered countering fifth columnists with practical considerations—including limited resources. The Tolan Committee found it "encouraging" that General DeWitt proposed delaying the wholesale movement of Germans and Italians until "his organization has gained experience with the Japanese."[22]

Initial Relocation and Internment

Perceived military necessity was the main reason for relocating German, Italian, and Japanese Americans. Moving them en masse, including Hawaiian Japanese, was constrained by economic considerations and winning the war. Relocation would, from the federal perspective, assuage public fears, remove fifth columnists from strategic areas, and solve the psychological need to avenge military losses. Pragmatism guided national and hemispheric policymaking. Canada and Mexico along with several Latin American nations acted and took early coordinated steps against their own Japanese populations, mainly those along their respective west coasts, months before the United States did (although Mexico, Canada, and the United States arrested and interned "dangerous" aliens immediately after Pearl Harbor). Relations, however, sometimes strained as the United States pressured its neighbors to take measures it was not yet ready to take itself.

When Raleigh Gibson, first secretary of the American Embassy in Mexico City, received instructions urging Mexico to take stronger actions against its Japanese nationals, the results were unexpected. On February 2, 1942, Gibson reported Mexican criticisms—continued U.S. inaction and Mexico's prior removal of "Japanese residents from areas considered of strategic importance by the United States"—to Cordell Hull. As Mexican officials had pointed out, Gibson's own country had not taken formal action against its own Japanese along the same coastline. Yet many, including California representative Leland Ford, saw Mexico's actions as both a precedent for and justification of steps California and the nation should take—particularly against Japanese Americans. On February 6, Ford followed suit and urged Hull to resettle Japanese based on Mexico's example.[23]

Maxwell Hamilton, chief of the Division of Far Eastern Affairs, thought Ford's suggestions "repugnant to many American concepts and would undoubtedly work unwarranted hardships on many individuals." Yet Hamilton, like so many, felt the war demanded "far-reaching defensive measures." The move would be temporary and somewhere inland. Japanese Americans would, with federal assistance as needed, "engage in legitimate activities." Meanwhile, public demands for the evacuation of Japanese Americans greatly intensified and peaked. More than twenty Latin American nations sent representatives to the third meeting of ministers of foreign affairs in Rio de Janeiro, January 15–28, 1942. They organized the Emergency Advisory Committee for Political Defense to coordinate hemispheric security measures, including deporting dangerous Axis nationals to the United States for temporary detention in exchange for member nations receiving their own nationals. More than a dozen nations cooperated, while a few, including Brazil and Mexico, established their own internment facilities, and others, including Argentina and Chile, took a more independent or neutral stance.[24]

Since Japan's invasion of China in 1937, Canadian officials had worried that Japanese soldiers disguised as fishermen were in British Columbia. The Royal Canadian Mounted Police began monitoring Japanese Canadians, and investigations intensified after Japan allied itself with Germany and Italy in September 1940. Pearl Harbor, for Canada too, proved Japanese treachery, revealed military unpreparedness, and increased a sense of vulnerability, especially in British Columbia. Canada declared war as Japanese victories in the Pacific highlighted Allied weaknesses and shocked military experts, arousing rage and humiliation. The enemy could strike anywhere. On Christmas Day, Japan took Hong Kong and twenty-five hundred Canadian prisoners. Pressured by public demands, Canada's authorities seized twelve hundred Japanese fishing boats, many at Vancouver Island—their captains familiar with Puget Sound's strategic waters. Japanese newspapers and schools were also closed. Japan's "wanton" and "treacherous" strike at British territory in the Pacific, said Prime Minister Mackenzie King, directly threatened "the defense and freedom of Canada."[25] As in the United States, rumors of fifth-column activity were widespread, as were reports of enemy naval activity just offshore. Many thought an invasion was imminent. On January 14, 1942, Canadian officials, acting before their U.S. counterparts, ordered a partial evacuation of their West Coast. The evacuees included all adult male enemy aliens—several thousand Germans, Italians, and Japanese.[26]

Since early January 1942, California politicians, and Generals DeWitt and Joyce, among others, had been advocating more vigorous control measures for enemy aliens near strategic coastal installations. As public demands for removing all Japanese along the West Coast intensified, the Canadian government went beyond its January 14 initiative establishing a one-hundred-mile "protected area" and required the removal of all enemy alien males over sixteen living west of the Cascade Mountains. On February 24, nine days after Singapore's fall and five after FDR's Executive Order 9066, Mackenzie King and his cabinet ordered the evacuation of "every person of the Japanese race." Order-in-Council PC 1486 empowered the British Columbia Security Commission to plan, supervise, and direct the forced evacuation. It began in mid-March and within weeks affected twenty-one thousand Japanese Canadians. Half went to road work camps and abandoned silver-mining towns hundreds of miles away—Slocan City, Greenwood, Kaslo, and Sandon, and newly constructed towns such as Tasme and Lemon Creek. Farmers went to labor in the sugar-beet fields of Alberta and Manitoba, and those considered "dangerous" or "dissidents" went to Canadian internment camps.[27]

Canadian and American relocation and internment policies were driven by similar considerations, including "exaggerated security fears, political opportunism, economic cupidity, and, above all, Caucasian assumptions of racial superiority." Canadians feared the "yellow peril" and believed that many Japanese were fifth columnists bent on aiding an imminent Japanese invasion and occupation of their West Coast. As in the United States, many Canadians thought it too coincidental that so many Japanese had chosen to live near dams and power stations. Authorities construed the absence of sabotage as evidence that something ominous and of massive proportions was in the works. Therefore, a concerted U.S.-led effort to quash fifth-column machinations began in earnest after Pearl Harbor. Governments throughout Central and South America as well as Haiti and the Dominican Republic acted against enemy aliens and citizens in the spring of 1942—arresting, detaining, and expelling them due to their "hostile origin."[28]

The State Department, noting how Canada and Mexico were handling their West Coast enemy populations, decided to cooperate with all hemispheric nations in carrying out "gunpoint relocations." U.S. efforts focused on Germans rather than Japanese or

Italians, as most officials, including FDR himself, believed that the one-million-plus Latin American Germans posed an imminent threat. Overreaction to widely published albeit largely erroneous reports led to 6,610 Latin American Germans, Italians, and Japanese being taken to the United States for internment and repatriation.[29]

Military necessity strongly influenced the government's decision to intern enemy aliens and citizens. So too did political, social, and diplomatic considerations. Arrest and internment numbers were roughly equal among German and Italian as compared to Japanese aliens, since all were seen as a threat. Officials exchanged undesirable aliens for Americans held by the Axis. In short, the multilateral wartime repatriation and exchange of enemy aliens and civilians served a number of purposes, including getting rid of "bottom of the barrel" types such as criminals, the insane, the ill and elderly, hobos, drifters, and the poor. Internment and exchange were pragmatic steps in ridding society of undesirables while obtaining individuals who, given their firsthand observations and knowledge of events in Nazi- or Japanese-occupied lands, might be useful.

The enormity of the Pearl Harbor debacle is hard to overestimate; nearly everybody expected another devastating attack, perhaps accompanied by an invasion. General DeWitt believed an attack was imminent and convinced civilians of the necessity for blackouts and other defensive measures. "This is war," he said. "Death and destruction may come from the skies at any moment." He called the few who disbelieved reports of Japanese planes flying over California "insane, foolish, and idiotic." Within seventy-two hours of the attack, Hoover's FBI took into custody nearly 4,000 enemy aliens, beginning a campaign that included the arrests of 16,062 aliens and 748 U.S. citizens by war's end. The FBI arrested nearly twice as many Germans and Italians as Japanese. DeWitt often told FDR that Japanese Americans were "organized and ready for concerted action," and he had frequently called for the simultaneous removal of all enemies—German, Italian, and Japanese—from the West Coast "at the earliest practicable date." FDR, preoccupied by the Japanese subversive and saboteur threat, accepted DeWitt's conclusion that "the very fact that no sabotage has taken place to date is a disturbing and confirming indication that such action will be taken."[30]

1. Fingerprinting a German American, 1917. Once at war, Woodrow Wilson proclaimed unnaturalized Germans alien enemies, believing the nation was swarming with spies and saboteurs. Wilson, his advisers, and the broader public viewed German Americans with distrust and suspicion, leading to the Alien and Sedition Acts and thousands filling out registration affidavits and being fingerprinted, as seen here in New York City. Library of Congress Prints and Photographs Division. https://www.loc.gov/item/2014706324/.

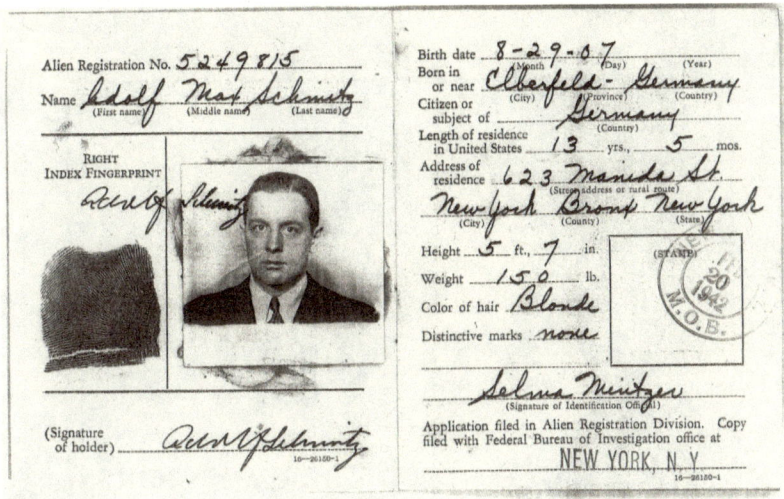

2. (*opposite top*) Germans interned at Fort Douglas, Utah, ca. 1918. The United States interned POWs as well as civilians, including 6,300 alien enemies, during World War I. Many ended up in camps such as Fort Douglas, which held a mix of over 1,000 POWs, alien enemies, and conscientious objectors. Library of Congress Prints and Photographs Division. https://www.loc.gov/item/2014705872/.

3. (*opposite bottom*) Australia registration of aliens notice, 1917. Nations took extraordinary measures against citizens and aliens during World War I, beginning with mandatory registration programs to counter sabotage and subversive activities in an age of total war. Even nations far removed from European battlefields acted. Australia interned 7,000 German aliens and naturalized citizens. National Archives of Australia. http://www.migrationheritage.nsw.gov.au/exhibition/enemyathome/wwi-australias-home-front-experience/.

4. (*above*) Adolf Max Schmitz's alien registration card, 1942. The June 1940 Alien Registration Act required the registration and fingerprint identification of all aliens. On February 1, 1942, Attorney General Francis Biddle announced "a new and important part of the job of making America safe." Now reclassified as alien enemies, nearly one million reregistered and submitted to blanket regulations and carrying certificates of identification like this one at all times. Courtesy Schmitz family collection.

5. World War II poster warning of enemy agents, 1940–41. Underlying U.S. relocation and internment was a ubiquitous belief in and fear of a fifth-column threat, and posters such as this one reminded citizens that subversives and enemy agents were a real and present danger. Courtesy Illinois State University Library.

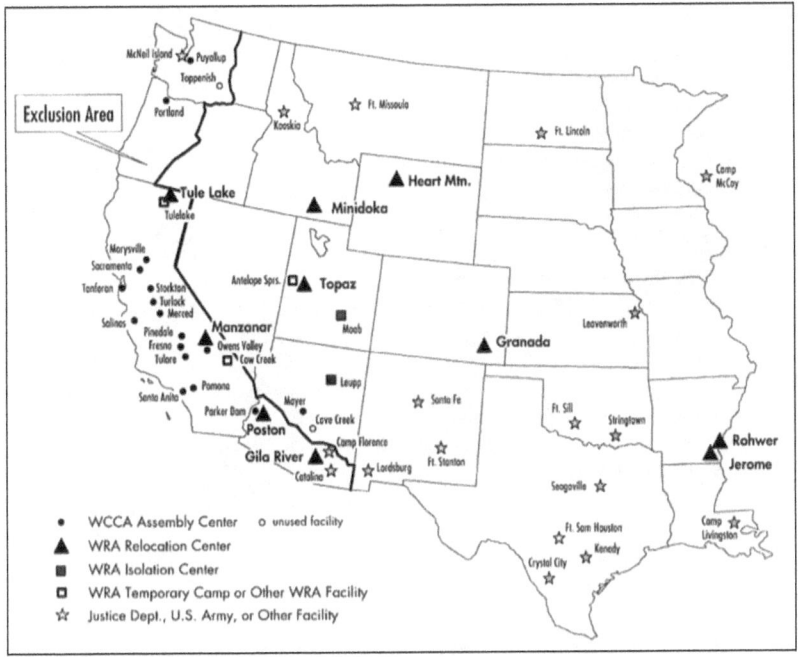

6. United States relocation centers and select internment camps. The War Relocation Authority (WRA) administered ten relocation centers, including Tule Lake, which became a segregation center in September 1943 as the military began expatriating or repatriating internees. Except for Tule Lake, these centers helped evacuees relocate outside the western defensive zone or unaffected areas of Washington, Oregon, and Arizona. The Wartime Civil Control Administration (WCCA) ran seventeen assembly centers, which expedited evacuee removal (voluntary and then forced). Citizen isolation camps in Moab, Utah, and Leupp, Arizona, housed internees who had psychological disorders. Image courtesy of National Park Service. NPS Map of World War II Japanese American internment camps.png.

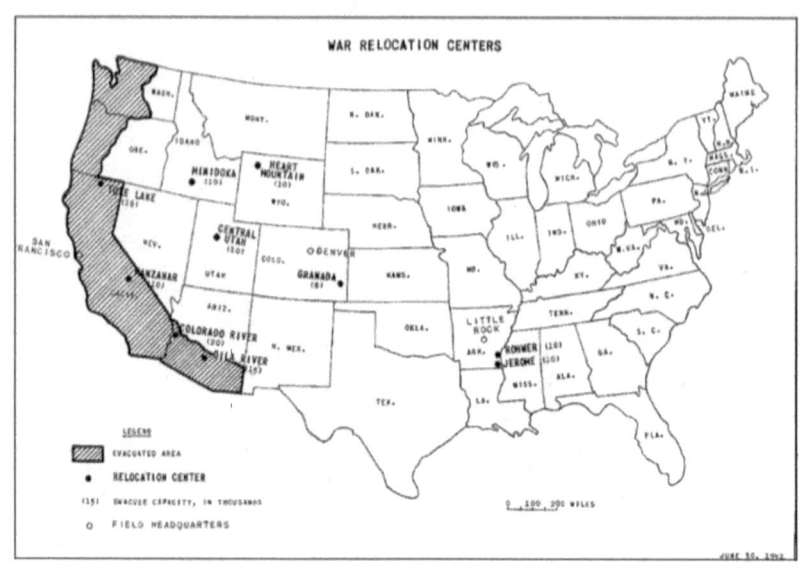

7. (*opposite top*) War Relocation Authority centers, 1942. Most maps of relocation and internment facilities, whether in academic texts or online, look like this one. Not depicted are the majority of facilities used by the United States to relocate and intern German, Italian, and Japanese Americans. Source: RG 65, National Archives and Records Administration.

8. (*opposite bottom*) War and Justice Departments internment camps. Besides WRA centers and WCCA camps, the INS operated eight internment camps and oversaw dozens of other facilities, including immigration stations and temporary structures used to detain aliens and citizens, from city, county, and federal jails to hotels, inns, and country clubs. More than fifty camps held Germans and Italians in twenty-eight states; San Juan, Puerto Rico; Pine Island, Cuba; and Sand Island, Oahu, Territory of Hawaii. Courtesy Art Jacobs and German American Internee Coalition.

9. Aerial view of Crystal City internment camp, ca. 1945–46. All internees went to INS camps. Crystal City, Texas, seen here in this aerial photo, was one of four primary INS facilities and was the only family internment camp used by any nation during the war. It reached its peak population in December 1944 with 3,374 internees but held, on average, 2,500 to 3,000 persons while in operation from December 12, 1942, until February 27, 1948. The camp's layout, perimeter fence, and nearby farmland and orchards are visible. Schmitz family collection, RG 59, National Archives and Records Administration; German American Internee Coalition; and University of Texas Institute of Texan Cultures at San Antonio.

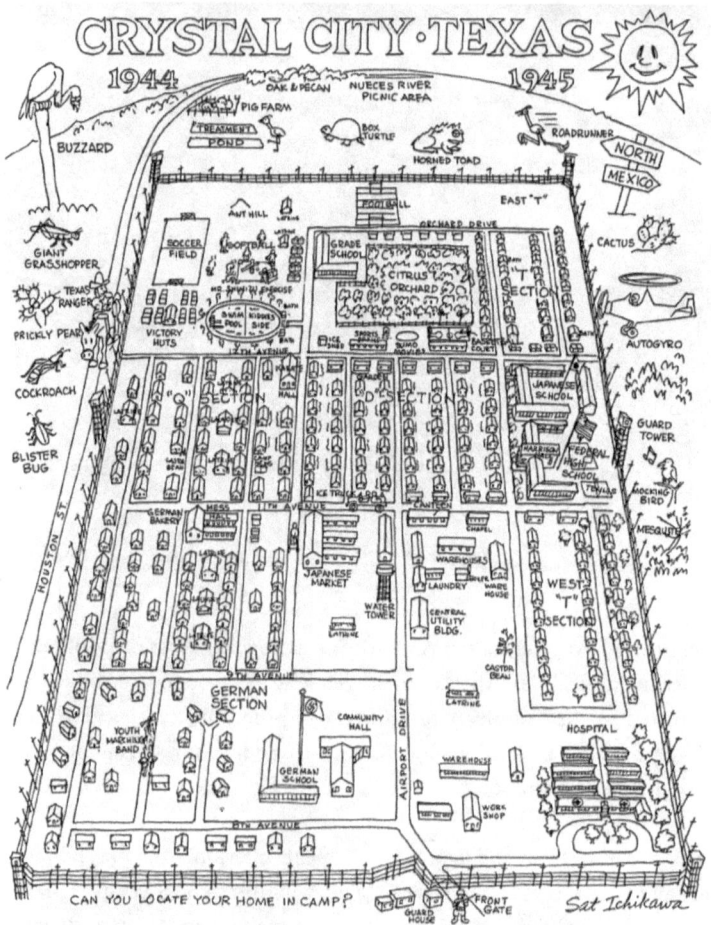

10. Drawing of Crystal City internment camp, 1945. By war's end, Crystal City camp resembled a small city (aside from the barbed wire and guard towers) and had 694 buildings on 290 acres. The camp's first internees, however, entered a 100-acre unfinished remote compound far from vital or vulnerable areas. The initial 140 acres outside the camp were devoted to farming, personnel residences, playgrounds, and storage areas. The INS added cottages, shelters, and Victory Huts along with 50 acres of additional land for farming. Each duplex and triplex had a toilet and bath while quadruplexes had communal toilets. Each unit had furniture, a kitchen sink, and an oil stove with oven. There was a seventy-bed hospital, dental clinic, chapel, grammar and high schools, administrative buildings, recreation centers, a barber and beauty shop, stores, and a community center. Densho Digital Repository, M. Nakagawa Family Collection, object ID: ddr-densho-64-5 and RG 59, National Archives. Densho Encyclopedia. http://encyclopedia.densho.org/Crystal_City_(detention_facility)/.

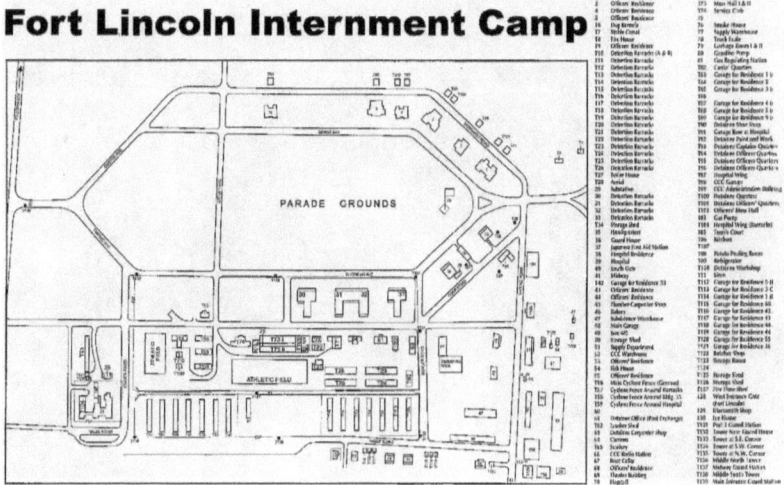

11. Drawing of Fort Lincoln internment camp, ca. 1944. Fort Lincoln, North Dakota, like Fort Stanton, New Mexico, and Fort Missoula, Montana, was rather remote, and the climate was often inhospitable. These converted forts held some 2,000 German and Italian sailors by May 1942. The map depicts many structures typical of INS camps. RG 59, NARA and German American Internee Coalition website.

12. Crystal City musicians, ca. 1945. Many internees experienced "barbed-wire disease," varying from boredom to depression traceable to detention and the loss of freedom. To boost morale, Crystal City, like other camps, offered many forms of recreation and leisure, including musicals, concerts, chess tournaments, plays, quiz shows, garden contests, art and handicraft shows, and sports as well as special holiday events, which often involved live music. Courtesy Schmitz family collection and German American Internee Coalition.

13. Crystal City band members, ca. 1945. While nearly all parts of camp life were segregated, music brought Germans and Japanese internees together and helped keep morale up among the thousands of internees. Courtesy Schmitz family collection and German American Internee Coalition.

14. German school students and teacher, ca. 1945. Camp officials prioritized education. Parents could send their children to a German, Japanese, or American school, where teachers taught English as well as reading, writing, and arithmetic in the students' respective languages. Courtesy Schmitz family collection and German American Internee Coalition.

15. Crystal City classroom, ca. 1945. The camp's kindergarten and elementary schools were segregated, but the high school integrated German and Japanese students. Because of the heat, classes were often scheduled in the morning and students had leisure time in the afternoons, sometimes spending many hours at the camp's pool. Louise Schmitz, the author's aunt, is in the front row, second from right. Courtesy Schmitz family collection and German American Internee Coalition.

16. Crystal City, German school, ca. 1945. Instructors were a mix of camp employees, internee volunteers, and local teachers. As camp officials believed most internee children would eventually return to Germany or Japan, their initial aim was to prepare the students for life abroad. For those parents who contemplated remaining in the United States, the camp's supervisor of education, Robert Tate, agreed to "an official school open to enrollment by any child, German or Japanese, who desired to continue or begin the 'American education.'" John A. Schmitz, the author's father, is in the second row, first from left. Courtesy Schmitz and Reseneder family collections and German American Internee Coalition.

6

Defeats, Rumors, and Reactions

> If the Japanese evacuation creates serious questions, it is because
> an entire group out of our population is being bodily removed....
> The numbers involved are large, but they are by no means as
> large, for the whole country, as those who will be involved if we
> generalize the current treatment of the Japanese to apply to all
> Axis aliens and their immediate families. Indeed, this committee
> is prepared to say that any such proposal is out of the
> question if we intend to win this war.
>
> —TOLAN COMMITTEE, *PRELIMINARY REPORT*, MARCH 19, 1942

The widely held belief in a fifth-column menace was reinforced by a series of spectacular Axis military victories before and after Pearl Harbor. Wild rumors told of enemy military actions, Japanese naval activity off the West Coast, aircraft carriers operating close to shore, and sinister insurgent activities. In June 1942 the sensational drama surrounding eight German saboteurs landing on East Coast beaches as well as the extensive media coverage of occasional Japanese submarine attacks directed against West Coast targets and U.S. ships seemingly heralded a much-anticipated invasion. When, not if, enemy troops arrived, alarmists argued, thousands of Japanese Americans loyal to their emperor would support them. The government acted as public demand for action against German and Japanese Americans peaked. Circumstances proved doomsayers correct and justified the relocation or internment of those now labeled enemies. Fear of an external attack aided by internal enemies led to relocating West Coast Japanese Americans en masse and interning Germans, Italians, and Japanese on a more selective but national basis given the regional and national political, media, and public demands for swift action. Even at war's end, rare attacks by Japanese balloons carrying explosives and anticipated strikes by German wonder weapons sustained public fears of and vindicated actions taken against enemy aliens and citizens.[1]

With no civil defense program, protecting the West Coast became a top priority as growing awareness that the East and Gulf Coasts, the Panama Canal, and interior and hemispheric defenses were woefully inadequate caused widespread anxiety and prompted many false alarms. On December 9 and 10, New Yorkers, Bostonians, and residents of dozens of New England cities experienced alerts, including two air-raid warnings. Hundreds of schools, industrial plants, and military bases closed as thousands of students, workers, and soldiers went home. The U.S. Army later acknowledged there were "definitely no enemy planes" associated with the first alert, while U.S. Navy patrol aircraft caused the second. In Washington DC residents saw machine guns on the Capitol as rare documents, including the Declaration of Independence and Constitution, went to safer places, including Fort Knox—where they remained until 1944.[2]

Military Defeats, Wild Rumors, and Initial Reactions

The U.S. Army, planning for and anticipating an attack along the East Coast, was relying on antiquated equipment, much World War I surplus and some dating back to the turn of the century. Ammunition was scarce, enough for a few days, after which, said one general in charge of West Coast defenses, the enemy "could have shot at us like pigs in a pen." The Army hurriedly moved more than three million tons of supplies, mostly to the West Coast, and by late January over 250,000 soldiers guarded military bases, key strategic positions, and major cities all along the Pacific. To protect coastline from Alaska to southern California, the Navy had only a dozen destroyers. An equal number of reconnaissance aircraft would be lucky to spot the Japanese fleet even within striking distance of major coastal cities, industrial sites, or defense plants.[3]

Numerous organizations and individuals acted swiftly to counter sabotage threats. The Federal Communications Commission (FCC) canceled the licenses of 50,000 ham radio operators. Eastern Air Lines banned express packages as well as Japanese passengers on all flights, and Norfolk's chief of police rounded up all fourteen Japanese aliens in his town. Construction workers hastily constructed dummy aircraft plants outside of Los Angeles to lure Japanese pilots away from real factories. Washington's annual Cherry Blossom Festival, still months away, was canceled, as was the upcoming New Year's Day Rose Bowl classic in Pasadena—the game was played, but in North Carolina. General DeWitt canceled or indefinitely postponed sports events, social conventions, political meetings, academic conferences, and most public gatherings that attracted crowds, fearing they were too tempting a target. Westbrook Pegler, a well-known nationally syndicated columnist, brashly proposed that for every American hostage the Axis murdered, the United States should kill "100 victims selected out of [America's] concentration camps," meaning German, Italian, and Japanese subversives.[4]

To wrest the initiative, Assistant Attorney General Wendell Berge, particularly concerned about anti-Japanese reprisals, addressed the nation's attorneys on December 8:

> State and local authorities in many parts of the country have apprehended Japanese aliens last night and this morning. The Attorney General is deeply concerned about this procedure. Notify all state and local authorities in your district immediately that arrests and detention of Japanese aliens are to be made only through the FBI. Advise proper state and local authorities and announce publicly that any complaint with reference to Japanese aliens should be made to the nearest FBI office and that no other action should be taken except through the FBI. . . . You are authorized to apply to the governor of your state for his cooperation.[5]

That same Monday morning, Los Angeles mayor Fletcher Bowron urged folks to stay home and use their cars only if necessary. California attorney general Earl Warren pleaded for calm even as he declared sabotage "an integral part of Axis warfare." He told the public and law enforcement to brace themselves, be vigilant, and contact the FBI about anything unusual. The *Los Angeles Times* put it simply: "They started it—we'll finish it."[6] The FBI received ten pouches of obscene and insulting mail directed to Japanese officials, including the Japanese ambassador to the United States, Kishisaburo Nomura. The following was typical:

> Remember, you back-stabbing, underhanded, smiling assassins, when we get through with you and yours, you will wish you had never copied the Hitler gangster. Not a single warship of yours will be left on the seas, every plane will be destroyed and for the lives you took at Hawaii we will take 100,000 alone for that outrage. Your Island will be reduced to ashes and you will become slaves to the Chinese. Remember this, you dirty, stinking, underhanded, double-crossing snake, and take this message back to your stupid emperor.[7]

Stories of suspicious Japanese activities and hundreds of arrests appeared in every major West Coast paper. The *Los Angeles Times* called California a "zone of danger" but assured readers that the city was "armed, ready for defense in emergency" and asked "alert, keen-eyed civilians" to assist "military authorities against spies, saboteurs, and fifth columnists." And after being "stunned by the sudden war start," came a "reaction as truly American as apple pie. . . . Defense and law enforcement agencies began operating. Citizens mobilized . . . the city shrugged off its amazement. . . . No more mufti. It's war." Some Japanese might be "good Americans," the *Times* continued, but who could tell? Besides, nobody could "take a chance in the light of yesterday's demonstration that treachery and double-dealing are major Japanese weapons." Headlines such as "Japanese Aliens' Roundup Starts: FBI Hunting Down 300 Subversives and Plans to Hold 3,000 Today" described the "great manhunt" that began Sunday night. The *Times* reported that the FBI, local law enforcement, and special officers had rounded up "close to 200 suspicious Japanese," were searching for "300 alien Japanese suspected of subversive activities," and would place into protective custody an additional 3,000 Japanese aliens "as soon as war is declared against Japan." FBI agents had arrested and questioned dozens of Japanese, entered homes confiscating cameras and guns, and stopped cars with Japanese drivers or passengers to seize contraband maps, binoculars, or radios. Acting on hundreds of tips, police and detectives scoured the countryside searching for "suspicious" Japanese using hilltops for "signaling" enemy ships, including submarines, and aircraft. To calm and reassure citizens, authorities publicized their efforts. Under the front-page headline "Hundreds of Japs Seized in L.A. Area," the *Los Angeles Daily News* ran the following:

> Hundreds of Japanese aliens last night were landed in Southland jails. Yesterday morning they were enjoying the United States brand of liberty when Japanese bombs began raining on Pearl Harbor. . . . The string of little brown men whom the FBI already had labeled as suspects began appearing at the jails . . . the roundup may continue . . . until the government has taken every possible precaution against enemy sabotage and espionage. . . . Francis Biddle is to apprehend Japanese aliens considered dangerous "to the peace and security of the United States." The action, Biddle said, was being taken under a section of the law that provides that alien enemies may be arrested "where an invasion or predatory incursion is perpetrated against the United States."[8]

The nation could accept no result, FDR stated on December 9, but victory, final and complete. Three proclamations empowered federal action against the nation's Japanese, German, and Italian aliens. Declaring them potentially dangerous to the nation's peace and safety, the 1798 Alien Enemy Act provided the legal precedent that in war "all natives, citizens, or subjects of the hostile nation or government . . . shall be liable to be apprehended, restrained, secured, and removed." A January 14 proclamation classified all citizens or subjects of Germany, Italy, and Japan as alien enemies and required them to obtain certificates of identification. Patterned after the June 1940 Alien Registration Act, by which 4,921,452 aliens registered at 8,000 post offices by that December, nearly 1,000,000 aliens re-registered in 1942, answering additional questions by FBI investigators. All enemy aliens now had to carry an identification certificate at all times. A July 17 proclamation applied the same to Hungarians, Romanians, and Bulgarians.[9]

Permanent controls were few in January 1942, but more restrictions came. All aliens had to report changes of address, could not enter or remain in prohibited areas, and were barred from flying, while permits regulated other types of travel. Roosevelt worried that restrictions would harm morale and cripple wartime production given the sheer number, political influence, and assimilation of Germans and Italians. During the summer of 1942, therefore, many European aliens returned to their homes in restricted zones. Convinced of the loyalty of most Italians, Francis Biddle announced that by mid-October they would be exempt from alien enemy regulations. Nevertheless, Italians, Germans, and Japanese who were believed to be dangerous or disloyal could be apprehended, interned, or face restrictions. An individual exclusion program had commenced and proceeded on a case-by-case basis.[10]

While rumors of Japanese fleet sightings circulated (enemy warships near the Golden Gate Bridge), newspapers asked readers not to overreact and called for restraint. "Be on the lookout for 'witch smellers'—letter writers proposing 'witless' forms of torment for the Italians and Germans," the *San Francisco Chronicle* urged. "Persecution of innocents won't win the war." When adult Nisei "expressed their horror over the attack and their loyalty to the United States, West Coast Americans appeared to accept them at their word." The string of Allied military losses in the Pacific, however, intensified hatred of the Japanese. Christmas news of the sinking of one Japanese submarine off California and another near the mouth of the Columbia River perpetuated fears of a Japanese invasion many believed likely even through June 1943.[11]

Knox's Findings and Roberts's Report

When Secretary of the Navy Frank Knox returned from Hawaii on December 15 after a flurry of fact-finding meetings with senior naval officials, he told reporters, "I think the most effective Fifth Column work of the entire war was done in Hawaii with the possible exception of Norway." Knox's initial Cabinet report credited Japanese success to their fishermen and spies, who, he believed, furnished crucial information and gave Japanese diplomats valuable intelligence. "There was a great deal of very active fifth column work going on both from the shores and from the sampans," Knox affirmed. As he urged Roosevelt and Stimson to remove all Japanese from Oahu, his public statements and private reports were accepted, repeated, and reinforced by newspaper reports and official statements. December 16 headlines read: "Fifth Column Treachery Told," "Fifth Column Prepared Attack," and "Secretary of Navy Blames 5th Column for the Raid."[12]

Stories of Japanese American treachery appeared by December 10. Disloyals allegedly aided enemy bombers and warships, including "an actual exchange of gunfire between Japanese fifth-columnists and American soldiers." Fictitious tales included the well-known account of Hawaiian Japanese cutting arrows in sugarcane fields to guide enemy aircraft to their targets; repetition and details typically included assurances of authenticity. Although Knox and others mentioned Japanese American heroism at Pearl (operating anti-aircraft guns), and nearly all treachery stories later proved false, papers nationwide vilified Japanese Americans. As Morton Grodzins observed:

> Pearl Harbor stories were matched by the space given to alleged evidences of sabotage intent on the mainland . . . given official credence by . . . contraband material gathered in police raids and by the statements of political and civic leaders that sabotage was planned. Congressman Martin Dies . . . made large headlines . . . stressing the potential fifth-column danger and the need for summary action. [HUAC's] *Yellow Book* was displayed with great prominence. More than six full columns were devoted to it by the *Los Angeles Times*; a page-one banner reading: "Children Born to Nippon Soil," a page-six headline reading: "Pacific Coast Jap Spying Exposed: Dire Peril Told in Dies Report." . . . Announcements of oil industry leaders, California congressmen, local officials, and "unnamed authorities" appeared with regularity. The total effect was an assumption of sabotage guilt in every paper and in almost every edition.[13]

Knox's emphasis of fifth-column treachery along with classified and confusing Pearl Harbor details accelerated the crackdown on alleged disloyals. Justice Owen Roberts's investigatory commission, created by Roosevelt shortly after the attack, reinforced Knox's claims. The report highlighted spying and espionage at Pearl, swayed public opinion, and pressured military and government action. A surge of bad news followed as evacuations, arrests, and increased control measures began. Those pleading for calm found themselves vastly outnumbered. Daily headlines called for action and testified that the war was going poorly, especially in the Pacific.[14]

The Roberts Commission's findings rightly revealed the military's unpreparedness but wrongly attributed Japanese successes to fifth columnists. Its report, made public on January 25, never claimed that "sabotage," "espionage," or "fifth column" activities were tied to the day of infamy. Yet the conclusions described widespread espionage activities conducted by "Japanese consular agents and others." The report supported a barrage of negative press, which found evidence of Japanese treachery everywhere, and intensified public concern and agitation for evacuating all Japanese—aliens and citizens. Removing enemies preemptively—primarily from the West Coast, but also along the eastern seaboard—was meant to prevent another Pearl Harbor and fifth-column uprisings.[15]

Action Demanded

As military losses mounted, labor and business groups, city councils, West Coast mayors, chambers of commerce, anti-fascist associations, military and law enforcement, the American Legion, and countless citizens demanded action. The media's change in attitude toward enemy aliens heightened demands for action. Rumors and fear encouraged a shift in reporting by late January and early February as fifth-column rhetoric intensified with the release of the Roberts Commission report. A vicious cycle was set in motion. As all remained quiet on the West Coast, many became convinced that Japan was planning or carrying out covert operations aided by Japanese Americans. By mid-February even Walter Lippmann, the nation's most influential liberal political columnist, normally "cautious and resistant to the hot breath of popular clamor," favored evacuating all West Coast aliens and enemy citizens:

The enemy alien ... or the Fifth Column problem is very serious and special. The Pacific Coast is in imminent danger of a combined attack from within and without. ... Japan could strike a blow that might do irreparable damage if accompanied by organized sabotage to which this part of the country is especially vulnerable. The Japanese navy has been reconnoitering the Pacific Coast. ... Communication takes place between the enemy at sea and enemy agents on land. These facts we shall ignore or minimize at our peril ... there has been no important sabotage on the Pacific Coast. From what we know about Hawaii and the Fifth Column in Europe, it is a sign that the blow is well organized and held back until struck with maximum effect.[16]

Conservative journalist Westbrook Pegler quickly followed suit, and added, "We are just sitting around waiting for the enemy to stab us in the back. We are so damned dumb and considerate of the minute constitutional rights of people whom we have every reason to anticipate with preventive action! The Japanese should be under guard to the last right now and to hell with habeas corpus until the danger is over." Tom Treanor reported "strange sights at [Los Angeles] harbor. ... The Japanese fishing colony on Terminal Island is sinister enough ... but nobody has done anything about this Japanese village. What kind of a war is this?" Columnist Henry McLemore wrote, "Nothing is done about the Japs. ... The government is treating the Japanese out here so nicely. ... California wants the Japs put away."[17]

Contra Costa County's district attorney boasted that, after handling the Japanese, "we are going after the Italians and Germans, and do the same with them." Los Angeles mayor Fletcher Bowron echoed the belief that German and Italian émigrés were Axis spies and that their taking out first papers was evidence of traitorous minds. Who knew when the "savage enemies of America and liberty disguised as refugees from Hitler" might strike? After being strongly rebuked by his superiors for urging the relocation and internment of all enemy aliens, General DeWitt pragmatically suggested handling Germans and Italians only after removing Japanese. Yet camps might become "breeding farms" as "Japs multiply like rabbits." Anti-Japanese agitators favored segregating the sexes or deporting them all—out in the ocean or in the middle of the desert. One California representative wanted Japanese Americans to have "the alternatives of sterilization or deportation." A Los Angeles resident asked the Justice Department to "exterminate them" or, instead of killing women and children, "sterilize them so that they can never produce any more of their kind." A Glendale resident wrote that "all loyal Japs" should be eliminated, taken "secretly and silently, securely blindfolded and hands bound behind them, then 'walk the plank' into the ocean . . . no one would be wronged."[18]

Peter Theberath and Iwao Matsushita

In the early hours of December 8, 1941, the FBI continued arresting several thousand aliens. One was Peter Theberath. His family experienced great hardship and personal loss, starting at 2:30 a.m. when the FBI came into their Milwaukee home and split up the family for reasons that remain unexplained. Agents took Peter and his wife, Marie, into custody and left the three children to fend for themselves. At Fort Oglethorpe internment camp, in May 1942, Peter wrote to Wilhelm, a relative in the Rhineland, Germany:

> Marie and I were awakened and taken into custody. I was in prison for 4 months. Marie was released on Feb. 11th, but *everything* was gone, *no children, no home.* In one word everything *robbed*, the children placed in separate homes, the mother *helplessly* thrown into *the street*. We arrived here on April 8th and no news yet from our family. The last time I saw John and Marie was in the prison on April 5th and I have not seen Gertrud and Friedrich since December 8th. These are ridiculous conditions. . . . All hope that the war will end soon.[19]

Peter's letter never made it past the U.S. National Censorship Office. Undaunted, in May 1943 he wrote to the Legation of Switzerland's Department of German Interests. The Swiss had a difficult time, as Peter, after four months in a Milwaukee prison, went to several internment facilities, including Fort Oglethorpe, Georgia; Camp Forrest, Tennessee; and Fort Lincoln, North Dakota. In April 1944 the legation found Peter and reported its findings to INS assistant commissioner W. F. Kelly:

> Since both parents were taken... the welfare authorities... sent the two children, Gertrud, 14, and Friedrich, 13, to the Milwaukee County Children's Home. No exact record is available... [for] the son John, then 17. The home was completely broken up and when Mrs. Theberath was released in February 1942, she found her home devoid of furniture and other personal property. No assistance was granted her.... Mrs. Theberath could have the children again if she found a suitable home. Mrs. Theberath was rather bitter and possibly antagonistic, which may have had some bearing on her case. It was mentioned that she was not competent to take proper care of the children. Since Mrs. Theberath could work as a cook in a private home for two years, at least some revision of such a serious judgment becomes necessary.
>
> The case seems to be a very disputable one, and... a more constructive, rehabilitative plan might have been found. Mrs. Theberath has undergone considerable mental stress. It is incomprehensible why no further effort was made to provide a solution best for both parents and the children.... Something has gone wrong somewhere.... Naturally, the woman must have become incoherent after all the agony she has gone through, and... [if] she is mentally unbalanced, the present situation certainly would not contribute anything towards an improvement.[20]

The Theberath case and others often found their way to Edward J. Ennis, director of the Alien Enemy Control Unit (AECU), or Major General Edwin Watson, FDR's military aide and appointments secretary. Most cases, however, never attracted much attention. Prior to their release, some internees had to swear not to divulge what had happened to them, and the FBI threatened to make life difficult if they did.[21]

The FBI arrested Iwao and Hanaye Matsushita on the night of December 7, and the agents advised, "You had better pack some things, take at least a tooth brush, but don't take any clothes; well, maybe a few clothes, but you won't be gone long." Yet Iwao and Hanaye spent two years apart—he in a Seattle jail and then Fort

Missoula, Montana, and she in the Minidoka Relocation Center, Idaho. Iwao was a member of the haiku society. There was also his community activism and choice of vocations (twenty years with Mitsui, a Tokyo-based trading firm, before studying English literature and continuing as principal of a Japanese-language school and a brief stint as faculty at the University of Washington). He was a member of the Seattle Camera Club, and shops in the United States and Britain had selected some of his photos for display. Being an intellectual of questionable loyalty was damning. That Iwao and Hanaye had lived in the United States since 1919 mattered little; that the FBI considered them dangerous did.[22]

These cases heralded future actions. Hoover's top-secret Custodial Detention Index had thousands of names. Considered for immediate arrest and detention were 636 German and 77 Italian aliens, 1,393 and 49 citizens thought sympathetic to Germany and Italy, respectively, and 1,694 German and 211 Italian Americans of unknown citizenship status. By December 9 the FBI held some 2,000 aliens, many arrested just hours before Pearl Harbor. All Japanese aliens were reclassified as enemy aliens (no right to habeas corpus), as were German and Italian aliens on December 11.[23]

Executive Order 9066

On December 10, 1941, a report estimating that "20,000 Japanese in the San Francisco metropolitan area were ready for organized action" reached the Ninth Corps Area staff. The commander approved and forwarded evacuation plans to Provost Marshal General Allen Gullion, recommended that "plans be made for large-scale internment," and hoped the War Department would find "areas for the detention of aliens." Concurrently, media reports, public pronouncements, Japanese submarine attacks, industrial accidents, nocturnal lights, unidentified aircraft sightings, field "arrows," and government findings suggested coordinated subversive activities directed from abroad. Word spread of Japanese invasion plans, disloyal activities, and sinister plots. The Justice Department, for example, charged those responsible for Detroit race riots with "seditious conspiracy." And many believed Nazi saboteurs caused the French liner *Normandie*'s sinking in New York

Harbor on February 9. *Time* called the days after Singapore's fall "the worst week of the war, the worst week of the century.... The fate of the nation was in the balance."[24]

On February 19, 1942, Roosevelt issued Executive Order 9066, authorizing the secretary of war to prescribe military areas "from which any or all persons may be excluded as deemed necessary or desirable." The order mentions no particular ethnic or racial group, nor does it specify any location, whether coastal or interior. EO 9066 also says nothing about relocation or internment. The order affected far more Japanese Americans, but also relocated thousands of Germans and Italians from both coasts. It did not relocate Hawaiian Japanese en masse, and far more Latin American Germans and Italians were interned than Japanese Americans in the United States. Racism there was, but it did not drive policy.[25]

Few trusted the Issei and Nisei. Official statements noted difficulties distinguishing "good" from "bad" Japanese. Privately, too, policymakers noted the "Japanese problem." Believing them unassimilable, unlike Germans or Italians, Henry Stimson wrote that the Nisei were more dangerous than their parents. "Their racial characteristics are such," he mused, "that we cannot understand or trust even the citizen Japanese." There were potential legal headaches, but the risk of a West Coast invasion supported by Japanese Americans was too great. Stimson accepted his and the government's inability to "understand or trust" Japanese as "fact." Thinking it best to evacuate all Japanese from "the most vital places of army and navy production," on February 11 Stimson phoned FDR requesting authorization for a mass West Coast Japanese evacuation. The president was, Stimson recorded, "very vigorous," and said to "go ahead on the line that I had myself thought the best."[26] Assistant Secretary of War John J. McCloy relayed the news to Colonel Karl Bendetsen, chief of the Aliens Division, PMG Office, San Francisco:

> The President, in substance, says go ahead and do anything you think necessary. We have carte blanche to do what we want to as far as the President's concerned.... If it involves citizens, we will take care of them too. There will probably be some repercussions,

but it has got to be dictated by military necessity, but as he puts it, "be as reasonable as you can."[27]

Roosevelt approved the War Department's removal of all "necessary or desirable" persons from prescribed areas as California representatives John Costello and Harry Sheppard warned that Japanese Americans constituted a "fifth column threat" and posed a "national hazard." Costello criticized Biddle for his ineffectiveness. Sheppard threatened to investigate Biddle's office "for the protection of white citizens," while others in Congress denounced the Justice Department for not protecting "against the hazards on the Pacific Coast."[28]

California's representatives celebrated EO 9066. "This is no time to apply civil liberties on questionable citizenship," said Sheppard. "No one with any knowledge of Jap psychology can apply civil liberties, it constitutes a national hazard." Bertrand Gearhart added that it was "time to stop talking of rights of individuals," while Alfred Elliott argued that any remaining Japanese would be "on our very front line" and would "invite sure and certain fifth column activities." It was "the height of folly to procrastinate." Even Jerry Voorhis, a liberal and Dies Committee member, praised EO 9066 as a "wise and proper move." Devoted quislings could get "even unwilling people to serve their interests." Evacuation was necessary for "self-protection." If anyone in Congress objected, nobody said so.[29]

Southern Congressional Reactions

California politicians led demands for action, particularly against the Japanese, but many in Congress did too. Three southerners unremittingly called for more controls. Along with Pacific Coast delegations, Representatives Martin Dies of Texas and John Rankin of Mississippi, along with Senator Tom Stewart of Tennessee, sought to deprive all aliens and Japanese citizens of their civil liberties. Rankin echoed Dies and his Texas committee's *Yellow Book*: "This is a race war, as far as the Pacific side of this conflict is concerned. The white man's civilization has come into conflict with Japanese barbarism. Christianity has come into conflict with Shintoism, atheism, and infidelity. One of them must be destroyed. I'm for catching every Japanese in America, Alaska, and Hawaii now and putting them in concentration camps. Damn them! Let's get rid of them now!"[30]

Rankin asserted, "You cannot regenerate a Jap, convert him, change him, and make him the same as a white man any more than you can reverse the laws of nature," adding:

> It is of vital importance that we get rid of every Japanese whether in Hawaii or on the mainland. They violate every sacred promise, every canon of honor and decency. This was evidenced in their diplomacy and in their bombing of Hawaii. These Japs who had been there for generations were making signs, guiding the Japanese planes to the objects of their iniquity in order that they might destroy our naval vessels, murder our soldiers and sailors, and blow to pieces the helpless women and children of Hawaii. Damn them! Let us get rid of them now![31]

In early March, Rankin again urged his colleagues to put "every single Japanese in a concentration camp for the duration of the emergency" and to keep Japanese men and women "absolutely separate," since otherwise, he warned, "they will use this internment time as an incubating period and in five years each family will emerge with five more children."[32]

The Japanese, said Senator Stewart, are among the country's worst enemies:

> They are cowardly and immoral. They are different from Americans in every conceivable way, and no Japanese should have a right to claim American citizenship. A Jap is a Jap anywhere you find him, and his taking the oath of allegiance to this country would not help, even if he should be permitted to do so. They do not believe in God and have no respect for an oath. They have been plotting for years against the Americas and their democracies.[33]

A year later Stewart wanted Stimson to "take into custody and restrain . . . any and all Japanese persons," regardless of citizenship. Stewart again assailed the Japanese: "Where there is a drop of Japanese blood, there is Japanese treachery. They bombed the open city of Manila and they stabbed America in the back at Pearl Harbor. They are not and never can be honest. There is no such thing as a Japanese not being a subject of the Emperor of Japan." Congress penalized violators who entered or left designated military areas. Public Law 503, passed with virtually no debate or discussion and without a single dissenting vote, gave (in the absence of martial law) any U.S. general power over anyone in a military area. Roosevelt signed the bill into law on March 21, and three days later DeWitt issued Civilian Exclusion Order No. 1 as the Tolan Committee issued its report.[34]

The Tolan Committee

On March 19, 1942, the Tolan Committee (named after Representative John Tolan of California) released its *Preliminary Report and Recommendations on Problems of Evacuation of Citizens and Aliens from Military Areas.* The hearings had opened in San Francisco on February 21 (with others in Portland, Seattle, and Los Angeles) and concluded there on March 12. The committee heard from 150 witnesses, listened to leading pro-evacuation advocates, and met with DeWitt, McCloy, and Tom Clark, coordinator for Enemy Alien Control. It supported removing West Coast Japanese but advised against a mass relocation of Germans and Italians from either shore. Harsh measures against Germans or Italians, the committee said, risked winning the war. Public opinion now shifted against the Japanese, who most now believed were disloyal and far more dangerous than Germans or Italians. Unlike the West Coast, there was no threat of an invasion on the East Coast, but there was outrage over Pearl Harbor and a desire to punish Japan and Japanese Americans.

While the Tolan Committee took testimony from Japanese American Citizens League (JACL) representatives, community members, and clergy, most witnesses "were a highly selected group." They included Governors Culbert Olson of California and Arthur Langlie of Washington as well as Mayors Fletcher Bowron of Los Angeles, Angelo Rossi of San Francisco, R. Earl Riley of Portland, Earl Millikin of Seattle, and Harry Cain of Tacoma. Local and state officials, city managers and police chiefs, leaders of agricultural and nativist groups (the California Joint Immigration Committee, American Legion, the State Federation of Labor, the Native Sons of the Golden West, and the California State Grange), and community leaders also testified. Hearing nearly every pro-evacuation voice made it "a conservative sounding board of public attitudes." Even JACL leaders cooperated. National Secretary Mike Masaoka testified to his organization's "complete agreement" with "any policy of evacuation" due to military necessity, and Treasurer Hito Okada agreed, "if necessary, from the danger standpoint." The findings included an overview, a survey of orders and decisions, and an analysis of the pros and cons of evacuating Japanese, German, and Italian Americans.[35]

Race did not determine relocation—except insofar as authorities claimed they could not establish Japanese American loyalty but could with German and Italian Americans. Above all, the sheer number of Germans and Italians shielded them from wholesale relocation. They had political power and had bolted Roosevelt's party in the 1940 campaign, and Democrats could not afford more of the same. They also enjoyed great economic leverage, as many tens of thousands worked jobs vital to the war effort. Their mass relocation would cripple the nation's ability to wage and win the war. The Tolan Committee called the 300,000 German and 675,000 Italian aliens along with their direct relatives "an army in themselves." Their movement, even if voluntary, much less incarceration for the war's duration, was "unthinkable." Generalizing the treatment of Japanese to "all Axis aliens and their immediate families" could cost the war. On March 29 the voluntary movement of Japanese Americans from West Coast military areas ended and DeWitt's forced mass removal of those remaining began. A compulsory but selective removal of thousands of German and Italian Americans continued too, but any serious thought of their mass evacuation was put to rest. Like the Japanese on the Hawaiian Islands, German and Italian Americans enjoyed safety in numbers.[36]

Numbers and Risks

German and Italian American numbers, along with their older age, assimilation, and vocations, shielded them from mass relocation. Prewar surges in citizenship applications, pledges of loyalty, and countless families who had someone serving in the armed forces spared many relocation hardships. For those deemed dangerous, hearing boards sifted "good" from "bad" Germans and Italians so that only a small minority faced internment. National security necessitated relocating or interning a few thousand persons, and along with Japanese policies this ensured a benevolent reciprocity—facilitating humane treatment for interned Americans overseas and expediting exchanges already in the works.[37]

Given the options, public pressures, and the imminent threat of a Japanese invasion and sabotage, government officials acted accordingly. Coastal vulnerabilities dictated the selective relocation of a few thousand Germans and Italians from militarily sensitive installations and industries as well as key ports along both coasts. Yet tens of thousands of Germans and Italians, indispensable to the war effort and Americanized, kept working in restricted areas. The reclassification of Italian aliens as "friendly" in October 1942 and the acceptance of German alien refugees from Nazi Germany also stifled plans to relocate them en masse. The same logic applied to all three enemy alien and citizen groups, given the resources, restraints, and the realization that all decisions were subordinate to winning the war. In its summary, the Tolan Committee wrote:

> The problem divides into two: the evacuation of Japanese, citizen or alien, and the evacuation of German and Italian aliens. Mass movement from prohibited west coast areas is necessary by the military problem of defending the coast.
>
> DeWitt proposes to postpone the movement of Germans and Italians until he has gained experience with the Japanese and . . . a partial movement will provide experience for later evacuation of other areas. The Japanese evacuation . . . numbers are large, but by no means as large, for the whole country, if we generalize the current treatment of the Japanese to all Axis aliens and their immediate families. Any such proposal is out of the question if we intend to win this war.
>
> There are in the three Pacific Coast States about 85,000 German and Italian aliens, of an average age of 60 years. Their average

length of residence in this country is 24 years. With family citizen members, they number 145,000. To move this group will tax public agencies. To incarcerate them ... would be a major undertaking. There are 300,000 German aliens and 675,000 Italian aliens. Together with their immediate citizen relatives, they are an army in themselves. It is doubtful our war effort could bear the consequences of shifting them to new settlements, even voluntarily. Their incarceration for the duration of the war is unthinkable.

There are 923,000 naturalized Germans and 929,000 naturalized Italians. Their children number in the millions. By blood and marriage, they are related to millions of citizens. There are 7,000,000 persons in families of whom at least 1 parent was born in Germany or Italy. Some more workable method exists for determining loyalty than uprooting 50 trustworthy persons to remove 1 dangerous individual. If strategic areas require special attention, evacuate everyone.[38]

Evacuation areas were an Army matter; a proposed War Resettlement Board would move enemy aliens under federal oversight. Relocation hearing boards would "issue certificates for all Italian and German aliens whose loyalty can be established" while "recommending internment should remain with existing enemy alien hearing boards." There were 58,000 Italian and 22,000 German nationals on the West Coast, with 52,000 Italians and 17,000 Germans in California. Relocating millions nationwide, especially along the East Coast, was not feasible, so selective relocation and secretive internment commenced.[39]

Other factors shielded Italian and German Americans from mass relocation. Over 97 percent of the Italians were over 25, and more Germans were in the 55–64 age range than any other 10-year group, and only 9 percent were under 25. By contrast, the Nisei averaged 18 years of age and comprised two-thirds of the continental Japanese population—79,642 out of 126,947. West Coast residents and officials did not fear 85,000 geriatric German and Italian aliens; they did fear 60,000 Japanese (30,000 men) between 10 and 40. The committee stressed key German and Italian differences: "These groups are the remainder of a much larger group who have become citizens. . . . [They] do not have the original stratification of the Japanese. . . . Whereas the Japanese have only one main economic base, vegetable production, the Americanization of second-generation Italians and Germans has permitted the original immigrant group to become absorbed in a great variety of occupations and industries."[40]

Besides age, assimilation, and economic arguments, the Tolan Committee asserted that many recently arrived Italians and Germans could help America win the war:

> Anti-Fascist and anti-Nazi refugees . . . are main[ly] intellectuals and professionals. . . . There are several thousand anti-Nazi refugees in Los Angeles with perhaps 10,000 in all on the entire west coast. Evacuation orders affecting German and Italian aliens will be less stringent than the Japanese. No one has proposed treating millions of second-generation Germans and Italians differently from other American citizens. Military orders will require that German and Italian aliens be evacuated from area 1-A, but, unlike the Japanese, will restrict but not prohibit their presence in area 1-B.
>
> Evacuation policies for German and Italian aliens on the west coast have direct nationwide import. . . . These aliens are elderly, 50 to 60 years. They have large families, and frequently their children are in the United States armed services. Many thousands are technically enemy aliens rather than citizens because of delays in naturalization. The tragic hardships and injustices of evacuation are most evident in the present plight of German and Italian anti-Axis refugees on the west coast. Many are becoming citizens.[41]

The committee's May 19 follow-up report further emphasized that extreme measures would "alter permanently those fundamental principles upon which this nation was built," adding that West Coast precedents "would prove especially embarrassing when applied to the much larger scale problems of the East Coast. With the announcement of General Drum's order [April 27], we find that this is exactly what has happened. Meanwhile hearing boards to eliminate wholesale evacuation of German and Italian aliens are not yet established." Furthermore,

There are almost 10 times as many German and Italian aliens as there are Japanese aliens and citizens in the United States. They are not geographically concentrated. . . . Some 700,000 Italian aliens and 300,000 German aliens are established throughout the United States. . . . These people are elderly, and their roots in America are deep. The American-born husbands and wives, sons and daughters of these aliens alone exceed 5,000,000. . . . This population pattern is inextricably woven into the life of America itself.

As to the dilemma German refugees faced as dual enemies, the committee stated:

These individuals in most cases . . . [are] stateless . . . and [had] their homes and properties confiscated. They have not resided here long enough in most cases to fulfill residence requirements for citizenship. The refugees are eager to assist authorities in singling out enemy agents, and to help the war against the Axis. . . . Among the refugees are renowned scientists, authors, and professionals. Approximately half of the 24,000 German aliens on the West Coast are refugees. Many thousands more are in . . . other parts of the country.[42]

Aside from the obdurate DeWitt, the War Department's Bendetsen, McCloy, and Stimson began siding with Biddle, the Justice Department's foremost voice of restraint. Stimson advised FDR against any mass relocation of Germans and Italians despite those, especially DeWitt, who kept pressing for the wholesale removal of West Coast Germans and Italians while others kept insisting upon a blanket East Coast evacuation. Biddle opposed any Atlantic seaboard mass evacuation as he had opposed the West Coast Japanese evacuation, but had then deferred to the Army, which cited military necessity. Evacuating East Coast German and Italian aliens en masse was unnecessary, and on May 20 Biddle stated so at a press conference: "A military area can be defended more effectively by keeping on doing as we are doing it now—examining individuals on suspicion. Mass evacuation is bad for the morale of the country, as the German and Italian bloc of our population is considerable." On May 26, Colonel Bendetsen announced the end of mass alien evacuations. In July, Roosevelt called for the reclassification of aliens, and by the fall, with the tide of war turning and the threat of invasion subsiding, cooler heads prevailed. Most German and Italian aliens stayed put even as officials relocated or interned individuals in "strict secrecy."[43]

Propaganda and Patriotism

While Americans differentiated between Germans and Hitler as well as Italians and Mussolini, a propaganda movement ensued. The 1939 film *Confessions of a Nazi Spy* portrayed German Bundists and domestic spies aiding Hitler. Vincent Sheean's *Not Peace but a Sword* (1939) told the gripping tale of Nazi violence, murder, and preparations for exterminating the Jews. Lillian Hellman's play *Watch on the Rhine*, produced in April 1941, and John Steinbeck's *The Moon Is Down*, a best-seller in 1942 and 1943, revealed the evils of Nazism, the risks of appeasement, and Germany's global aims. In March 1942, *Life*'s "Six Ways to Invade the U.S." explained that Axis forces posed a real and imminent threat and that each method of invasion would use enemies among us: "As one man," *Life* warned, "a hundred thousand German, Italian, and Jap Fifth Columnists rock the country with explosives, wrecks, and sabotage." *Collier's* noted that Nazi agents aided by "unthinking dupes" were "at it again, reporting fake flu epidemics in Army camps, false wholesale desertions, etc. . . . the object is to destroy morale."[44]

Before Pearl Harbor, news reports warned that Japanese American fishing boats would "sow mines across the entrance of our ports, Sierra passes and tunnels will be blocked, and Japanese farmers will send their peas and potatoes and squash full of arsenic to the markets." In the following weeks the *Los Angeles Examiner* reported "armed Japanese in lower California ready for invasion," Governor Olson warned that the state might soon see combat, and the *Los Angeles Times* ran articles by the nationally syndicated columnist Henry McLemore, who wrote:

> We are at war. California is our key state . . . its airplane industry and its shores offer the most logical invasion point. So why are we so beautifully courteous? Everywhere that the Japanese have

attacked to date, the Japanese population has risen to aid the attackers. Pearl Harbor, Manila. What is there to believe that the same wouldn't be true in California? California wants the Japs put away until this thing is over. I am for immediate removal of every Japanese on the West Coast.... They are a serious menace. You can't tell me that an individual's rights have any business being placed above the nation's safety. If making 1,000,000 innocent Japanese uncomfortable will prevent one scheming Japanese from costing the life of one American boy, then let 1,000,000 innocents suffer. Okay, let them howl. Herd 'em up, pack 'em off.[45]

Even the progressive *San Francisco Chronicle* was changing its stance. On January 31, 1942, an editorial proclaimed: "America's long-ridiculed attitude of sweetness and light to enemy aliens has been blasted out of existence. Hundreds of thousands of Japanese, German, and Italian nationals saw for the first time, the grim specter of concentration camps, mass evacuation of families, revocation of business licenses, doctors and dentists thrown out of work, a savage hunt to crush secret organizations. Some of the most savage enemies of America and liberty have come disguised as refugees from Hitler."[46]

Time showed how to distinguish between one's "Korean and Chinese friends" and "the Japs": the latter were hairier and more arrogant yet hesitant, nervous, and shifty—they would "laugh loudly at the wrong time." Their buck teeth, spectacles, small size, and peculiar ape-like walk were proof of being subhuman. In January, Stanley High's "Japanese Saboteurs in Our Midst" appeared in *Reader's Digest*. A Los Angeles respondent wrote that "all the conquered nations have suffered disaster from fifth columns ... the treachery of Japanese fifth columns in the Philippines and Hawaii. Yet apathetic, tolerant America goes right on—a lackadaisical, complacent republic!" As evacuation demands peaked, *Time* warned, "California Is Japan's Sudetenland"—Japanese Americans were ready to strike.[47]

Geoffrey Gorer, an English social anthropologist, published the most influential academic analysis of "Japanese character structure" during the war. The Japanese had an unassimilable nature, he told fellow academicians through presentations and scholarly journals, and then the American public through mainstream magazines. In "Why Are Japs Japs?," *Time* described Gorer's *Themes in Japanese Culture*. Gorer noted that the Japanese worldview was "more consonant with an isolated and primitive tribe than with a major industrialized nation." Ultimately, "the Japanese can never feel safe unless, as their more bombastic military speakers have proposed, the Mikado rules the whole earth."[48]

Reports of sabotage, military strikes, and suspicious activities nearly all proved false but heightened national anxieties. There were tales of Japanese farmers using "arrows," fields of flowers pointing arrow-like at a nearby airport, and tomatoes pointing to an air-training field. Rumors spread along the East Coast too. Rural fires, mysteriously burning in arrow-like shapes, "pointed" to major cities; mysterious lights, on land and at sea, directed at power plants, dams, or beaches—places often "encircled" by Japanese Americans on the West Coast or German Americans on the East. The only known arrow was twenty feet long painted atop a Warner Brothers sound stage; it pointed to a nearby Lockheed aircraft factory. Jack Warner added huge letters LOCKHEED—THATAWAY.[49]

With rumors rampant and public anxiety rising, Roosevelt wrested the initiative. In January 1942 FDR sent Lowell Mellett, coordinator of government films, to meet with the War Activities Committee in Hollywood. Avoiding the term "propaganda," the government would "tell the truth," provide "facts and figures," or publicize "information" to educate and inform the public. By March, Hollywood was at war, and by June Roosevelt had created the Office of War Information (OWI). Elmer Davis, its director, released government data via films, radio announcements, and newspaper and magazine articles. *Sunday in Hawaii, Yellow Peril, Yellow Menace, Spy Swatters, V for Victory, Casablanca*, and Frank Capra's well-known *Prelude to War* convinced Americans they were battling evil. One notable *Prelude* scene had a "conquering Jap army" marching triumphantly in Washington DC. *Prelude to War* was one of seven films in the celebrated *Why We Fight* series, made for the War Department and shown to every soldier sent overseas and to civilians in theaters nationwide. Roosevelt entrusted the OWI "to coordinate the dissemination of war information by all federal agencies" and use the press, radio, and movies to showcase government "policies, activities, and aims." The OWI inspired correct thinking and encouraged proper behavior. The president wished to avoid World War I excesses yet well understood the value of controlling information through publications, motion pictures, and radio programs. "I am perfectly willing to mislead and tell untruths if it will help us win the war," FDR confided.[50]

Fostering patriotism and vilifying the enemy, newspapers, magazines, novels, films, radio, comic books, and popular slogans spread diabolical enemy stereotypes. Exposés depicted the enemy's use of fifth columnists. The White House, the War, State, and Justice Departments, and the FBI and HUAC warned of a scourge of spies, subversives, and fifth columnists ready to strike, probably on the West Coast. Radio commentators like John B. Hughes promoted anti-alien and anti-Japanese propaganda. Such inflammatory broadcasts warned of Japanese American colonies near defense installations. Hughes suspected Japanese Americans of using radios to send military information and receive sabotage or espionage instructions. Californians accused Japanese fishermen of slipping photos of defense installations and overviews of San Francisco and Los Angeles to Japanese diplomats or naval officers, who forwarded them to Japan. Martin Dies predicted a "tragedy that will make Pearl Harbor sink into insignificance."[51]

Comic-book characters joined the fray. Captain America and Superman battled domestic enemies. Dick Tracy hunted down "the Mole." Joe Palooka joined the Army. Don Winslow, serving in the Navy, searched for a saboteur on the battleship *Vermont*. Jane Arden trailed foreign agents, and Tim Tyler learned from a sailor's last gasps that a "foreign spy" was to blame. A *Little Joe* cartoon, "Give Till It Hurts?," appeared in papers nationwide on December 26, 1943: a mother gives Christmas gifts to Japanese internees, against the advice of a cowboy postal officer. Later she received a gift from them: "I knew they'd understand." The gift explodes and she screams, "Oh-h-h, those awful, inhuman beasts! They tried to kill us!" The cowboy replies, "Yep, I still claim Japs jest don't understand kindness." Popular poster slogans such as "Wake Up, America!"

"Attack Now!" "Production or Destruction," "The less said, the less dead," "A slip of the lip may sink a ship," "Enemy agents are always near; if you don't talk they won't hear," "Enemy Ears are Listening," "Keep mum Chum," and "Loose Talk can Cost Lives!" urged citizens to consider their impact on the war effort. Careless talk had led to disaster, as "Rumors cost us lives" noted: "U-Boat Captain Kills 22 sailors, Laughs as He Torpedoes Lifeboat Leaving Doomed Vessel." Similarly, "Only 3 Miles Out, It All Depends on Me" showed an unarmed freighter torpedoed, cut in two, and sinking.[52]

Best-selling books in 1941 alerted readers to sinister fifth-columnist machinations and national threats. *Time* featured Curt Riess's *Total Espionage* as a vignette under "Great Improbabilities" in its December 1 issue. *Harper's* had Edward Aswell's "The Case of the Ten Spies," while *American Magazine* printed J. Edgar Hoover's "War Begins at Home." Another notable work was Ladislas Farago's *German Psychological Warfare*. William Shirer's *Berlin Diary*, John Gunther's *Inside Latin America*, Winston Churchill's *Blood, Sweat, and Tears*, and Douglas Miller's *You Can't Do Business with Hitler* urged citizens to jettison their principles for security's sake. The nation, Shirer wrote, "is in the midst of a grim war knowingly harboring an aggressive Fascist Fifth Column whose open and avowed purpose is to make us lose the war."[53]

Shortly after Pearl Harbor, popular author and editor Carl Van Doren endorsed one of the war's best-sellers: "*Sabotage!* will make history as well as be it." Journalists Michael Sayers and Albert E. Kahn's *Sabotage! The Secret War against America* exposed a seemingly genuine fifth-column threat. Sayers and Kahn claimed they uncovered sensational evidence of Axis saboteurs' plans and operations and traced "Nazi and Japanese conspiracies aimed at wrecking or obstructing the American war effort." Sabotage, they argued, "has become the problem of every patriotic man and woman, for it directly affects their security and their very lives." Nazi sympathizers and Japanese agents, *Sabotage!* warned, were preparing coordinated acts of sabotage and espionage against industry and transportation aimed to cripple the economy and undermine morale. It was an unnerving exposé full of case histories—names, addresses, maps, and letters.[54]

Sabotage! began with the following on its frontispiece:

We may be sure that Hitler and Japan will cooperate to do the unexpected.... In any event, the psychological and sabotage offensive in the United States and Latin America will be timed to coincide with, or anticipate by a few weeks the height of the military offensive.

We must be especially prepared to stifle the fifth columnists in the United States who will try to sabotage not merely our war material plants, but even infinitely more important, our minds.

—Vice-President Henry A. Wallace
May 8, 1942

The foreword added to Wallace's warning:

This book is about Axis sabotage. It deals with a weird political underworld of spies and saboteurs. It portrays the agents and conspiracies of a system, reaching into the United States, which relies upon wrecking, terror and treachery as major weapons in its war to enslave the world.... The use of arson, explosives, and assassinations to strike at the enemy's home front has been common to all modern wars. But with the Nazis, sabotage became state policy. Nazi Germany itself is the creation of professional spies and saboteurs.... Their saboteurs assume the importance of a Second Army, operating within other nations.

Axis saboteurs are at work in the United States today.... It is impossible to understand the workings of these saboteurs without a full awareness of Axis plotting in America during the years that preceded the attack on Pearl Harbor, and without recognizing the role that certain Americans ... played and are still playing—some wittingly, some unwittingly—in aiding Axis sabotage.

A piece of candy or chewing gum could become a "very effective incendiary bomb," and the "chiclet bomb" could easily be used on "docks or elsewhere." An employee could set a bomb at work while casually "speaking to the boss." Terror weapons (disguised as household or workplace items) included the cabbage-bomb (or any camouflaged vegetable), fire-pencil, fire-envelope, can of food, piece of coal, and, of course, the "saboteur's favorite weapon: the 'fiery cigar.'" Japanese saboteurs could easily cripple Los Angeles and its war industries by poisoning or destroying the city's aqueduct system. Police found a member of the secret Black Dragon Society with "a short-wave radio set, expertly-drawn maps of Hawaii's fortifications, and complete plans of the Los Angeles water supply system." Before Pearl Harbor, Japanese saboteurs

> moved in by droves to take up residence and carry on business in the immediate vicinity of important United States military establishments, oil storage tanks, oil wells, harbors and forts in California. After December 7, FBI agents uncovered caches of guns, ammunition, explosives, maps, charts, high power cameras, signaling devices, short-wave radios, and other equipment of spies and saboteurs. Following the Nazi pattern, Japanese Consulates . . . had been converted . . . into centers of espionage-sabotage activity.

Sabotage! was a call to arms. "The ghosts of secret destruction," the authors stated, were still "walking through the American countryside" searching for opportune targets whether they be on farms or in factories, aboard ships or down mines. The book ended with the following prognosis: "America's enemies are skillful, powerful, and ruthless. For more than ten years they have been building their underground machinery in this country. This vast and intricate apparatus of secret war cannot be smashed overnight, but inevitably it will be smashed by an American people fully aware of the character and methods of the Axis saboteurs and of all who aid them in the United States."[55]

Movies, too, dealt with subversion. Of the thirty-eight war pictures in production between July and October 1942, twenty-four dealt with espionage and sabotage. The Office of War Information's newly acquired Bureau of Motion Pictures argued that the constant barrage of depressing and portentous imagery was bad for morale. Yet by the fall of 1942, with the tide of war shifting, the invasion threat abating, and no major acts of sabotage or espionage, the public remained intrigued by saboteurs and fifth columnists even as books dealing with home-front problems lost their appeal. Notably, one book dealing with the home front became a best-seller. John Roy Carlson's *Under Cover: My Four Years in the Nazi Underworld of America—The Amazing Revelation of How Axis Agents and Our Enemies within Are Now Plotting to Destroy the United States* (1943) warned Americans to be cautious still. "I found," Carlson wrote, "that many otherwise fine Americans were propagating the lies and the 'party line' originally advanced by Hitler's agents and doing it sincerely in what they believed to be good Americanism." Furthermore, "most of the saboteurs of Democracy looked and acted like ordinary men and women, went quietly about their work of destruction, lived on Park Avenue as well as Yorkville, came from some of our best families, and the most efficient among them were American-born and boasted of their ancestry."[56]

Not surprisingly, hostility, mainly directed against West Coast Japanese Americans, often led to cases of mistaken identity. Chinese were mistakenly jailed. A Portland man answered a knock at his door by a uniformed Japanese, shouted "The invasion is here!," and rushed back inside. The "invader" was a U.S. soldier. In Smithfield, North Carolina, a woman serving meals at a Salvation Army post detected an unusual accent from an itinerant stranger and called police. Julius Klink could not convince authorities that he was an American. Ten days later, cleared by the FBI, Klink left prison a free man.[57]

Japanese American Loyalty

German and Italian Americans had many well-known advocates as well as thousands of refugees who told horrific stories of Nazi persecution. Japanese Americans lacked such advantages as officials at all levels tried to determine their fidelity. Although the War and Justice Departments did not believe mass evacuation necessary in January 1942, they agreed on implementing an alien registration program immediately, allowing FBI searches of aliens' residences, and barring all alien enemies from designated strategic areas. With the Roberts Commission report's release on January 25, Californians felt enemies were among them. All Japanese "looked alike," and none could be trusted. One San Diego district attorney argued the contrary: "You can always tell a Jap," but Germans and Italians "can get by." West Coast residents nevertheless focused on the Japanese.[58]

By early 1942 the media had their insidious enemy within. *Liberty* magazine's "Japanese Spies and What They Did: There Was a Pattern behind It All" revealed how a few "humble" Japanese were really "highly placed and influential people" representative of hundreds of Japan's "super spies." Newspapers focused a great deal of attention on a book titled "Sankoku Domei to Nichibei Sen," translated as "The Tripartite Alliance and the Japanese-American War." Papers publicized it as "a Japanese '*Mein Kampf*.'"[59] Headlines like "Japanese Here Sent Vital Data to Tokyo" and "FBI Seizes Jap Uniforms in Raids on Coast" warned readers of Japanese perfidy. The *Los Angeles Times* summarized the dominant attitude well: "Lincoln Would Intern Japs: Bowron Says Civil War President Would Move Aliens If in Office Today."[60] A *Los Angeles Times* editorial, "The Question of Japanese-Americans," claimed that a "viper is nonetheless a viper wherever the egg is hatched . . . a leopard's spots are the same":

> So a Japanese-American, born of Japanese parents, nurtured upon Japanese traditions, living in a transplanted Japanese atmosphere and thoroughly inoculated with Japanese thoughts, Japanese ideas and Japanese ideals, notwithstanding accidental citizenship, almost inevitably . . . grows up to be a Japanese, not an American in his thoughts, in his ideas, and in his ideals, and is a potential and menacing, if not actual, danger to our country unless properly supervised, controlled and, as it were, hamstrung.[61]

Most Americans agreed and so many wrote their elected officials, including President Roosevelt. R. W. Borchert of San Diego typified the mood:

> There is so little action concerning the menace of fifth columnists . . . particularly the Japs. . . . Send all the Japs to the sugar beet and cane sugar sections of the U.S., where there is a labor shortage. How long are we going to let those traitorous barbarians strut among us seeking every means of destroying us, storing arms and ammunition right under our noses and within stones throw of our war industries . . . ?
>
> Minorities must of necessity suffer, and the only safe and sane course is to put the screws on them ALL and get them out of dan-

ger zones at once and before they stab us in the back here at home. HAVE WE FORGOTTEN PEARL HARBOR? The Pacific Coast... is most vulnerable and most coveted in the eyes of the Japs.... Are you going to be guilty of making the Pacific Coast another Pearl Harbor?[62]

Arthur Wolff of Los Angeles could not understand why one "loyal" Japanese did not "step forward and forewarn us" about Pearl Harbor. "My plea," Wolff wrote the president, "is not based on hysteria." One Japanese American saboteur, he added, could do "one hundred times more real damage here than a fleet of Jap planes dropping bombs at random."[63]

Lest elected officials did not get the point, Frank Schilling of Los Angeles wrote:

> Mr. Biddle does not seem to be in any great hurry to remove this very serious danger, but is concerned with constitutional questions— the rights of aliens and citizens of dual nationality, who will not hesitate, if they have an opportunity, to stab this nation in the back, in the stomach, or in any place they can reach.
>
> How much is the Emperor, that slant eyed god of the heathen, concerned with the rights of the white man in Japan? How much is Hitler, or his dummy in Rome, concerned with the rights of our citizens? Why be so considerate of the Jap, the German, the Italian, and their offspring? Remove Biddle and appoint a HARD BOILED gentleman, one not afraid of doubtful constitutional rights of traitors.... Give us hard fisted fighting men. This is a time for hard and grim work.[64]

Others, too, wrote the president and many included newspaper clippings to help make their case. Frank Miller of Montgomery, Alabama, wanted all Japanese "put in a concentration camp. Japs are like Indians—the only good Indian is a dead Indian. If these aliens are not locked up, we will have sabotage constantly." After Singapore's fall, attorney W. H. Weddell of San Bernardino wrote, came "accusations of Fifth Columnists and sabotage. Is our government going to sit by and allow such actions here on the Pacific Coast?"[65] J. D. Lee, who grew up in Los Angeles but was living in

Birmingham when the war began, was like nearly all on the coast and most across the nation, and saw Japanese Americans as the main threat:

> Every day we hear broadcasts from the Pacific Coast relative to the "open and dangerous" situation regarding the Japanese, German, and Italian population, particularly the Japanese. . . . I know the treachery of the Japanese—their cunning, their over-polite backstabbing, and their utterly false faces. The government would do the nation a favor by putting every Japanese on the Pacific Coast in a concentration camp for the duration. Confine the Germans, put the Italians on probation. I do not think the Italian population is as dangerous. An Italian seems to be a nature and home loving creature and does not think for himself as the Germans and Japs do.[66]

German and Italian American Loyalty

While few stood up for Japanese Americans, many did on behalf of their German or Italian neighbors—whether friends or refugees. Margaret Utz of Santa Cruz, like countless others along the West Coast, wrote the president:

> I can't get out of my mind the plight of my good neighbor, Mrs. Righetti. She said, "What's the use! We have to move any day!" There were tears in her voice. She poured out her heart. . . . So now these peaceful, law abiding people, who built up the community life, own their attractive homes, who pay their taxes, must be moved away, through no fault of theirs. They are not criminals or enemies. Just unfortunate . . . caught in the web of injustice.
>
> Keep our country from committing a great injustice, of which, when all the hysteria is over, we shall be thoroughly ashamed! A German friend, a harmless old "alien" though at heart a loyal American, neglectful in taking out citizen papers, was found drowned, body washed up on the beach. I knew the old man. It makes me sick. He had brooded over having to leave his little home in the evacuation order, and he jumped over the cliffs. . . . Our country will get the same kind of reputation for cruelty and persecution as Germany regarding the Jews.[67]

Wolfgang Zu Putlitz wrote "Your German American Neighbor and the Fifth Column" for *Harper's*. He stated: "For people like myself—Germans recently arrived after having fought against the Nazis—the position will not be pleasant." Trying to mollify his readers, Putlitz unintentionally supported their suspicions:

> I myself hope that a German State will eventually be founded which will take its place in the family of Occidental nations. Germans will be needed to serve as mediators between an exhausted, suspicious, politically stupefied and vanquished people and their conquerors. There are many Germans who feel, as I do, that they can contribute more to the peace of the future by remaining German than by adopting another nationality. Nothing is clearer than that such Germans will be able to do more for the non-German world by remaining German than by abandoning their country. I have not taken out "first papers" and do not intend to apply for them. In applying for "first papers" one is asked to renounce one's nationality and to swear that it is one's intention to become a citizen of the United States. For some us, nevertheless, it is impossible to take this oath.

For many readers, this was damning evidence of fifth-column circumspection and double-talk. Yet Putlitz cautioned:

> There is a small sector where isolated elements of danger may lurk. I refer to those immigrant citizens who have had a hard time in this country, and for whom adherence to the Nazi idea is a cheap fashion of taking their "revenge" against the country in which they failed to make good. This is a pocket of pus for which the whole community, and not the German American community alone, must take responsibility. . . . Twenty-five years ago, discrimination could only create misery for its victims: in our day, it would bring formidable aid to the enemy.[68]

Thousands of refugees, many having endured Nazi persecution, had to assure authorities of their benign intentions. Mrs. Ernst Offenheimer's tragic story reached U.S. Supreme Court justice Felix Frankfurter in February 1942. He forwarded her letter to Francis Biddle, noting "the imponderables" of war:

Being a refugee from Nazi oppression I can't help wondering that I and many others are called "enemy aliens" on both sides of this world-wide struggle. We were the first victims of Nazi Germany.... When war started, Norway discovered Quislings. Belgium interned refugees.... In France, refugees were put behind barbed wire. This is a war between two fundamentally divergent ideals, not limited by state boundaries. How can a man understand if one persecutes the persecuted? Shall we be used involuntarily once more to deter suspicion?

Do with us whatever you like. You will never succeed in converting us into your enemies. Agitation has grown against us and one is quickly degraded and marked. There should be Americans who understand the problem and are willing to help us. We are enemies of Germany, enemies of everything connected with Germany, enemies of your enemies, your friends and allies. Can you help and will you help? May I add, that by explaining the problem to the public as outlined, one of the many ways to win this war will be achieved.

Frankfurter admired Biddle's "libertarian attitude," his "sensitive understanding of the feelings of those victims of Hitler in this country whose technical legal status may be that of enemy aliens." Perhaps he could identify with "their psychological plight" and "fortify their spirits and enlighten American opinion." Biddle received many such letters and regretted he could not "classify Germans as non-alien enemies," but conceded such situations were "troublesome." Frankfurter did not expect Biddle to reclassify anyone. The letter was, he offered, an eloquent and informative "cri de coeur."[69]

Some Jews, such as Dr. Arthur Mayer and wife, Margarethe, sought asylum after losing their citizenship in 1935 by the Nuremberg Laws. Hitler's regime expelled Dr. Mayer from his hospital post as medical director and forced Margarethe to give up her membership in the International Actors' Union and her job as professor of the Academy of Dramatic Art. The Gestapo arrested and threatened them both. They fled Germany and accepted Harvard professor Merrill Moore's invitation to come to America. After immigrating in the spring of 1938, they applied for and received first citizenship papers. Dr. Mayer then passed California's medical board examination. In January 1941 the German consul at Los Angeles revoked their German citizenship. They then notified Alien Registration of their status change. By November, every non-Aryan German living abroad was expatriated and their property seized by decree.

With mutual declarations of war between the United States and Germany on December 11, 1941, they were "compelled to register as enemy aliens," the Mayers stated. "We are in reality not enemy aliens, but imbued with a great love and admiration for . . . the United States, which gave us asylum at a time when we, as Jews, were deprived of every right, dispossessed and robbed of our property by Hitler." The Mayers conveyed their hardships:

> Being compelled to undergo the vicissitudes of oppression, wandering, and finding a new home, almost broke our health and spirit, and it was only with the finding of a new home in this asylum for the oppressed [that] we began slowly to regain our health, our spirit, and our trust in humanity. We call upon you to exercise your kind and good offices and help us, to remain where we are, unmolested, to pursue our honorable and sincere endeavor to make our honest living undisturbed, and thereby being of a service to ourselves, to suffering humanity, and to the great land of our adoption, the United States of America.[70]

Yet the Mayers, along with thousands of other newly classified alien enemies, were forced from their homes for months, the duration of the war, or beyond.

Some wrote Roosevelt while others pleaded their case through newspapers and magazines. On February 14, 1942, Albert Liotta, a citizen, wrote FDR on behalf of his eighty-six-year-old father, Vincent. Liotta wondered why his dad, a U.S. Army veteran and resident of fifty-five years (but lacking citizenship papers), bedridden and in ill health, had to move from the restricted area where he and his parents lived. "Surely this country of liberty and justice," Liotta wrote, "can come to no harm from this poor old man. Can he not be allowed to spend his last few remaining days in his own home near his children in peace? The deadline is February 24, so will you please give us an answer immediately?" On March 24, an overworked Edward Ennis and overburdened AECU advised Albert to contact his local military commander, as the secretary of war now had jurisdiction over West Coast military areas—the advice came too late for the Liottas.[71]

Ordinary citizens and charitable organizations created to aid émigrés worked doggedly for those who had fled the Nazis and highlighted internationally renowned anti-fascist refugees. Notables included Arturo Toscanini, Thomas Mann, and Albert Einstein. Together, these highly respected intellectuals and well-known artists, along with thousands of refugees, used the media or appealed directly to the highest levels of government for compassion and consideration. Biddle tempered FDR's concerns, as Justice Department official Jerre Mangione, liaison with relocatees and internees, noted:

> The Attorney General's selective internment policy was derived from the experience of the British government with its own aliens of enemy nationality. In the panic that seized the British when the Low Countries and France collapsed, the government mass-interned almost eighty-five thousand [sic] German and Austrian refugees, many of them avowed enemies of Hitler who had fled to England for safety. After a few months the public came to its senses and began condemning the government's wholesale internment policy. The government later admitted it had victimized "some of the bitterest and most active enemies of the Nazi regime," and returned to its initial policy of selective internment.[72]

Refugee stories influenced Biddle just as testimonials did the Tolan Committee. Their advice in turn swayed Stimson and FDR, who sympathized, eased restrictions against German and Italian Americans, and decided against their large-scale relocation. Instead, a highly selective and secretive movement of individual aliens and citizens took place based upon military necessity. Stimson wanted to retain a mass evacuation option in case of an "outbreak of fifth column activities." The lack of a military threat to incite aliens partially eased FDR's fear, as did the constant mail the White House was receiving. A number of famous anti-Nazi refugees, including

Giuseppe Borgese, Bruno Frank, and Bruno Walter, joined Toscanini, Mann, and Einstein in mid-February and wrote Roosevelt:

> We draw your attention to a large group of natives of Germany and Italy who by present regulations are, erroneously, characterized and treated as "Aliens of Enemy Nationality." Such persons have fled and sought refuge in the United States.
>
> Many of those people, politicians, scientists, artists, writers, have been among the earliest and most farsighted adversaries of the governments against whom the United States are now at war. Many of them have sacrificed . . . and risked their lives.
>
> The "Application for a Certificate of Identification" provides . . . an opportunity to make additional statements. . . . But, so far, these victims of Nazi and Fascist oppression, these staunch and consistent defenders of democracy, would be subject to all the present and future restrictions meant for and directed against possible Fifth Columnists.
>
> Mr. President . . . a clear and practical line should be drawn between the potential enemies of American democracy on the one hand, and the victims and sworn foes of totalitarian evil on the other.[73]

Gerhard Hiller, a Jewish refugee from Germany, received first citizenship papers in July 1940 and wanted Biddle to know about a regulation that affected him and "thousands of other victims of Hitler's Nazi Regime as well." Hiller wrote:

> The German government issued a decree on November 25, 1941, depriving German citizenship of all Jews who have left Germany. . . . The German government made clear that it considers all Jews as enemies. Such persons in this country must not be classified as "enemy" aliens by the authorities. These people despise Hitler.
>
> These people . . . persecuted by Nazis . . . could never be guilty of sympathizing with the Regime that has brought about their expatriation. I cannot speak too strongly of the psychological damage brought about by including under the heading of "enemy" aliens, those of German origin who are using every bit of their energy to aid the United States to achieve complete VICTORY.

I would suggest that boards or tribunals be set up for thoroughly investigating aliens before placing them in the category of "friendly" aliens. Assuring you of the sincere appreciation of the thousands of people who find themselves in this classification, for what consideration you can give.[74]

Attorneys helped too, including Chase Kimball, who wrote Biddle in September: "This is primarily a war of ideologies, not simply a war between nations. Despite that fact, our government is treating many German and Italian political refugees from fascism as alien enemies. Hitler has taken away German citizenship, and it is clear they are much stronger against him than most American citizens. Exempt from enemy alien restrictions all persons who are refugees."[75]

Government studies of German aliens revealed that many were bona fide refugees. Some had been stateless since 1933. Others had family members serving in the military, and tens of thousands had been residents for decades. Ennis wished to expand Biddle's Columbus Day exemption of Italian aliens by adding German refugees and longtime residents. On October 20 he asked Thomas Cooley, Review Section Chief, AECU, to look into it. By month's end, Donald Perry of the Alien Registration Division found that 122,270 German aliens matched the criteria—36,681 refugees, 5,847 with a family member in uniform, and 79,742 who since 1917 had been living in the United States.[76]

7

Dual-Coast Relocation and Nationwide Internment

> Looking back into our own history... our people have had much experience in evacuation. Colonists left their farms to seek protection from Indian attack.... In time of flood and hurricane, large segments of our population have been obliged to leave their homes and possessions to avoid further disaster and unnecessary exposure to danger.
>
> —WAR DEPARTMENT, "EVACUATION OF CIVILIAN POPULATION, 1941"

Initially, there was to be no difference in the government's treatment of alien enemies—regardless of race or ethnicity. The question of what to do with citizens of German, Italian, and Japanese descent was, for a time, unanswered. Constitutional rights, national security, political repercussions, economic effects, public morale, and Axis reciprocity were all factors that shaped relocation and internment policies and procedures. The early course of the war had a tremendous impact. Seemingly everyone—from FDR to military brass, top government officials, esteemed intellectuals, Hollywood notables, nationally syndicated columnists, business executives, local politicians, and civic leaders to the public and media at large—blamed Japanese fifth-column perfidy for the Pearl Harbor fiasco. With the news of each passing Japanese victory, an angry and fearful public (especially along the West Coast) readily accepted the propaganda that then fueled demands for action against the greatest perceived threat—Japanese fifth columnists.

West Coast Actions

Nearly all West Coast politicians recommended relocating enemy aliens and Japanese Americans. Tacoma's mayor was the only representative of larger cities in Washington, Oregon, and California to oppose the plan, while California's entire congressional delegation, meeting in Washington DC on January 30, unanimously called for the mandatory removal of all enemy aliens and dual citizens from areas designated vital to the nation's security. "The thought in mind, of course, is to prevent any Fifth Column activity or aid to the enemy," proclaimed California representative Leland Ford a week before the meeting. His statements to Congress as well as correspondences with cabinet members and other officials between mid-December 1941 and mid-January 1942 indicate the rapidly changing public, political, and military attitudes about Japanese Americans. Two declarations by Ford well reflect the shift. The first is his rebuttal to fellow House member Rankin's call for "deporting every Jap who claims, or has claimed, Japanese citizenship, or sympathizes with Japan in this war" on December 15, 1941:

> These people are American-born. They cannot be deported whether we like it or whether we do not. This is their country. [When] they join the armed forces, they must take the oath of allegiance, and I see no particular reason at this particular time why they should not. I believe that every one of these people should make a clear, clean acknowledgement [of loyalty].

The second is his letter of January 16, 1942, to Hoover, Knox, and Stimson:

> All Japanese, whether citizens or not, should be placed in inland concentration camps. This may be hard to do [but] if an American-born Japanese is really patriotic . . . he would be making his contribution to the welfare of this country. If he is sincere in wanting to help us, he should be willing to do this. As against this sacrifice, millions of other citizens are willing to lay down their lives, which is a far greater sacrifice than being placed in a concentration camp. Of course, if they are not loyal enough to do this, perhaps they ought to be placed in the camp anyhow.[1]

The earliest calls for evacuating enemy aliens and citizens came one month after Pearl Harbor. Legislative efforts for and then demands of evacuation soon followed. Ford was the first congressional representative to seek action. On January 6, among the many telegrams and letters sent by his constituents, he received a telegram from movie star Leo Carillo (who was part of a prominent Californio family) asking for legislation requiring all Japanese truck farmers living along the California coastline to move inland. Ford immediately sent it along with his endorsement to Cordell Hull. "I thoroughly agree," he wrote. There could be "complications," Ford admitted, because "land might be operated by native-born Japanese." Nevertheless, he argued, "these are war times and I do not believe we could be any too strict," especially "in the face of the treacherous way in which they do things." Ford then amplified his concerns. On January 20 on the House floor he argued that for a "patriotic" Japanese American "to submit himself to a concentration camp" would be but a "small sacrifice." He then told the *Los Angeles Examiner*, *Los Angeles Times*, and *San Francisco Examiner* that the Japanese, aliens and citizens, should be moved inland, far from the coast. Many saw a clear and present danger to coastal cities, California, and the nation. In a radio speech on February 9, Ford stated that interning all Japanese was "very humanitarian," avoiding the "heartaches from separating families."[2]

Ford sent at least seven more messages to top officials in January, including Hoover, Knox, Stimson, Hull, and Biddle, and consistently urged moving and interning the Japanese. In his initial letter to Biddle, as with the others, Ford referenced and sometimes enclosed some of the many letters and telegrams from California's "outstanding citizens . . . men of standing . . . men of well-balanced judgment [who] know what they are talking about," including one Mr. Le Roy, the vice president of the Southern California Gas Company:

> This morning's dispatches from Malay stated that the Japanese have been infiltrating behind British lines by coming ashore. . . . Local Japanese planters have no doubt provided the Japanese Army in advance with complete information. Japanese farmers along the

> Pacific Coast have given valuable military information to the Japanese Empire. There is no reason to believe that the Japanese in California are any different from Japanese anywhere else. To let these men continue to sit and farm vegetable lands along our seashore . . . seems unbelievable.

Although he had opposed treating California's Japanese population harshly in mid-December, Ford changed his mind amid a difficult reelection campaign. On January 4 he telegrammed Hull requesting rigorous checks on Japanese Americans because of their "treacherous" behavior. As noted, from January 16 to January 20 Ford had shared his concerns with Stimson, Hoover, Knox, and his fellow congressmen, among others. "It no doubt has been brought to your attention," Ford then wrote Biddle on January 23, "that many of the commanding positions in the coastal area are occupied by the Japanese." Even worse, Ford had learned from "a man who ought to know" that "Japanese are permitted within 100 yards of our camouflaged coast defense guns." Ford saw difficulties with a mass evacuation but prioritized preventing "fifth column activity." His letters concluded: "I would like to know what action you propose to take. This question is of very vital concern to the people of California. Occupying the position that they do, there is nothing in God's world today to stop them from signaling submarines or communicating with them, and if this is not stopped, I make the prediction that it is going to be disastrous for the people who occupy the California coastline."[3]

Ford's January 23 letter to Biddle, sent as the Roberts Commission's report was issued, echoed thousands demanding a Japanese American evacuation. Biddle responded the next day:

> My dear Mr. Congressman:
>
> As you know those who were considered dangerous have already been interned. A registration is being made of all Japanese and plans are now being considered. After this registration is complete, it will show precisely who are Japanese citizens and where they are living, and then further steps will be taken.[4]

Biddle could not envision interning citizens without suspending the writ of habeas corpus, but he welcomed suggestions. One came from William Palmer, an attorney who worried particularly about California's Japanese operating fishing boats "capable of long trips, readily transformable into mine layers and mine sweepers." On January 7, Palmer requested government-issued executive warrants to intern such men for the war's duration if deemed dangerous to the public safety. By month's end, California attorney general Earl Warren called the Japanese situation the "Achilles heel of the entire civilian defense effort" and cautioned that "unless something is done it may bring about a repetition of Pearl Harbor."[5]

Stimson could not assuage the concerns of Ford, DeWitt, and others who demanded an immediate and total removal of West Coast Japanese. Although Stimson was willing to help, he was reluctant to accept responsibility and with his staff took a week to mull over his department's next steps. Stimson's recommendation to Biddle and response to Ford (drafted by Bendetsen) highlight the dilemma he faced:

Attorney General Biddle:

General De Witt has expressed great apprehension because of the presence on the Pacific Coast of many thousand alien enemies. As late as yesterday, 24 January, he stated that shore-to-ship and ship-to-shore radio communications, undoubtedly coordinated by intelligent enemy control, were continually operating. A few days ago it was reported by military observers on the Pacific coast that not a single ship had sailed from our Pacific ports without being subsequently attacked. General De Witt's apprehensions have been confirmed by recent visits of military observers from the War Department to the Pacific Coast. The alarming and dangerous situation just described . . . calls for immediate and stringent action.

Dear Mr. Ford:

The internment of over a hundred thousand people, and their evacuation inland, presents a very real problem. While the necessity for firm measures to ensure the maximum war effort cannot be questioned, your suggested proposal involves many complex considerations. Responsibility and authority for internment has been delegated by the President to the Attorney General. Those ordered interned by the Department of Justice are turned over to the Army for custody. The Army is prepared to provide internment facilities in the interior to the extent necessary.

The Army is submitting recommendations to the Attorney General for designation by him of restricted areas on the Pacific Coast. This, together with the pending alien registration directed by the President, should formulate the basis for a definite program of security from fifth-column activity emanating from this source. I take the liberty of suggesting that you present your views to the Attorney General.[6]

Initial steps aimed at all enemy aliens were under way. On February 2, orders required enemy aliens to register with the Western Defense Command as the FBI began its "spot" raids of their homes and the creation of strategic areas continued. West Coast residents, especially Californians, protested these steps as inadequate, and their representatives listened. By mid-February, a month after Ford's speech demanding the removal of all West Coast Japanese, California politicians, annoyed and frustrated, demanded satisfaction.

Most legislators, even those of California, the state with the greatest number of Japanese by far, wanted all West Coast enemy aliens—Germans, Italians, and Japanese—and their families removed. On January 30 the Pacific Coast delegation, made up mainly of California's representatives, met with the War Department's Karl Bendetsen and the Justice Department's James Rowe and Edward Ennis on Capitol Hill. Dissatisfied with how the Justice Department was handling the alien enemy situation, the delegation called for the War Department to take charge, and, notably, did not press for the removal of any citizens—whether of German, Italian, or Japanese descent. In short, even the most vociferous advocates of alien removal, the Pacific Coast congressional delegation, did not single out Japanese Americans. Instead, it was the military that led the call for the large-scale West Coast removal of Japanese Americans. Bendetsen and DeWitt both well knew that the inclusion of family members with enemy aliens meant most Nisei.[7]

Conversations and correspondence between DeWitt and Bendetsen prior to and after the Pacific Coast delegation meeting reveal that all considered Japanese Americans the nation's primary threat and top priority. On January 24, DeWitt telephoned Bendetsen expressing fear of sabotage and fifth-column activities and erroneously stated that Japanese Americans were communicating with the Japanese navy. Five days later, and just four days after the Roberts report was released, which directly (but incorrectly) linked the Pearl Harbor disaster to fifth-column treachery, DeWitt, on the eve of Bendetsen's meeting, informed him of the mounting public pressure to remove all West Coast Japanese. DeWitt's rapid change in attitude reflected the Roberts findings along with the sharp rise in public demands for federal and military evacuation of the Japanese. It also reflected private warnings from California governor Culbert Olson, Attorney General Warren, and others who would hold him personally responsible for sabotage or subversive activities, which DeWitt believed imminent. He notified Washington on January 29:

> There's a tremendous volume of public opinion now developing against the Japanese, . . . aliens and non-aliens, to get them off the land, and in Southern California . . . they want and they are bringing pressure on the government to move all the Japanese out. As a matter of fact, it's not being instigated or developed by people who are not thinking but by the best people of California. Since the publication of the Roberts Report they feel that they are living in the midst of a lot of enemies. They don't trust the Japanese, none of them.[8]

The next day, Bendetsen accurately told DeWitt that the delegation was "pretty well stirred up," but then suggested that, "out of military necessity" along with "irresistible" public sentiment, certain areas would become "prohibited to everybody concerned."

The following day Bendetsen went even farther and inaccurately reported to his boss, Provost Marshal General Gullion, that the Pacific Coast delegation was "calling for the immediate evacuation of all Japanese from the Pacific coastal strip including Japanese citizens age 21 and under." The delegation's summary recommendations of January 30, while giving the War Department immediate and complete control over all alien enemies and citizens holding dual citizenship in designated critical areas, made no specific mention of the Japanese and wanted

> 1. Designation by War Department of critical areas throughout the country and territorial possessions. 2. Immediate evacuation from critical areas of all enemy aliens and their families, including children under 21, whether aliens or not. 3. Temporary internment of evacuated aliens and families in available CCC [Civilian Conservation Corps] camps pending completion of long-range resettlement or internment program. 4. Opportunity and federal assistance to dual citizens living in critical areas for voluntary resettlement as patriotic contribution. 5. Federal assistance to all uninterned alien enemies and dual citizens whose means of livelihood are affected. . . . 6. Development and consummation as soon as possible of complete evacuation and resettlement or internment program covering all alien enemies and dual citizens wherever located.

DeWitt wanted all German and Italian aliens as well as all Japanese residents from designated areas moved immediately and simultaneously. On January 31, he privately recorded: "The steps now being taken by the Attorney General through the FBI will do nothing more than exercise a controlling influence and preventive action against sabotage; it will not, in my opinion, be able to stop it. The only positive answer to this question is evacuation of all enemy aliens from the West Coast and resettlement or internment under positive control, military or otherwise." His multiple conversations with Bendetsen and Gullion on January 31 and February 1 went even further: "I include all Germans, all Italians who are alien enemies and all Japanese who are native-born or foreign born . . . evacuate enemy aliens in large groups at the earliest possible date. . . . Put them to work in internment camps. I place the following priority: First the Japanese, the most dangerous; the next group, the Germans; the third group, the Italians. We've waited too long as it is. Get them all out."⁹

That same day, Biddle, Rowe, Ennis, and Hoover met with McCloy, Gullion, and Bendetsen. Biddle wanted a joint press release to show that all were "in agreement on control measures" and emphasized that his department "would have nothing to do with any interference with citizens" or suspend habeas corpus. He recalled that the three War Department representatives concurred, adding, "the military situation did not at this time require the removal of American citizens of Japanese origin." After heated exchanges, the War Department flexed its muscle. Nobody could be "soft" on the Japanese, and they knew it. The press had been merciless with Biddle, accusing him of "pussyfooting" with mass evacuation. Gullion bluntly asked him: "Do you mean to tell me that if the Army, the men on the ground, determine it is a military necessity to move certain citizens, Jap citizens, that you won't help us?" McCloy added: "You are putting a Wall Street lawyer in a helluva box, but if it is a question of the safety of the country [and] the Constitution . . . Why the Constitution is just a scrap of paper to me."¹⁰

Growing impatient, on February 18, Ford, now one the loudest voices clamoring for internment, told his fellow conservative Republicans that he had called Biddle's office

> and told them to stop fucking around. I gave the Justice Department twenty-four hours' notice that unless they would issue a mass evacuation notice I would drag the whole matter out on the floor of the House and Senate and give the bastards everything we could with both barrels. Justice Department officials had given the West Coast group the runaround long enough, and if they would not take immediate action, we would clean the goddamned office in one sweep. I cussed at the Attorney General and his staff just like I'm cussing you now, and they knew damn well I meant business.¹¹

California's city and county governments targeted Japanese Americans, and many agencies acted prior to federal action. San Buenaventura's City Council's Resolution no. 1880, for example, declared that a threat to its own security and that of "the entire Pacific Coast" existed because of the war and "the presence of Japanese in large numbers" along the coast. It urged removing "such persons within 200 miles of the Pacific Ocean," resolved that "all dangerous enemy aliens of any country should be removed," and also urged "federal authorities having jurisdiction to cause the evacuation of all such persons" from the Pacific Coast. On February 9 the council passed and adopted the resolution.[12]

Evacuation and other demands reached a crescendo over the next few weeks as Japan won a series of military victories. The vitriolic campaign against the Japanese was so successful that by late March, 62 percent of those polled felt the nation should be fighting Japan first as compared to 21 percent who thought it should be Germany; revealing the public's thirst for vengeance, 67 percent approved of all-out war against Japan, including attacking its civilians. Yet most felt that Germany was a greater threat and, aside from the months after Pearl Harbor, often feared German enemy aliens more. Irrational fears that most Americans had of fifth columnists coupled with a powerful desire to exact revenge for a continuing series of American defeats in the Pacific helps to explain the apparent discrepancy in public thinking.[13]

The Japanese had to go. Major Clarence Harbert, commanding officer of the Japanese American Branch of the Office of the Provost Marshal General (PMG), offered shaky and circular logic:

> Many American-born Japanese, while technically citizens, were loyal to Japan. . . . Ties of society and blood were so strong that necessary information could not be obtained. . . . [A] general and justifiable mistrust of the Japanese caused a series of official acts, such as curfews, to curb their activities. The Japanese drew closer together and . . . felt that an invasion might come shortly and wished to be on the right side. Japanese fanatics, both alien and citizen, increased the distrust, this led to further restrictions. These actions had a demoralizing effect. . . . There was insufficient information upon which to distinguish the loyal from the disloyal, and the peril to the West Coast was so great that no risk could be taken. Military necessity required the immediate handling of the whole

group, and any well-meaning citizen was obliged to undergo a temporary limitation of his normal rights and activities.

PMG figures revealed that nearly 92 percent of enemy aliens (1,010,078 of 1,101,936) came from Germany and Italy. In order to "preclude damage to or destruction of vital war installations or materiel" and guard against "espionage and subversive activity," Gullion authorized the Alien Employment Program (AEP). While many were "disloyal or potentially subversive individuals," he believed the alien population included "a large percentage of experienced mechanics and technicians whose skill is greatly needed." As a result, from March 9, 1942, when the PMG assumed responsibility for the AEP, until June 30, 1945, over 207,000 requests for work on classified and aeronautical War and Navy Department contracts were handled. The program denied 5,400 aliens but approved over 201,000 after separating the "loyal from disloyal." Gullion noted that the FBI had found "no case of enemy inspired sabotage." Using the surplus labor from 200,000 loyal aliens aided the war effort and had a "positive propaganda" affect that "influenced the loyalty of any alien." Gullion argued for the same policies if they were later required.[14]

Policies aimed at West Coast Japanese aliens and citizens soon differed from those directed at Germans and Italians, as relocating all of the latter was simply out of the question. Stimson proceeded cautiously as his War Department explained that, "looking back into our own history," forced movements have hardly been unique occurrences, as "from early colonial days, our people have had much experience in evacuation." Relocating Japanese en masse was acceptable, but not Germans or Italians. On February 3, McCloy and Chief of Staff General George Marshall phoned DeWitt for advice and assurance that he and Gullion were not committing the War Department to relocating citizens without proper authorization. Stimson, McCloy, and Marshall prioritized safeguarding West Coast military installations, but they were not committed to a mass relocation of aliens or citizens. That same day, Stimson, McCloy, Gullion, and Bendetsen met, and when DeWitt learned from Gullion that Stimson and McCloy were against "any mass movement" and "interfering with civilians unless it can be done legally," he backpedaled, afraid of creating a political firestorm, embarrassing the War Department, and being censured by his superiors. Yet DeWitt and the War Department soon implemented key policies.[15]

From early to mid-February, Hiram Johnson, California's senior Republican senator, fearing a Japanese invasion, took charge of the Pacific Coast congressional delegation. On February 13 the delegation unanimously recommended to Roosevelt "the immediate evacuation of all persons of Japanese lineage and all others, [dangerous] aliens and citizens alike, . . . from the strategic areas of California, Oregon, and Washington." Gullion convinced McCloy that anything less would be "too little too late." Stimson followed suit and told Roosevelt that the military should remove all West Coast Japanese. Bendetsen's machinations and Gullion's steadfast belief in the Japanese fifth-column threat brought DeWitt, key War Department civilians, and Roosevelt himself to support relocating them en masse. Bendetsen, Gullion, and DeWitt were unsuccessful, however, in doing the same to Germans and Italians, as top military and civilian leaders, including Roosevelt, realized its impossibility and impracticability. A mass relocation of Germans or Italians would cost the war. Yet preemptive action was required. In June 1942 the War Relocation Authority noted:

> Japanese aliens are enemies and enjoy no civil rights. The President has absolute control over their detention. Citizen Japanese may be detained for the national safety, and other classes of citizens need not be affected. Chances are good that the courts will sustain the detention of Japanese at relocation centers.
>
> Resident Japanese cannot be distinguished from disguised Japanese soldiers landed by parachute or small boats. . . . If the possibility of invasion is present (as recent events on the West Coast clearly show), the removal of all Japanese from vital defense localities, and restrictions on their movements in other areas within range of feasible sea or air attack, is undoubtedly justified.
>
> Evidence has shown a) Japanese are much more likely to engage in sabotage and fifth column work than any others, b) it is impos-

sible in advance to distinguish between the loyal and disloyal, and c) there is serious present danger from the free and uninhibited movement of the disloyal, it would be reasonable to take preventive measures against all citizen Japanese. It is the Japanese government's position that . . . all persons of Japanese extraction, as Japanese nationals, are liable to military and other service for Japan.[16]

West Coast Public Opinion

Few Californians championed Japanese American civil liberties after Pearl Harbor. The potency and cogency of local, regional, and national pressures for federal action combined and intensified in late January and February 1942. While some defended Japanese Americans as well as German and Italian Americans, most did not. The vast majority of letters, telegrams, editorials, and articles were hardly conciliatory and called for stringent treatment and no quarter. In California this was especially true for Japanese Americans, as racism, xenophobia, and the backlash stemming from Pearl Harbor coalesced with the fear of an imminent Japanese West Coast invasion.

In January, Mrs. Blum of Los Angeles wrote what became a typical letter to FDR:

> Today we are mourning the thousands of dead who have been wantonly sacrificed at Hawaii—wantonly because of the utter failure of the men in charge to thoroughly comprehend dangers that were lurking just around the corner. Are we to learn nothing? Are we, in California, to go on complacently believing that the Japs living in our most vital defense areas will do less for their mother country than did the Japs at Hawaii, the Philippines, Malaya, and Hong Kong?
>
> Is the West Coast to become another PEARL HARBOR before the necessary steps are taken? It is far better to misjudge a few Japanese who might be loyal to this country—but the all important thing to do NOW is to get all Japanese out of these vital areas—as far away from the coast as possible. Those Japanese who mean no harm to this country can take no offense. I beg, please see that definite steps are taken NOW to protect our Pacific Coast.

Lilah Maria White of Santa Monica was one of thousands who wrote Biddle at the height of public anger and calls for action. On February 9 she wrote: "Dear Sir: What are we waiting for? Another Pearl Harbor? As a mother whose only son is serving with the U.S. Navy—at sea—and the wife of a U.S. Navy man on active duty, I *beg* of you to take steps *immediately* to free our strategic zones of Japs—*all* Japs—at *once*."[17] Others worried about the nation's black population colluding with the Japanese:

> [Westbrook] Pegler's column made very clear the importance of the Negro people's attitude toward the war. The enemy's agents in our town are not neglecting an attempt to create a Japanese-Negro anti-white-race fifth column. The Japanese colony and the Negro colony in San Francisco are close enough neighbors to provide many contacts.
>
> It isn't propaganda of the ridiculous Nazi kind. It takes advantage of real discrimination as well as propaganda the Communists have used in past years to sell the Negro on the idea that, although pacific by nature, he has often been forced into American military enterprises—and paid off in dirt.
>
> Japanese agents are trying to stir up strife right in our own town—and at a time when the Japanese problem may mean such tragedy for loyal Japanese-Americans. Who do you suppose is tearing down air-raid shelter signs and defacing other notices designed to prevent confusion and save lives? Now is the time for Jap spies to do their stuff.[18]

On February 4, Governor Olson delivered a much-publicized radio report, followed the next day by the mayor of Los Angeles, Fletcher Bowron, who also took to the airwaves in his first public address. They falsely cited statewide Japanese fifth-columnist preparatory work, much of it likely coming from DeWitt, and emphasized that inaction could well lead to another Pearl Harbor. Hysteria and public hostility skyrocketed. By mid-February, public demands for federal and military intervention against the Japanese peaked. A vicious cycle ensued as political pressures for federal action increased, the military provided politicians and the public false or grossly exaggerated accounts of enemy actions and subversive activities, and the public put incredible pressure on their elected officials and the military to act before it was too late. On February 10, Mrs. Kate Ford of Bakersfield wrote Biddle a letter typical of those sent to and received by local, state, and federal officials at the height of the removal demands:

> The United States is at war. We are fighting for our existence. We are fighting ruthless nations that will prosecute this war by every means, fair and foul. Democratic institutions we have struggled to build are being threatened. Why is our government not doing all in its power to see that this war is won? Why does our government allow thousands of Japanese . . . to reside where they can cripple us? With the memory of Pearl Harbor and Manila . . . why . . . postpone the removal of all Japanese from the Pacific Coast area—where they are a serious threat to our defense program, our war industries, and our lives?
>
> Americans on the Pacific Coast do not care to wait until Japanese saboteurs have struck a damaging blow. . . . Act at once in the removal of all Japanese from the entire Pacific Coast area. We expect you to do all in your power to eliminate the Japanese threat to West Coast security. Do all in your power to force this step toward eventual victory. Let's protect our home front![19]

Dr. Grover Walters of Tacoma wrote Roosevelt and warned of Japanese poisoning food. A neighbor, he added, whose "farm adjoins Japs," said that "she and other Americans cannot trust them." Walters urged that Japanese workers be federally supervised or that they find "other lines of activity" which would be "safer for all." Albert Elliston of Los Angeles wrote: "I live in the heart of a Japanese neighborhood" and "90 percent or more, alien as well as American born, are pro-Japan. The little half-naked Jap kids tear around here with toy pistols shouting 'Heil Hitler!' We are very likely to have trouble with these Japs. They really hate us." An anonymous "John Democrat, one of thousands" of Los Angeles argued the same and pleaded for Biddle to receive his letter "instead of the waste basket." He wrote:

> Why move some poor sap of an old alien, when his sons, who think and talk and honor Japan stay in these vital areas? . . . Send your

agents to talk to the average person on the street or to any police chief and you will get a clearer picture of what is going on as to the people's wishes here. For safety, we want all the Japs moved from the coast NOW. The young Japanese have been the troublemakers in the past weeks, not the aliens and the people are getting a belly full of it.

Many, including "John Democrat," who wrote their elected officials enclosed a newspaper clipping or two from those especially who gave "a very clear view point of what the people of California think." One favorite, not surprisingly, was Henry McLemore, who well summarized the mood: "If making one million innocent Japanese uncomfortable would prevent one scheming Japanese from costing the life of one American boy, then let the million innocents suffer. Let them howl." Members of patriotic groups, including Robert Duncan of the Veterans of Foreign Wars, shared such views:

> The United States is in danger of invasion. Enemy aliens are a constant menace. . . . Enemy aliens and children are a possible fifth column aid to enemy activities. The defense of the Pacific Coast against Japanese aggression is surely greatly hampered by these nationals and their sympathizers. We can expect to have the repetition of their activities as at PEARL HARBOR to happen here. . . . This POST requests that all enemy aliens be removed from the Pacific Coast region.[20]

Method in the Madness: Calculating Costs

During the war, five different U.S. agencies detained, relocated, and interned enemy aliens. Two more helped control the detainees, relocatees, and internees while still others oversaw their property. The FBI used enemy alien warrants to arrest and detain thousands of civilians. After a hearing, officials determined whether to intern, parole, or release the detainee. The FBI delivered enemy aliens directly to INS internment camps and Border Patrol detention stations while authorities lodged other detainees temporarily in county jails and local prisons. The FBI often seized and jailed enemy aliens without notifying their families or anyone else; these individuals often "disappeared for as long as two weeks, leaving businesses in operation, cars parked on the streets which were taken by the police for over-parking, and families totally without knowledge of their whereabouts."[21] While the public remained largely unaware of the plight of German and Italian aliens or Latin American nationals, the relocation of the Japanese was publicized and well known.

Edward J. Ennis, AECU director since its creation in December 1941, responded to citizens' concerns about Japanese American maltreatment. On March 12, 1942, three weeks after Executive Order 9066, Ennis informed Los Angeles residents that the government's policy was "one strictly in accordance with the rights and privileges guaranteed by the Constitution. At no time shall either citizens or loyal aliens be discriminated against because of race, creed, or color." James Rowe, responding for the attorney general, informed the president of Woodbury College in Los Angeles that he could "rest assured" that the Justice Department would "continue to protect the civil liberties of citizens and non-citizens alike." Rowe continued: "So long as aliens and minority groups continue to conduct themselves in accordance with the law, they need fear no interference."[22]

All the while, the FBI was rounding up aliens for dubious reasons and from tips provided by jittery citizens fearful of alien nationals and by vigilantes determined to prevent an enemy uprising. Some eagerly informed on their neighbors, others settled personal grudges, while still more reported aliens who violated curfew or entered restricted zones. Many months had passed since April 30, 1941, when Hoover directed agents to "clarify, consolidate, and supplement instructions" regarding "persons who should be considered for custodial detention pending investigation in the event of a national emergency." Selecting aliens and citizens for detention or internment rested greatly on this memo and public perception. The Japanese, most believed, were more dangerous and less assimilated than their European counterparts. Governor Olson said one could not tell loyal from disloyal Japanese since all "look alike," but at least they were "easily identifiable." Warren added, "When dealing with the Caucasian race we have methods that will test their loyalty." DeWitt remarked, "a Jap is a Jap," while Rankin asserted "once a Jap, always a Jap; you cannot regenerate a Jap, convert him and make him the same as a white man any more than you can reverse the laws of nature." Mayor Bowron mused, "When the final test comes who can say but that 'blood will tell'?"[23]

Two days after the Roberts report was released, Governor Olson warned DeWitt and others that unless immediate action was taken, "people may take things into their own hands." Roosevelt agreed with Olson's assessment as DeWitt, head of the WDC, called for removing all West Coast enemy aliens. Stimson recommended forcing enemy aliens from Category A areas (places prohibited to aliens deemed vital to security and conducting the war that included waterfront and key military, industrial, and defense areas). Although Roosevelt and Biddle would later overrule DeWitt, since Germans and Italians were "numerous, politically influential, well assimilated, and widely dispersed," all German, Italian, and Japanese aliens would nevertheless be evacuated from West Coast Category A areas by February 24. Category B areas would be restricted to aliens, but there was some confusion as to specifics: for example, enemy aliens had limited (restricted) use of the San Francisco–Oakland Bay Bridge (Category B), but all access points and approaches (Category A) to the bridge were prohibited to them. More significantly, as the War Department was wresting the initiative from the Justice Department, DeWitt pressed for large areas of the West Coast to be designated prohibited rather than just restricted and that citizens as well as enemy aliens be subject to removal. Where they would go nobody quite knew, and neither the War Department nor the Justice Department knew how to handle the thousands of persons displaced by this initial evacuation order.[24]

The January 29 Justice Department directive led to the forced evacuation of all enemy aliens from West Coast Category A areas. It established prohibited and restricted zones and regulated the movement of enemy aliens. Biddle's follow-up orders throughout February moved and placed further restrictions upon thousands of German, Italian, and Japanese aliens. Not until June 27 could European aliens return to their homes and jobs in the exclusion areas. For these evacuees, it took months before life returned to some semblance of normalcy. The California congressional delegation typified the mood of local and state politicians when it unanimously approved evacuating and interning (the "humane resettlement") all aliens and dual citizens, fearing that doing otherwise would invite a disaster even greater than Pearl Harbor.[25]

Germans and Italians were not relocated en masse from either coast as Roosevelt and key advisers carefully weighed their options. After the initial post–Pearl Harbor rush of emotions, most officials calmed down and calculated the economic, social, military, and political effects their decisions would have on waging the war both abroad and at home. Japanese Americans did not hold jobs vital to national defense. Additionally, "nearly four of every ten worked on small vegetable farms, and the rest were in domestic service or in businesses catering to a Japanese clientele." Few held white-collar or skilled blue-collar jobs due to discrimination. Politically unimportant and poorly assimilated, Japanese Americans lacked advocates. Only 130,000 resided in the continental United States, and most, 112,000, lived along the West Coast. The opposite was true for German and Italian Americans—they were far too numerous, politically important, and well assimilated, and sober officials understood the genuine impossibility of their mass relocation.[26]

Japanese Americans had long been the targets of racial discrimination, and legal barriers perpetuated cultural and physical differences. There were "laws against intermarriage with whites, legal exclusion from swimming pools and dance halls, and extralegal bars to employment and to middle-class housing districts." The 1924 Immigration Act prohibited further Japanese immigration and made the 47,000 Issei ineligible for naturalization. Many state laws had long denied Japanese Americans the right to vote and own land. They then had "no reason to absorb American concepts about civil liberties. Rejected by Americans, they clung to many of their old traditions."[27]

Roosevelt himself tempered relocation and internment policies. In the 1940 election, Republican Wendell Willkie campaigned well and picked up a substantial number of antiwar ballots cast by German, Irish, and Italian Americans. Roosevelt won, though by a much narrower margin than in the previous two elections, and there is little doubt that only the specter of war allowed him to win an unprecedented third term in office. FDR could not afford the personal and political cost of alienating German and Italian Americans as he once again assumed office during a crisis-filled atmosphere and perhaps entertained notions of running one more time if conditions permitted and the times required it.

Method in the Madness: Evacuation and Internment

A few individuals, some with strong preconceived ideas of enemy aliens and civilians, guided dual-coast evacuation and internment measures amid a complex chain of events. These included Generals Emmons, DeWitt, and Joyce; Assistant Secretary of State (Special Division) Long; Secretaries Hull, Stimson, and Knox; and Biddle, Hoover, and Roosevelt. Politics, economics, and the military threat, internal and external, affected the treatment of so-called domestic enemies. The public and media created an environment amenable to and supportive of government policies vis-à-vis enemy aliens and citizens. Although actions taken against German, Italian, and Japanese Americans during the crises weeks of early 1942 may have appeared haphazard and even chaotic, there was method in the madness.

While thousands of aliens endured incarceration as the threat of invasion and calls for evacuation from the West Coast peaked in the spring of 1942, thousands more remained largely unaffected by the West Coast mass evacuation. Officials who demanded the mass relocation and internment of all three enemy alien and citizen groups were rebuffed. To be sure, the consensus among top policymakers, including FDR himself, was that fifth columnists were dangerous. Yet locking up every potential subversive was simply out of the question.

Benevolence did not spare millions of German and Italian Americans living throughout the nation from mass relocation or over a hundred thousand Japanese Americans on the Hawaiian Islands from incarceration; rather, it was their great numbers and their economic, social, and political influence that did. German and Italian aliens were the overwhelming majority of the nation's enemy alien population. As the fortunes of war improved by the summer of 1942 and the likelihood of a West Coast invasion ebbed, the highly publicized removal of Japanese Americans along with sensational stories of interned dangerous Germans and Italians reassured the public, although authorities kept warning everyone to observe their neighbors' conduct. It was unnecessary, officials stressed, to relocate Germans and Italians en masse from major cities specifically and the East Coast generally because, unlike the Japanese, one could distinguish between the good and bad. Finally, with no East Coast peril and a greatly reduced West Coast threat, most Germans and Italians returned to their homes.[28]

Military Necessity: General DeWitt

Roosevelt and key officials argued that relocation and internment decisions were justified on military grounds. After Pearl Harbor, those charged with the nation's defense, including DeWitt and Hoover, took no chances. Preparations, years in the making, allowed the FBI and military to arrest and relocate suspected subversives quickly. Hyphenated Americans were caught in the crossfire of war. Recent immigrants who had escaped Hitler's Germany were arrested and interned because of their association with the Nazi regime. Others, victims of a hemispheric dragnet, found themselves rounded up in Central and South America, forcibly taken to the United States, charged with illegal entry, and then interned—pawns in an international alien exchange. Initially, nearly everyone wanted Italian and German aliens to be treated like the Japanese. Walter Lippmann, recalled Biddle, "came out on February 12 for evacuation of the West Coast. He did not mention Japanese Americans as such, and his logic would have had to include German and Italian American citizens as well as Japanese, which would have made a sizable evacuation."[29]

On February 1, DeWitt told Bendetsen that he wanted all German and all Italian alien enemies and all Japanese evacuated at the "earliest possible date." He deemed the Japanese the most dangerous: "We've waited too long. Get them all out." Governor Olson told fellow Californians in a well-publicized radio address on February 4: "It is known that there are Japanese residents of California who have sought to aid the Japanese enemy by way of communicating information, or have shown indications of preparations for fifth column activities." Over the next two days, Mayor Bowron similarly warned residents of Los Angeles: "Right here in our own city are those who may spring into action at an appointed time in accordance with a prearranged plan wherein each of our little Japanese friends will know his part in the event of any possible attempted invasion or air raid.... We cannot run the risk of another Pearl Harbor episode in Southern California."[30]

DeWitt perhaps had the greatest say relocating enemy aliens and citizens. Now sixty-two, he was nearing the end of a lengthy though relatively obscure career, having served in the Spanish-American War, Philippine campaigns, and World War I as a quartermaster and supply officer before becoming quartermaster general in the 1930s. In December 1939, as part of a series of initiatives designed to improve military readiness, the Army gave DeWitt command of the Fourth Army and the Ninth Corps Area. The War Department gave him and the three others, including General Hugh Drum (DeWitt's East Coast counterpart), great authority over their commands. From San Francisco's Presidio, DeWitt's WDC guarded America's coastline from Alaska to the Mexican border.[31]

DeWitt feared that members of the nation's thirty-five hundred Japanese organizations would aid a West Coast invasion—thought to be imminent—and knew that Admiral Husband E. Kimmel and General Walter C. Short, responsible for Hawaii's security, had been charged with dereliction of duty and their careers ended disgracefully. Now accountable for defending the entire West Coast, DeWitt received daily reports of Japanese surface and air units nearby. Learning from G-2 staff that subversives were aiding Japanese military efforts, he warned Rowe and Bendetsen of the Justice and War Departments in early January. Testifying before the House Naval Affairs Committee in April 1943, DeWitt insisted Japanese were dangerous and that there was no way to determine their loyalty. The subversive threat never abated, he felt, even with Allied air and naval superiority throughout the Pacific. In June 1944 the WDC reported that the Japanese, while only one-tenth of one percent of the nation's population, had "a highly developed and well integrated economic and social life." Intelligence agencies knew "the number and types of existing organizations" but focused only on those "suspected of being actually subversive." The report warned that "many activities indulged in prior to war take on a different significance during wartime."[32]

Military Necessity: West Coast

Guam fell on December 10, Wake Island on December 23, and Hong Kong on Christmas Day. If December was bad, January and February were worse, bringing news of Manila's capture and Singapore's fall. Most of the Allied navy was gone, destroyed in the Battle of the Java Sea. On the home front, as time went by without an attack or invasion, it seemed more likely that something major was in the works. On February 21, Earl Warren testified as much to the Tolan Committee:

> Unfortunately, many of our people and some of our authorities ... are of the opinion that because we have no sabotage and no fifth-column activities in this state since the beginning of the war that means that none have been planned for us. But ... that is the most ominous sign. ... The sabotage [and] fifth-column activities that we are to get are timed just like Pearl Harbor was timed and just like the invasion of France and of Denmark and of Norway and all of those other countries.

Missing warning signs, overlooking clues, and underestimating Japan's capabilities while overestimating America's own had proved costly. There had been radar blips, delayed messages, and the sinking of a midget submarine just outside the harbor entrance. The military "had not forgotten," Biddle later reflected, "that they had been caught with their pants down at Pearl Harbor" and, he continued, "did not propose to be put in that awkward position again, or to take any chances." Fear of sabotage was so great that General Short, commander of U.S. Army forces on Hawaii, misunderstood alerts and prepared for an internal attack—lining up his aircraft wingtip-to-wingtip. Robert Shivers, the FBI's Special Agent in Charge in Hawaii, later testified in front of the Roberts Commission: "If there should be an out-and-out attack on this island by the Japanese Navy, reinforced by their air arm . . . expect 95% of the alien Japanese to glory in that attack and to do anything they could to further the efforts of the Japanese forces. . . . Some second- and third-generation Japanese . . . American citizens . . . would join forces with the Japanese attackers. . . . Some of them may think they have suffered discrimination, economic, social, and otherwise."

All along the West Coast, confusion, misinformation, and false alarms followed Pearl Harbor. Fire-engine sirens woke San Francisco residents three times before dawn on December 8. Messages and reports placed the Japanese fleet anywhere from just off San Francisco to Los Angeles to San Diego, so DeWitt held emergency meetings with city defense councils. There was no doubt, he told reporters, that thirty Japanese carrier-based planes had flown over San Francisco the night before. Why no bombs fell and searchlights found no aircraft remained unknown. When reporters pressed, DeWitt angrily rebuffed them: "Death and destruction are likely to come to this city at any moment. These enemy planes were over our community. . . . They were tracked out to sea. . . . It might have been better if some bombs had dropped to awaken this city."[33]

Memories of Japan's treachery resurfaced in mid-December, when I-class subs patrolled from Cape Flattery, Washington, to San Diego, California. Sometimes operating within sight of land, these new long-range boats engaged several U.S. ships, striking fear into mariners and mainlanders alike. The first attack, on December 18, damaged the tanker *Samoa* off Eureka. Eight more attacks off California's coast resulted in two tankers sunk and one freighter damaged. Shore targets, including cities, could be next as the holidays neared. One Fort Ord officer wrote, "The little yellow bastards may try a fast one and bomb, sabotage, or shell this area." In fact, Japan's military tabled plans for shelling coastal cities on Christmas Eve, the same time a B-24 crew claimed to have sunk a submarine just fifty miles from the Columbia River's mouth. In February two Japanese subs reached the West Coast, and an anxious public and a nervous WDC overreacted to the shelling of oil-storage tanks near Santa Barbara on the night of February 23 just as FDR addressed the nation in his first fireside chat since Pearl Harbor.[34]

More than sixty-one million listened eagerly as Roosevelt explained a new kind of war. Many followed along with their maps as they learned of a global war on "every continent, every island, every sea, every air-lane in the world." No longer, Roosevelt disclosed, could the broad oceans protect America. The struggle would be protracted and against odds not unlike those which George Washington's troops once faced. FDR promised to stay the course and expressed ebullient confidence in ultimate victory. The speech strengthened the public's resolve. The *New York Times* remarked that the president's address was "one of the greatest" of his career. The following night the "Battle of Los Angeles" occurred as antiaircraft batteries opened up and pumped some fourteen hundred shells into the air trying to bring down what turned out to be a stray weather balloon. Nevertheless, citizens knew that both they and the military were at war.[35]

Earl Warren had been looking at maps too—especially ones revealing a "disturbing situation" in California. According to Warren's testimony before the Tolan Committee, "From Marin County [just north of San Francisco] to the Mexican border virtually every important strategic location and installation has one or more Japanese in its immediate vicinity. . . . Undoubtedly, the presence of many of these persons in their present locations is mere coincidence, but it would seem equally beyond doubt that the presence of others is not coincidence. . . . Some of our airplane factories in this state are entirely surrounded by Japanese." On April 23 the War Department warned DeWitt, who in turn alerted coastal residents to expect an attack or invasion. General Marshall's staff anticipated carrier-based strikes along the coast, in the Aleutians, or on Alaska itself. Roosevelt issued Executive Order 9165 the following month, protecting "essential facilities from sabotage and other destructive acts." Japan's attack upon the Aleutian Islands in June, followed by its occupation of Attu and Kiska, increased fears of further attacks aided by West Coast Japanese Americans.[36]

Military Necessity: The Internal Threat

Officials feared sabotage, yet targeting aliens could turn them into quislings, deny much-needed skills and labor, and give the Axis an "excuse for retaliation" against Americans abroad. Roosevelt's January 14, 1942, proclamation required all (now enemy) aliens to reregister and obtain a certificate of identification. The Department of Justice's Enemy Alien Unit would carry out the program, and so, on February 1, Biddle announced that the Justice Department had begun "identifying all German, Italian, and Japanese aliens, 14 years or older," adding:

> The identification program is another part of the job of making America safe. Because of the disloyal few, the many must be inconvenienced. They must submit to certain blanket regulations . . . where they may go and where not . . . permission for travel. The identification program is a necessary part of our wartime protection.
>
> Your government is taking every precaution against espionage, sabotage, or fifth column activities. . . . Persecution can easily drive people, now loyal to us, into fifth column activity. Economic discrimination against loyal aliens deprives us of important skills and manual labor. . . . Let's not give the Axis countries any excuse for retaliation against innocent Americans living abroad.
>
> The great majority of so-called enemy aliens came to our shores to escape persecution, enjoy democracy, and raise their children in a free world. These people are loyal to our ideals and our government. Let's encourage that loyalty.

Biddle referenced initial steps, including the June 28, 1940, Alien Registration Act, that dealt with subversive activities and sabotage, alien groups to be deported, and the fingerprinting and registration of all aliens. That drive began on August 27 and concluded on December 26. The INS received over three million requests for information, many from employers holding war contracts. Such initial steps had laid the groundwork for those taken after Pearl Harbor. The program had come a long way, as within a few weeks of Biddle's announcement nearly one million had reregistered, having answered additional questions such as "whether they had relatives living abroad or serving in the armed forces of a foreign country."[37]

For anxious officials charged with the nation's defense, such steps had come just in time. During the summer of 1942, spectacular events taking place along the eastern seaboard showed that the enemy could come ashore, change clothes, and, with the help of sympathizers, destroy the nation from within as doomsayers had warned. It mattered little that the so-called invasion was pathetic, ineffectual, and downright farcical; it mattered much that invaders had crossed the ocean, scrambled onto shore, mingled with locals, and tried to do harm. Fear and a heightened sense of vulnerability supported relocating and interning enemy aliens and civilians.

On June 27, Hoover held a press conference and announced that the FBI had hunted down and captured German saboteurs; two days later the *New York Daily News* ran the headline "FBI Captures 8: German Agents Landed by Subs." Extensive and detailed coverage of the events and subsequent trial electrified the nation and brought Hoover unprecedented praise, including petitions for the Medal of Honor. The announcement reassured the public yet worried others. On July 7, members of the Counterintelligence Group of the Military Intelligence Division met to discuss security matters. Under the auspices of the PMG since October 29, 1941, the MID investigated applicants for military jobs and employees with access to classified information, worked on the military's "Counter Fifth Column Plan," and coordinated with the PMG's Internal Security Division. Both now agreed that, to date, "very few and minor instances of sabotage that could be attributed to hostile subversives" had occurred. Yet these and other investigative agencies argued that the absence of subversion likely indicated that the fifth column was "highly disciplined and possibly waiting for a zero hour when a concerted, well-planned major sabotage attack against war production may take place." Such fears, however ungrounded and illogical, were buoyed by submarines off-loading spies and saboteurs.[38]

West Coast Relocation and Hawaiian Pragmatism

Executive Order 9066 forced 20,000 Italian and German aliens along with 100,000 West Coast Japanese to move from newly designated prohibited areas in February and March 1942. Deciding what to do with thousands of suspected disloyals was tricky. DeWitt and others had incomplete, unreliable, or even erroneous information under stressful and changing circumstances. All the while, nobody wanted another Pearl Harbor. Generals DeWitt and Joyce, therefore, intended to evacuate all German and Italian Americans from all prohibited zones. On January 8, two admirals responsible for coastal defense likewise urged removing all enemy aliens along with those Japanese American citizens who could not prove "actual severance of all allegiance to the Japanese government" and urged that they be "classified as enemy aliens."[39]

Americans calling for action against Hawaii's Japanese joined those demanding the evacuation of West Coast Japanese. Since December 19, Navy Secretary Frank Knox had been advocating the mass removal of Japanese from Oahu to other Hawaiian Islands. A White House discussion dealing with Stimson's concern about the "dangerous Japanese in Hawaii" took place on January 30 and then continued among high-ranking military officers and cabinet members who wrestled with the "delicate and dangerous" situation over the next ten days or so. On February 12, William Donovan and Atherton Richards, two of Roosevelt's key advisers, also favored evacuation based on the Japanese threat to Hawaii's security, while General Marshall recommended against relocating Oahu's or Hawaii's 100,000-plus Japanese en masse and instead urged the immediate evacuation of only the most dangerous 20,000. Knox agreed. On February 27 Stimson surprised FDR, who had anticipated that the Japanese, at least on Oahu, "should be removed," by shrewdly arguing against any large-scale evacuation and neatly summarizing the pragmatic reasons why. By March 13 FDR had backed down, though he felt that the military could relocate those 20,000 most dangerous Japanese. Yet here, too, the president deferred to reality, and in the end Stimson's rational approach carried the day and only 1,100 Japanese, along with dozens of Germans and Italians, went to mainland camps. Selective action meant minimal disruption to Hawaii's economy and America's war effort.[40]

The nation could ill-afford disrupting the flow of goods to the front or antagonizing substantial portions of its own population. Whereas the Japanese were a small, powerless minority on the vulnerable West Coast, they constituted the largest portion of Hawaii's plantation workforce and, at nearly 40 percent of the population, an indispensable part of the overall economy in a place under martial law and teeming with soldiers. Although the FBI had already arrested and relocated several thousand "dangerous" persons, including Germans and Italians, on June 7, following the Battle of Midway, DeWitt announced that the removal of 100,000 Japanese from Military Area No. 1 was complete. With that, Speaker of the House John McCormack asked about Hawaii's Japanese. Stimson responded: "Our greatest difficulty in dealing with the problem is the economic aspect. The Japanese population is so interwoven into the economic fabric of the Islands that if we attempted to evacuate all Japanese aliens and citizens all business, including that concerned with the building up of our defenses, would practically stop."[41]

West Coast to East Coast

The War Department initially intended to handle German and Japanese Americans exactly the same. Believing Germany was behind the Pearl Harbor attack strengthened the argument to deal with German aliens first; some, even on the West Coast, considered them the greater threat. But the 20,000 Nazi refugees there along with another 112,000 on the East Coast mattered. Thousands avoided forced evacuation or incarceration as the government determined who had fled Hitler's Germany as exiles versus those who posed as wolves in sheep's clothing. Officials often assumed aliens were a security risk. "Nazis have been exploiting the 'Jewish refugee' problem for the purpose of espionage and other subversive activities in the Western Hemisphere," argued Hoover.[42]

The goal, above all, was "our ultimate victory." Winning the war was the top priority. On February 7, Biddle shared with FDR his concerns about events and the effect West Coast Japanese policies would have on East Coast Germans and Italians:

> We believed mass evacuation at this time inadvisable, that the FBI was not staffed to perform it . . . there were no reasons for mass evacuation and I thought the army should be directed to prepare a detailed plan of evacuation in case of . . . an air raid or attempted landing on the West Coast. I emphasized the danger of the hyste-

ria, which we were beginning to control, moving east and affecting the Italian and German population in Boston and New York. Generally, he approved, being fully aware of the dreadful risk of Fifth Column retaliation in case of a raid.[43]

In May, Roosevelt, Biddle, Stimson, McCloy, DeWitt, Hull, and New York lieutenant governor Charles Poletti, among others, discussed expanding EO 9066 to include the East Coast, allowing for the mass apprehension and evacuation of enemy aliens and citizens there. Gullion proposed extending the military area (exclusion zone) across the nation, thereby regulating the residence and movement of several million aliens and citizens. Discussions also focused on the West Coast and the Hawaiian Islands. Remarkable consistencies in policies and practices emerged, as Biddle noted on May 14:

> I am very much opposed to any ... mass evacuation of ... the East Coast area. It would be bad for national morale; it would seriously interfere with the war production program; and it would inflict a very great injustice upon hundreds of thousands of innocent people whose continued loyalty, and there has never been any serious question of their loyalty, is essential to our ultimate victory.
>
> There are approximately 706,000 non-citizens of German, Italian, or Japanese nationality ... in the sixteen states comprising the Eastern Defense Command: 514,172 Italians, 189,190 Germans, and 3,373 Japanese. Add to this number the children and family members who are American citizens, and you have a total in excess of 1,100,000. We could not possibly evacuate any such number of persons, as was done with the Japanese on the Pacific Coast, without the most serious consequences.
>
> The FBI has apprehended the disloyal and dangerous enemy aliens—a total of about 8,000 out of 1,100,000, or seven-tenths of one percent! There is no evidence of organized, enemy-instigated sabotage, and no reason to suspect our enemy alien population of disloyalty.[44]

Millions of German and Italian immigrants lived along the East Coast. Five million out of New York City's seven million residents were immigrants or their children, and hundreds of thousands of these were Germans and Italians. Many, including Hugh DeLacy, chairman of the American Committee for Protection of Foreign Born, argued, "America must have the utmost support and sacrifice of every single person in the country." New York's immigrant population was especially important: "They can strengthen tremendously our victory effort and it is essential that every handicap to the complete mobilization of the foreign born be eliminated." Officials knew this, and a liberal exclusion policy resulted.[45]

General Hugh Drum's Eastern Defense Command (EDC) was in charge of fifty-two million persons spread out over fifteen entire states, most of Florida (minus the Panhandle), and the District of Columbia. On May 16, Drum issued Public Proclamation No. 1, noting that the EDC was "inhabited by millions of loyal citizens and hundreds of thousands of persons not yet citizens" and that "the economic life of this large portion" of the population "should be disturbed as little as may be consistent with national defense and internal security." Since the Atlantic and Gulf Coasts were "particularly subject to attack and espionage and acts of sabotage," this would require "the adoption of military measures necessary to establish safeguards against such hostile operations."[46]

On April 22, Stimson had picked Drum to carry out the duties imposed by EO 9066 for the EDC. All Selective Service Boards, post offices, courthouses, and town halls within the entire Eastern Military Area would display for public inspection the full text of the proclamation on posters, which included a strict warning: "Willful violation of any such restriction or order by an alien enemy, or repeated careless violations, even if not willful, are cause for expulsion, internment, or prosecution; similar violations by persons other than alien enemies are cause for expulsion or prosecution."[47] Drum's proclamation established the EDC's unilateral authority to relocate, intern, or prosecute foreign nationals as well as expel or prosecute citizens, and it confirmed the Justice Department's authority over enemy aliens. The government relocated thousands of German and Italian aliens and interned thousands more from the East Coast. Most, feeling they had little choice, went without a fight. Others did not.

On May 7, 1943, Olga Schueller, age fifty-three, had had enough. She and a hundred others living in and near Philadelphia now had to "leave the vicinity for sections of the country where they could not jeopardize the war effort." Schueller decided to defy Drum's April 26 order to quit the region. Her plight caught the attention of the *New York Times*. "The case of Mrs. Schueller," the *Times* reported, "was said to be the first of its kind on the Eastern coast, although hundreds of aliens and citizens have been transported inland by the government from the West Coast since the war began." In an unprecedented act, Schueller challenged the order in court, claiming that Congress had abrogated its legislative power to General Drum and that the exclusion order violated her right to due process under the Fifth Amendment. She did not want to leave her home of fifteen years.

A resident of the United States since 1911 and a citizen since 1920, Schueller had one son serving in the Navy and another working in the Edward Budd Manufacturing Company plant, a vital war production center. Yet she now had, per Drum's order, just ten days to leave not just Philadelphia but the coast. What about her restaurant? She told reporters: "If I went away it would look to my customers and friends as though I had done something. I haven't done anything." When asked about allegations of subversive ties, she responded: "It is true that I am president of the ladies' auxiliary to the Bavarian Charity Society. I am also an officer of the German-American Federation, that was at one time known as the Central Bund, but when the war came along, we dropped the German title. What's the matter with that? The members are patriotic American citizens."[48]

Enemy Alien Challenges

A *Japanese American Daily News* article of February 7, 1942, reflected the growing sense of hopelessness. A wave of hate after the "backstab Sunday at Pearl Harbor" increased in fury, threatening to engulf California's Japanese: "They're all alike, you can't trust any of them!" Denying this, the author argued that thousands of Japanese are citizens "loyal only to the United States. They have no ties in Japan. Their love of democracy is sincere and genuine." As proof, many offered to move inland voluntarily before conditions worsened. Frank Ohye, a Japanese-born resident who had lived in California since 1919, proposed the following:

> Evacuate all Japanese from California; place them on government farms east of the Rocky Mountains for the production of vegetables and other foods needed in the defense of America.... In the status of selective service, they could be of more service to the country, and family groups could remain together. It would also do away with complications that now arise where they intermingle with Americans of other races. As loyal Americans, we desire to do what is best for our country.[49]

German and Italian Americans faced similar challenges. Hoover's FBI had arrested over seven hundred German and Italian aliens by December 9. The federal government had moved thousands of them too from the West Coast and thousands more from selected East Coast areas based on their potential threat to defense installations and industrial centers. They, like their Japanese counterparts, felt humiliated, outraged, or betrayed, and wrote to the Roosevelts, the State and Justice Departments, congressional representatives, state officials, or anyone who might help. Ennis's AECU and James Rowe's office received and responded to those letters, including those of Mr. B. Eiteneuer, who had lived in Oakland, California, for twenty-nine of his thirty-one years in the States when he was "branded an 'alien enemy.'" On February 9 he wrote: "Mr. President, I have never been nor do I ever intend to be an enemy of this nation. I have never by word or deed committed an act unfriendly to this government nor have I ever belonged to any organization or associated with anyone hostile to this country." Eiteneuer had left Germany at fourteen; he sailed on different ships for several years before coming to America at age twenty-one. In 1911 he took his first citizenship papers and served in the U.S. Cutter Service (later the Coast Guard) and the U.S. Naval Auxiliary Service, both of which honorably discharged him.

Eiteneuer conceded that "our country must be safeguarded and protected from dangers within as well as without" but hoped the government would not be "harsh and cruel to those not deserving such treatment." For the loyal thousands, he proposed the following:

> Permit . . . alien enemies . . . conducting themselves as good citizens and will bear strict investigation and can give a satisfactory account of their activities to take an oath of allegiance to the United States. Let them retain their homes and work to help this country. . . . I am willing to take this oath. . . . I ask to work and defend this country and prove my good will. I offer my services . . . in the armed forces or civilian defense. Consider my suggestion, from my heart—God bless America.[50]

Refusing to Fight

Unscrupulous motives influenced internment policies. Aliens were arrested and interned for refusing to fight the Axis. The lack of evidence in most cases was often so obvious that in October 1942 it drew the attention of Edwin Clapp of the Attorney General's Office, who informed Edward Ennis:

> Military Intelligence in New York has been submitting . . . the names of alien enemies who indicated to their Draft Boards that they would not fight against one or more of the Axis nations. On this basis and following an examination by U.S. Attorneys . . . these alien enemies have been sent to Ellis Island for deportation pending hearings and presidential warrants.
>
> In almost all cases, there is no further derogatory information presented or developed. In spite of all this, the U.S. Attorneys and their Hearing Boards appear to consider this sufficient for internment . . . of every alien enemy who is not willing to fight against the country of his birth.[51]

Clapp spoke with Harold Kennedy, an attorney for New York's Eastern District, who noted that "the alien enemy procedure might well deprive the Army and the civilian war effort of the services of persons otherwise able-bodied and capable of performing many valuable functions." While the "facts upon which the warrants were requested were exceptionally brief," Kennedy admitted, "they represented the opinion of experienced Assistants who would not care to be responsible for the release of the subjects." Under the circumstances, Clapp conceded, attorneys could issue warrants.[52]

Many aliens had a tough choice: fight or face internment. On November 19, Clapp informed Ennis that the FBI and the Army were applying considerable pressure upon the United States Attorneys' offices in New York City. Kennedy's office wanted an AECU policy statement "where the sole charge is the refusal to fight." Clapp noted the request's seriousness:

> The name of every alien enemy who objects to military service is transmitted automatically to MID, FBI, and the U.S. Attorney. Kennedy takes the position that refusal to fight for the United States indicates a divided allegiance and a sympathy to the enemy cause which merits internment. I only know of one alien enemy who refused to fight whom Kennedy's office has not prosecuted to the hilt.
>
> The Alien Enemy Program was not designed to enforce the Selective Service Law. That certainly is the only valid ground upon which any action against most of these subjects can be based. As long as the Department of Justice will process these persons who object to fighting, the Army will continue to refer them to us.
>
> Note Willie Brandt. [Kennedy's office represented] Brandt as a dangerous alien enemy. Now Brandt has been inducted into the Army and his dangerousness has disappeared. From Kennedy's office comes this: "I do not believe that this man is dangerous or potentially dangerous to the national security. I held him principally on the ground that he refused to fight in the armed forces of the United States."
>
> The problem of the alien enemy who refuses to fight can be solved by other agencies without subverting the Alien Enemy Program and depriving the Army and civilian population of the services of willing and able-bodied alien enemies.

Clapp then wrote to Kennedy directly regarding the Nicola Gelao case:

> An alien enemy's refusal to fight is based on any number of divergent reasons.... In relatively few of these cases is there any real internal security problem involved. To apprehend all such individuals with a view to interning them for the duration seems a perversion of the powers of the Alien Enemy Program.
>
> This is not to be taken as an indication that nothing should be done.... Where there is a genuine internal security problem, I

believe it should be treated as such. Where such does not exist, alien enemy proceedings should not be instituted.[53]

Reinhold Niebuhr, professor of theology at Union Theological Seminary, raised similar concerns. Niebuhr wrote Biddle on behalf of a German émigré, Arnold Borsig, who had arrived in 1929 on a visitor's visa and learned that "he must choose between entering the Army or being interned." Niebuhr knew Borsig well and assured Biddle that there was "absolutely no question about his honesty or integrity as an opponent of the Nazi regime." Ultimately, Niebuhr concluded, "internment would be the wasting of a man. Émigrés of his type are being used effectively outside of military service." Clapp forwarded a copy of Niebuhr's letter to Ennis with the caption "FIGHT OR INTERN!!"[54]

All aliens completed a questionnaire, and men answered whether they objected to military service; those who did were classified as 4-C, unacceptable for induction. FBI agents then used executive warrants to "search the alien enemy's premises and question him," after which they were "almost automatically ordered detained at Ellis Island pending hearing." Clapp stated that "the vice of the procedure . . . lies in the fact that refusal to fight is made the basis for an immediate apprehension without clarification of the subject's reasons and without any investigation. If any of the persons so apprehended were really dangerous, it would be next to impossible to discover it." He concluded:

> The ideal solution would be the removal of these individuals from the civilian population and their employment in some useful capacity. Every alien enemy reported as objecting to military service should be made the subject of a complete investigation. If . . . sufficient to warrant internment, the subject should be processed as an ordinary alien enemy. All others, including those paroled or released by the Attorney General, should be inducted. This would solve all the problems.[55]

Dangerousness

Hoover thought the Justice Department was paroling or releasing too many aliens, especially former members of "dangerous" organizations, prior to their hearings. He requested that hundreds of cases "be reviewed and that orders of internment be entered." A February 1942 circular, he noted, listed organizations "subject to the direct control of radical nationalistic elements." An alien enemy, "even without active participation . . . should be interned unless there are special countervailing factors." Hoover railed: "Membership in these militaristic groups, which have openly assisted the Japanese war effort, should be seriously considered when it involves the Issei, the vast majority of whom are undoubtedly loyal to their mother country. It is not believed that the internal security is strengthened by the release or parole of individuals who have proven their loyalty to Japan. . . . It is urged that each of these cases be reviewed and interment ordered for all of these aliens."[56]

Despite Hoover's warnings, Biddle and Ennis increasingly viewed the FBI's methods as unlawful and ineffectual. By the summer of 1943, Biddle had had enough and informed Hoover and Assistant Attorney General Hugh Cox:

> These individual danger classifications . . . serve no useful purpose. The detention of alien enemies is being dealt with by the Alien Enemy Control Unit. . . . There is no statutory authorization or other justification for keeping a "custodial detention" list of citizens. . . . This classification system is inherently unreliable. The evidence used was inadequate; the standards . . . defective; and . . . to make a valid determination as to how dangerous a person is in the abstract without reference to . . . relevant circumstances is impractical, unwise, and dangerous. I direct that the classifications should not be used for any purpose.
>
> A copy of this memo should be placed in the file of each person who has been given a classification. Each card should be stamped with the following: "This Classification is Unreliable. It is hereby Cancelled, and should not be used."

Biddle's explicit directive did not stop Hoover. He technically complied and on August 14 instructed SACs that henceforth

> investigations of individuals (other than alien enemies) who may be dangerous or potentially dangerous to the public safety or internal

security of the United States shall be a "Security Matter" not "Custodial Detention." The phraseology, "Custodial Detention," shall no longer be used to designate the character of the investigation.

Security Index cards . . . should be considered as strictly confidential, and should at no time be mentioned or alluded to in investigative reports, or discussed with agencies or individuals outside the Bureau other than . . . representatives of the Office of Naval Intelligence and the Military Intelligence Service.

Hoover kept up the extralegal practices by not using the FBI's central records. Unaware of this, Ennis informed Biddle on December 3 that many of those arrested or interned had been released, especially after case reviews, and assured him that "applications for review are denied in the more serious cases," but "in other cases, applications for review are processed by reconsidering the file." Rehearing involved a special hearing board composed of "the most able board members" at the internment camps where it "has the benefit of the conduct record of the internee and the views of the custodial authorities." The results went to the original hearing board for its input before any possible change in the internees' status. After tabulating the results of the special hearings, Ennis found that "in 75% of the cases the order is changed and usually from internment to parole."[57]

Good aliens were often judged bad Americans. Eleanor Roosevelt, after reading the *New York Times* article "Some Useful 'Enemy Aliens,'" asked Biddle's help for those like anti-fascist writers Brecht, Remarque, and Feuchtwanger as Thomas Cooley vented to Ennis:

A recurrent item . . . is the influx of FBI memoranda protesting the action recommended by the hearing boards and the Attorney General. . . . The hearing board in this case, at which an agent of the Bureau was present, recommended parole. . . . After review, the Attorney General entered an order upholding the board's recommendation. . . . Hoover addressed a memo to the Attorney General, sending copies to Mr. Ennis, suggesting that the facts set forth therein should be reconsidered and the subject's internment ordered for the duration of the war. Hearsay testimony was introduced. There was no supporting data.

Nowhere is there any mention of the facts (1) that both the alien's sons are at present serving in the United States armed forces (2) that the subject is a member of a society called the Alpenland and (3) that the subject has made a second effort to become a citizen since the expiration of his first papers about 1930.

Allegations about his pro-Nazi attitude have been made. Some of the hearsay is plainly erroneous and the hearing board concluded that he could safely be paroled. The memo is only a partial and inaccurate statement. Omission of any favorable evidence and tendency to present anonymous hearsay as proven facts clearly prevent it from fulfilling [its] function. Its concluding recommendation clearly exaggerates legitimate inferences from available evidence.[58]

8

Internment, Repatriation, and Exchange

> We could not obtain the release of our own citizens from enemy control unless we exchanged their citizens for them, and amongst those citizens the enemy powers will naturally insist, just as we have insisted, that persons of certain qualities and desirability be exchanged.
>
> —SECRETARY OF STATE CORDELL HULL TO ROOSEVELT, AUGUST 27, 1942

During the war, the United States government orchestrated and implemented an extensive movement of people. The results were impressive. Moving tens of thousands of civilians during turbulent and hazardous times required coordination and cooperation. The State Department's Special Division was established on September 1, 1939, to deal with the diplomatic problems arising from increasing tensions in Europe. This included handling large numbers of Americans held by enemy nations along with foreign nationals, many of whom were believed dangerous and residing throughout the Western Hemisphere. Repatriation efforts began before U.S. entry in the war and continued during and after it. With careful advanced planning, State Department officials from 1936 through 1941 addressed diplomatic missions and consular establishments, and suggested how the repatriation of U.S. nationals and related problems might best be handled. Officers in the field had arranged, as circumstances permitted, to protect and assist Americans living abroad.[1]

Great War precedents, fifth-column fears, and protecting Americans abroad influenced the individual internment program. Authorities arrested and interned citizens and aliens due to their "dangerousness." Internees were subject to repatriation and exchange. As bartered commodities, ensuring their benevolent treatment meant that belligerents closely scrutinized the treatment their nationals received and promised reciprocity—humane treatment if all went well and reprisals if there was maltreatment. Belligerent nations applied the tenets of the Geneva Prisoners of War Convention of 1929 to all civilians, including internees, yet the possibility of neglect or abuse always existed. The State and Justice Departments as well as the FBI arrested, incarcerated, and deported thousands throughout the Americas. The ONI, MID (G-2), AECU, and FBI (the four protective agencies) collaborated and then cleared or detained potential repatriates as the State Department negotiated internee exchanges with Germany and Japan.[2]

Repatriation was either voluntary or forced. Some willingly joined the internee head of family, but most were coerced. National and international conditions influenced the growth and development of the internment, repatriation, and exchange of thousands throughout Europe, Asia, and the Americas. Exchanging civilians, diplomats, and POWs among European belligerents began in the spring of 1940, while repatriating destitute Americans began in September 1939 and continued throughout 1940 and 1941.[3]

The initial deportations established a basic repatriation framework. The foreign affairs ministers of the American republics met in Rio de Janeiro from January 15 to January 28, 1942, and affirmed their solidarity and cooperation. They approved severing diplomatic relations with the Axis powers, coordinating police and judicial measures, controlling dangerous aliens, and investigating acts of espionage, sabotage, and subversive propaganda. The United States would act as a liaison between Latin American nations and Germany and Japan, helping with exchange efforts, while the ministers organized the Emergency Advisory Committee for Political Defense (CPD), which coordinated hemispheric security measures, including deporting dangerous Axis nationals to the United States for temporary detention in exchange for their own nationals. Meetings in Washington DC during July and August 1943 further defined inter-American internment and repatriation policies. Resolving logistical, legal, political, and diplomatic issues would be a complex and lengthy undertaking—lasting well after the cessation of hostilities.[4]

Beginnings

Germany's invasion of Poland set into motion a flurry of events. State Department officials, including Adolf Berle, George Messersmith, Sumner Welles, and Cordell Hull, discussed assisting Americans in areas affected by war. Roosevelt created and then asked Breckinridge Long to head the State Department's new Special Division, which received $500,000 to help repatriate Americans. Yet Long was stingy doling out money and thought tourists "caught in a jam" should fend for themselves and not criticize "the government's inability to evacuate them." Despite such personal feelings and the Special Division's many obstacles, during the final months of 1939 over 75,000 foreign nationals and Americans returned from Europe. While there were still nearly 51,000 Americans in Europe by May 1941, the Special Division, which began operations on September 1, 1939, with only twelve Foreign Service officers and nineteen clerks and stenographers, helped return 130,000 Americans by January 1941.[5]

During the spring of 1940, Britain and Germany exchanged thousands of nationals. When Belgium, the Netherlands, and France collapsed in May and June the exchanges stopped; as conditions stabilized a few months later, they resumed on a much greater scale. By December the State Department authorized repatriating imperiled or destitute Americans from occupied France. First Secretary Maynard B. Barnes of the U.S. Embassy in Paris reported to Washington the results of recent repatriation efforts. Special railway cars kept the movements hidden as American Red Cross and American Express Company personnel accompanied persons from Paris, Nantes, and Bordeaux to the Portuguese border, where Lisbon officials met them. German military authorities granted group exit visas. The exchanges and evacuations required cooperation and coordination among many nations as well as organizations and agencies, public and private, national and international. The State Department reminded Germany and Britain:

> During 1914–1918, nearly all belligerents interned enemy aliens. This meant widespread and unnecessary suffering to thousands of innocent persons. It evolved . . . into a general practice as a consequence of reprisals. . . . It was unjust to punish these unfortunates. . . . Just as nations have abandoned the idea that prisoners of war are hostages for the good behavior of the enemy, so the same idea in respect to civilians might be held.[6]

Many internees were released quickly. From January 1939 to January 1941 more than 30,000 Americans returned from Europe along with 2,500 from the Far East. By October 1940, with Japan occupying much of China and northern French Indochina, the ss *Mariposa*, *President Coolidge*, and *Monterey* returned Americans from Hong Kong, Beijing, and Chinwangtao. Over the next year the American President Lines diverted five of its ships to take Americans to San Francisco, the State Department provided loans, and the Maritime Commission compensated owners or operators of private vessels who helped. In the spring and summer of 1942, the first of several global exchanges took place as 40,000 Americans remained in Europe and 7,000 were in the Far East.[7]

Hemispheric Planning

Foreign affairs ministers from twenty-one nations in the Western Hemisphere met in Rio de Janeiro from January 15 to January 28, 1942, to articulate their resolve and solidarity. They organized the CPD to coordinate hemispheric security measures, including deporting Axis nationals to the United States for temporary detention in exchange for their own nationals. Delegates also discussed strategic materials, transportation facilities, their economies, and relations with the Axis. They addressed subversive activities and enemy aliens, and emphasized hemispheric political cooperation, military preparedness, and economic collaboration. The CPD reiterated its "complete solidarity and determination to cooperate jointly for mutual protection" until the war's end:

Acts of aggression of non-military character, including systematic espionage, sabotage, and subversive propaganda are being committed, inspired by and under the direction of the Tripartite Pact and states subservient to them, and the fate of formerly free nations of Europe has shown them to be both preliminary to and an integral part of a program of military aggression.[8]

The CPD would establish and enforce "extraordinary measures of continental defense." Latin American officials, like their counterparts to the north, felt threatened and sought to "maintain and expand" their surveillance systems to prevent subversive activities by foreign nationals, as individuals or groups, "that originate in or are directed from a foreign country" and are intended "to interfere with the efforts of the American Republics to preserve their integrity and independence." Furthermore, the republics should combat anti-democratic propaganda and control "organizations directed or supported by non-American States . . . whose activities are harmful to American security . . . and terminate their existence if they are centers of totalitarian propaganda."[9]

All aliens registered with and regularly reported to authorities who strictly supervised and controlled them—detaining, interning, or restricting their movements. Enemy nationals could not possess or use aircraft, firearms, explosives, radios, or have "implements of warfare, propaganda, espionage, or sabotage." Aliens faced limitations on travel and residency changes (unless moved by decree) and could have nothing to do with Axis organizations or interests. On the other hand, the CPD sought to protect all non-dangerous aliens so they could live and work without discrimination or other abuses.

The committee punished obstructionists and required full disclosure of any ties to political parties, clubs, societies, and institutions—whether social, humanitarian, sporting, educational, technical, or charitable—directed or supported by any non-American nation. Suspects were surveilled. Preventing the spread of fascist ideology, sabotage, or espionage was top priority, so the CPD recommended detaining or interning suspicious persons for the war's duration. These potential troublemakers could then be swapped for nationals in Nazi-occupied Europe. Member states coordinated police and judicial functions, and a database of registered enemy aliens and civilians later helped deport uncooperative Germans, including those indicted or condemned for international offenses or subversive activities. Believing that Germany had organized and coordinated hemispheric espionage and sabotage efforts, delegates wanted to stymie such threats.[10]

To present a unified front, representatives shelved local or regional conflicts. Their efforts laid the groundwork for an inter-American internment and exchange program that soon targeted all Germans, viewing national identity as proof of guilt. The Justice and State Departments drafted resolutions that specifically mentioned deporting persons "to another American republic for detention when adequate local detention facilities are lacking." The United States was taking charge of hemispheric security, offering to pay for the removal, transportation, and incarceration of enemy nationals, and promising cooperating nations the inclusion of their respective officials and nationals in any exchange with the Axis. From the outset, more than a dozen states cooperated, and even Argentina, the last holdout, was arranging to swap Japanese diplomats for its own when the war ended.[11]

Exaggerated fears of and poor information about seditious activities guided internment efforts, as did the vast scope and direction of the U.S.-led deportation, detention, repatriation, and exchange program. Efforts focused on arresting, interning, and expelling dangerous Germans but also included Japanese and some Italians. Aside from Peru's and Panama's Japanese focus, authorities aimed to get rid of Nazi operatives. Most viewed German and Japanese Americans, especially aliens, as the greatest threat nationally and Germans hemispherically. By war's end the FBI arrested 16,062 aliens, among them 7,043 Germans, 3,567 Italians, and 5,428 Japanese, and had 360 agents acting as attachés in embassies throughout Latin America to assist national police forces. Washington pressured its good neighbors to combat the alleged threat aggressively, and most did so by forcibly deporting 6,610 persons (4,058 Germans, 288 Italians, and 2,264 Japanese) to the United States and thousands more directly to Europe and Asia.[12]

Sounding the Tocsin

Washington had little confidence that any Latin American nation could control its own alien enemy population. Policymakers regarded their southern counterparts as mildly apathetic at best and grossly negligent at worst. By February 1942, most anticipated a hemispheric calamity. Military strategists predicted leaders of Axis cells recruiting and leading hundreds of thousands, even millions, of Germans and Japanese against national governments. The United States therefore took charge of hemispheric security and pressured other nations to follow suit as the CPD rubber-stamped its initiatives.[13]

Latin American propagandists warned of impending danger, urged their respective governments to act, and appealed to Washington for help. As with their fellow northern activists and alarmists, the themes used and predictions made were strikingly similar. Hugo Fernández Artucio, an activist, broadcaster, and lecturer, traveled from Uruguay to warn Americans of the Nazi menace. Thousands of German soldiers, he announced, were "distributed throughout" the continent's "political underground." Adolfo Tejera exaggerated Nazi economic and propaganda efforts in his 1938 novel *Penetración Nazi en America Latina*. Argentine writer Ernesto Giudici compiled selected anti-fascist articles he had written for *Crítica*, the most popular Spanish daily in the world, in *Hitler Conquers America* and detailed Nazi economic and political advances.[14]

Other popular writers echoed such concerns. Journalist Carleton Beals was perhaps the leading Latin America watcher of the day. "It is Hitler's boast," Beals warned in *The Coming Struggle for Latin America* (1938), "that when he has subdued Europe," Latin America "will drop into his hands like an over-ripe fruit." Chapters such as "Swastika over the Andes" and "Don Quixote Rides the Pampas" highly embellished potential dangers. John Gunther also highlighted such mysteries and intrigues: *Inside Latin America* (1941) was the classic study of Central and South America and became a top-ten best-seller in 1941 and 1942. Gunther reflected, "I traveled 18,938 miles by air and by train, boat, and car. There are twenty different republics . . . I visited them all." He met seventeen presidents and many ordinary people before conveying two key findings: first, do not expect "advanced political development from people who live perpetually at 12,500 feet"; and second, Latinos were rather indifferent about German subversives. While at a dinner in Bogotá, he explained, "I hoped to hear about the Fifth Column and the Panama Canal, but no one would talk about anything except Marcel Proust."[15]

Fears of Axis hemispheric intrigues abated little over time. The July 1940 *Newsweek* exposé "Nazi Pipeline" related clandestine German activities of July 1915, briefcase contents that "disclosed a vast espionage system," with recent "secret packages found on two alleged German undercover agents . . . a new Nazi diplomatic pipeline from San Francisco through Central America," and "200 Reich technicians, chemists, businessmen, and diplomatic passport holders" in Latin America. Similar stories regularly appeared in dozens of popular magazines, periodicals, and journals. Beals depicted a fascist plan to conquer Brazil in *Dawn over the Amazon* (1943). The action-packed romance novel told how Amazon treasures could support a powerful civilization. Engineering would create air-conditioned cities, rid the jungles of dangers, end petty feuds, and bring work, peace, and prosperity to all when the united Americas defeated military invaders. Such fanciful scenarios were not so outlandish. Anti-fascist propagandists and anxious politicians had long warned of the fifth-column specter. With ever-increasing frequency, credible sources described Nazi intrigues. Ivy League professors Carl Friedrich and Edward Earle warned of Nazi propaganda and how German troops first infiltrated a nation disguised as tourists or refugees. After fostering chaos, dissention, and doubt about the government's credibility, the nation would be suitably "softened up" from within to allow a traditional attack.[16]

Reports and Reactions

The government and military had long been planning to deal with enemy nationals as the FBI, MID, and ONI monitored German, Italian, and Japanese Americans. In 1939, secret presidential directives put the FBI in charge of hemispheric anti-propaganda, anti-subversive, anti-sabotage, and counterespionage activities. Official reports described fifth-column threats and detailed Nazi plans to conquer Latin America. By February 1941, Adolf Berle's influential and widely circulated report, *The Pattern of Nazi Organizations and Their Activities in the Other American Republics*, led many U.S. diplomats to believe New World Germans supported the Nazis. Pearl Harbor proved the enemy's reach and, anticipating *Luftwaffe* strikes into Brazil from Senegal, Berle echoed Roosevelt's concerns of Nazi military plans and resident German machinations.[17]

Two months later, Vice President Henry Wallace, convinced of Axis offensives in Latin America, including the Canal Zone, urged Roosevelt to take immediate action. Although focused on the "German menace," Wallace privately told FDR that "the Japanese plan an advance from Peru, by Japs in that country, on Guayaquil and strategic nearby points." Roosevelt, convinced subversives contributed to Nazi successes in Europe, took the threat seriously. Thus began a hastily conceived and poorly executed program of repatriating and exchanging diplomats and correspondents followed by allegedly dangerous individuals for nationals held by Germany and Japan. Beyond ridding the hemisphere of such persons, German- as well as Japanese-owned businesses and farms would become available to investors through expropriation processes.[18]

Roosevelt wanted a broad coalition against the Axis that would yield greater U.S. influence throughout Latin America during and after the war. Hull, an advocate of hemispheric unity and free trade since becoming secretary of state in 1933, articulated Washington's concern that danger was not limited to a possible military invasion. It was "more acute in its indirect form of propaganda, penetration, organizing political parties, buying some adherents, and blackmailing others." At the 1938 Lima Conference, Berle had called for solidarity to rebuff foreign intrusions by way of a "north-south Axis." Although Argentina, Chile, and Uruguay were not so cooperative, anti-Axis efforts led to the Declaration of Panama in October 1939, which established a hemispheric security zone. Domestically, finding and detaining aliens was accomplished thanks to the FBI's index of aliens and citizens, the June 1940 Alien Registration Act, and FDR's January 1942 proclamation.[19]

United States Intervention

The United States intervened in Latin American affairs ostensibly to fight threats that most leaders knew were largely nonexistent. Washington pressured its neighbors to reduce or stop their trade with the Axis and diverted the export of crucial raw materials to its own shores. Meanwhile the Export-Import Bank offered more than a dozen nations some $130 million in loans. U.S. investments in Bolivian tin increased, as did holdings in Venezuelan oil. Nevertheless, the overriding goal was to contain German and Japanese power and fascist ideology. To that end, the United States acquired bases in Panama and Guatemala, helped build Brazilian warships, and supported some regimes and undid others, all the while prodding its good neighbors to fight the Axis—including its supposed fifth-column legions. The efforts bore fruit when, at the Rio de Janeiro Conference of January 1942, every nation except Argentina and Chile agreed to sever diplomatic relations with the Axis. By year's end a dozen Latin American nations had bilateral alien exchange agreements with the United States, and by war's end nearly every nation had interned hundreds if not thousands of enemy nationals and repatriated and exchanged many more for their own nationals held by Germany and Japan. Even Argentina and Chile finally broke off diplomatic relations with the Axis and participated in repatriation and exchange efforts. From start to finish, the United States directed nearly all aspects of these efforts.[20]

On May 8, as the movement of over two thousand Latin American nationals and diplomats ended and the first American-European exchange began, Wallace delivered an impassioned speech, "The Price of Free World Victory," to the Free World Association at Madison Square Garden. It dealt with the hemispheric threat and what to do about it:

> Hitler and Japan will cooperate to do the unexpected. The psychological and sabotage offensive in the United States and Latin America will be timed to coincide with or anticipate the height of the military offensive. We must be especially prepared to stifle the fifth columnists in the United States who will try to sabotage our war material plants, and infinitely more important, our minds.

> We must expect the offensive against us on the military, propaganda, and sabotage fronts, both in the United States and in Latin America, to reach its apex during the next few months. No compromise with Satan is possible. But they cannot prevail, for on the side of the people is the Lord. He giveth power, we who fight in the people's cause will never stop until that cause is won.[21]

The following month, an FBI *Bolivia Today* report showed Bolivia's 12,000 Germans dressed as Nazi storm troopers; it neglected to mention that only 184 of 3,500 German Bolivians were Nazi Party members, while the other 8,500 were Jewish refugees![22]

The United States never seriously questioned its evolving interventionism. Nor did officials doubt their judgment, question their paternalist responsibilities, or distrust their own self-asserted superiority. Even as the war ended, Edward Stettinius, the new secretary of state, unwittingly quipped that Mexico was "a good neighbor, a strong upholder of democratic traditions, and a country we are proud to call our own." Once the overestimation of the subversive threat was realized, it was too late. With a self-designated mandate to interfere hemispherically, the hunt for subversives took on a life and momentum of its own as economic benefits and political influence proved irresistible for business executives and Washington elites. Policy implications were far-reaching.[23]

Negotiating the First Exchanges

Through the legations of Switzerland and Spain, the United States, Germany, and Japan began arranging for the exchanges of officials and non-officials in January 1942. The success of two major American-European exchanges, consisting of five trips from New York to Europe and two from Lisbon to the United States, required five major movements of German, Italian, and Japanese nationals and diplomats from Latin America. By the summer, U.S. officials had orchestrated the repatriation of nearly all aliens brought to its shores and exchanged them for its own and Latin American nationals held by Germany and Japan. Yet the State Department's priority was exchanging official personnel, a point that Hull had stressed two weeks into the war when he informed Germany that only after official personnel were exchanged could civilians be repatriated.[24]

Germany made it clear by mid-January that it would mutually repatriate and exchange Americans in Nazi-occupied Europe with Germans throughout the Western Hemisphere. Japan similarly proposed exchanging all persons "regardless of their number or their qualifications (usefulness)." The State Department agreed on February 5. By month's end, Japan requested vessels to accommodate those non-officials not included on the first exchange so that "all persons concerned" would be repatriated quickly. On March 13 the State Department concurred, desiring that after all officials, press, and Red Cross personnel and families were embarked, priority would be given to "Persons objectionable to the Japanese. Persons from areas under Japanese control remote from Tokyo and Shanghai. Women, children, and the aged and infirm according to urgency. Quasi-officials and their dependents. Officers and employees of American organizations (commercial, religious, philanthropic)."[25]

Exchanges saved millions in relief costs for interned Americans abroad and expenses for interning enemy aliens domestically. But aside from logistical problems and lack of available resources, Hull and Roosevelt had misgivings about exchanging non-officials. On January 22 Hull stated that the United States would repatriate only diplomats, families, and staff due to "insufficient space" and would not include any non-officials "except as dependents of officials, press representatives, and Red Cross." Yet belligerents were detaining thousands of "dangerous" foreign nationals for the upcoming exchanges.

Exaggerated security concerns and reciprocity affected internee treatment. On February 5, the day after the U.S. Army defined its twelve restricted areas and the same day Allen Gullion called for evacuating Japanese Americans en masse, Stimson wrote Hull:

> General MacArthur has reported ... that American and British civilians in areas of the Philippines occupied by the Japanese are being subjected to extremely harsh treatment. The unnecessary harsh and rigid measures imposed, in sharp contrast to the moderate treatment of Filipinos, are designed to discredit the white race.

> I request that you strongly protest this unjustified treatment of civilians, and suggest that you present a threat of reprisals against the many Japanese nationals now enjoying negligible restrictions in the United States, to insure proper treatment of our nationals in the Philippines.[26]

Washington needed internees to ensure the safety of Americans held abroad. Holding and repatriating enemy aliens was a widely supported national safety measure. The difficulty was deciding who and how many to intern: too few would demonstrate a lack of resolve, while too many would alarm the sizable German and Italian American populations.

Reciprocity issues could make headlines. In September 1942, Assistant U.S. Attorney Frank Parker wrote Edward Ennis about a story that, if true, "makes one's blood boil but it is a ticklish situation. If we bludgeon the people concerned, they may retaliate on the other side." The *New York Times* article "Enemy Aliens Spit on Flag" noted:

> Axis nationals in custody here are spitting on the American flag and abusing guards. Prisoners are getting special food, the finest medical service, and liberal recreation. That situation is contrasted with the treatment of American nationals by the Japanese and refusal of safe conduct to a Red Cross ship loaded with badly needed clothing and medical supplies for our nationals, prisoners in Japan.
>
> Ellis Island is the type of country-club detention our government offers civilian Axis nationals. There are several hundred Germans, Italians, and Japanese awaiting alien hearing boards or transfer to internment camps. The Germans are arrogant and impertinent. The Japanese are stubborn. One well-fed paunchy Japanese spat at a guard and told him, "When Tojo come he kill American."[27]

In January 1943 another *New York Times* article, "Nazis Hold 14 U.S. Women," revealed that Germany pressured Norway to deport American women who then went to Liebenau internment camp in Württemberg, Germany. "The women were arrested as hostages just before Christmas because of alleged United States maltreatment of German citizens," the article stated. "Their deportation to Germany was kept secret, but friends in Norway are said to have received postcards from them marked 'Concentration Camp Liebenau.'"[28]

First Voyages

Agreeing to exchanges was relatively easy. The difficulty lay in the organization, logistics, coordination, and technical issues that required resolution and agreement even as Germany and Japan insisted on the return of certain persons. On January 28, 1942, FDR gave Long authority to remove "undesirable and untrustworthy aliens" from Latin America. Concurrently, the FBI had arrested 243 Italian, 1,301 German, and 1,566 Japanese aliens, while the Justice Department held 261, 1,361, and 1,450, respectively. By April 13 the State Department had 4,206 persons and the War Relocation Authority received its first Japanese relocatees, while internment facilities held several thousand more.[29]

Negotiations among the Allied and Axis powers went in fits and starts. Handling diplomats and their staffs began on January 16 when a special train took over one hundred persons from Union Station, Washington DC, to the Greenbrier Hotel in White Sulphur Springs, West Virginia. There the State Department and INS held them pending an exchange with U.S. officials. By February 10 an agreement in principle was reached with Germany and Italy. Cordell Hull needed a final list of officials for transport to Portugal, while Sumner Welles added that several hundred non-officials might also be included. Welles asked his Axis counterparts to review their list of those who wished to return to Europe and requested a list of non-official Americans desiring to come home. Officials representing the belligerents and the protecting neutral powers Spain, Sweden, and Switzerland resolved minor difficulties. Germany, for example, wanted its diplomats and nationals returned directly from South America and certain persons sent promptly.[30]

There were five major movements of German and Italian aliens from Latin America between January and June 1942. The *Santa Lucia* left Colombia on January 21 with 111 persons (officials and nationals) en route to New York City. After their arrival a week later, INS authorities sent officials to the Greenbrier Hotel, while the Army interned the rest at Ellis Island and Camp Upton, Long Island. It was the largest group of Axis nationals to arrive since U.S. entry in the war, and all were "closely guarded and kept in seclusion by State Department agents, armed Coast Guardsmen and a detail of soldiers carrying riot guns," reported the *New York Times*. Several months later the Army moved twenty-five men, fifteen women, and nineteen children to White Sulphur Springs, and after repatriating diplomats and their families and staffs, U.S. efforts focused on expelling dangerous foreign nationals.[31]

The next forced repatriation of Latin American aliens ended on April 20, when the *Etolin* docked in San Francisco, bringing 525 nationals from Peru, Ecuador, and Colombia. New Orleans received the *Acadia* first on April 25 with 654 nationals and officials from Bolivia, Peru, Ecuador, and Colombia, and then again on May 17 with 493 passengers from Colombia, Ecuador, and Venezuela. The *Shawnee* docked in late June with 526 passengers from Peru and Bolivia. Its arrival brought the total number of Latin nationals on these five voyages to 2,308 (1,601 Germans, 113 Italians, and 594 Japanese). In addition, more than one thousand other enemy nationals were deported. By May 7, eighteen nations had deported 3,050 persons (1,366 Axis officials and 1,684 non-officials, many of whom went directly to Europe or Asia). By summer's end the United States had repatriated most of the German and Italian aliens sent from Latin America.[32]

As of May 1 the Army and the Justice Department held 8,700 enemy aliens. The Red Cross reported that the Axis had interned 675 Americans and held 132 as prisoners of war. A month later the numbers had risen to 929 and 932, respectively. Not only was the increase worrisome (Germany and Japan interned 466 and 448 Americans respectively while Italy held 15), but Japan was now holding 929 American POWs, compared to only 3 by Germany. Fears of Japan's anticipated coastal invasion and the number of incarcerated Americans prompted the relocation and internment of Japanese Americans.[33]

By the summer of 1942 the United States was in a strong position to exchange its own internees, but there were objections to and haggling over who should and should not leave. The protective agencies cooperated and approved potential repatriates. If the State Department agreed, then logistical, coordination, and communication difficulties were tackled. Finally, some of the repatriates themselves did not want to go voluntarily. Despite the difficulties, thousands of Latin American Germans and Japanese joined German, Italian, and Japanese Americans bound for Lisbon and Gothenburg. Secrecy was paramount. Most repatriates had little advance notice of their departure—especially Latin American nationals. Albert Clattenburg, a Special Division assistant chief, stressed the absolute avoidance of mentioning repatriation to Germans "until 48 hours before they leave the camps to avoid their conniving with other internees in unfavorable reports regarding the camps or other communications to be taken to Germany which might be contrary to our interests."[34]

The State Department and protective agencies grossly overstated Axis, especially Nazi, hemispheric encroachments. Labeling someone "pro-Nazi," "fascist," "pro-Hitler," or "particularly dangerous" was often enough to result in arrest and internment. Most had no option but to endure deportation, internment, and repatriation. Despite pressure from its own and British intelligence (typically objecting to one third of proposed repatriates), the United States honored its exchange agreements with its Latin American neighbors. Notwithstanding the potential security risks, the State Department repatriated several thousand Axis nationals during the summer of 1942—gambling that they would be less dangerous back home.[35]

The five exchanges from the United States to Europe included 902 officials and correspondents (565 Germans, 243 Italians, 49 Hungarians, Romanians, and Bulgarians, and 45 reporters) along with 2,141 nationals (1,824 Germans, 270 Italians, and 47 Hungarians and Bulgarians). The United States held 3,663 Germans by December 1942 (2,819 German Americans and 844 Latin American Germans in Army and INS camps). At the same time, Germany interned 1,027 out of an estimated 2,500 Americans it had.

The voyages (three by the *Drottningholm* and one each by the *Nyassa* and *Serpa Pinto*) brought 313 officials (147 Americans and 166 Latin Americans), 1,683 non-officials (1,422 Americans, 252 Latin Americans, and 9 Canadians), and 23 journalists back.[36]

In all, the United States helped repatriate 4,557 Germans, Italians, and Japanese to their respective countries during this first round of exchanges from May to August 1942. In return, it received 3,299 persons: 2,722 Americans (1,300 from Japan and 1,422 from Germany) and 577 Latin American nationals. The U.S. sent 279 tons of relief supplies aboard the *Gripsholm*, which Japanese authorities and the Red Cross distributed. Afterward, U.S. officials privately expressed great disappointment about the repatriated Americans. Hull, Long, and Biddle, among others, described them as "nonsubstantial persons," "destitute," "undesirable," "lame and blind," "not a benefit to our war effort," and not "representing business or commercial interests." Aside from possible spies and saboteurs returning with these undesirables, U.S. officials used Germany's revocation of its safe-conduct promise as a violation of the exchange agreement and halted the exchanges.[37]

As Germany and Japan interned more Americans and the first exchanges ended, Roosevelt told Hull: "I believe that we should be very careful in repatriating any enemy aliens to Germany. All German aliens in America are potential, if not actual, spies and the Americans in Germany are not." FDR added: "While I think it is tough on the Americans who must remain in Germany throughout the war, I nevertheless think that Germany gets the best of the exchange." Although returning diplomats divulged vital war-related information and the subsequent arrival of nationals afforded an opportunity to gain even more intelligence (which Americans coming from the Far East aboard the *Gripsholm* provided), foreign nationals had become bartered goods as the exchanges paused and Germany demanded "all manner of persons."

Germany was getting sailors, pilots, reservists, engineers, mechanics, machinists, factory workers, and "leaders and members of espionage and propaganda organizations." Japan wanted "particular individuals," but Washington told Tokyo no more "than they already know." Biddle warned FDR of repatriating those who would imperil the nation's security. The Navy expressly objected to including any Hawaiian Japanese, as they would "undoubtedly convey accurate and vital information" to Japan; the State Department warned against sending Tokyo "experts and engineers" who knew "technical processes of industry, including making machine tools, munitions, tanks, and airplane engines." Then there were fishermen: Frank Booth, a former financial adviser for Nippon Kogyo Kabushiki Kaisha, was "an authority on Japanese fisheries and canneries, with special reference to operations in Russian waters" and was the type of person Tokyo should not have.[38]

The Dilemma and the Shift

The first exchanges ended in August 1942 for security reasons and the ultimate goal of winning the war. The dilemma was ridding the hemisphere of dangerous aliens without aiding the enemy. All repatriated males between sixteen and fifty swore "not to bear arms for the duration." Still, they might get non-combat duty, work in war-related industries, or pass on privileged information. So now repatriating the "inherently harmless"—women, children, and elderly men, the insane and sick, hobos and drifters, and "obnoxious" and "bottom of the barrel" types—became "particularly desirable."[39]

American officials, having earlier exchanged "persons without regard to number or to their usefulness," now reassessed the policy. A change occurred for several reasons. First, repatriated Americans were undesirable. Second, two-thirds of Latin American repatriates were poor, older residents who had lived in the Americas since the 1920s, not dangerous agents, saboteurs, or quislings. Finally, security agencies increasingly objected to repatriating "able-bodied young men, skilled technicians, and trained observers" who would benefit the enemy. As the Axis was getting a better deal, the exchanges stopped. Still, 6,610 Latin Americans were forcibly deported and then interned in the United States.[40]

By late 1942, Washington shifted its policy from repatriating dangerous nationals to inherently harmless ones. While negotiating with Japan, officials noted:

> We have so far been unable to include . . . persons requested to whose repatriation the agencies object. We are already suspect in Japan's eyes. . . . We can refrain from admitting that there are domestic difficulties . . . and negotiate a new understanding.
>
> The reasons . . . to carry on the exchange as negotiated are: 1) To save Americans from indescribable suffering in Japanese internment camps. 2) To send urgently needed medical and food supplies. . . . We can be certain that if we withhold Japanese nationals desired by Japan, she will hold out those whom we wish most to get . . . our highest type citizens. It would seem elemental that we do not invite retaliation until we have exhausted every means of avoiding it.
>
> We can escape criticism for a breakdown in the exchange if we make Japan "a reasonable offer," namely 4,500 Japanese for 4,500 Americans. Japan's refusal . . . will place upon Japan responsibility of breaking the exchange. Unless . . . we contemplate withholding [those] so dangerous that their release could not be justified by the value of the *quid pro quo* of (1) and (2) above, this government must expect severe criticism. There have been indications of a Congressional investigation. Such an investigation might be embarrassing.[41]

Special Agent R. L. Bannerman stressed similar concerns and goals: exchanging equal numbers without selecting from Japan's priority list and speeding up negotiations, as many Americans, including diplomats, were still in the Far East. Detaining those of value while expelling undesirable persons was advantageous. Balancing these priorities, however, proved difficult.[42] Ennis's response to Biddle's repatriation question is telling:

> Pursuant to your suggestion that alien enemies deportable for the commission of crimes involving moral turpitude should be considered for internment, representatives of this office have gone through the Immigration files for all aliens of enemy nationality ordered deported on this ground and have divided them into those who should clearly be interned pending deportation that it is unnecessary to give them a hearing and others to be given a hearing to determine internment or parole. . . . Alien enemies . . .

may be detained for the duration of the war and then deported if we cannot include them in the present repatriation.⁴³

Certain Qualities and Desirability

As internee numbers grew steadily, on August 15 Roosevelt asked Hull about the exchanges; he felt they were benefiting the Axis. Hull replied on August 27 and explained why they had become commodities—in effect, bartered goods. Repatriates should not benefit the enemy; rather, they should be criminals, mental incompetents, and the insane along with the elderly, sick, disabled, and women and children—the bottom of the barrel. Hull wrote Roosevelt:

> Responding to your note about repatriation of further enemy aliens, particularly Germans, I may say that there are no negotiations under way except as hangovers from the original agreement. The original agreement was terminated by us after two shiploads [*sic*] had been exchanged. It was very apparent that the persons we were receiving were not such as to benefit our war effort. Consequently, the arrangement was terminated.
>
> I am quite in agreement and my associates in the Department have been in thorough accord with the proposal to prevent the return to Germany of persons who would be helpful to the German cause, but . . . we could not obtain the release of our own citizens from enemy control unless we exchanged their citizens for them, and amongst those citizens the enemy powers will naturally insist, just as we have insisted, that persons of certain qualities and desirability be exchanged.⁴⁴

On August 29, Long and his colleagues discussed removing all Latin American enemy aliens to the United States. The grandiose plan, though never realized, presumed America's right to dictate policy to its neighbors. As Germany and Japan demanded specific persons, the State Department devised delay strategies even as some expressed concern about such practices. Long wrote Assistant Chief of Staff General George Strong:

> As you are aware, this government has agreed to repatriate Japanese nationals from the Hawaiian Islands as well as from the con-

tinental United States. It is necessary to repatriate a token number of Japanese from Hawaii in exchange for American nationals from Manchuria and Korea. . . . This is particularly desirable in order that the Japanese Government will have no hesitancy in including on the next exchange vessel the remainder of Americans from remote areas under Japanese control. . . . Realizing there may be certain Japanese whom the military authorities may consider advisable to hold as long as possible, the Department of State desires to leave to the discretion of the military authorities to select . . . those to be repatriated at this time.[45]

Two Special Division personnel, James Keeley Jr. and George Brandt (chief and assistant chief, respectively), echoed widespread exchange concerns. Keeley's comments to and request of Brandt are revealing:

If we continue to stall and fail to give the names [Japanese from Hawaii] to the Spanish Embassy will it not get suspicious? It has repeatedly asked for them and our reply whether a list is available is getting a bit weak. They have every reason to believe that we should know the names of those we brought here. Yet if we give a list of the 173 it will include the names of 104 whom the Navy says cannot go. It is as De Molina [Spanish Embassy] says "One Grand Puzzle." We have not yet solved it, can you solve it?[46]

On September 15, after the initial exchanges, protective agency representatives met for an extended review of repatriation. The ONI's Commander Wallace Wharton was dissatisfied. John Burling, assistant director of the AECU, noted that agreements had been negotiated without any agency input and that repatriation was improperly handled. Burling wrote:

The investigative agencies should consolidate their objections and should inform the State Department that no person was to be repatriated if objection was made. . . . This Unit had been opposed to the manner in which repatriation was being handled from the first. . . . It was alleged that the President had approved the program.

If there were persons whom the State Department felt it necessary to repatriate in order to get back American citizens, [it] would then request the investigative agency to reconsider its objections on the basis of man to man trading.

Ennis stated that the details of horror brought back by the first American repatriates had affected the public and possibly the President to such an extent that further repatriation would be carried on even at the expense to internal security.[47]

Secretary of the Navy Frank Knox echoed such concerns. On October 29 he wrote:

> The Navy Department recommended reconsidering the repatriation from the Hawaiian area of certain Japanese who had the opportunity of obtaining military and naval information. In reply, the State Department stated that the exchange agreement between this government and the Japanese government had been negotiated on a reciprocal basis.... In order to prevent important, current, military and naval information from being transmitted from the Hawaiian area to the Japanese government ... it is recommended that Japanese repatriates from Hawaii be brought to the mainland for a period of at least four months prior to their return to Japan.[48]

A Few Good Americans?

As Americans arrived from the Far East aboard the *Gripsholm* in August, the State Department created interview lists, desiring information about Germany or Japan. One person had "long experience in Japan" and could "throw some light on conditions." Another was a "walking encyclopedia regarding all industrial activities in and about Yokohama." Still another was "well informed on the Japanese oil industry" and had news about "coal liquefaction." Of use were those with technical or industrial knowledge or had "prolonged and intimate association with the Japanese."[49]

Despite the desire to exchange civilians along with injured POWs, there were fears that the Axis was sending spies and saboteurs disguised as refugees and undesirables. A State Department memo in November 1942 articulated the dilemmas and desires of realizing a coherent, comprehensive, and consistent repatriation and exchange policy:

The United States government has received the hearty cooperation of the other American Republics [for] the expulsion of aliens of enemy nationality and other dangerous aliens. We could repatriate, intern, or hold them in escrow for bargaining purposes. . . . Our experience in this matter and general observation of Axis methods lead to the conclusion that all German nationals without exception, all Japanese nationals, a small portion of Italian nationals, and . . . refugees from Central Europe are all dangerous and should be removed as rapidly as possible.

By offering designated groups of Axis nationals, particularly women, children and elderly men, safe-conduct to Europe . . . we can develop a considerable voluntary evacuation of German and Italian nationals. For persons whose repatriation we cannot permit, there exists the alternative of internment. If the local government is unwilling to transfer aliens or the numbers involved are too great, . . . this government might lend personnel, funds and material for strengthening the local internment program and bringing it up to an acceptable standard.

It is particularly desirable that the repatriation of inherently harmless Axis nationals may be used to the greatest possible extent in obtaining the repatriation from Axis territory of nationals of the other American Republics whose presence in enemy territory gives the enemy a certain amount of bargaining power.[50]

In May 1943 the CPD echoed the State Department's concerns. Its June 5 report to member nations reaffirmed "Axis plans for political conquest of the American republics, as part of the totalitarian scheme for world domination." There had been "careful and intensive preparations," including dispatching "a multitude of agents, trained in the techniques of totalitarian penetration, to operate under the close direction of the Axis governments." Oftentimes, "continuous streams of agents" came "disguised as diplomats, businessmen, scientists, artists, immigrants, technicians, tourists, refugees, heads of cultural and religious missions, etc." These emissaries worked with embedded "groups and colonies of Axis nationals" to start "espionage, sabotage, and military operations." As in Europe, these fifth-column steps, aimed at "undermining local governments, institutions, and democratic principles," had reached "a high stage of perfection."⁵¹

Hemispheric security necessitated interning dangerous Axis agents and nationals. Given the option of internment or repatriation, the committee concluded, "internment is greatly to be preferred" and "should be pursued as the basic security policy." The CPD added that thousands already repatriated knew much of vital hemispheric "military, political, and economic developments" and would be "of great value to the Axis." The CPD faced the same issue that plagued Washington—how best to get those of "equal or greater weight" in the exchanges—and summed up the situation this way:

> Bearing in mind the value received by the Axis powers from the return of their informed, trained, or able-bodied nationals, and the concomitant threat to American security, the crucial question is whether the return of any non-official Americans still in territory under Axis control is required by security considerations of equal or greater weight. The solution [is] careful examination of individual cases ... whether the security risks inherent in the loss of control over particular Axis nationals are outweighed by advantages resulting from the return of American nationals. ... No Axis national ... of dangerousness or substantial usefulness to the Axis war effort should be repatriated, except upon an exchange basis.
>
> The American republics are able to exert a bargaining power in negotiations with respect to repatriation or exchange, when they act in concert. ... There has been understandable concern [about] the safety and proper treatment of our nationals. The American republics ... are in a superior position. ... The Committee urges that the American republics regard the nationals held by the Axis, and the Axis nationals within this hemisphere, as common pools of hemisphere interest, not as separate groups to be bargained over individually.⁵²

Interning dangerous aliens for months, the war's duration, or even beyond was better than sending them to the Axis or back to their homes in Central or South America. In short, just after the first round of exchanges, Washington reversed course. Ridding the

Western Hemisphere of dangerous aliens was not such a good idea after all.[53]

Exchange Hiatus

Stalled negotiations halted the exchange program by November 1942. The timing was unfortunate, as talks had included releasing Axis-held Jews for U.S.-held Germans. A chance to save thousands of Jews and free many internees was lost. Keeley explained:

> The German government by refusing further safe conduct . . . terminated the arrangements under which American nationals, in Germany and German-occupied territories, interned or at liberty, were being exchanged for German nationals of similar status in the United States. That exchange brought to light circumstances that apply with even greater force to the exchange under study.
>
> 1. The British government refused safe conduct to hundreds of German nationals whose activities in this hemisphere or technical qualifications were such that their return to Germany would be more detrimental to the allied cause than their detention in the United States. 2. The protective agencies of this government, for similar reasons, refused the repatriation of many German nationals. 3. Many of the Americans received in exchange were of questionable value to the country and certain of them were found to be active Nazi agents.
>
> It is almost impossible to separate the bona fide from the mala fide in such an assemblage of people as would come to the United States. There are political and other considerations. . . . While there is widespread sympathy in the United States for these suffering refugees, it is doubtful if the American people as a whole would support such a project. The relatives of those Americans still in Germany, especially those interned, would expect those Americans to be repatriated before the *quid pro quo* that could be used to ransom them were used to bring alien refugees here. Further efforts to repatriate those Americans had to be abandoned for compelling reasons of national security.[54]

D. W. Smith, State Department staff, made some important points to Keeley:

> A further exchange [of interned Germans for Americans interned in Germany] would be contrary to the national welfare. Many [interned Germans] are well-trained espionage agents who would contribute to the enemy's knowledge of our war plans and industrial production, or have technical skills of value to the enemy.
>
> It is not likely that a proposal to exchange Germans in the U.S. for Jews held by the Nazis could be implemented unless the national welfare were subordinated to the welfare of Jews in Germany and German-occupied territory.[55]

The hiatus and policy shift from August to December 1942 achieved several interrelated goals, ensuring a benevolent reciprocity as thousands more civilians were later exchanged. Deteriorating condition in the Far East troubled many, including Senator Elbert Thomas, who believed that Japan had refused to apply the civilian exchange arrangement provisions to Americans "captured on the Philippines, Guam, and Wake Island." U.S. officials worked doggedly to repatriate "all Americans in Japanese hands." There was less worry about Germany, as it was "living up to the provisions of the treaties." Nevertheless, Washington was concerned about all American internees.[56]

Hemispheric Evaluations and Preparations

From July 28 to August 10, 1943, diplomats representing nearly all of the American republics met in Washington DC to review political defense structures, particularly the control of dangerous aliens. The CPD issued a report that formed the legal basis to prevent subversive activities. Addressing concerns of the Justice Department's Special War Policies Unit (SWPU), headed by Lawrence Smith, the committee's focus included certificates of identification; registering dangerous aliens; detention, internment, expulsion, and repatriation; preventing the abuse of citizenship; international travel; and acts of political aggression. Significantly, the report reflected the recent U.S. repatriation and exchange policy shift—from repatriating dangerous to inherently harmless aliens while keeping dangerous or useful Axis aliens interned in U.S. camps.

Inaccurate information and outright duplicity characterized much of the repatriation program—the result of a grossly exaggerated Axis, particularly Nazi, hemispheric threat. Repatriates were victims of poor timing and guilt by association; nearly all were living in the wrong place at the wrong time. Most interned aliens faced repatriation, and while renunciants volunteered for deportation, many resisted. Some stayed in the United States. Others, not so fortunate, were forced to move to neutral Switzerland or Sweden or, after May 1945, into impoverished areas of the defeated Axis nations. Beyond the requests of those few wishing to go, most initial repatriates fulfilled Washington's wish of getting rid of dangerous aliens, diplomats, and POWs while having its own citizens, prisoners, and officials returned. The results, however, were hardly satisfactory. Long described arriving Americans as "destitute," Biddle called them "undesirable," and Keeley reported to the CPD that the United States was "repatriating Axis aliens on an exchange basis only, with due regard to Hemisphere security considerations." Clattenburg noted U.S. cooperation with Latin America in handling aliens: negotiating for their exchange, moving them to the U.S. for immediate or postwar repatriation, and issuing safe-conducts to facilitate independent exchanges with the other republics.[57]

Fourteen Latin American nations now had bilateral agreements with the United States and had sent 4,656 Axis aliens to the U.S for detention, internment, or repatriation (of which 2,242 had been repatriated in 1942 while many of the other 2,414, plus an additional 1,954 brought after July 1943, remained in U.S. custody for the war's duration or beyond), and nearly every country in South and Central America had repatriated and exchanged enemy nationals for their own held by Germany and Japan (most under direct U.S auspices). By war's end, eighteen nations had sent 4,058 Germans, 288 Italians, and 2,264 Japanese to the United States for detention and internment or for repatriation. As late as November 1, 1945, there were still 1,447 internees who languished in camps under the alien enemy program.

Of the 6,610 Latin American aliens brought to and interned in the United States during the war, 4,325 repatriated themselves voluntarily. These 3,135 German, 253 Italian, and 937 Japanese nationals felt they had no choice but to join their head of household or were pressured, threatened, or impelled to "repatriate voluntarily." Another 837 voluntarily repatriated themselves after the war. U.S. officials also orchestrated the movement of thousands more directly from Latin America to Europe and Asia. Many of these joined internees in both the initial and final exchanges at the end of the war and beyond.[58]

New Thinking, New Exchanges

By the fall of 1943 repatriation and exchange efforts resumed amid deteriorating conditions in Germany and Japan and concerns for the well-being of American internees and POWs. The Swiss Legation reported the abuse of Americans in Japanese hands. Hull received the news in December 1942 and Japan's response in May. Tokyo claimed the incidents were due to "special circumstances in areas that had been fields of battle." Washington countered that the regions had long ceased to be "scenes of active military operations." Updates revealed that nearly all Americans were victims of Japan's "inhuman cruelty or callous failure to provide the necessities of life." Meanwhile, the United States had "consistently and fully applied" the Geneva Convention provisions to "all Japanese nationals," whether internees, detainees, or evacuees, with "high standards of housing, food, clothing, and medical care." Washington concealed Japan's "outrages" and demanded immediate corrective measures and punishment for provision violators so it could reassure the public that American captives were receiving proper treatment.[59]

Repatriating the inherently harmless meant emptying camps of undesirables along with some internees wanting to leave and others refusing deportation. Even as Allied military fortunes improved, Biddle responded on August 20 to FDR's concerns about national-security risks in a proposed repatriation of Latin American German nationals:

> Your letter [of August 10] points out that it is improbable that these German nationals while in detention have been able to obtain infor-

mation which would endanger us. You suggest it may be far less harmful to repatriate these persons now than it would have been some time ago. These facts decrease, although they do not entirely eliminate, the potential threat of these persons.

This proposal requires us to exchange 750 to 900 German nationals for 266 U.S. nationals and 530 nationals of other American Republics. The FBI has objected to 38 Germans. The question whether the exchange should be made is primarily one for the State Department, but is it possible to avoid repatriating these relatively few skilled Germans whose training and experience will be of direct assistance to the German military forces.[60]

A second series of American and Japanese internee exchanges, set for the summer of 1943, built upon the groundwork laid in December. Japan held 8,000 Americans, whose treatment was deteriorating. At least 4,500 "would be of advantage" if repatriated. They were "persons of great value . . . being forced to render services" to Japan's war effort. The *Gripsholm* would bring needed supplies to POWs and was currently "idle at a cost to the government of $6,500 per day." FDR approved the State Department's plan for removing Germans, Italians, and Japanese from South America, exchanging Japanese and American nationals, but not repatriating any more German Americans to Germany.[61]

With the exchanges nearly set to resume, on August 23 Clattenburg asked Special Agent R. L. Bannerman to communicate the following to all agencies: "It is hoped that after the exchange of Americans and Japanese is completed it will be possible to proceed until all 8,000 Americans in Japanese hands have been brought back. Japan's attitude will be largely governed by the treatment of Japanese returning from the U.S. It is important to avoid incidents in connection with the examination and embarkation of Japanese nationals."[62]

The United States now held 4,962 Germans along with thousands more Japanese, and by April 1944 more than 300 State Department agents helped move 12,134 Axis officials and non-officials on 137 separate train movements without incident—no escapes, protests, or Geneva Convention violations. Repatriates went from twelve hotels and inns (serving as internment centers) and INS and Army facilities going to embarkation points where they left the country and were then exchanged for their Axis-held counterparts. The *Gripsholm* left New York City on September 2 with 1,330 Japanese Americans and 1,600 tons of badly needed relief provisions to be distributed to interned Americans.[63]

The resumption of exchanges in late 1943 and early 1944 was largely successful. The Swiss, Spanish, and Swedish Legations in charge of German and Japanese interests accepted all repatriates "to be exchanged against bona fide" U.S. and Latin American nationals. Washington also exchanged internees and German Americans for POWs. Weighing domestic matters as well as broader national and international concerns, the belligerents prioritized those they most wanted returned and repatriated. Cooperation among the State and War Departments, FBI, and INS determined internee outcomes—forcible repatriation, remaining interned, staying in the states, or returning to Latin America. In short, internees served as "exchange bait," mere pawns bartered at the whim of authorities: as discussions with Germany resumed in April 1943 to exchange persons on a "quid pro quo basis," Long informed Welles that the "U.S. is offering 299 (of 757 demanded by Germany) in exchange for 265 Americans" and would "have a pocket of 221 persons available to be used . . . should it become necessary to increase our offer."[64]

On December 1, 1943, nearly fifteen hundred Americans arrived in New York after spending almost two years in Japanese internment camps. They were instructed to be "close-lipped with reporters," especially about atrocities, because, as one Navy public-relations officer put it, publication "makes it difficult to deal with the Japanese over the release of the 6,300 American civilians" still held. Nevertheless, repatriates talked. Upon the *Gripsholm*'s arrival after sixty-four days at sea, some revealed "chilling tales of Japanese cruelty," while others described "considerate or even friendly treatment." One repatriate said that the guards at a camp in Shao Shing, Chekiang Province, China, "had been very kind to the children," while another noted that the Japanese officers would sing "popular songs with the internees while one of them played the piano." Mainly, however, the news was bad. There was a "lack of nutritious food, proper hospitalization and medical attention, general filth, and, finally, the brutal Jap attitude." And so it went: "we were the enemy . . . whether soldier or civilian." They "hated us" and "showed us who is top dog here in the Orient." Another, from the Philippines, beseeched officials to "get Americans in Manila home," recalling "their mental attitude is going down" while food and clothing were "major problems." Many lost ten to forty pounds while interned, but coming home changed that. The ship's physician saw "most passengers gain from eight to twenty-five pounds."[65]

As the second exchange was ending, the State Department tried but failed to negotiate a third wartime exchange with Japan. Receiving news about the maltreatment of its nationals held in U.S. camps, Japan began investigating. Spain and Switzerland, the protecting powers, finally reported that the internees were well treated. The fact-finding process, however, was lengthy and delayed the exchange until after the war. Also, Japan's insistence on the return of several hundred pearl divers and captured pilots held in Australia sparked a vigorous debate between the British and Douglas MacArthur, who repeatedly opposed returning those with vital information about Australian waters and Allied forces. By the fall of 1944 MacArthur finally acquiesced, but Britain lacked enough internees to trade. As fighting in the Pacific came ever closer to its home islands, the plight of Allied POWs and internees became increasingly desperate.[66]

New Situations, New Problems

By the fall of 1944, as the new series of exchanges continued with Germany, the State Department realized that many deported Latin Americans were "undoubtedly relatively harmless" and had been "selected for expulsion through error." It was impossible to send all internees to Germany or Japan or return dangerous ones to Latin America. Moreover, officials did not want any Latin American internees to remain in the United States after the war. Clattenburg well understood the increasing difficulties "in disposing of the enemy nationals brought here." At a secret meeting of select department officials on August 31, he noted:

> A certain number of the individuals will want to stay in the United States. . . . While it might be desirable to . . . return all internees to the enemy state of which they were nationals, this would be incompatible with United States government policy and would be unacceptable. On the other hand, in the absence of an international commitment it would be practically impossible to resist requests for the return to other American republics of most dangerous types of individuals.

Officials agreed to adopt Britain's and Canada's classification system:

> A) Dangerous: Persons whose deportation from this Hemisphere should be insisted upon. . . . B) Probably dangerous: Persons whom we would prefer to see return to their homeland but who might be allowed to return to the other American republics if those republics should insist upon it. C) Probably harmless: Persons who might be allowed to elect whether to return to Germany or to the American republics whence deported.[67]

Although Germany was treating its internees well, ensuring a benevolent reciprocity for future exchanges, alarming news hinted at what might happen should talks fail: several thousand Latin American nationals of "certain European racial or political minority groups" might be subjected to forced labor, torture, or even death. The CPD stressed:

> There are in Axis-occupied territory two thousand individuals who possess certain documents, issued by American Republics, which reflect a right of admission or protection. Apparently, with the deliberate purpose of using such persons as a medium of exchange for German nationals abroad, the German government has detained a majority of those individuals in concentration camps.
>
> The German government has apparently concluded that the various American Republics are not determined to protect these persons or to accept them for exchange purposes. It has consequently subjected them to measures applied to racial or political minorities who have no claim to American protection. These

measures are notoriously of the most brutal character, involving forced labor and other extreme cruelties. Persecution of minority groups has recently intensified.

Only the most urgent and decisive steps will prevent the annihilation of these persons. Documents issued or permits granted must be respected. Exchange proposals must be promptly worked out for liberating such persons.

It resolved to address the "desperate plight of those in Germany" with the aim to protect, rescue, and exchange them for "certain German nationals in the Western Hemisphere."[68]

More transatlantic exchanges took place in late 1944 and early 1945. In December, Lee Seward, a State Department representative at Fort Stanton, received a directive from Chief Special Agent T. F. Fitch, who stressed the necessity of unusual caution moving German internees for the *Gripsholm*'s upcoming voyage. Repatriates were under strict guard and forbidden any outside communications. Authorities prohibited internees, prior to their release, from discussing camp life, whether critical or laudatory, with anyone. After a screening process and list adjustments, officials frisked or strip-searched repatriates for concealed articles as camp authorities examined and transferred their baggage. Armed guards monitored and held them incommunicado until they boarded an exchange vessel. Guards on trains and buses kept the public away. Such were now standard practices.

While secrecy was important, the State Department occasionally granted the media access to confidential releases. The United Press, for example, covered the journey of 312 Americans from Baden-Baden to Lisbon in February 1944. One repatriate said that "France is impatiently awaiting an Allied invasion," another spoke of "food shortages and cold," and still another "outwitted the Nazis" by pretending to be a nurse "to get better food." A public release of January 5, 1945, announced that the *Gripsholm* would leave New York for Marseille to exchange seriously sick and wounded POWs. German civilians and aliens from Mexico were also exchanged for U.S. nationals and other Latin Americans. Repatriates moved through Switzerland in two separate operations.[69]

Homeward Bound

Internees, as "pockets of persons" held "in escrow for bargaining purposes," had hopes for the future. Some desired to go back to their old rural communities or familiar city streets, provided, of course, they had not lost their homes, businesses, or property due to vandals, collection agencies, foreclosures, or tax collectors. Others, disillusioned by their treatment and incarceration, returned to Germany or Japan despite the risks and worsening conditions. Still more were forcibly deported during and after the war. Some could opt to stay or leave while others successfully resisted repatriation or deportation. Yet thousands of forced repatriates found themselves unwelcome, met by suspicious and distrustful compatriots. Soldiers met those who returned to Germany and Japan after the war and led them to camps where they endured many more weeks or months behind barbed wire. Former German American internees, for example, ended up in camps such as Asperg or Tredennick after processing at places like Stuttgart or Ludwigsburg.[70]

The January 7, 1945, sailing of the *Gripsholm* illustrates repatriation cooperation and complexities. The vessel took 856 Germans from the U.S. and 102 from Mexico along with 183 POWs from the U.S. and 21 from Canada. There were 429 internees from Crystal City and 114 from Seagoville, 47 from Fort Stanton, 208 from Fort Lincoln, and 58 from Ellis Island. Border Patrol and Army guards as well as State Department and FBI special agents accompanied repatriates throughout—from camps to ships. Most went to Pier F in Jersey City by special train, though Army guards delivered the POWs. Each was limited to three suitcases and one hundred dollars along with personal effects—clothing, linen, blankets, kitchen utensils, antiques, art, baby carriages, passports, and birth certificates. Prohibited items included furniture, garden tools, electrical appliances, sewing machines, radios, typewriters, cameras, mechanical equipment, binoculars, and firearms. Repatriates could not take food, gold (except jewelry), instruments (except for doctors), photographs, prints or sketches (except portraits), and documents of any kind.

After the Customs examination, repatriates could not access their baggage until they arrived at a foreign exchange port. Once at Jersey City, officials cleared the pier area. After final State Department and Export Control Office verification checks, repatriates sailed under safe-conduct assurances with Swedish and Swiss representatives. Once under way, adults had time to reflect while children would often play. Rudolf and Berta Plaschke's two sons, Alfred and Paul, too young to understand the U-boat menace, spent most of their time exploring the ship. Others, such as Art Jacobs, were going to a place only their parents knew. Some were hopeful and optimistic, others anxious and despondent. U.S. officials said the trip was "without incident" and noted that the German repatriates "were extremely quiet." The return voyage included checking passenger lists, answering questions and complaints, filling out security questionnaires, and distributing money for onboard spending. Problems included fights organized by Polish Americans who "beat up certain German American passengers." Officials reported the brawls as "a healthy reaction" and other scuffles "over nothing in particular." As the *Gripsholm* neared New York, the civilians, who had obeyed "any command," emerged "as individuals" and the "American strain . . . began to assert itself."[71]

Ethics of Internment, Repatriation, and Exchange

In November 1943, J. M. Cabot of the U.S. Costa Rican Embassy had seen enough and expressed his concerns to his superiors:

> Herewith is the kind of thing which I have been fearing and . . . may well rise to damn us. . . . Our Embassy . . . has sent a formal note to the Costa Rican Foreign Office referring to . . . a list of enemy nationals "approved by the Enemy Alien Control Unit . . . for internment in the United States." . . . I recognize some of the names as those of Costa Rican nationals. We should invite State Department's attention to the dangers of this course and we should rap the Embassy sharply over the knuckles for such an indiscreet act.

Laurence Knapp, chief of the SWPU's Latin American Section, replied to the embassy, admonished Cabot, and enunciated U.S. policy:

> The note handed to the Foreign Minister smacks of intervention in its phrasing and that in the circumstances prevailing vis-à-vis

Costa Rica, it was probably unwise to employ this formal avenue of approach at all. With that criticism, based as it was on the special facts . . . I would not presume to disagree; if I were to exercise judgment, I would criticize the tenor of the note transmitted.

The important thing . . . is that Mr. Cabot recognizes that it is desirable for the missions to make use of the CPD recommendations, which were designed to assist them to avoid charges of intervention by placing the program on the basis of hemisphere approval and character, and only questions the method the Embassy employed in this case in referring to them.

Cabot responded by commending alien deportation policies while urging that the written record should not reveal Washington-based initiatives:

> I am not opposed to deportations in general. . . . The written record in each deportation case should show that the deporting government had requested our collaboration. I think it is undesirable for the written record to show that the initiative came from us. . . . I am disturbed at the Embassy's action (a) because . . . we are not self-appointed administrators of CPD recommendations, which, as Mr. Knapp says, were designed to avoid charges of intervention on our part, (b) because it is not for United States officials to determine what individuals have a sufficient Axis taint to necessitate their deportation from the territory of another sovereign state, and (c) because we certainly do not have the right to tell another sovereign government which of its citizens it should deport, or to what country they should be deported.

Anxious about the disclosure of coerced repatriation practices, Cabot concluded:

> I fear that in the post-war period unfriendly leaders in the other republics may use incidents such as this to demonstrate that behind the facade of Good Neighborship the United States was really interfering in the internal affairs of the other republics. I see no reason why we should give them *written* evidence to bolster such an assertion. If we really must take the initiative and exert pressure

in connection with deportations, it should at least be done with great discretion.

On this point at least, the Justice and State Departments concurred. Stealth was paramount with all aspects of internment, including repatriation and exchange.[72]

In the spring of 1942, Biddle and others suggested interning and repatriating undesirables, convicts serving sentences from larceny to murder, mental incompetents, and the insane along with the elderly, sick, disabled, and women and children—in sum, the bottom of the barrel along with those believed highly dangerous. By the fall, officials wanted to rid the country of any convicted of moral turpitude, narcotics, prostitution, or admitted to a crime before entering the United States. An alien enemy could also be interned or deported if "a member of or affiliated with an organization, association, society, or group that writes, circulates, distributes, prints, publishes, or displays, or that has in its possession written or printed matter advising, advocating, or teaching the overthrow by force or violence the United States government or forms of law."[73]

Officials also repatriated aliens for administrative or other compelling reasons. One German deportee from Ecuador was suspected of espionage activities and being a "good German" who "favors Hitler." In November 1944, as *Gripsholm* readied to go to Europe, Lieutenant Commander Peter Belin of the ONI phoned Sidney Lafoon of the Special War Problems Division to let him know that some civilians were not cleared. Lafoon recorded Belin's reaction: "He [Belin] hopes that we will continue to work on the 'bottom of the barrel' principle. I told him that was our intention and we would not repatriate anyone whom they would like held back unless there were compelling reasons to do so."[74]

The FBI and ONI sometimes objected to certain repatriates. One, for example, had "made false answers regarding Nazi Party membership on her 1940 alien registration form" and was indicted in New York for perjury. The most famous case involved Fritz Kuhn. In December 1944, Kuhn was one of 131 nationals requested by Germany but not cleared by the investigative agencies. The Military Intelligence Service stated:

> Fritz Kuhn [is] ... the convicted fuehrer of the German American Bund. Because of his wide personal contacts, organizational ability, and probable propaganda value to the enemy it is believed that his repatriation at this time is militarily inexpedient, because of his present potential value to the enemy and his probable value in any anti-American underground activity with which American commanders may have to deal after the occupation of Germany.[75]

Kuhn eventually was repatriated, but not until September 1945, and afterwards he spent much of his time in and out of internment camps and prisons until freed in 1950.

Some officials suggested using internees for psychological evaluations—testing and classifying their basic emotional structure under adverse conditions via the Stewart Emotional Response Test. The INS and AECU cautiously deliberated the issue, as any hint of abuse could have a serious impact on interned Americans. INS commissioner Earl Harrison solicited Ennis: "Don't rack your brains too severely, but what is your offhand opinion with respect to the attached [Stewart Test]? Under the spirit of the Geneva Convention we could scarcely use the interned aliens as guinea pigs."[76] Ennis replied:

> Personally, I like to encourage these studies, but the Germans have been so careful to match our conduct concerning internees that they might consider it a matter for some kind of reprisal in kind. Perhaps you might see Dr. Stewart, find out precisely how information and reactions would be obtained from the internees, and whether the results could be withheld until after the war, and if it seems like a useful project scientifically, ask the State Department if they perceive any objection to it.[77]

Officials had to be careful. Talk of sterilized Japanese internees, for example, nearly proved disastrous as Japan immediately threatened to do the same to its American internees. The United States and the neutral protecting powers quickly proved that the rumors were false; nevertheless, Stimson informed Japan that if Americans were mistreated, they could expect "dire consequences" in the form of "severe retaliation."[78]

Repatriation Results

During the war and up to July 1946, the United States repatriated 10,770 nationals, including 1,325 Germans (225 officials and 1,100 non-officials), 1,556 Italians (78 officials and 1,478 non-officials), 7,818 Japanese (635 officials and 7,183 non-officials), 51 Hungarians, and 5 Romanians. Of the Japanese Americans, it is unclear how many of the 5,620 renuncants or 11,229 non-renuncants were among the non-officials received by the INS. It is also unclear whether any of the 4,724 War Relocation Authority center relocatees sent to Japan during and after the war were among the Japanese repatriates.

The United States received 6,610 aliens from eighteen Latin American nations for internment and repatriation. Of these, 1,447 (with 560 more from other nations) were being held as of November 1, 1945. Two months later it was 1,370, and in February, nine months after Germany's surrender and six months after the atomic bombings of Japan, over 1,000 Latin American Germans and Japanese still languished in various camps, and the Justice Department held thousands more. By October 1, 1945, INS facilities (Fort Lincoln, Santa Fe, Tule Lake, Crystal City, and Ellis Island) held 3,911 persons along with 1,029 voluntary internees. A month later the postwar numbers peaked at 8,264 with 1,018 more self-interned. Including those from Latin America and elsewhere, the number swells to 11,289 persons. By February 1, 1946, the Justice Department held 6,101 internees (4,549 along with 498 volunteers from the U.S. as well as 1,054 from Latin American and other countries) and by March 1 the number stood at 4,004 internees.[79]

With Truman's proclamations of July 14 and September 8, 1945, empowering and directing the removal of alien enemies, the plight of the remaining internees worsened. INS commissioner Ugo Carusi instructed all district directors to act and by December the expulsion of these last undesirable aliens began. While some successfully resisted, most went against their will, some as late as July 1947, part of a forced migration of people who witnessed horrific scenes in Germany's ruins. Meanwhile, in July and August 1945 Chile and Paraguay sent even more persons to the United States for deportation to Germany. Aliens had been used as "exchange bait"—that is, deported and repatriated in exchange for those interned abroad—yet Washington claimed it had cooperated with its neighbors to "prevent Axis-inspired elements" from threatening "the security or welfare of any American republic," but in fact it had coerced compliance with its policies.[80]

Voluntary and Forced Repatriation

Repatriation was either voluntary or forced. While some fought deportation orders successfully, officials pressured most voluntary internees, especially from Latin America, to repatriate. Many were dependents—children and wives who had little choice given the conditions. Others, including 5,620 of 16,849 Japanese internees, were renunciants—those who refused to sign a loyalty oath and agitated for deportation. The 1944 Denaturalization Act, building on the 1940 Nationality Act, allowed aliens and citizens to renounce their allegiance. Consequently, renunciants were subject to internment and expatriation. With the exception of renunciant deportees, voluntary repatriates fell into three groups: those arrested in the United States who were or were not deportable, and those taken from Latin America. Non-deportable aliens who no longer wished to leave posed a special problem. Legally, the government could not coerce them and typically refrained from doing so.

The majority of voluntary repatriates never gave their assent. Indeed, Germans were often "pressed and threatened" by others or officials or "by a desire to avoid arrest and persecution." Complicating matters, U.S. authorities could not legally deport voluntary repatriates who had committed no crime, as repatriation and deportation were separate legal processes. Officials also listed family members under the "heads of the families" regardless of their immigration status. Aliens (Latin American deportees excepted) could not be compelled to return to their country of origin unless requesting or accepting repatriation. Yet, as with the *Gripsholm* voyage of January 7, 1945, INS assistant commissioner W. F. Kelly instructed district directors to recognize that "this privilege was not to be granted to any alien" on the sailing list if there was "an outstanding order of deportation." The U.S.-led policy of forced repatriation and expatriation, especially of internee children, profoundly affected many thousands for the rest of their lives.[81]

After the war in Europe ended, forced expatriation and repatriation continued. In August 1945, Commissioner Carusi wanted the Justice Department to expedite alien deportations and ordered a review of all cases, including those showing any change in status, and in January 1946 the State Department posted notices in all INS camps:

> If the country that deported you to the United States requests the return to its territory of *all* [its] aliens ... the United States government will agree.... Otherwise, the United States government ... That is, the State Department will decide either (1) to release you from internment or (2) to hold you for possible deportation. In case (2), you will have an opportunity for a hearing and the country that deported you ... will be consulted before a final decision is reached.
>
> In deciding, the State Department gives "great weight to American family ties." This means ... that if you have a wife who is a Latin American citizen or a child born in the Americas, expect to be released unless you were a spy, saboteur, or a leader in Nazi or enemy activity.[82]

The notices also answered internee questions. One was "Why have I not been given a hearing?" The State Department replied that it was releasing all who "did not appear dangerous" and added that "if you cannot be released, you will be given an opportunity to request a hearing." Another question was "If I am released, may I remain in the United States?" The answer: "No, your entry was not made under the immigration laws, and you must therefore depart promptly." If any wished to reenter, they "should apply to an American Consulate." Finally, how long must one wait? The answer: "It is difficult to say exactly," but going back to one's country would likely mean being held for two months while those expecting deportation proceedings could expect a much longer wait.

Some internees remained if they posed no threat under parole, but officials forced many to leave. The case *Citizen's Protective League et al. v. Tom C. Clark* tried to stop alien enemy removal but was decided unanimously by an appellate court on May 2, 1946, in the government's favor. Alien enemies, under guard, had to follow removal orders, "settle personal and business affairs, provide for the recovery, disposal, and removal of personal goods and effects," and leave the United States within thirty days of notification. Some applied to the State Department's Exit Permit Unit, claiming that they had permission for legal entry, which was rarely true. The Justice Department also revoked the naturalization of former enemy nationals in cases of fraud or illegality.[83]

9

Internment Camps and Relocation Centers

> We could repatriate them, we could intern them, or we could hold them in escrow for bargaining purposes.
> —STATE DEPARTMENT MEMORANDUM, NOVEMBER 3, 1942

During the war the United States interned 31,275 enemy aliens and citizens, including 6,610 from Latin America, and relocated 140,000 German, Italian, and Japanese Americans. Nearly all were innocent victims of war and fear. Authorities targeted these unfortunates, most living in vital or vulnerable coastal areas, and arrested and repatriated thousands more, mainly Germans, from Latin America. While there were different reasons for relocating Issei and Nisei en masse as opposed to the more selective relocation of German and Italian nationals and citizens, the U.S. government interned roughly the same number of Japanese as German and Italian Americans. Internment ensured a benevolent reciprocity of treatment while enabling exchanges during and after the war. None of the forcibly evacuated Germans or Italians ended up in War Relocation Authority centers, as did the Japanese, but they still suffered humiliations and restrictions. Relocatees, including thousands of Germans and Italians forced from their homes along both coasts and other areas nationwide, should not be confused with aliens and citizens interned in INS facilities. All internees received a formal hearing during which the government brought specific charges against them. The civilian hearing boards then made recommendations to Edward Ennis, director of the Alien Enemy Control Unit.

Alien Enemy Hearing Boards

Hearings were typically quite informal. Charles Gordon, a lawyer who wrote for the *National Lawyers Guild Review*, described the process:

> Shortly after the outbreak of war, Alien Enemy Hearing Boards were set up throughout the country.... Hearings are held in each case, after written notice to the alien. The Boards are not bound by any rules of procedure or evidence. They may consider any type of evidence, oral or written, in the alien's absence, and the nature of such evidence need not be disclosed.... The alien may submit affidavits and oral testimony ... but the Board may limit the number of witnesses. Stenographic record of the testimony need not be made. The alien may be accompanied to the hearing by a relative or adviser, who is not permitted to make any objection or argument.
>
> The Board only makes a recommendation to the Attorney General for unconditional release, parole under designated conditions, or internment for duration of the war.... The Attorney General reviews each file and enters the final order. After apprehension by the FBI, the INS detains the alien.... If internment, the alien is transferred to Army custody. If conditional release, the alien is paroled under the aegis of a loyal citizen. General supervision of parolees is entrusted to the INS. Detained or interned aliens are entitled to treatment equal to that accorded prisoners of war.
>
> The courts hold that national safety during war is a necessary incident of sovereignty, and the President's determinations of the danger of enemy nationals and measures necessary to combat such danger are not subject to judicial review. The courts have invariably refused to challenge the President's actions in apprehending dangerous alien enemies.... It is presumed that the President has acted lawfully, and the [alien enemy] is properly in custody.[1]

Very few aliens retained lawyers. For those who did, the government forbade representation in hearing rooms. The public and media were excluded. There were no records of alien, FBI, or informant testimonies. Hearing boards were often biased and the trials unfair. James Rowe later called California's boards "pretty thin stuff," while Edward Ennis testified that "every alien enemy was given a hearing," which typically lasted half an hour, and then his office decided if the accused was freed, paroled, or interned—whether at large (working under U.S. Forest Service or another agency's supervision) or to be forcibly or voluntarily repatriated. Of the 9,100 aliens examined by early 1943, officials interned 4,100, paroled 3,700, and released 1,300. Because the War and Justice Departments operated independently and usually disagreed about policies, an array of internment, detention, assembly, relocation, and citizen isolation centers arose.[2]

Many waited months or even years for a decision. Others found themselves released after a case review. Ennis assured Biddle that "applications for review are denied in the more serious cases," but others had their files reconsidered. Rehearing involved a special board held at the camp whose custodial authorities could access the internee's conduct record. Results went to the original board for its input before any possible status change, and "in 75% of the cases the order is changed and usually from internment to parole."[3]

Arrests and Restrictions

The FBI had taken 620 Germans, 98 Italians, and 1,212 Japanese into custody by December 9, 1941. A month later there were 2,599 enemy aliens in over one hundred city, county, or federal jails. This concerned Hull, so he asked Biddle to act quickly to avoid "any retaliatory measures against American nationals" by the Axis. Biddle assured Hull of INS compliance, while Roosevelt, acting upon Justice and War Department advice, ended the possibility of a mass relocation of Germans and Italians on May 5, 1942, and instead opted to remove them from either coast, or anywhere, and intern enemy aliens hemispherically. "The control of alien enemies," Roosevelt told Stimson, is "primarily a civilian matter except of course in the case of the Japanese mass evacuation on the Pacific Coast."[4]

On May 15, with little publicity, defense commanders under Executive Order 9066 issued individual exclusion orders that forcibly evacuated thousands of Germans and Italians, aliens and citizens, along both coasts and throughout the nation and its territories based on military necessity. On May 26, Karl Bendetsen announced in a nationwide broadcast that "no further mass evacuation is contemplated either on the West Coast or on the East Coast." Roosevelt saw Germans and Italians as distinct problems on opposite coasts requiring solutions different from the Japanese. The first was a national civilian matter demanding discretion and resolution on an individual basis. The second was a West Coast military matter requiring the mass removal of Japanese along with Germans and Italians. The military danger to the West Coast coupled with the internal fifth-column menace guided policymaking. The West Coast solution would not disrupt the war effort, and nearly all supported the relocation of the main perceived threat—Japanese Americans.[5]

Aliens were controlled by exclusion, travel limitations, certificates of identification, prohibited articles, conduct, and arrest and internment. Regulations of December 7 and 8, 1941, and January 14 and February 5, 1942, allowed aliens to travel locally, commute to work, go to school, and attend religious services. None, however, could "reside in, enter upon, remain in, or be found within any area designated a prohibited area." Those permitted in restricted areas obeyed additional rules. Seven days' written notice was required to travel or move. The alien provided his name, home and business address, certificate of identification, and a detailed itinerary of the trip's purpose, persons and places to be visited, means and route of transportation, and travel dates. If the Justice Department and FBI approved, the alien received an endorsed statement copy and could travel only with documentation. Those who traveled often on business saw a magistrate, stated the need, and provided required information. Authorities could always prohibit a trip, cancel it in progress, or deny any travel if it might risk public safety or threaten national security. No alien could fly. Any status change entailed alerting the U.S. Attorney, the Alien Registration Division, and the FBI.

Radios were surrendered—including transmitters and shortwave receivers. Cameras, also prohibited, were handed over to local police. Under special circumstances, aliens could petition to keep radios or cameras. Only in "extraordinary and exceptional cases" could they possess or use firearms or other prohibited articles. U.S. marshals inventoried, transported, and stored confiscated items. Any alien not in compliance was subject to "apprehension, detention, and internment" and, if found aiding or inducing any other enemy alien to "fail to comply with any of the regulations," could also be "arrested, detained, or interned for the duration." Fear, circumstantial evidence, and mere hearsay led to action taken against thousands who then suffered numerous hardships.[6]

Internees: Where, Why, and Who

They came from Anchorage and Atlanta, Baltimore and Birmingham, Chicago and Charlotte, Dallas and Detroit, Honolulu and Houston, Los Angeles and Louisville, Miami and Milwaukee, New Orleans and New York, Phoenix and Philadelphia, Providence and Portland, San Diego and San Juan. They also came from Bogotá and Buenos Aires, Montevideo and Mexico City, Santiago and São Paulo. Internees, due to an initial lack of adequate housing, were held in internment or prisoner-of-war camps or makeshift facilities. They spent months or years in facilities scattered worldwide—from Africa, the Middle East, and Asia, including China, the Philippines, Hong Kong, Java, and Japan, to Europe, including France, Denmark, Germany, and Italy. Ensuring their safety proved difficult and sometimes impossible. Hundreds, if not thousands, died.

Internees, from the allegedly dangerous to the inherently harmless, were held "in escrow for bargaining purposes." A November 1942 memo for Thomas Cooley, chief of the AECU's Review Section, directed authorities to intern aliens who were "of the hobo or drifter type," those who were "single and looked to German organizations or societies for diversion or interest, thus becoming exposed to German propaganda," and those who "made frequent trips to Germany." But "a German alien who had family ties as well as financial interests here and who made no return trips to Germany was invariably released or paroled." The selection criteria targeted the alien poor, many of whom had lived through the Great Depression, were often not well educated, and lacked business, legal, or social connections. Their detention hardly detracted from the war effort.[7]

There was a more unscrupulous reason for internment: the military gained soldiers. For some, their only crime was refusing to fight the Axis. Edwin Clapp informed Edward Ennis that the FBI and the Army were pressuring officials who were arresting aliens into giving them a choice: fight or face internment. Few criticized such policies and practices, and most who did spoke out belatedly or anonymously. Biddle, for example, knew there were serious flaws and tried to remedy some of them, usually with little success. By the summer of 1943 he concluded that the FBI's "dangerousness" classification system served "no useful purpose" and declared that the evidence used was "inadequate," that the applied standards were "defective," and that stereotyping aliens was "impractical, unwise, and dangerous." He ordered a stop to the FBI's custodial detention system. One among many high-ranking officials testified that hemispheric internment was haphazard and ineffectual:

> American authorities presented evidence to local authorities that X was dangerous and asked that he be sent for internment; in other instances, local police decided that Y's liberty was prejudicial to the security of the Americas and sent him along on the boat.... No thought was given to specifying what was to be done with an individual beyond the fact that he was boarding an American vessel heading for the United States.[8]

Internees held a wide variety of jobs before their incarceration. The Japanese at Fort Sill, Oklahoma, for example, included sugar beet contractors, farmers, cooks, barbers, fishermen, doctors, priests, teachers, clerks, secretaries, merchants, tailors, students, grocers, mail carriers, vegetable shippers, and carpenters. There were fruit stand owners, saki brewers, dancers, hotel operators/managers, chemists, gasoline attendants, poultry farmers, watchmen, launderers, teamsters, cobblers, florists, reporters, newspaper owners, photographers, janitors, drill operators, interpreters, managers, honey-bee men, orange pickers, smelters, laborers, and card dealers. The list was seemingly endless.

Relocatee and internee demographics reveal consistent dealings with the nation's perceived enemies. During the first half of 1942, authorities forcibly removed 10,000 to 20,000 European aliens from both coasts living in or near militarily sensitive or vulnerable areas. Most Germans came from states with large German American populations. From December 7, 1941, to June 30, 1945, the FBI arrested 7,043 German aliens: 2,292 were from New York, 756 from New Jersey, and 388 from Pennsylvania; approximately 350 were from the Southeast, 300 from Texas, and 572 from California; over 250 were from the Northwest, and roughly 800 came from Wisconsin, Illinois, Michigan, Ohio, Indiana, and Missouri. The FBI also arrested 3,567 Italian and 5,428 Japanese aliens along with 121 German, 29 Italian, and 598 Japanese American citizens.

No mass relocation of Japanese on the Hawaiian Islands or Germans or Italians anywhere occurred because of the catastrophic economic effects. With no threat of a German or Italian invasion, unlike Japan's with the West Coast, relocatee numbers reveal an even (albeit heavy-handed) national-security approach. The same logic applied to Latin America, and since authorities saw Germans as the greatest threat, they arrested, deported, and interned them in far greater numbers than the Japanese. Of the 6,610 persons deported and interned in the United States there were 4,058 Germans, 288 Italians, and 2,264 Japanese. The War Department and other agencies simultaneously conducted their own evacuation, relocation, and internment programs.[9]

Barbed-Wire Disease

The War and Justice Departments managed a great variety of internment and relocation facilities. More than fifty camps in twenty-eight states held German, Italian, and Japanese citizens and aliens. The military had a detention center in San Juan, Puerto Rico, and the Justice Department operated a camp on Pine Island, Cuba. Camps had mess halls, shops, laundries, gardens, swimming pools, golf courses, schools, hospitals, libraries, soccer fields, and theaters, so were not concentration camps save for the encompassing barbed wire and guard towers. Attempts to escape were few, only twelve in all, and only one lasted more than a few hours: a determined Nicaraguan who eluded Camp Kenedy's guards for three days trying to reach the Mexican border.

For most, the worst part of their experience was "barbed-wire disease." Doctors and nurses found many of their patients suffered from depression. Crystal City's hospital staff treated daily up to sixty patients whose "ills were often imaginary—traceable to detention, the fence, the loss of freedom." Although barbed wire provided a palpable reminder of confinement, several camps lacked it, while others scarcely needed it. Tule Lake lacked barbed wire until it became a segregation center in September 1943. Crystal City's inner fence was so permeable that German kids "escaped" daily from the camp swimming pool to go play and climb trees in the nearby grapefruit orchard while Japanese men often labored in the fields beyond. Manzanar's three wires kept children from wandering into the desert and prevented animals from entering the compound. A photographer, Toyo Miyatake, said anybody could easily walk through Manzanar's cattle-guard barbed wire, "but nobody wanted to." Living in a gilded cage, internees felt betrayed by a nation that professed its respect for the natural, inalienable rights of the individual. Moreover, internment meant alienation in postwar society. Bitter memories and FBI warnings made former captives reluctant or afraid to talk. Indelible emotional scars endured as the fence became a symbol of guilt and condemnation. Jerre Mangione recalled that one prisoner wrote his wife and "begged her to release their pet canary from its cage. 'No living thing should be caged up. When I am free, I want to live in a house without locks, even without doors. It will be made up of windows, the view must not be obstructed by anything.'"[10]

Internee dependents suffered severe financial hardship. Many wrote to the Bureau of Public Assistance, including its director, Jane Hoey, requesting aid. By October 1942, she noted a sharp rise in their "widespread economic distress." Hoey wrote Hoover, who then asked Earl Harrison to give her the name, address, and number of dependents of everyone the FBI held. "Steps were being taken," said Hoover, to "diminish the number of extreme hardship cases." Internees could "petition to have their dependents, regardless of innocence or guilt, united with them in family internment camps." Yet, he admitted, many dependents "do not wish to undergo the severe restriction of camps," and other paroled or released alien enemies "find themselves in distress because of their status or because their apprehension and hearing have disrupted their employment." As families struggled, Hoover noted that those "who were not embittered" by their internment "tend to become so." He then removed dependents, by voluntary transfers to family camps, to lessen the chance of security problems and a dependent's becoming a potential danger.[11]

Kurt Heinrich Rudolf Peters

A few camp employees and commanders acted on behalf of suffering internees, sometimes with positive results. Bert Fraser, in charge of Fort Missoula, Montana, wrote his superiors and sympathetic lawyers in support of Kurt Peters, who endured three years of internment before joining the Navy. After his induction, Peters appeared in uniform before a judge who granted his citizenship papers and said "go have a beer." Getting that particular beer was an ordeal.

Kurt Heinrich Rudolf Peters was born in Hamburg, Germany, in 1920 and by 1938 was a radioman aboard freighters (to avoid Wehrmacht service). In August 1939 he was working aboard the Standard Oil tanker *Peter Hurll*. The ship was docked in New York City when Germany invaded Poland, and Peters suddenly found himself stranded as Standard Oil replaced its German crew with Americans. As German sailors began receiving arrest warrants for overstaying their visas, Peters tried to get American citizenship while enrolling at Columbia University. None of that mattered when he was arrested on September 21, 1940. After several hearings he was interned at Ellis Island and then Fort Lincoln in May 1941. There he met Bert Fraser, then a camp supply officer.

Fraser recognized that Peters was a victim of circumstances. In August 1941 he wrote to a lawyer friend of Kurt's that Kurt was an "honest and industrious young man [who] has a real desire to become an American citizen," and added that "now is the time for we Americans to really show our belief in freedom and democracy by helping those who are deserving." If Peters was deported to Germany, Fraser warned, it would likely mean a "long prison term, or even death." Kurt's efforts to naturalize became well known, as did his fight to resist deportation. In January 1942 he was told to expect a decision shortly. Eight months later he was still waiting and again wrote the INS:

> My conviction that I am spiritually on the right side has grown irrevocably. I sincerely wish to convert my statements into action and prove that I am spiritually in full alliance with America and every ideal it stands and fights for; but as long as I am handicapped and sentenced to idleness, I certainly cannot do that.
>
> I am fully aware this case requires a thorough and profound investigation, particularly when ruthless public enemies have often betrayed your trust and good will. . . . The best proof for my loyalty and devotion would be an opportunity to do my share in this war. I am willing to do everything the government considers most appropriate. It hurts me infinitely to be detained. . . . As I am a licensed radio-operator, I am willing to join the American Merchant Marine. . . . I implore you to realize that you decide over a man's life who cherishes nothing so highly as Americanism.

Fraser forwarded Kurt's letter along with these recommendations to Ennis:

> Several of the German boys worked for me the entire time at Fort Lincoln and I know their characteristics and anti-Nazi feelings. I would not hesitate to assume responsibility for Kurt Peters and Fred Bruning. They are trusted . . . work hard, and are loyal. . . . They are far more deserving than many individuals I have seen released from the camps.
>
> Living among these people for so long you soon choose between the bad and good. . . . These boys are worthy, an asset rather than a danger or liability. It is my duty as an American to help anyone who is deserving, regardless if they are unfortunate enough to bear the stigma of "enemy alien." These boys are certainly "friendly aliens."

On Columbus Day in 1942, Biddle announced that Italian Americans were no longer enemies. INS commissioner Ugo Carusi added, "Our government understands how devoted the Italian people are to the principles of liberty . . . you have the government's friendship and confidence." The claims stung German internees, yet

Kurt did not give up. Fraser kept championing him, and by April 1943 Kurt finally had a favorable hearing. In June, Biddle ordered Kurt paroled. Eleven months passed before Kurt finally became a citizen and had his beer.[12]

The First Camps

Thousands of internees spent months or years in camps that workers were building at a furious pace now that the nation was at war. The need for them was obvious. By January 7, 1942, there were 1,265 German, 231 Italian, and 1,208 Japanese alien detainees. Preparations had begun a year earlier to ready Forts Missoula, Lincoln, and Stanton to receive 10,000 persons, but work had fallen behind schedule as detainee numbers rose swiftly and the War and Justice Departments discussed relocating all West Coast enemy aliens fourteen or older. Ellis Island, which had been converted into an alien detention camp in December 1939, was overcrowded too. By February 18, the day before EO 9066, the FBI had arrested nearly 4,000 alien enemies. On March 3, General Richard Donovan and others discussed steps to detain them. Army G-4 (supply and evacuation) had facilities for roughly 25,000 in "Type B" Civilian Conservation Corps camps (56 to hold 16,000 and 39 more expected by March 31 with a capacity of 8,500). Army "Type A" facilities, with provisions for guards, included Forts Sill, Sam Houston, and Bliss, which could hold 600, 900, and 1,350 internees, respectively. A camp in Florence, Arizona, was nearly ready, and facilities in Stringtown and Lordsburg were under construction. The Army was also preparing "Type C" facilities—private and municipal properties such as military housing, racetracks, and fairgrounds—to hold 22,350 persons.[13]

By May 11 the Army held 1,094 Japanese, 735 Germans, and 102 Italians along with 23 others, while the Justice Department had 3,331 Japanese, 2,028 German, 1,255 Italian, and 91 others along with 1,818 additional aliens awaiting internment and another 5,563 awaiting a decision—release or internment. Slightly more Germans and Italians than West Coast Japanese were interned or in custody. Only five of nineteen camps were completed, although fourteen temporary ones were in use. The Army needed all of these facilities as it had 2,289 internees and soon received another 2,316 while the Justice Department had 6,557 enemy aliens in custody. Meanwhile, authorities released 594 and paroled 768 enemy aliens. Captain Earl Edwards, chief of the Army's Operations Branch, figured that by year's end the Army would need to house 52,000 persons (excluding West Coast Japanese handled by the WRA). By July, a dozen facilities held over 3,000 aliens and nearly 3,000 more soon followed. There were tens of thousands more, mostly Japanese, who were being forcibly moved and would have to be managed.

Relocation camps had to house 90,000 Japanese Americans from coastal assembly centers plus 17,000 who left their homes as five major movements from January to June 1942 brought 1,401 Germans, 53 Italians, and 526 Japanese aliens from Latin America to the United States, though most were repatriated by early fall. Taken arbitrarily in mass sweeps, most were innocents, as officials later admitted. Thousands more followed as Washington overreacted to widely published albeit erroneous official and media reports that millions of Latin American Germans, and maybe some Italians, were an imminent threat.[14]

Camp Crystal City, Texas

There were four basic camp types used during and after the war. First, the INS operated eight internment camps and oversaw dozens of other facilities. The military administered POW camps, and the Army initially housed internees along with the INS until May 1943, when it began receiving more POWs and the INS took charge of all internees. Second, War Relocation Centers (WRCs), established by EO 9102, which created the WRA, were under civilian control. The WRA administered ten Relocation Center Camps, including Tule Lake, which became a Segregation Center in September 1943 as the military began expatriating or repatriating internees. Aside from Tule Lake, these centers helped evacuees relocate outside the western defensive zone or unaffected areas of Washington, Oregon, and Arizona. An evacuee could leave a WRC by taking a loyalty oath and offering proof of employment. Third, the Wartime Civil Control Administration (WCCA) ran seventeen Assembly Centers, which expedited evacuee removal (voluntary and then forced). Finally, there were two Citizen Isolation Camps in Moab, Utah, and Leupp, Arizona, to house internees who had psychological disorders.[15]

By the spring of 1942, the government forcibly evacuated thousands of West Coast Germans, Italians, and Japanese; during the summer and fall, most evacuees were relocated or interned. Relocatees went to WRCs in California, Idaho, Utah, Arizona, Wyoming, Colorado, and Arkansas. All internees went to INS camps. These included four primary facilities in Bismarck, North Dakota; Missoula, Montana; Santa Fe, New Mexico, and Crystal City, Texas.

The United States interned 31,275 enemy aliens during the war: 16,849 Japanese (including 5,620 renunciants), 10,905 Germans, and 3,278 Italians along with 52 Hungarians, 5 Bulgarians, 25 Romanians, and 161 others. Most were aliens, although several hundred German and Italian American citizens (not including children) lost their freedom. Moreover, 6,610 internees arrived from nearly every Latin American nation. Because internment adversely affected entire families, the INS established Crystal City, the only family internment camp used by any nation during the war.[16]

Prior to Crystal City's opening, two facilities in eastern Texas housed enemy aliens. In early 1942 a Farm Security Administration (FSA) migratory labor and former Civilian Conservation Corps camp reopened near the small town of Kenedy. Located fifty miles southeast of San Antonio, Camp Kenedy was for males only, mostly Germans and Japanese. Yet Kenedy's 3,000 internees soon represented seventeen nations due to the influx of those brought from Latin America. In nearby Seagoville (Dallas outskirts), the INS used a federal correctional women's institute. Originally for females, Seagoville later held couples in prefabricated Victory Huts while single women lived in dorms.

The INS had on file another migratory labor camp. Situated between Uvalde and Carrizo Springs, 120 miles southwest of San Antonio and 30 miles from the Mexican border, was Crystal City. The FSA transferred the property, and on November 6 and 7, 1942, INS representatives visited the site. Four factors favored its conversion into a family camp: first, 41 three-room cottages and 118 one-room shelters existed; second, adequate utility services for

2,000 people were in place; third, winters were mild; and fourth, the camp was located far from vital or vulnerable areas. Originally intended to hold only 2,000 Japanese, facilities and services rapidly expanded. Nicholas Collaer, a career Border Patrol officer whom Harrison had chosen to run the camp, soon became overworked and anxious managing disputes between the German and Japanese internees. His wife and three children did not take well to the sun's intense heat or the camp's primitive conditions, and soon the Collaer family was off to Philadelphia, where Collaer began his new job as acting assistant commissioner for alien control. To oversee operations Harrison next named Joseph O'Rourke, whom Jerre Mangione praised as one "who combined the skills of a seasoned diplomat with the expertise of a first-class social worker and psychologist." Internees, Mangione recalled, lauded O'Rourke's efforts.[17]

As the first internees, 115 Germans, arrived on December 12, 1942, from Ellis Island, joined by 15 more from Camp Forrest days later, they entered a 100-acre unfinished compound. Camp conversions had begun a month earlier, but the handful of INS officials and construction workers had not yet completed the ten-foot-high perimeter fence with floodlights and guard towers. With so few guards, the Border Patrol provided assistance and surveillance. The initial 140 acres outside the camp was devoted to farming, personnel residences, playgrounds, and storage areas for equipment and maintenance supplies. Thirty-five German families, 130 persons, began living in a roped-off section of camp that had twenty-nine cottages. With population growth, the INS added duplex, triplex, and quadruplex housing units, more three-room cottages, one-room shelters, and Victory Huts. Hoping to give internees as normal a life as possible, each duplex and triplex had a toilet and bath, while the quadruplexes had communal toilets. Each unit had furniture, a kitchen sink with cold running water, an oil stove with oven for cooking and heating, and essential utensils and dishes. Internees helped build and farm on 50 acres of additional land purchased by the INS. By March, the camp held 378 Germans and 145 Japanese. Reaching 3,374 internees by late 1944, Crystal City resembled, aside from the barbed wire and guard towers, any other small city. Officials and internees had built 519 structures at a cost that exceeded $1,000,000. There was a seventy-bed hospital, dental clinic, chapel, grammar and high schools for German and Japanese students, administrative buildings, recreation centers, a barber and beauty shop, stores, and a community center. By war's end, the camp had 694 buildings on 290 acres.

Joseph O'Rourke, who succeeded Collaer in June 1943, inherited many managerial problems, including difficulties between internees and employees. Mabel Ellis of New York's YWCA noted that Crystal City's isolated location gave employees "little more freedom than the internees." O'Rourke was well aware of this, but he could not stop the high attrition rate of personnel:

> Selling these employees on the internment program was an obstacle in itself, which, in effect, squeezed the staff members in between the natural demands of an internee group and a corps of workers who were convinced in their own mind that anything received by the internees was too good and too much. Naturally, this condition did not alleviate the general suspicions and accusations of a hostile public whose ration cards would not permit them to enjoy as much meat, sugar, etc., as nationals of enemy countries in government custody.

The INS showed off what Collaer described as "one of the best, if not the best, internment camp ever operated by any country." The official INS documentary about Crystal City, *Alien Enemy Detention Facility*, begins with a shot of the American flag fluttering in the breeze as "My Country, 'Tis of Thee" echoes in the background, and ends with a "view of Old Glory being raised to the top of the flagpole." The twenty-minute narrated film depicts camp officials caring for the 3,600 German and Japanese detainees who live, work, and play "under a tradition of American standards of decent and humane treatment." The images bear this out. Children frolic in the pool, blocks of ice and bottles of milk are delivered, classical notes drift through the air played by German musicians, women and men buy food and clothes in the camp's many canteens, Germans fix cars and make furniture, Japanese gardeners till the soil, and mail trucks pick up and deliver parcels.[18]

Despite O'Rourke's efforts to make life bearable or even pleasurable for internees, stress often led to severe bouts of depression and other detention-related ills. Many developed a deep and abiding animus toward authorities and a nation ostensibly fighting the "good war." But O'Rourke well managed the camp's growing diversity as more Germans came from disparate places, including Camp Kenedy and Costa Rica. On March 10 even more Germans along with Japanese women and children arrived from Seagoville. That same day, the first camp birth occurred. A German male began life as a citizen behind barbed wire under the watchful eyes of armed guards. A steadily evolving mix of people arrived from many camps and relocation centers.[19]

The population grew steadily, peaking at the very end of 1944 with 3,374 internees (2,371 Japanese, 997 Germans, and 6 Italians). Numbers fluctuated with arrivals and departures, births and deaths, but typically ranged from 2,500 to 3,000 persons. Camp demographics varied, too. For example, Germans exceeded Japanese until July 31, 1943. The next month the Germans were the minority until 1,330 Japanese repatriates left for New York City to board the *Gripsholm* in exchange for U.S. and other Western nationals. In February 1944 the Japanese became a majority again, this time for good.

All camps scaled down in the summer of 1945. Yet nearly two months after V-E Day, Crystal City held 2,548 Japanese, 756 Germans, and 12 Italians. From its inception through June 1945 it received 4,751 internees (including 153 births), released or paroled 138, transferred 73, interned at large 84, and repatriated 354 Germans in February 1944 and 600 more in January 1945 along with 169 Japanese in August 1943. Seventeen internees died there. Except for two Japanese girls who drowned in the pool and one German boy hit by a truck, the deaths were from natural causes. After June 1945, several thousand more arrived, mainly Japanese repatriates, and half of them left for Japan on December 3. Most of the remaining 1,168 Japanese stayed though the summer of 1946, but were all released by year's end. The camp officially closed on February 27, 1948, and the last internees, all Germans, went to Ellis Island, where many stayed until June 1948—three years after the war's end in Europe.[20]

Crystal City Camp Life

The children were O'Rourke's primary concern. They should have fond memories, he felt, so that they could "grow up to be good American citizens." Earl Harrison once saw children getting ready to "play war," but they never did. When he and O'Rourke asked why, the kids responded that nobody wanted to be "the enemy" but "everybody wanted to be on the American side." Many children had typical experiences: soccer, baseball, volleyball, basketball, and tennis; swimming at the pool that internees converted from an irrigation reservoir; recitals, films, dramas, musicals, and festival days. A nightly family ritual involved walking the camp's perimeter; as the evening offshore breeze made the climate tolerable, hundreds exercised, pondering their situation and contemplating the future. Mangione recalled that the older children had a tough time. "We're supposed to be Americans. We were born here. So why should we have to live in a prison camp like we were criminals? We haven't done anything to be punished for. And neither have our parents." O'Rourke conceded that it was a "tough problem," telling the teens and adults that they were "victims of a lousy war and the only thing to do is to make the best of the situation." He did his best to keep everyone busy with "lectures, courses, sports, gardening, and all kinds of hobbies."[21]

Officials prioritized education. Parents could send their kids to a German, English, or Japanese school, where teachers taught reading, writing, and arithmetic in the students' respective languages. Kindergarten and elementary schools were segregated, but the high school integrated German and Japanese students, who had a library with 3,500 volumes plus texts. Worship and spiritual life were important, and families could attend religious services at the camp chapel. The internees themselves improved the camp's aesthetics and spent $50,000 of their own money adding rooms and porches to their residences in addition to beautifying the camp through gardening and landscaping projects. Such endeavors boosted morale, but internees felt embittered. As Mangione noted during his two-month-long camp visits, "many of the occupants represented no threat to the national security; had they been accorded due process of law, they would probably never have been interned." Investigators who reexamined cases usually found that charges had been based on flimsy or nonexistent evidence, unreliable witnesses or accusers who had a particular ax to grind, or vague hearsay and speculation about political loyalties.[22]

Dr. Amy Stannard, the officer in charge of Seagoville, noted that some female internees suffered from deep psychological wounds that would never heal. Despite the government's later claim of having given "extra careful consideration of evidence in the case of any woman," Dr. Stannard's findings were substantiated. Crystal City staff also noted distinct changes in the attitudes of women and children who voluntarily interned themselves. Swiss, Swedish, and Red Cross representatives saw changes too in the "hearts and minds" of voluntary internees. Camp administrators argued against voluntary internment because national values and ideals would lose their hold over American-born women and children who, as internees, were subjected to anti-American sentiment:

> It is the general opinion of our staff that voluntary internment should not be permitted.... Pro-enemy sentiment is in the majority, and under this daily influence, typical American boys and girls have been changed in heart, attitude, and behavior.... [It] is only logical that a human being will be affected when he is completely removed from American influence. This office greatly admires the children of interned parents who have weathered the storm of public sentiment outside a camp, and we do not attempt to restrain our emotions when we see these children, many of whom are members of our military forces, visit their parents who are here as dangerous enemy aliens.
>
> We can see no objection to women, actually interned themselves, being joined with their husbands, but we would caution extra careful consideration of evidence in the case of any woman, since our observation has formed the opinion that a woman, because of her usual emotional state, will generally develop an anti-American complex through internment, even if no such prior attitude existed.[23]

Some internees supported Hitler or Mussolini, while a few Issei and Nisei staged rallies to convince others to renounce their allegiance to America and return to Japan. The Hokoku Seinen Dan club tried to instill pro-Japanese values and, in the only instance of group violence, Japanese at Santa Fe conducted military exercises and threw rocks at the guards. Members terrorized others and threatened bodily harm until they "renounced their American citizenship and joined the club. The goal was to go to Japan and fight against the United States." Officials indexed aliens into two groups based on their repatriation status. While many non-repatriates "sympathized with the cause of their fatherland . . . a large number evidenced a pro-American attitude." Officials acknowledged that some were trying to "incur favor," but there was no doubt that American loyalty was "strictly genuine on the part of others." Conversely, the repatriates "loudly blew the horn of loyalty to their home country and branded the others as traitors."[24]

Most internees viewed the war as "a fight between his father and mother." As the Axis began losing, many canceled their repatriation petitions and rethought their politics. The Internal Relations Office found that after Germany's surrender there were no longer any Nazis in Crystal City. After U.S. troops reoccupied the Philippines, few Japanese at the Santa Fe camp demanded repatriation and signs of American loyalty increased noticeably. As more Pacific victories followed, one Japanese internee stated: "We licked the hell out of those Japs on Iwo Jima." When camp officials told another that they were cutting work hours to save money, he remarked that it would "clear enough money to buy at least two machine guns a week." Despite "difficult and trying situations," the day-to-day routines had gone well. Overall, the Crystal City staff felt, internees "highly respect the administration. They have, of course, grumbled at times, but we have no doubt that each individual realizes that the treatment accorded by this government has gone far beyond the 'must' requirements outlined in the international agreement to which we are a signatory."[25]

Because the United States met and often exceeded Geneva Convention standards, newspaper and magazine articles occasionally rebuked camp administrators for giving internees better food and medical care than most Americans had. They responded that, by convention, all internees had to be fed equally in quantity and quality to U.S. soldiers. Internees also provided much of their own food and health care—thus cutting costs while allowing self-help. Ivan Williams, Santa Fe's commandant, expressed frustration that public relations had created concerns about the internment program because "we have been too secretive." Williams decried the lack of publicity explaining camp conditions and ventured that "not one person in fifty knew about the terms of the Geneva Convention."[26]

Crystal City's organizational structure mirrored those of other camps. Six divisions carried out camp administration. Headquarters had an officer in charge and an assistant with administrative and fiscal employees. Supply was responsible for procurement, distribution, and property control accounting. Liaison was created for miscellaneous contacts with internees and work between camp officers and aliens. Surveillance oversaw the general custody of internees and prevented escapes. Maintenance was responsible for the upkeep of buildings and utilities. Finally, there was Medical, a division critical for internee health. By war's end, there were seven principal divisions—Administrative; Surveillance; Internal Security; Maintenance, Construction, and Repair; Internal Relations; Education; and Medical—subdivided, in turn, into sections and units. Eventually 150 personnel worked under the seven organizational units. Some 200 additional employees served as artisans and laborers. Every office grew in personnel and size and the camp resembled a typical town, excepting the barbed wire, armed guards, and lack of basic freedoms for its intended inhabitants.[27]

War Relocation Authority Camps

Roosevelt issued EO 9066 on February 19, 1942, because winning the war required "every possible protection" against espionage and sabotage to national defense material, premises, and utilities. The WCCA and WRA, established on March 11 and 18, respectively, restricted alien movement. DeWitt, who set up the WCCA, was in charge of defending the entire West Coast—including Alaska. Karl Bendetsen left as chief of the Aliens Division, PMG's Office, to head the Civil Affairs Division of the WCCA and its seventeen interim assembly centers. These held evacuees until more permanent relocation centers could be built. The WRA had the formidable task of relocating aliens from designated military areas. Milton Eisenhower led the effort until June 1942, when Dillon Myer took over and served until the program's end in June 1946. A confidential memo of April 7, 1942 reveals internment and evacuation differences:

> Enemy aliens deemed unsafe are placed in internment camps, under guard, and . . . are held in accordance with the provisions of international law. The enemy alien program is handled by the Department of Justice. The evacuation of a military area is an entirely different matter. The military commander of such an area can determine who shall remain in the area, and under what condition, who shall be removed from the area, or who may enter. . . . However, once outside of a military area, citizens of the United States are free to come and go as they please.

The WRA ran ten permanent relocation centers that housed Japanese Americans. Three opened by June and seven more by the fall of 1942. Nine remained open until November 1945, and Tule Lake up to March 1946. Relocating Japanese evacuated from prohibited West Coast military areas, the WRA admitted, was far more difficult and dangerous than originally anticipated. Driven by fifth-column fears and "stern military necessity" with the coast likely a "zone of combat," the Army moved the Japanese far from strategic areas, railroads, highways, or places where communication or interaction with outsiders might occur. The agency envisioned a five-point program whereby relocatees would engage in useful public work, agricultural production, manufacturing, employment, and create a self-supporting group in remote areas where they would be "no burden to the government." Relocation centers became communities, complete with schools, hospitals, churches, and libraries, yet they were remote and desolate. None enjoyed a hospitable climate, and weather conditions at Minidoka, Heart Mountain, and Topaz were so harsh that winter temperatures typically reached 30 degrees below zero. Relocatees suffered from isolation, and boredom was commonplace.[28]

A series of crises punctuated evacuee life. Most went from Army assembly to WRA relocation centers from the spring of 1942 to

February 1943; from then to January 1944 occurred registration and segregation, which preceded a draft crisis lasting for much of 1944–45 alongside the release of nearly all remaining Japanese—a process begun in the summer of 1942 even as thousands entered the camps. After the trauma of being forcibly moved came Stimson's January 1943 announcement of an all-Nisei combat unit. Two questions on a form given to all Japanese relocatees over seventeen years of age caused considerable problems, as they artificially created "loyal" and "disloyal" Japanese. Friends and families were ripped apart as the Army moved the "disloyal" to Tule Lake and the "loyal" to other relocation centers. The reinstitution of the draft for relocatee citizens sowed further bitterness as many felt abused, betrayed, and ostracized. While many would not serve, others did to demonstrate their loyalty. Two-thirds of those who returned home met with some hostility and violence, but mainly found their fellow Americans welcoming; one-third started anew in places like Chicago, Denver, Salt Lake City, and New York City—far away from their former homes and neighbors.[29]

Getting In and Out

Americans expressed rancor to relocatee and internee news—humane treatment, releases, riots, strikes, and disturbances—by writing local newspaper editors and even Roosevelt himself, especially about Japanese relocatees. Forgetting or overlooking their loss of property, jobs, and freedom, separation from friends and family, and the stigma of "enemy," thousands wrote the WRA, the FBI, and the War, State, and Justice Departments sharply criticizing the persons and policies responsible for freeing the Japanese "in spite of their assertions of disloyalty." Californians, noting how "Japs here are being petted and coddled," were especially bitter, and letters by Oroville residents typified national attitudes. Jay Spencer stated, "We do not want the Japs. Send them back to Japan where they belong." Minnie Hedge, a self-proclaimed "native daughter of California," wrote, "We the people of the Pacific Coast do not want *any* of the Japs turned loose out of the internment camps and we especially do not want them to come back here." Another asked Roosevelt: "Why are we giving our boys' lives to fight the

Japs when the Japs we interned created riots and demonstrations against our government are now given their freedom? Give them the front line, the firing squad, or going back to Japan." Mrs. H. G. Shannon wrote: "If we don't get them out of here and back to their own country where they belong, this country won't be safe to walk down the streets. Get rid of the rats here, either ship them back or shoot them or make them fight for our good." Mrs. Grace Walker said: "We are giving our boys' lives, and why coddle the Japs who create riots, and now give them their freedom to do worse. Why not the firing squad or back to Japan. Please no more freedom for Japs." Governor Earl Warren himself warned of a "second Pearl Harbor" as numerous town committees expressed their shock and outrage.[30]

Some Japanese Americans renounced their citizenship, others sought to prove their loyalty, requesting enlistment in America's armed forces or joining work projects for the war effort, and still more campaigned for their freedom through petitions, letters, and the courts. Kiichi Nishino wrote Roosevelt on the first anniversary of Pearl Harbor. Like many, he was torn, expressing regret that he was "not allowed to take any part in the armed forces or war industry," but added: "I wish to reaffirm my loyalty to this land of my adoption, and to express my support of your policies in an all-out war effort."[31]

Many doubted the loyalty of Japanese Americans, and fears intensified with the release of thousands of relocatees. Washington DC's *Evening Star* reported this on May 29, 1943:

> The Dies Committee disclosed today it had found evidence that many of the Japanese discharged from the ten relocation centers . . . had received training in an espionage school operated by the Imperialistic Black Dragon Society of Japan. The Jap secret agents, according to Robert E. Stripling, chief investigator for the committee, are member of the Butoki-Kai and were taught at the North American School of Military Virtue how to carry out a program of destruction. . . . The organization has 10,000 members in the United States.
>
> "The Japanese are being released at the rate of 1,000 a week to run willy-nilly all over the country," declared Mr. Stripling. "There

is no way of determining which are loyal to this country and which are loyal to Japan." Army questionnaires ... disclosed that 4 per cent unhesitatingly vowed allegiance to Japan. A great many other Japanese were loyal to Japan and ... many of those disloyal to this country would be released.... The Japs, in returning some of their nationals in this country to Tokyo for training in the sabotage school, had followed the plan of Germany ... the eight Nazi saboteurs who landed on the Atlantic Coast from U-boats last summer had left the United States for training in a sabotage school near Berlin.

Numerous California town committees expressed "shock" and "outrage" when they learned of the release of relocatees and indicated that they did "not want the Japanese evacuees back during or after the war." The *Palo Alto Times* put it this way: "All of the reasons which justified the relocation of the coast Japanese in the first place hold equally strongly, if not more so, today."[32] By November the citizens of Livermore, California, feared a Japanese uprising by freed relocatees and demanded that the FBI investigate Dillon Myer. The city clerk wrote:

> Even after Myer's attention has been called to the danger to the country of relocating over 14,000 disloyal Japs from Tule Lake, he persists in ... releasing many thousands of other Japs, giving the flimsy argument ... that "there has not been a single report of a subversive act." ... Jap leaders advised them not to commit any sabotage until invasion by the Japs comes.... Their ruse is to disarm suspicion and get practically all of them released, ready to all strike at once—wrecking trains, burning food warehouses and crops, poisoning or polluting city water supplies, etc., so as to paralyze our war effort.... The Japs could use their cargo submarines and bring arms and ammunition for these 5,000 or 6,000 disloyal Japanese and the many others who would doubtless join their invading force ... ready for use by the Japs when the invasion and uprising come. In a letter I received from Myer, acknowledging receipt of my letter to the President, his signature shows, according to books on graphology, that he is dishonest—the small letters decreasing in height toward the end of the word. Last, but perhaps

not least, the name Myer shows him to be of German ancestry, but how lately from Germany, I do not know.[33]

Fear was palpable. One writer had watched "in horror" as released Japanese were "buying all the butcher, kitchen and other knives" in town and "shopping in radio stores for wire" for some "oriental purpose." The FBI and WRA were "incompetent," believed another, and of "decided sympathy with our enemies." Relocatees, said others, had "set up a program" to aid a Japanese invasion and had "cached stolen food in the desert for expected paratroopers." This was "madness" for G. G. Orcutt, who feared Japan "would have our country before long." Mrs. Edna Deatrick's views were typical:

> We should not abuse these enemy peoples, but . . . we are not a nation of soft-headed fools. Like small children, the Japanese need good instruction and examples of democracy and a good measure of discipline to make them better Americans with more respect for us than the kid-glove handling they've had so far. They are utterly insolent and very treacherous and none of them should be turned loose. . . . They should be deported.

Another asked who was running the WRA as "yellow blood thirsty hog-wild Japs" were freed. Mrs. Edna Hesting wrote to the War Department, "America went soft, and is still soft. Who knows, maybe one of those yellow devils is running the WRA."[34]

After the war, many wrote local politicians and state representatives who, in turn, sent colorful letters to FDR and Biddle. In December 1945, Geo Porter, Montana's state treasurer, wrote: "Send them back to Japan, no one in Montana wants them, if they must stay, keep them near Washington, D.C." During the war, at Santa Fe, a committee representing the two thousand Japanese asked camp officials to heighten the perimeter barbed wire to keep nearby residents from attacking in retaliation for American casualties and setbacks in the Pacific as they had done the previous year. Many never attempted escape, fearing the hostility they would surely encounter. Those leaving the camps, temporarily or permanently, were advised by FBI agents and other officials to say nothing of their experience.[35]

Those granted temporary leave agreed to follow a prearranged travel route and to abide by censorship regulations, meaning no mention of the camp or their experiences, whether critical or laudatory, to anybody. Prior to an internee exchange in November 1944, Chief Special Agent T. F. Fitch notified key officials of the following:

> The Germans must be held incommunicado during the entire trip until placed aboard the exchange vessel. . . . A guard must be stationed at the end of each car on a 24-hour basis. . . . Each German will have a lapel identification tag showing his name, car number, berth, and train. . . . Germans must at all times be held under strict guard and afforded no opportunity whatsoever to pass or receive written or verbal communications after customs examination. Please be governed in strict conformity to these instructions.

Some, like novelist Rex Stout, who led the Society for the Prevention of World War III, fervently argued against releasing German internees. Convinced that enemies lived among them, Stout wrote Attorney General Tom Clark in August 1945:

> It is incumbent upon us to warn the American people concerning . . . Pan- and pro-Germanism. Sympathy with the enemy can do incalculable harm . . . such sentiments can rot away the foundations of a stable world order. We hope you will . . . give the public a complete list of dangerous enemy aliens . . . and their whereabouts. . . . We can guard against those in our midst. . . . Nazis are resuming agitation on behalf of the Fatherland. They are enemy aliens released from internment. Public opinion demands stamping Nazism out. . . . The FBI's scrupulous regard for civil liberties and the fact-finding accuracy of its investigative work are famous. The arrests were for good reason. But the FBI was hampered in its work by the many Enemy Alien Hearing Boards. Most were composed of reputable citizens, but Mr. Biddle handpicked the boards. Thus, many were grossly naïve when dealing with glib enemies.
>
> Americans have a right to security. . . . The press must be free to report on the enemies of our country. Many of them are as much a menace to American society as thieves, murderers, and rapists

whose activities we record in print and on the air. . . . The most effective, indispensable defense weapon of our democracy is a factually informed public opinion.

At war's end, Italian Americans fared better. Twelve were interned and two hundred were paroled, and nearly all had been out for months or years with no problems. Assistant Attorney General Herbert Wechsler wrote Biddle suggesting that all Italian alien orders change from parole to release. By September 1945 Crystal City held eight Italians, and by year's end there were none in any camp and nearly all parolees were released.[36]

Reciprocity and the Geneva Convention

While the INS expected internees to obey regulations, internees expected officials to adhere to the 1929 Geneva Convention. The United States and Germany had signed the treaty, but Japan had not. This fact concerned Hull and Biddle and their respective departments. The U.S. wished to avoid retribution against its citizens in Nazi-occupied Europe and the Japanese Empire. On December 27, 1941, Japan began to cooperate with the International Red Cross Committee's Central Prisoners of War Agency at Geneva. On February 4 the U.S. learned of Japan's intention to apply the Geneva Convention regarding prisoners of war on a reciprocal basis. Three weeks later Japan agreed to apply the same with civilian internees. Both nations agreed to treat enemy aliens and citizens equally, yet as the war progressed, numerous protests, nearly always between the U.S. and Japan, alleged ill treatment of their nationals, and both threatened harming internees as a retaliatory measure "in kind" to any initial abuses.

Occasionally, negative reports, news, or publicity about Japanese American internees appeared in Japan's papers while similar stories of mistreated Americans reached Washington. The State and War Departments tried to reconcile official reports, media statements, and internee complaints of abuse, especially to avoid reprisals. Although rumors, hearsay, or speculation formed the basis of most accounts, they often led to accusations, counter-accusations, and threats. In November 1942, when the Spanish Embassy sent an unsatisfactory report noting abuses of internees to Japan, Tokyo immediately protested the alleged mistreatment, charging that U.S. authorities had failed to protect Japanese subjects "from violence and vigilantes." U.S. officials swiftly responded, protesting alleged Japanese mistreatment of Americans and launching an internal investigation as well as inviting the Spanish Legation and the Red Cross to investigate and report. A positive review and Tokyo's acceptance would "repose confidence" in America's treatment of Japanese; more importantly, the findings would be "in the interest of, and in justice to all concerned." Washington also assured Tokyo that it would promptly take "appropriate remedial action" where "there may have been isolated cases in which irresponsible subordinate officials failed to comply with the provisions of international law."[37]

Despite such assurances, Hull told Stimson that he remained worried that Japanese officials would endorse "reprisals on American citizens in Japan." If true, U.S. officials would threaten retaliation against Japanese internees. Top officials in Washington, Tokyo, and Berlin made it clear that their governments would retaliate in kind against any verified mistreatment of their own nationals, wherever they might be held. Bizarre stories circulated: soldiers, acting on orders, reportedly poured "boiling water on victims, cut their ears off, gouged out their eyeballs, sliced off tips of their noses, amputated their arms, and mutilated their legs." Rumors spread of physical or mental abuses, sexual misconduct, and torture. There was even talk that U.S. officials were sterilizing Japanese internees, which nearly proved disastrous as Japan immediately threatened to sterilize U.S. civilians unless it received contrary proof. The Red Cross promptly verified that the rumors were false, and Hull told Japan to expect "dire consequences" if any Americans were sterilized or mistreated in any way.[38]

Americans often worried about the safety and well-being of U.S. soldiers and civilians in enemy hands, and thousands asked the State Department if Japan or Germany was mistreating captives. Officials answered that because the United States was applying the Geneva Convention to prisoners of war and interned civilians, it expected the same in return:

> Reports received through the Swiss Government and Red Cross do not indicate that American prisoners of war in Japanese hands are being mistreated.... The Japanese Government intends to apply the Geneva Convention to prisoners of war. This Government has informed the Japanese Government of its intention to apply the Geneva Convention, not only to prisoners of war but also to any civilian enemy aliens interned by the United States and has expressed the hope that the Japanese Government will do likewise.
>
> The treatment of Japanese prisoners of war and Japanese nationals in the United States will naturally be influenced by the treatment accorded American prisoners of war and American nationals under Japanese control.... Swiss government representatives inspect places of internment and report upon the conditions. Such inspections are provided for under the Geneva Convention. You may rest assured that the Department will take further action as circumstances may suggest.[39]

In August 1942, Assistant Secretary of the Navy Ralph Bard received a letter from his brother, who, like so many, was asking about Japanese Americans and the safety of soldiers and citizens held by Japan. He also asked about the differences, if any, between relocation and internment and who was involved and why. Bard wanted an expert's opinion and asked Breckinridge Long, head of the SWPD since January 1940. Long told Bard that many confused relocation from designated West Coast military areas with the nationwide but selective enemy alien program under which Japanese subjects and other potentially dangerous aliens are interned. Japan is, Long added,

> reminded of the presence on American territory of numerous Japanese subjects and has been told that their treatment will naturally be influenced by treatment accorded to American nationals in Japanese hands.... The reports from the Swiss and Red Cross are much more satisfactory than press reports. These reports are confidential.
>
> Our task of... pressing the Japanese to maintain humanitarian standards in the treatment of prisoners of war and civilian internees... is attended with great difficulties. Preparing internment and

detention facilities for thousands of people was difficult and carrying out the evacuation of 120,000 persons of the Japanese race on the Pacific Coast was and continues to be even more difficult.

Prisoners of war and internees in Japanese hands are of special concern to us, being as they are in the hands of a nation so different in standards and background.... We should continue to raise Japanese standards of treatment of American citizens by constant vigilance and immediate protest as necessary. We should avoid any general public statements to the effect that the Japanese are faithless or barbarians.... It might lead to a complete collapse of Geneva Convention standards, which could result only in the increasing misery of American citizens in Japanese hands.

Reciprocity was the guiding principle as to how and why Japan, Germany, and the United States treated their respective relocatees and internees, which was done fairly well overall.[40]

The same concepts applied to Hitler's Germany. In October 1941, for example, Albert Clattenburg of the State Department's Special Division and W. F. Kelly of the Justice Department's Special Defense Unit noted the negative publicity from such articles as the *Brooklyn Daily Eagle*'s "Long Island Gets Alien Detention Pen: Concentration Camp Nearing Completion on Upton Grounds." Since the camp's "old winterized six-man tents" would house seven hundred German aliens, Hitler might "react vigorously" to such news and retaliate with equalizing measures by "confining Americans in tents" too. Germany was struggling to shelter all its POWs and civilian internees. Officials knew that some, including British POWs, "had lost extremities because of the cold" the previous winter, and feared "Americans would undoubtedly have a less satisfactory experience than the Germans confined to tents in this country." Hull directed the American Legation in Bern to get lists of Americans—officials and nationals—to protect them and their property. Just after Pearl Harbor, he announced liberal policies treating internees at least as favorably as POWs. Washington's benevolent treatment hinged upon Berlin's reciprocal efforts and U.S. officials never wavered from this stance. On many occasions, the State Department demanded punishment for German officials who mistreated Americans and threatened reprisals if Germany did not take "prompt and adequate punitive measures."[41]

The INS sent telegraphic instructions about enemy alien treatment within hours of America's entry into the war. Written instructions followed on December 12 but proved inadequate as relocatee and internee numbers quickly swelled. On April 28, Major Lemuel Schofield, special assistant to the attorney general, combined the instructions into one comprehensive order, known as "Instruction No. 58." Copies went to all who handled alien enemies. Officials were to observe the spirit and letter of the Geneva Convention at all times. Protecting and humanely treating detainees, particularly against violence, insults, and public curiosity, was top priority:

> The basis underlying our treatment of alien enemy detainees is reciprocity, and nothing must be done or permitted to be done whereby any ground may exist for the charge that the Geneva Convention has been violated or ignored, thereby providing an excuse under the guise of retaliation for harsh treatment and cruel abuse of nationals of this country in the hands of our enemies.
>
> Reports as to our treatment of alien enemy detainees are made ... to belligerent nations by diplomatic representatives of the protecting powers. Representatives will make visits of inspection from time to time by arrangement with the Central Office. Representatives of the International Red Cross and similar organizations will also make visits. Full access must be accorded and opportunity afforded to talk to internees and to receive any complaints they care to make.

Instruction No. 58 had twenty-three rules categories. "It should be remembered," Schofield wrote, "that these are minimum standards. Full discretion to exceed them is given to district directors and officers in charge of detention camps in the interest of the health and personal welfare of detainees but always consistent with the responsibility of adequate security." The rules covered humane treatment and living quarters, sanitation and exercise, food and clothing, work and recreation, religious services and visitors, internal relations and censorship, money and medical care, information and discipline, and canteens and bedding. Every camp posted a copy of the Geneva Convention so detainees could consult it and all officials would follow its spirit and letter at all times.[42]

The primary responsibility of camp commanders and INS personnel was to treat all internees humanely. This meant adequate living quarters; sanitary installations; exercise facilities; sufficient amounts and types of foods; clothing, linen, bedding, and towels; and articles such as soap, shaving, writing and sewing materials, and tobacco. Internees could have a canteen, engage in sports and intellectual diversions, and observe their faith—including conducting religious services once a week, and if requested, "representatives of religious faiths must be allowed to visit." They could also see anyone during established visiting hours. Supervised visits were "as liberal as local conditions" allowed, and officials answered inquiries from outsiders—including relatives, friends, counsel, or other persons with proper reasons—provided their replies did not bring publicity or deal with the charges, evidence, or disposition of the case in general.[43]

Strict censorship applied to all internees. Camp commanders expurgated incoming mail—from newspapers and magazines to the unlimited number of parcels and letters one might receive. Internees could send telegrams plus two letters and one postcard per week (not including letters by camp representatives written on their behalf). They could not discuss "adverse conditions and morale" or camp information, including "addresses, arrival date and place, comparison of camps, complaints or criticism of treatment, interrogation centers, unfavorable references to health of interned persons, and criticism of capture." Internees could not criticize the United States, its armed forces or agencies, or the Red Cross; nor could they discuss "military information," "enemy propaganda in any form," or "enemy activity in camps." Finally, they could not "invent details," send pictures, photographs, maps, sketches, or drawings, or circumvent restrictions.

Internees kept valuables (except money or dangerous items) and received receipts for all confiscated property, although officials forced many to part with items of great sentimental value. U.S. Customs, for example, seized Carl Boden's stamp collection given to him by his son Tom, because the Customs Service Philatelic Division declared some "enemy stamps." Far more significantly, many lost their homes, businesses, or both. Officials disposed of enemy alien property while the FBI seized dangerous items, including cameras, letters, and diaries. On order of the Treasury Department, federal marshals padlocked all Japanese businesses and organizations. All property, "if not retained on the premises was turned over to the Alien Property Custodian for disposal."[44]

The Trading with the Enemy Act of 1917, as amended by Roosevelt's Executive Order 9095, authorized the Alien Property Custodian (APC) to exercise jurisdiction over enemy alien property. The APC had great discretion with each case. If an internee's family members could protect their property or when power of attorney went to a friend or acquaintance, there was usually no need for APC intervention or interference. If, however, national interests required confiscating property, then officials did so, regardless of any prior arrangements. The APC could issue supervisory orders whereby it would administer the alien's property. One major problem was what to do after an arrest while a detained individual or family awaited a hearing. Here, too, the APC acted on a case-by-case basis, but assets were always frozen once the alien was interned, although these could be released up to $180 per month for the internee's or dependent's use.

Internees could keep up to ten dollars, make withdrawals from their account, and spend their money at canteens and small businesses that other internees operated and ran. The Justice Department and INS felt that detainees, if cooperative, might "manage the internal affairs of the camp relating to work, recreation, education, and general welfare, including the operation of canteens and the administering of welfare funds." They could also appoint a representative in dealing with Justice Department or INS officials.[45]

Daily medical inspections were conducted, and necessary health care was provided free of charge. Sick detainees went to an infirmary or hospital, depending on the nature of the illness or emergency. Government documents and eyewitness accounts attest to the quality of medical care internees received. At Crystal City alone, doctors performed 204 major and 881 minor operations, provided 9,225 immunizations, and made 11,107 house calls. There were only seventeen deaths there, fourteen from natural causes and three that were accidental (two drownings and an auto mishap). Charges, then and now, that INS camps were death traps or that evacuees died of "lack of medical attention" are not supported by facts, whether government records or internee accounts. WRA reports indicate that the relocation centers had "the lowest incidence of disease anywhere in the United States" and "experienced the highest live-birth rate anywhere in the nation."[46]

End Times

In September 1945, Red Cross representative W. Ferrett noted that there were 653 German internees and 1 Italian internee at the Ellis Island INS camp. There were also 354 "men and women of various nationalities held: immigrants whose papers were not in order, or who were in transit, foreigners who were being deported for one reason or another, the majority being seamen who stayed after their ships departed." The Ellis Island station, in use for over four years, was located next to the Statue of Liberty. Male internees lived in dorms, each with about 150 beds. Women had more privacy, living in rooms with two or three beds. Lodgings were satisfactory, the food "good and plentiful." Internees could buy canteen food and prepare it themselves, receive it from visitors, or eat in a common mess hall. Sanitary and health conditions were good. The sick went to the island's hospital. Religious services along with leisure and physical activities were available to all. While nobody lodged any formal complaints, many did have requests, worries, and concerns. Many felt like prisoners since they could not see or talk to the opposite sex (only married men could see their wives). They could not even talk through the bars from one area to another. "Existing rules," officials replied, "did not permit any changes."

Uncertainty about the future was commonplace. Ellis Island authorities noted cases "where the internees will be separated from their families and sent back to Germany . . . and it is not yet known who will be deported and who will be set free." Some feared going where they would have no relatives or friends. For others, deportation meant family separation. Hearings, many felt, were "not held impartially." The Red Cross report noted this especially about Latin American German internees:

> The accused never have the opportunity to defend themselves effectively and they state that it is the same person who is deciding the case, so no appeal against the decision is possible. We will discuss this with the State Department.
>
> Persons of German origin arrested on order from U.S. authorities were... interned for the duration in camps for civilian internees, and are now to be deported to Germany against their will, although most of them lived in the new continent for a long time. These internees have in most cases spouses and children.... Some internees were born in America and cannot speak German.... Some persons are old and it will be very difficult to adapt again to conditions in Germany or find livelihood there.[47]

Elsewhere internees expressed the same basic fears and concerns. Arthur Jacobs, interned in Crystal City in 1945 at age twelve, recalled that while camp life was fine, the mental consequences, including stigma and shame, were difficult to accept; he expressly detested his family's forced repatriation. How could one explain internment?

Internee newspaper articles support Jacobs's views. Camp Forrest's *The Latrine* often referred to the internees' "small new world." Numerous articles mention the importance of extending comradeship, cooperation, and compassion for all newcomers. *The Latrine* highlighted special holiday events, musicals, chess tournaments, plays, quiz shows, garden contests, art and handicraft shows, and soccer games. The *Crystal City Times* likewise accentuated the positive to boost morale, especially around holidays and after the war. An article in its New Year's edition of January 1946 titled "Down Memory Lane" noted a prayer by Robert Louis Stevenson: "We thank Thee for this place in which we dwell; for the love that unites us; for the place accorded us this day; for the hope with which we expect the morrow; for the health, work, food, and the bright skies that make our lives delightful; for our friends in all parts of the earth, and our friendly helpers in this foreign isle."

Coeditors Rosie Taniguchi and Robert Oda wrote:

Two and a half years ago, we came to this center where only a few facilities were set up.... It was a challenge to transform this barren place into a more livable, lively refuge. Yes, we had cause to be thankful for this haven when the outside world seemed threatening. We won the confidences of friends, and worked with them on the carnival, field meets and numerous activities which helped to keep up morale. But now these various undertakings shall only linger as memories of the good ole days spent in a community of friends from all parts of the world.

To part from such dear friends—the repatriates and the Hawaii bound—has hit us hard. Words within our grasp cannot even begin to tell of the sorrow that wells within our hearts. We are pretty tough about a lot of things, although much of it is nothing but empty bravado. Our eyes are burning but we are holding back the oceans of tears that are surging against the aches of our will power. We must "buckle up," face the circumstances, and realize that we have a hard trek ahead of us down the road of life.[48]

Perhaps *Latrine* editor Hans Hasenkox best expressed internment sentiment and the psychology of captivity in a short piece titled "New Year's Eve."

In retrospect, many of us believe that we have in spite of our present troubles, bettered ourselves somewhat. Do you remember when some of us had to spend this day under the most dreadful circumstances last New Year? You never thought the day or the time would pass. The Company you had to endure was horrible to behold. You and yours made the acquaintance of the Jailhouse for the first time in your life. Some of you already were placed in camps and others were still free.

Well, meanwhile we have somewhat hardened against this fate of ours, but reflecting on all, time will eventually pass until the day arrives that we can go home. Let that be our consolation and guidance for all actions. Let us relish the thought that this world at present in turmoil will once more become a peaceful place to live in. Then we shall look back and know that we withstood this trial in our life brave and manly. It made us stronger and perhaps better human beings. We feel it will come to pass this coming year and that the end of the year will find us once more in harmony with all and ourselves. We shall glory again in the Freedom of action, thought, and mind.

In this spirit, we wish you a happy New Year, happy in the thought of good things to come, happy in the realization, that we will be once more joined with our families and friends, happy because we withstood all trials and tribulations and come forth triumphant in the end.[49]

The total number of internees was 31,275, including those received from abroad and so-called volunteers. This number included 10,905 Germans, 3,278 Italians, 11,229 Japanese, 5,620 Japanese American renunciants, 52 Hungarians, 25 Romanians, 5 Bulgarians, and 161 persons of unlisted or unknown origin. The total includes some 6,000 German Americans, 3,000 Italian Americans, and 9,000 Japanese Americans. Latin American internees totaled 6,610 repatriates and included 4,058 persons of German, 288 of Italian, and 2,264 of Japanese heritage. Voluntary internees included some who joined the head of family or others authorities pressured, threatened, or urged to "repatriate voluntarily." In addition, 120,313 Japanese and 20,000 to 40,000 German and Italian Americans were forcibly relocated.

Internee numbers fluctuated greatly during the war as new groups arrived and authorities paroled, released, or repatriated others. The United States held 6,238 in June 1944 and 11,289, including 9,803 Japanese and 1,451 Germans, in October 1945. The number dropped to 9,757 in November and 6,470 by December 1945, and these remaining internees became increasingly agitated. Repatriating those still classified as enemy aliens continued despite the cessation of hostilities. Ellis Island received transfers from overcrowded camps who wanted a hearing, while officials sent many from Seagoville and other camps as they closed. Couples, accustomed to being together, were separated at Ellis Island. Gertrud Neubacher bitterly complained about being "unable to endure further physical hardship and, above all, mental strain," since, as she pointed out, "we have gone through several years of internment already" and authorities were now reneging on their promise to keep married persons together.[50]

By May 1946 America's camps still held 1,624 internees: 1,125 Japanese, 497 Germans, and 2 others. Most closed that year, but a few remained open and operational. Ellis Island held hundreds of Germans in 1947, many of whom contacted politicians or anybody who might help. Astutely observing that the country needed help against new enemies—the Soviet Union and communist ideology—internee Martin Hoisl wrote:

> Germans and German Americans are intensely anti-communistic; unfortunately, in spite of this fact, millions of these people are still engaged forcefully in slave labor and thousands are held in concentration camps here as well as abroad.
>
> As one of the latter category, apprehended one year after V-E Day, on May 1, 1946, I am imprisoned and, although I am a lawfully admitted resident with no criminal or otherwise dishonorable record, I am destined to be deported without charges and without due process of law. It is not necessary to elaborate on what this will mean to my family, from whom I shall be separated for many years to come, and to myself. But I may mention here that Justice Robert Jackson at the Nuremberg Trial declared concentration camps, the persecution of minorities, and deportation proceedings as "crimes against humanity."
>
> In view of the aforementioned facts, I appeal to you, Sir, to propose or give your support to legislative measures that will restore freedom to all civilian internees and remove from their wives and children the constant state of worry and fear for the ultimate fate of their beloved-ones.[51]

Elizabeth Guldemont, a citizen concerned about German American internees, also wrote in early 1947:

> It is hard to believe that the extirpation of the German people and the holding of prisoners of war and civilian internees for an indefinite period will help teach the "democratic ideal of tolerance" or will be a "character-building process."
>
> It constitutes an especially sad chapter of our times that within the shadow of the Statue of Liberty hundreds of men, women, and even children—our German civilian internees—are still held

behind barbed wire fences and, without due process of law and without charges, are destined to be deported to the misery in Germany within the near future.

I, an American citizen, therefore request respectfully that you will give this matter your most serious attention, that you will take immediate steps to correct this unbelievable state of affairs and propose appropriate legislation for the liberation of these unfortunate victims of war hysteria, and that you will find out what goes on behind the walls of Ellis Island, New York.[52]

By May 1947, despite such protests, 160 German internees remained at Ellis Island. Crystal City held 1,028 Japanese in June 1946 and 106 Germans in March 1947, some of whom were desperate. Rev. Hugh Lavery of Los Angeles decided to help and successfully petitioned for the release of fourteen Japanese teenage girls from Crystal City in the fall of 1946, while the next spring Walter Steiner, spokesperson for the camp's Germans, petitioned Thomas Cooley, chief of the AECU's Review Section:

> This is a cry for help!
> The days, the months, the years roll by, and our nerve tension is near the breaking point. When will our punishment stop? The war is over for nearly two years. Please stop the heartache we are suffering for more than five years! We are not getting any younger and we will have to start anew in life again sometime, so please let us return to our American homes. We did learn our lesson!

A few weeks later, Cooley informed Steiner that the AECU considers "the facts in each individual case carefully" and if "a change of status is warranted, the alien is advised." Yet Crystal City did not close until February 27, 1948, and its last internees, all Germans, went to Ellis Island, where many remained until June. By August there were still 174 German alien enemies held under removal orders, and as late as April 1949 authorities held 36 Germans (still referred to as alien enemies) whose cases were pending in a number of district courts and appellate courts. Finally, by June 1949 there were no longer interned Germans in the United States. An investigative process that had begun with the hunt for German subversives fifteen years earlier had finally ended.[53]

Mike Masaoka, director of the Japanese American Citizens League, was concerned about America's aliens, particularly the Japanese. How was it that in March 1947, and through "no fault of their own or lack of interest, as alien Japanese have never been extended the privilege of becoming naturalized citizens," these "resident Japanese aliens" were still "enemy aliens"? It was high time, Masaoka believed, to afford "our resident Japanese aliens and their citizen children every possible consideration, the least of which is the removal of this arbitrary and now indefensible classification. We submit that the arbitrary wartime classification of all aliens coming from nations with which we were at war is no longer justified either by the facts or by public policy." As to America's relocatees, the vast majority of whom were Japanese Americans, roughly three-quarters were still in WRA camps by the spring of 1944. Nearly 80,000 of the 89,933 Japanese in WRA camps on March 4 remained incarcerated at year's end. On January 2, 1945, the War Department lifted the West Coast exclusion orders. Nevertheless, by August, with the war ending, the United States still held 44,000 Japanese, roughly one-third of all relocatees. By the end of 1945 there were still 12,545 relocatees in WRA centers, and as late as March 1, 1946, the government still held 3,026 Japanese Americans at Tule Lake and INS facilities including Fort Lincoln, Santa Fe, and Crystal City. On March 20, 1946, Tule Lake Relocation Center closed, forcing the remaining thousand relocatees to move again. The WRA itself finally closed on June 30, 1946.[54]

Conclusion

> I was hungry and you gave me food, I was thirsty and you gave me drink, I was a stranger and you welcomed me.... Truly I say to you, as you did it to one of the least of my brethren you did it to me.
>
> —MATTHEW 25:35, 40

During the first few months of 1942, widespread fear of an external attack aided by internal enemies made the decision to act against those labeled as enemies relatively easy and largely well supported. Relocating West Coast Japanese Americans en masse and German and Italian aliens in smaller numbers from both coasts as well as interning German, Italian, and Japanese aliens and citizens on a more selective and pragmatic basis seemed prudent—especially given regional and then national political, media, and public demands for immediate action. Officials reasoned that they could far better ensure the safety of Americans and citizens of other Allied nations trapped in Nazi-occupied Europe and the Japanese Empire by interning German, Italian, and Japanese nationals residing in the United States and throughout the hemisphere. The United States then bartered its internees for those interned abroad. Interning and exchanging thousands of nationals helped guarantee a benevolent reciprocity and assure the safety of those who remained at large. Internee exchanges meant that the Axis and Allied powers mutually benefited by getting their own citizens back while concurrently expelling first dangerous or potentially dangerous troublemakers and then those considered harmless. As exchanges proved successful, demonstrating the good faith of all sides, the possibility of mistreating internees and other nationals remained low—a priority for all participant nations.

The different but parallel roads enemy aliens and citizens traveled led to a common end for thousands of German, Italian, and Japanese Americans. For many reasons, Americans eagerly sought and easily found scapegoats in their midst. Convinced of the urgent need to ensure the nation's safety, most did not mind the sacrifice of relocation, internment, or repatriation others had to make for the common good and many convinced themselves that these selected persons would not mind so much either. Weeks, months, or even years of such service to the state would therefore inure them to their lot at worst or demonstrate their loyalty at best. All so-called enemies suffered. The government relocated far more Japanese than it did Germans and Italians. It did so based first on the sheer number of Germans and Italians living throughout the nation; second, upon the lesser perceived external and internal military threat posed by them, and third, Germans and Italians had achieved a high degree of social and cultural assimilation by then. That the fifth column was essentially nonexistent and a Japanese West Coast invasion unrealistic mattered little. Few seriously questioned the premises upon which the nation's dual policies of relocation and internment rested. What mattered was belief in a fifth-column menace and fear of a West Coast invasion.

Washington's actions were reminiscent of Miguel Cervantes's Don Quixote who, in a famous scene, battles windmills that the romantic visionary supposed were giants. The rueful knight believed that fortune guided his actions and that slaying giants would bring great riches in his righteous war. The "removal of so foul a brood from off the face of the earth" was indeed a "service God will bless."[1] Like Don Quixote, Americans battled windmills. Unlike Cervantes's romantic visionary, the government, supported by the public, did much more. Americans created, castigated, and then incarcerated alleged enemies: all this, despite lack of evidence, or worse, evidence to the contrary. As the rueful knight adhered to his outdated chivalric code in an age in which nobility could exist only as madness, so too did Americans battle an ominous foe that they themselves created within a self-made culture of fear.

Questions concerning the status of aliens, fundamental issues of citizenship, and what to do about potentially disloyal aliens and citizens during war were hardly novel topics. The United States and other nations had certainly faced such vexing difficulties before. What was new was the tendency among the belligerents in a total war context to act with increasing severity against all perceived enemies—foreign and domestic. World War I served as the catalyst for this change, especially the treatment of enemy aliens. By the tens of thousands, aliens were arrested, interned, and deported. Twenty years later, belligerent nations once again had to manage and control enemy aliens (commonly referred to and conceptualized as "fifth columnists"). The United States, for its part, now faced three enemy groups—German, Italian, and Japanese Americans— and the steps taken to deal with them closely resembled actions taken against German Americans during the Great War. Overall public acceptance of such anti-alien policies in both wars inhered in a broader tradition of intolerance and suspicion of outsiders combined with the exigencies of a nation at war to protect its citizens and institutions and, ultimately, to prevail.

When the United States finally went to war in December 1941, many top civilian and military officials, including the President, along with the general population, had already come to accept as fact that fifth columnists were hard at work undermining the nation's defenses and sacred institutions—paving the way for Axis troops to finish the job. Allied losses and Pearl Harbor were proof enough of what quislings could do, and then, ironically, the lack of sabotage or subversive activity on American soil in the first months of 1942 surely meant that the enemy was planning devastating attacks with inside help. If German, Italian, and Japanese aliens and citizens intended to prove their loyalty or somehow counter accusations of disloyalty and fifth-column activity, the ability and means to do so vanished quickly.

The combination of firmly established and accepted precedents, entrenched fears of and a widely held belief in fifth columnists, overzealous officials committed to the nation's safety, and the government's desire to exchange enemy aliens and disloyal citizens for Americans trapped abroad made the treatment of perceived enemies not only predictable, but almost inevitable. The cost in civil liberties, shattered dreams, and disrupted or even destroyed lives was high. Some committed suicide; others became embittered, feeling their adopted nation had abandoned them, while still others proved their loyalty by serving in the nation's armed forces. Thousands of citizens and aliens who wanted to help America's war effort or just go about their lives as they had done for many years, even decades, found they could not do so. Their hopes, especially those of Japanese Americans, largely disappeared along with most of the Pacific Fleet on that fateful Sunday morning and rapidly faded with each successive Japanese military victory. In addition, unknown to German, Italian, and Japanese aliens and citizens, contingency plans and preparations were well underway and had been largely agreed upon long before the United States formally entered the war. The fate of enemy aliens and even potentially disloyal citizens was decided long before December 7, 1941. What remained unanswered was when the government would act, how it would handle hundreds of thousands or even millions of potential enemies in the United States and throughout the hemisphere, and how many labeled as enemies would suffer and to what extent.

This has been the story of how government policies affected thousands of ordinary people during an extraordinary time in America's history. It is the story of the treatment that many, whom the government considered enemies, endured in a democracy under stress. What remains unknown is how our nation will continue to act toward those whom it fears and labels as enemies among us. Perhaps we can learn from scripture and accept that when an alien resides with us in our land, we should not oppress the alien. Perhaps, then, the alien who resides with us shall be as a citizen among us. Maybe, then, we shall love the alien as ourselves. As we journey through the twenty-first century, we will need to come to terms with our own diversity, especially in times of great duress.

NOTES

Abbreviations

CLCF Closed Legal Case Files
CWRIC U.S. Commission on Wartime Relocation and Internment of Civilians
FDRL Franklin Delano Roosevelt Library, Hyde Park NY
HF   Headquarters Files
NA   National Archives, Washington DC
NACP National Archives, College Park, Maryland
PMG   Provost Marshal General
SAC   Special Agent in Charge
SDCF State Department Central Files
SWPD Special War Problems Division of the Department of State
SWPU Special War Policies Unit of the Department of Justice

Introduction

1. German, Italian, and Japanese aliens living in the United States became enemy aliens by definition when the United States entered World War II against Germany, Italy, and Japan. The terms "enemy aliens" and "alien enemies" are technical and dehumanizing descriptors that imply such persons were "dangerous" or "threats" or "enemies" of the United States rather than nationals of enemy nations. This reclassification affected all aliens of German, Italian, or Japanese descent. By German Americans, Italian Americans, and Japanese Americans, I mean aliens living in the United States who for various reasons had not naturalized (become U.S. citizens) and U.S. citizens of German, Italian, and Japanese heritage, some of whom the FBI or others considered dangerous or potentially dangerous to the nation's security. The phrase "enemy aliens and citizens" refers to German, Italian, and Japanese aliens and their families, including children (citizens), whom most Americans viewed as a genuine threat. Japanese Americans consisted of Issei, first generation immigrants from

Japan forbidden by U.S. law from becoming naturalized citizens; Nisei, those born in the United States and therefore citizens; and Kibei, American-born citizens raised and educated in Japan. To some degree, all three groups of citizens were viewed as potential enemies, but most believed Japanese Americans, aliens and citizens, were the most dangerous or disloyal, followed by German American and then Italian American aliens and citizens. The phrase "enemy aliens and citizens" connotes both a technical and legal classification with a broader view of German, Italian, and Japanese Americans (aliens and citizens) as potential or actual enemies.

2. Fiset, *Imprisoned Apart*, 30–31; W. C. Bruppacher, Legation of Switzerland, to W. F. Kelly, regarding Peter Theberath, April 20, 1944. Legation of Switzerland Document (Department of German Interests), and W. F. Kelly to Edward J. Ennis, concerning the Theberath case, July 22, 1942, SWPD, RG 59, NACP.

1. Pejoratives, Precedents, and Prejudice

1. Kraut, *Huddled Masses*, 148.

2. Francis Walker, noted economist and anti-immigrationist, spoke of the clash of old-stock Americans and newly arrived immigrants as a struggle for existence. "On the key roll call, the Senate vote was 76-2 against the Japanese." Daniels, *Concentration Camps USA*, 21.

3. "Japanese Invasion: The Problem of the Hour," *San Francisco Chronicle*, February 23, 1905. The 100,000 claimed was four times the actual number. Even by 1940 there were fewer than 127,000 Japanese, and they made up just 1.4 percent of California's population. U.S. Department of Commerce, Bureau of the Census, Washington, Sixteenth Census: 1940, *Population: Japanese Population of the United States and its Territories and Possessions*, December 9, 1941, Series P-3, no. 23; Daniels, *Prisoners without Trial*, 7–8; Daniels, *Concentration Camps*, 29–30; Barone, *Our Country*, 20; "Japan Sounds Our Coasts: Brown Men Have Maps and Could Land Easily!," *San Francisco Examiner*, December 20, 1906; Friedrich Nietzsche, *The Gay Science*, trans. Walter Kaufmann (New York: Vintage, 1974), 121.

4. Josiah Strong's *Our Country: Its Possible Future and Present Crisis* (1885), which sold over 500,000 copies, is a good example. Strong, a Congregational minister, called attention to the perils threatening America's Christian civilization. Many, including Roosevelt, viewed the Japanese as irremediably alien, hence unassimilable and potentially (if not probably) dangerous.

5. Chan, *Asian Americans*, 204n1.

6. Online Catalog of the Library of Congress, 51116785: *Re-elect James D. Phelan, U.S. Senator, and let him stop the silent invasion*; see also Daniels, *Concentration Camps USA*, 10, and *Prisoners without Trial*, 7–11.

7. Okihiro, *Margins and Mainstreams*, 135–37.

8. Hunt, *Making of a Special Relationship*, 227; Daniels, *Prisoners without Trial*, 7; Kraut, *Huddled Masses*, 17–18. Numerous newspaper articles, including those by the *San Francisco Chronicle*, claimed that all Japanese immigrants were spies and Japanese men, typical headlines noted, were a "peril of national proportions," a "menace to American women" and an "evil in the public schools."

9. Lea, *The Valor of Ignorance*, xxi. From 1913 to 1924, "'war scares' smoldered in the imagination of governmental officials, military leaders, and patriotic citizens," adding to fears of Japanese aliens along with spies and agents as potential threats. Corbett, *Quiet Passages*, 202n17.

10. Okihiro, *Margins and Mainstreams*, 136. Okihiro adds: "Although apparently 'fantastic,' the Bureau report conceded, the menace was real and must be taken seriously" (136).

11. House Document no. 89, *Congressional Record*, 67th Cong., 1st sess. (1921), p. 4, quoted in Daniels, *Concentration Camps USA*, 19.

12. "National Security League," Hearings before a Special Committee of the House of Representatives, *Congressional Record*, 65th Cong., 3rd sess. (1919), p. 2013, quoted in Kennedy, *Over Here*, 67. The NSL was one among many so-called pro-preparedness groups that combined advocating for national defense preparation and polices with a militant patriotism that included anti-alien and pro-nationalist beliefs and rhetoric.

13. O'Connor, *The German-Americans*, 437; U.S. Department of Commerce (compiled by U.S., Bureau of the Census), *Statistical History of the United States from Colonial Times to the Present*, Series C 88–114, 56–57; Fifteenth Census: 1930, Population (General); Sixteenth Census: 1940, Series P-9, no. 2; Records of the Alien Information Bureau, Alien Civilian Internees, 1941–1946, War Dept. #466J, "List: Enemy Aliens Apprehended in U.S. by FBI," PMG, box 1, RG 389, NACP; Rippley, *The German-Americans*, 198, 209; U.S. House, Special Committee on Un-American Activities, *Investigation of Nazi and Other Propaganda*. The House Special Committee's report is located in SDCF, 1910–49, Class 8, Internal Affairs of State, box 4729, RG 59, NACP. For census data see also Wattenberg, *Statistical History of the United States* and https://www2.census.gov/library/publications/decennial/1930/abstract/00476589ch02.pdf for 1930 and https://www.census.gov/library/publications/1941/compendia/statab/62ed.html for 1940.

14. Rippley, *The German-Americans*, 180. Significantly, key officials knew that "if all the American-citizen descendants of enemy nationals had been interned during World War II, the United States would have had thirty million people in camps" (Girdner and Loftis, *Great Betrayal*, 125). First papers, also known as declarations of intention, are documents by which an applicant for U.S. citizenship begins the naturalization process; significantly, the person renounces allegiance to his or her country of origin's government.

15. Beers, "Protection of American Citizens Abroad," 828; Fenwick, *International Law*, 710.

16. Schwarzenberger, *Manual of International Law*, 192–93.

17. Hershey, *Essentials of International Public Law*, 566.

18. Saunders and Daniels, *Alien Justice*, 11, 71; Krammer, *Undue Process*, 14–15.

19. Tindall and Shi, *America*, 354.

20. Baker, *American and Japanese Relocation*, 58; Tindall and Shi, *America*, 354.

21. Canedy, *America's Nazis*, 1–2.

22. *Personal Justice Denied*, 17–18; Dimock to Attorney General, June 13, 1941, CLCF, folder "January–February 1942," box 5, RG 60, NACP; Weinberg, *Foreign Policy of Hitler's Germany: Diplomatic Revolution in Europe*, 133.

23. "The sound of the blast was unearthly, and the tremor was felt 100 miles away in Philadelphia. The night sky over New York Harbor turned orange. People were jolted from bed and windows within 25 miles. The Statue of Liberty, less than a mile away, was damaged. . . . The epicenter of the blast, a small island called Black Tom, all but disappeared in what was then the largest explosion ever in the U.S." Richard Pyle, "90 Years Later, N.J. Blast Still Shrouded in Mystery: German Sabotage Believed to Be Cause of Explosion," July 31, 2006, http://archive.boston.com/news/nation/articles/2006/07/31/90_years_later_nj_blast_still_shrouded_in_mystery/; W. Wilson, *Public Papers*, 5:60–67.

24. *New York Times*, November 20, 1917; Luebke, *Bonds of Loyalty*, chapter 8, "Superpatriotism in Action," esp. p. 255.

25. Kennedy, *Over Here*, 67–68; Luebke, *Bonds of Loyalty*, chapters 8 and 9; *Life*, June 13, 1918, reprinted in Luebke, *Bonds of Loyalty*, 276.

26. Kennedy, *Over Here*, 31, 75–76, 79–81, 290; Bennett, *The Party of Fear*, 184; Sperry, *The Tentacles of the German Octopus in America*, 2.

27. The NSL's agenda of "patriotic education" was to inculcate civil obedience, foster patriotism, promote good citizenship, and require a "correct knowledge of history." Campuses became focal points for political indoctrination. Kennedy, *Over Here*, 57; Rippley, "Ameliorated Americanization," 221; Rippley, *The German-Americans*, chapters 14 and 15.

28. O'Connor, *The German-Americans*, 430.

29. Luebke, *Bonds of Loyalty*, 240–44, 268–70.

30. Kennedy, *Over Here*, 67–68. Kennedy points out that Prager, rejected by the Navy, was seized by a mob, "stripped, bound with an American flag, dragged barefoot and stumbling through the streets, [and] eventually lynched to the lusty cheers of five hundred patriots." Jurors found Prager's killers not guilty of their "patriotic murder" (68). The *Washington Post* declared on April 12, 1918: "Enemy propaganda must be stopped, even if a few lynchings occur," and noted that "in spite of excesses such as lynching, it is a healthful and wholesome awakening." See also "Seized Records of Enemy-Controlled Organizations," 131.3.2, RG 131, NACP. Groups from which records were seized included the German Railroads Information Office (New York City), German-American Bund, Deutsches Haus, Deutscher Klub of Dallas, German American Athletic Union of North America, Federation of Italian World War Veterans in the United States, and the Dante Alighieri Society of New York.

31. Diamond, *Nazi Movement in the United States*, 58. There was "an inverse relationship between the degree of persecution endured by a German American group and the threat it posed. Erstwhile champions of German imperialism and the German American Alliance escaped unscathed while harmless German-speaking Mennonites and Hutterites—rural, separatist, pacifistic, nonresisting, apolitical—were ridiculed, harassed, beaten, painted, tarred, robbed, and betrayed in the name of American democratic ideals." Luebke, *Bonds of Loyalty*, 311–12.

32. Luebke, *Bonds of Loyalty*, 328–31. "Most Germans thought of themselves as Americans totally loyal to American democratic ideals. . . . Mostly the German Americans wanted to forget what had happened. Families gave up speaking German in

their homes. Programs for the maintenance of language and culture withered and died.... They were thoroughly Americanized" (50–51, 329–30).

33. W. Wilson, *Public Papers*, 3:423–24; Luebke, *Bonds of Loyalty*, 144–46.

34. Kennedy, *Over Here*, 24; Luebke, *Bonds of Loyalty*, 145–46. Kennedy adds: "In an otherwise dull address, one observer remarked, 'The most enthusiastic applause was for [Wilson's] attack on hyphenated Americans'" (24).

35. Statistics from Kennedy, *Over Here*, 24; Luebke, *Bonds of Loyalty*, 211.

36. Andrew, *For the President's Eyes Only*, 79.

37. Andrew, *For the President's Eyes Only*, 75–79.

38. Katz, *Secret War in Mexico*, 350–55; Stokesbury, *A Short History of World War I*, 221.

39. Nagler, "Internment of German Enemy Aliens," 71.

40. Quoted in Patterson, *America in the Twentieth Century*, 20.

41. Rippley, "Ameliorated Americanization," 217.

42. Diggins, *Mussolini and Fascism*, 12.

43. Sixteenth Census: *Foreign-Born Germans and Italians*. Census figures showed 314,715 alien Germans out of 1,237,772 born in Germany and 695,363 alien Italians out of 1,623,579 born in Italy. See also Fox, *Unknown Internment*, 4, 8.

44. Fox, *Unknown Internment*, 20–21.

45. Perrett, *Days of Sadness*, 230.

2. Fifth-Column Fears and Foreign Challenges

1. Dr. Charles Fama, *Beware of the Menace of Fascism in America*, May 1927, SDCF, 1910–49, Class 8, Internal Affairs of State, box 4729, RG 59, NACP.

2. Diggins, *Mussolini and Fascism*, 27-28; Harvey to Child cited and quoted Diggins, 262.

3. Salvemini, *Italian Fascist Activities*, 8–9. A telegram to Rome put the Order of the Sons of Italy's membership at 300,000.

4. Diggins, *Mussolini and Fascism*, 292–93. For the opinion poll see *Fortune*, October 1935, 170–73.

5. *Congressional Record*, LXII, Pt. 9 (Washington DC, 1930), May 22, 1930, p. 9390; Report 2290, U.S. Congress, House of Representatives, 71st Cong., 3rd sess., Special Committee on Communist Activities in the United States, January 17, 1931; "Investigation of Communist Propaganda," January 22, 1931, SDCF, 1910–49, Class 8, Internal Affairs of State, box 4727, RG 59, NACP. Quoted material is available at http://www.fas.org/irp/ops/ci/docs/ci1/ch4b.htm.

6. D. F. Schmitz, *The United States and Fascist Italy*, 78; conversations with the Italian ambassador, January 6 and January 14, 1932, SDCF, 1910–49, Class 8, Internal Affairs of State, box 4728, RG 59, NACP.

7. Goddard to Hoover, March 1, 1931, SDCF, 1910–49, Class 8, Internal Affairs of State, box 4728, RG 59, NACP.

8. Austin to Hoover, March 1, 1931, Hoffman to Hoover, February 28, 1931, Hartmann to Hoover, March 2, 1931, Kast to Hoover, March 2, 1931, and Bentz family to Hoover, March 1, 1931, all in SDCF, 1910–49, Class 8, Internal Affairs of State, box 4728, RG 59, NACP.

9. Valenti to Stimson, August 8, 1932, SDCF, 1910–49, Class 8, Internal Affairs of State, box 4728, RG 59, NACP; Cannistraro, introduction, x–xvii; Diggins, *Mussolini and Fascism*, 143; D. F. Schmitz, *The United States and Fascist Italy*, 134 and 135–52; Girolamo Valenti, "Mussolini's Agent Fosters Fascist Propaganda in the U.S.," *La Stampa Libera*, January 24, 1934.

10. Cannistraro, introduction, xii.

11. Diamond, *Nazi Movement in the United States*, chapters 3 and 4; Frye, *Nazi Germany*, chapters 2–4; "1,500 Nazis Here Told to Disband," *New York Times*, April 27, 1933; "Hitlerites Confirm Ban on Nazis Here," *New York Times*, April 29, 1933. By 1936 there were seventy-four official and unofficial agencies of Auslanddeutschtum (Germany's racial or ethnic linking of all expatriate Germans globally). A. L. Smith, *The Deutschtum of Nazi Germany*.

12. See Leuchtenburg, *Roosevelt and the New Deal*, chapter 12; A. L. Smith, *The Deutschtum of Nazi Germany*; Hawgood, *The Tragedy of German-America*, 287–308.

13. See Kuhn, *Awake and Act!*; Kuhn, "What Are We?," *Deutscher Weckruf und Beobachter*, October 7, 1936, quoted in Diamond, *Nazi Movement in the United States*, 218. The term "fifth column" originated in the Spanish Civil War as sympathizers inside a city stood ready to aid approaching soldiers and take control. Weinberg observed, "No two major powers were on better terms with each other than Germany and the United States before 1933, and the destruction of that relationship must be considered one of the signal events of the 1930s" (*Foreign Policy of Hitler's Germany: Diplomatic Revolution*, 133).

14. "Deportation Urged for Hitlerites Here," *New York Times*, September 25, 1933; film *The March of Time: Inside Nazi Germany* (Time, Inc., 1938).

15. Frye, *Nazi Germany*, 16, 21–22. "The directive recognized the prevalence of an anti-German attitude in most countries of the New World, and it repeatedly exhorted Nazi operatives to use the utmost caution in order to mask the sources and intentions of the propaganda. . . . In the Western Hemisphere the central task would be to develop sympathy for the Reich's foreign policy." The Nazis would "consolidate, gain control over, and enhance the power position of German elements [and] win influence over public opinion in the Western Hemisphere in order to improve Germany's international position and weaken the power of American governments to provide effective opposition to Nazi policies and actions" (Frye, *Nazi Germany*, 22, 31).

16. Breuer, *Hitler's Undercover War*, 3.

17. "Attention! Protestant Ministers and Protestant Christian Americans: Stop, Read, Think and Act," circular, April 10, 1933, SDCF, 1910–49, Class 8, Internal Affairs of State, box 4729, RG 59, NACP.

18. "Historical Sketch on Origin and Extent of Nazi Activities in United States," Confidential Committee Print, 1933, SDCF, 1910–49, Class 8, Internal Affairs of State, box 4729, RG 59, NACP.

19. Winslow to Hull, Fascist Pressure on Naturalized American Citizens—The Case of Aurelio Toppano, October 19, 1933, SDCF, 1910–49, Class 8, Internal Affairs of State, box 4728, RG 59, NACP.

20. Dominian to Hull, Necessity of Legislation to Prevent Fascist Political Agitation in the United States, November 6, 1933, SDCF, 1910–49, Class 8, Internal Affairs of State, box 4728, RG 59, NACP.

21. In March 1933 the German government decided that local Nazi units or "cells" in the United States should dissolve. On April 16 the Foreign Section of the NSDAP ordered it so. See "Nazi Actions Here Bring an Inquiry," *New York Times*, October 10, 1933, 1; "Reich Is Worried over Our Reaction," *New York Times*, March 23, 1933, 11; "1,500 Nazis Here Told to Disband," *New York Times* April 27, 1933, 10; "Hitlerites Confirm Ban on Nazis Here," *New York Times* April 29, 1933, 8; Hodgdon to Carr, November 14, 1933, SDCF, 1910–49, Class 8, Internal Affairs of State, box 4729, RG 59, NACP.

22. U.S. House, Special Committee on Un-American Activities, *Investigation of Nazi and Other Propaganda*; Ogden, *The Dies Committee*, 33. The McCormack-Dickstein Committee became the House Un-American Activities Committee (HUAC) in May 1938 through HR 282. HUAC is also known as the Dies Committee after Representative Martin Dies of Texas.

23. Hitler stated: "The Reich must embrace all Germans for the purpose of uniting and maintaining the most valuable racial elements of this nation [and] for the purpose of raising the German nation gradually and safely to a dominating position." *Mein Kampf* (Munich: Franz Eher, 1934), 439, reprinted in *The German Reich and Americans of German Origin*, 16–17; "Address by George Viereck at Madison Square Garden," May 17, 1934, SDCF, 1910–49, Class 8, Internal Affairs of State, box 4729, RG 59, NACP; House Report 153, 74th Cong., 1st sess., Serial 9890.

24. Irons, *Justice at War*, 19–20; Roosevelt to Chief of Naval Operations, memo, August 10, 1936, folder A 8-5, box 216, RG 80, NACP.

25. "General Program for Foreign Service Officers," August 31, 1936, folder "Rupture of Relations," box 76, SWPD, RG 59, NACP; "Policy of U.S. Government in Regard to Repatriation of U.S. Nationals," 1944, "Vol. 22: Exchanges of Civilian Nationals by Belligerents," box 8, SWPD, RG 59, NACP. U.S. vessels included the *Orizaba*, *Shawnee*, *Iroquois*, *St. John*, and *Acadia*.

26. *Life*, like most magazines, extolled the Russian people's courage and the Red Army's heroism but avoided lauding communism or praising the Soviet regime. Fussell, *Wartime*, chapter 9, "Type-casting."

27. UVA Miller Center, Presidential Speeches, FDR Presidency, October 5, 1937: Quarantine Speech. On December 12, 1937, Japanese aircraft sank the U.S. gunboat *Panay* in Chinese waters while Japanese troops took Nanking and initiated widespread killing, raping, and execution of noncombatants—later known as the Rape of Nanking.

28. Goodwin, *No Ordinary Time*, 103.

29. Goodwin, *No Ordinary Time*, 320.

30. "Nazi Units in United States List 1,000 Aliens," *New York Times*, March 23, 1933; "Nazis' Hand Seen in Activities Here" and "Hitler Men Said to Be Ready to Send Report of 'Sabotage' to Reich Authorities," *New York Times*, September 24, 1933.

31. "Educating for War," *New Republic*, November 8, 1933; "Nazi Agent Called in Federal Inquiry," *New York Times*, November 9, 1933; "'Mr. X' at Hearing Details Nazi

'Plot,'" *New York Times*, November 15, 1933; "German Day Set; Nazi Note Curbed," *New York Times*, December 2, 1933.

32. Leuchtenburg, *Roosevelt and the New Deal*, 276. "The success of Huey Long," Leuchtenburg wrote, "seemed evidence that fascism could come from within, not through a coup d'état, but with the acquiescence of the people" (275).

33. Theoharis, *Spying on Americans*, 67.

34. Biddle, *In Brief Authority*, 107; Theoharis, *The Boss*, 95.

35. Stimson, letter to the editor, *New York Times*, March 6, 1939; Roosevelt to Chief of Naval Operations, August 10, 1936, box 216, RG 80, NACP; President's Secretary File (PSF) 197, FDRL; Irons, *Justice at War*, 20; Robinson, *By Order of the President*, 56.

36. Gentry, *J. Edgar Hoover*, 205; Theoharis, *The Boss*, 172; Andrew, *For the President's Eyes Only*, 88; Theoharis, *Spying on Americans*, xi–xii.

37. Hoover to SACs, *Hearings on Intelligence Activities*, 94th Cong., 1st sess., 1975, vol. 6, FBI, 562–63, quoted in Theoharis, *Spying on Americans*, 69–70.

38. Gentry, *J. Edgar Hoover*, 206–7; Theoharis, *The Boss*, 172–76; Theoharis, *Spying on Americans*, 68–69; Andrew, *For the President's Eyes Only*, 88–89.

39. Theoharis, *The Boss*, 165n.

40. Theoharis, *The Boss*, 5, 182.

41. Prentias Gilbert, Chargé d'Affaires, to Hull, October 28, 1937, Subject: Action taken concerning German National Socialist Activities, no. 3718, pp. 1–3, 13, SDCF, 1910-49, Class 8, Internal Affairs of State, box 4729, RG 59, NACP; Representative Citron to Hull, July 21, 1937, and Senator Capper to Hull, April 8, 1938, SDCF, 1910–49, Class 8, Internal Affairs of State, box 4730, RG 59, NACP.

42. Dies, *The Trojan Horse in America*, 348.

43. Vooros testimony before Dies Committee, *New York Times*, August 19, 1939, quoted in Canedy, *America's Nazis*, 201.

44. *The German Reich*, front jacket and preface.

45. *The German Reich*, 18–44. The editors note that some 33–35 million Germans live outside the Reich, including 15 million in the Western Hemisphere, 8 million in the United States, and 500,000 in Canada.

46. Leuchtenburg, *Roosevelt and the New Deal*, 280; "Nazi Bund Rally, Protected by Free Speech, Attacks Democracy," *Scholastic Magazine*, March 11, 1939, 9; "Bund Banned," *Time*, March 14, 1938, 15–16; "U.S. Citizens Drilled by Bund in 28 Camps: Nazis on the March in Intensive Training Used in Hitler's Rise," *Brooklyn Daily Eagle*, March 26, 1938. The *Eagle* claimed it had material from "government sources, substantiated by documentary and photographic evidence."

47. Address by Fritz Kuhn, August 10, 1937, SDCF, 1910–49, Class 8, Internal Affairs of State, box 4730, RG 59, NACP.

48. U.S. Congress, House, Special Committee on Un-American Activities, *Special Report on Subversive Activities*, 1–4.

49. U.S. Congress, House, *Special Report on Subversive Activities*, 1–4.

50. Dieckhoff quoted in Canedy, *America's Nazis*, 86, 158–61; Dies, "The Real Issue Is Plain," 731–34. Dies declared that, according to the testimony and documentary evidence his committee received, "There is no question that . . . the German Amer-

ican Bund is closely allied with the Nazi movement in Germany; that it receives its inspiration and encouragement from the Nazi government and is deeply sympathetic with the Nazi movement" (731). Kuhn grew increasingly desperate as he and the Bund struggled. With membership declining and funds drying up, America's führer staged a grand spectacle, but like so many other provocative exhibits, the rally at Madison Square Garden on February 20, 1939 (attended by some twenty-two thousand), backfired as fights broke out and a far larger angry mob awaited them outside the venue. See Canedy, *America's Nazis*, 194–97; Hart, *Hitler's American Friends*, 38–45; and Diamond, *Nazi Movement in the United States*, 324–31.

3. Dire Preparations

1. Moss, *Nineteen Weeks*, 243–44; Perrett, *Days of Sadness*, 89; Krammer, *Undue Process*, 9–10.

2. From 1913 to 1933 the Bureau of Immigration and the Bureau of Naturalization existed within the Labor Department. Executive Order 6166, on June 10, 1933, established the INS in the Labor Department.

3. Stanley Karnow used the term "minimum candor" to describe the Johnson administration's choice of a "deliberate tactic to disclose only the barest essentials without blatantly lying" (*Vietnam*, 414). Roosevelt and Hoover acted similarly, battling alien enemies and potentially disloyal citizens.

4. "Proclaiming the Neutrality of the United States," *Federal Register* (September 6, 1939), vol. 4, no. 171, pp. 3809–12.

5. Kennett, *For the Duration*, 65–66; Lingeman, *Don't You Know*, 35–39.

6. Krammer, *Undue Process*, 15; Nagler, "Internment of German Enemy Aliens," 71. Britain's Home Office, founded in 1782, was responsible for immigration, security, and policing.

7. M. M. Anderson, *Hitler's Exiles*, 19–21.

8. Gillman and Gillman, *"Collar the Lot!,"* 23–27.

9. Scherman, *Life Goes to War*, 79. The pictorial section is titled "The menace of invasion arouses every Englishman."

10. Conference with Mr. Patterson, in Charge of Internment for the British, "Interoffice #1," April 18, 1941, SWPU, box 9, RG 60, NACP; U.S. Congress, House, *Fourth Interim Report of the Select Committee*, 281; Gillman and Gillman, *"Collar the Lot!,"* 45, 173, 222–25. Britain had largely halted their internments by July 1940, and the 27,000 persons included merchant sailors. Roosevelt, along with Breckinridge Long and Sumner Welles, in part due to the rampant anti-Semitism that existed in the United States (there were over one hundred active anti-Semitic organizations), believed that refugees generally and Jewish refugees specifically (because, the reasoning was, they were easily coercible) could be spies and saboteurs—dangerous regardless even if it was just a small percentage. See Friedman, *Nazis and Good Neighbors*, 213–14.

11. Conference with Mr. Patterson.

12. Quoted material from Theoharis, *Spying on Americans*, 74, and *The Boss*, 140–41, 178, 195; Irons, *Justice at War*, 14–15; Fox, *Unknown Internment*, 152. Classification depended upon perceived dangerousness. Those thought most dangerous were "A"

category, "less dangerous" were "B," and suspected "sympathizers" were "C." Hoover to all SACS, June 15, 1940, "To and from Justice Re: Enemy Aliens," box 129, SWPD, RG 59. See also HF, War Dept. #439A, PMG, boxes 5, 16–19, RG 389, NACP.

13. Confidential and Strictly Confidential Memoranda to State Department and FBI, November 6, December 14, 27, and 28, 1939, and January 22, 1940, SDCF, 1910–49, Class 8, Internal Affairs of State, box 4731, RG 59, NACP.

14. Hoover to all law enforcement officials, September 6, 1939, "Economic Defense," SWPU, box 4, RG 60, NACP. See also Theoharis, *From the Secret Files*, 184.

15. Theoharis, *Spying on Americans*, 74.

16. Hoover to SACS, December 6, 1939, "Internal Security," RG 65, NACP. Hoover's list had actually been created several years earlier. Theoharis mentions a still-secret May 1934 presidential directive that authorized Hoover to "conduct a limited investigation of the activities of American Nazis and American Nazi sympathizers" as well as Secretary of War George Dern's January 1936 request for the FBI to "conduct appropriate investigations into so-called subversive activities." After a private meeting with Roosevelt in August 1936, Hoover instituted a broad surveillance program and created an elaborate filing system containing indexes and dossiers on "subversive" persons. The "suspect list" became known in June 1940 as the Custodial Detention Index (CDI)—those of German, Italian, and Japanese ancestry whom the FBI would arrest and incarcerate in the event of a national emergency. There were numerous revisions and updates to include new enemies; the CDI was later renamed the Security Index (SI) and then the Administrative Index (ADEX). Theoharis, *From the Secret Files*, 179–83; Theoharis, *The Boss*, 171–77; Theoharis, *Spying on Americans*, 67–70.

17. Hoover to SACS, December 6, 1939, "Internal Security," RG 65, NACP, and FBI HQ Files. The registration act referred to is the Foreign Agents Registration Act (FARA), which sought to ensure that the public and lawmakers knew the source of information (propaganda) intended to sway public opinion, policy, and laws. Source: FARA website.

18. Proclamation, "Export of Arms, Ammunition, and Implements of War," *Federal Register* (September 7, 1939), vol. 4, no. 172, p. 3819; Proclamation, "Proclaiming a National Emergency," *Federal Register* (September 9, 1939), vol. 4, no. 174, p. 3851; Theoharis, *Spying on Americans*, 40–42; Theoharis, *The Boss*, 199.

19. Christgau, *"Enemies,"* 19–21; memorandum from Lemuel B. Schofield, Special Assistant to the Attorney General to Francis Biddle, August 13, 1941, CLCF, "January–February 1942," box 5, RG 60, NACP; for Fort Stanton, see https://www.fortstanton.org/. The *Columbus*'s crew were categorized as enemy aliens (no longer distressed seamen) once the United States entered the war.

20. Brinkley, *Washington Goes to War*, 41–45; "U.S. Seizes Axis Ships," *New York Times*, March 31, 1941.

21. Detention Reports: May 31, 1946, Records of the Alien Information Bureau, Records Relating to Alien Civilian Internees, 1941–1946, War Department decimal filing system #466J, folder "Detention Reports," PMG, box 2, RG 389, NACP; Bolino, *Ellis Island Source Book*, 42; Christgau, *"Enemies,"* 19–21; Fox, *Unknown Internment*, 38, 152, 164.

22. State Department: "Various American Agencies Holding Civilian Enemy Aliens," June 19, 1942, folder "Enemy Aliens in U.S.—General," box 129, SWPD, RG 59, NACP; Culley, "A Troublesome Presence"; UVA Miller Center, Presidential Speeches, FDR Presidency, December 29, 1940: Fireside Chat, Arsenal of Democracy Speech; Schofield to Biddle, August 13, 1941, CLCF, folder "January 1942," box 5, RG 60, NACP; for Fort Stanton, see http://www.fortstanton.com.

23. Perrett, *Days of Sadness*, 58–60, 155–57, 217; Leuchtenburg, *Roosevelt and the New Deal*, 299–304. See also Leuchtenburg's chapters 12 and 13. Patriotic citizens joined home defense corps and became informants. In its June 3, 1940, issue, *Time* noted that "hundreds of gossips wrote the FBI volunteering to spy on their neighbors."

24. FDR condemned Mussolini for stabbing France in the back. Blum, *V Was for Victory*, 150.

25. Mangione, *An Ethnic at Large*, 271–75. Congress passed the Smith Act on June 28, 1940. U.S. courts regularly upheld the Naturalization Act, by which the government could revoke citizenship. The October 1940 act targeted Bundists and any naturalized citizen who corresponded with persons in Germany, showed sympathy for Germany, or criticized U.S. foreign or domestic policies. Attorneys accused them of fraud (misrepresenting or concealing facts) or violations of naturalization laws. By the fall of 1941, Edward Ennis, an INS employee, worked alongside Harrison and Biddle developing internment processes. One of Ennis's responsibilities was deciding whom to intern. He became head of the Alien Enemy Control Unit on December 22, 1941, and his hearing and review boards later decided whether to intern, parole, or release aliens. Harrison, for his part, served as INS commissioner from July 1942 to July 1944.

26. U.S. Department of State, *Report of the Delegation*, pp. 6–8 (the report of the Emergency Advisory Committee for Political Defense is located in folder "To and from Justice Re: Enemy Aliens," box 129, SWPD, RG 59, NACP); Hoover to SACs, December 6, 1939, "Internal Security," RG 65, NACP and FBI HQ Files.

27. Theoharis, *The Boss*, 198–201.

28. Perrett, *Days of Sadness*, 89; Hoover to all SACs, June 15, 1940, folder "To and from Justice Re: Enemy Aliens," box 129, SWPD, RG 59, NACP; Gellately, "The Gestapo and German Society." Some compared the FBI's intelligence-gathering methods with Hitler's Gestapo and Stalin's Cheka.

29. Hoover to McGuire, August 21, 1940, FBI HQ Files, quoted (and available in full) in Arthur D. Jacobs and Joseph E. Fallon, *The World War Two Experience*, section 1, vol. 4 of *German-Americans in the World War*, ed. Don Heinrich Tolzmann (Munich: K. G. Saur, 1995) [hereafter cited as Jacobs and Fallon, *World War Two*]. See also https://www.foitimes.com/internment/vol.htm. Excerpts of this and other primary source documents can be found at https://www.foitimes.com/internment/chrono.html. Hoover quoted in Theoharis, *The Boss*, 175, 195. See also "Chronology of Alien Enemy Material, January 3, 1941," "Interoffice Memoranda, no. 1," box 9, SWPU, RG 60, NACP. The FBI investigated 4,500 people on its suspect list for over eighteen months; 1,800 were tentatively classified as aliens.

30. Memo for the Attorney General from Smith, September 23, 1940, SWPU, box 4, and Chronology of Alien Enemy Material, "Interoffice #1," January 3, 1941, SWPU, box 9, both in RG 60, NACP.

31. Miles, memo on Counter-Fifth Column, "Civilian Protection," July 29, 1940, SWPU, box 3, and Hoover to Stimson and Stimson to Hoover, "Interoffice #1," January 3, 1941, SWPU, both in box 9, RG 60, NACP.

32. Memo for Smith, Re: Proposed Plan Alien Enemies, June 26, 1941, CLCF, folder "Jan.–Feb. 1942," box 5, RG 60, NACP; Theoharis, *The Boss*, 175, 224–29.

33. "Establishment of the SD," November 18, 1944, box 78, SWPD, RG 59, NACP; Corbett, *Quiet Passages*, 1–7; Messersmith to Harrison, November 25, 1939, box 208, Breckinridge Long Papers, LOC. By April 1941 the FBI had concluded that the Nazis "have been exploiting the 'Jewish refugee' problem for the purpose of espionage and other subversive activities in the Western Hemisphere." The OSS agreed. Theoharis, *The Boss*, 194–96; Lees, "National Security and Ethnicity," 113–14. The protecting neutral powers included Spain, Sweden, and Switzerland.

34. Goodwin, *No Ordinary Time*, 100, 173–74; Fox, *America's Invisible Gulag*, 313n23.

4. The Fifth-Column Threat

1. "These Are Signs of Nazi Fifth Columns Everywhere," *Life*, June 17, 1940; "Trojan Horses," *Newsweek*, April 29, 1940; "The Bunders' Resume," *Newsweek*, June 24, 1940; "Nazi Pipeline," *Newsweek*, July 22, 1940; Kirchwey, "The Fifth Column," *Nation*, April 27, 1940; Moss, *Nineteen Weeks*, 244 (*Harper's* quotation); survey data from "Public Opinion, in a Compound of Dread and Determination, Goes on a War Footing," *Fortune*, supplement, July 1940.

2. Stent, *A Bespattered Page*, 252–53; Weinberg, *A World at Arms*, 107–12. Lord St. Oswald, a *Daily Telegraph* reporter, may have been the first to use the term "fifth column." Weeks before, however, Franco's General Emilio Mola had boasted that a fifth column of spies, saboteurs, and sympathizers in Madrid joined his four columns of troops marching on the city.

3. Gillman and Gillman, *"Collar the Lot!,"* 73.

4. "Fifth Column Dossier," *Newsweek*, August 26, 1940, 29.

5. "Crescendo of Nazi Propaganda Charted in Princeton Analysis," *Newsweek*, September 16, 1940, 54.

6. Margaret Schmidt, "I Married a Nazi," *Reader's Digest*, March 1940, 89. Condensed from *Eve's Journal*, October 1939.

7. Perrett, *Days of Sadness*, 216–30. From 1938 to 1942 a "case of national jitters" gripped the United States—fear that a fifth column had penetrated the nation, engaged in a campaign of subversion.

8. Fear of enemies within by self-categorized whites is a recurrent theme in United States history, whether those perceived enemies were Native Americans, blacks, Tejanos, or various immigrant groups. In 1854, Know-Nothing Party newspapers "attacked Germans and Mexicans as hostile to democracy and to the native-born." Bennett, *The Party of Fear*, 144, 184. In 1905, especially on the West Coast, newspapers warned of the "Yellow Peril," a "Japanese Invasion, the Problem of the Hour," bent on molesting white American women, corrupting white children, taking jobs from white men, and destroying America's white culture.

9. Moss, *Nineteen Weeks*, 243.

10. Frye, *Nazi Germany*, 173; Rauschning, *The Voice of Destruction*.

11. Gillman and Gillman, *"Collar the Lot!,"* 274. "Bluntly stated," Gillman and Gillman conclude, "the United States asked Britain how to do it."

12. Hoover to Jackson, April 1, 1941, quoted in Theoharis, *Secret Files*, 187.

13. Sondern, "Hitler Looks to South America," 47–50.

14. For fifth-column context, see Frank L. Kluckhohn, "Washington Alert to 'Fifth Column,'" *New York Times*, June 2, 1940; Joseph Shaplin, "Outlawing Is Urged for Fifth Column," *New York Times*, June 24, 1940; Moss, *Nineteen Weeks*, 243–44. Roosevelt press conference quoted in Moss (244), who cites an unnamed *New York Times* article of June 6, 1940.

15. UVA Miller Center, Presidential Speeches, FDR Presidency, December 29, 1940: Fireside Chat, Arsenal of Democracy Speech.

16. Carter to Roosevelt, November 7, 1941, box 573, RG 210, NACP; U.S. Commission on Wartime Relocation and Internment of Civilians, *Papers of the U.S. Commission on Wartime Relocation and Internment of Civilians*, reel 3, p. 638 [hereafter cited as CWRIC, *Papers*].

17. "Roosevelt Proclaims Unlimited Emergency," *New York Times*, May 28, 1941; UVA Miller Center, Presidential Speeches, FDR Presidency, May 27, 1941: Fireside Chat, Unlimited National Emergency Speech. For the context of the speech see Goodwin, *No Ordinary Time*, 236–40. Roosevelt's concurrent proclamation stated that "an unlimited national emergency confronts this country, which requires that its military, naval, air and civilian defenses be put on the basis of readiness to repel any and all acts or threats of aggression directed toward any part of the Western Hemisphere." The full text can be found at UC Santa Barbara, American Presidency Project, Roosevelt documents, Proclamation 2487.

18. Buhite and Levy, *FDR's Fireside Chats*, 192; UVA Miller Center, Presidential Speeches, FDR Presidency, September 11, 1941: Fireside Chat, On the Greer Incident. As U.S. officials trekked across the Colombian countryside searching for the elusive (and fictitious) airfields, President Eduardo Santos protested FDR's assertion and U.S. actions. Hull later expressed his "very deep regret." Hull, "Reference to Air Field in Colombia," September 17, 1941, reel 28, Cordell Hull Papers, Manuscript Division, LOC.

19. Sondern, "Hitler Looks to South America"; *Life*, June 10 and 17, 1940; *Fortune*, August and October 1940; *Foreign Affairs*, January 1941; *Collier's*, June 22, 1940; *Nation*, March 4, 1939; *Newsweek*, August 26, 1940; *New Republic*, June 29, 1938, and December 2, 1940; *New York Times*, June 28, 1938. Most fifth-column stories focused on Germans before Pearl Harbor and on the Japanese afterward. Many dozens of stories told of fifth columnists and Trojan horses at work in numerous European nations prior to Nazi military victories. The infamous *War of the Worlds* broadcast of October 30, 1938, regarding an alien invasion, did not help matters. Neither did *Life*'s caption "These Young Americans Are Nazis" with a photo of a few boys of the Bund's "Order Guard" enjoying a picnic and a swim—a "vilification" of the "American way of life" at Camp Siegfried, Long Island (*Life*, June 17, 1940)—or the many

hundreds of articles appearing throughout the mid- to late 1930s, including those with subtitles such as "Nation-Wide Plot by Nazis Charged: Moley Magazine Reports a Coast-to-Coast Organization to Supplant Democracy," under the title "Hitlerism Invades America," *New York Times*, March 30, 1934.

20. J. A. Thompson, "The Exaggeration of American Invulnerability," 28; Conn and Fairchild, *United States Army in World War II: Framework*, 32–34, 95–96, 272–74. Hints of a Nazi-inspired coup in Uruguay seemed to prove Hitler's intentions. The United States created RAINBOW 4, which assumed a German-Italian-Japanese coalition and included plans for military operations in Brazil to thwart anticipated Axis hemispheric encroachments.

21. Kimball, *The Juggler*, 118, 253n35. The famous (but fictional) map FDR presented publicly in October 1941 was "the product of the fertile imagination of an overzealous local Nazi who perhaps was trying to curry favor with his superiors. Roosevelt was able to use it to strengthen the interventionist cause." Hilton, *Hitler's Secret War*, 204.

22. Memo: "The Japanese Question in the United States: A Compilation of Memoranda, by Lt. Com. Kenneth D. Ringle," 1942–1945, folder "WRA, June–December 1945," box 19, SWPD, RG 59, NACP.

23. Carter to Roosevelt, November 7, 1941, box 573, RG 210, NACP; CWRIC, *Papers*, reel 3, p. 638.

24. Roosevelt to Stimson, November 8, 1941, box 573, RG 210, NACP; CWRIC, *Papers*, reel 3, p. 656; Daniels, *Concentration Camps USA*, 27–29; "The Japanese Question in the United States"; Moss, *Nineteen Weeks*, 244.

25. Andrew, *For the President's Eyes Only*, 94. Numerous magazine and newspaper stories implicated domestic enemies or implied that subversives caused many unexplained events, from local disasters to widespread international instability.

26. Theoharis, *The Boss*, 203; *Congressional Record—Senate*, vol. 86, pt. 1, 76th Cong., 3rd sess., p. 680, pt. 6, pp. 6773, 6775, quoted in Friedman, *Nazis and Good Neighbors*, 53.

27. Krebs's 1941 best-seller was a stunning international success, selling more than a million copies in the United States alone. *Book of the Month Club News* called it "full of sensational revelations and interspersed with episodes of daring, desperate conflict, torture, and ruthless conspiracy." *New Republic* said it was "exact and truthful," while the *Nation* praised it as a "historical document of the first rank." For the descriptions, see *Book of the Month Club News* quoted in Amazon and Barnes and Noble overview of *Out of the Night*; Bertram Wolfe, *New Republic*, January 27, 1941; and Franz Hollering, *Nation*, January 18, 1941. Valtin, *Out of the Night*, 600–602; Fox, *Unknown Internment*, 38. Fox writes that Krebs's testimony in May 1941 "became the catalyst for repression. The roundup of alien enemies in the United States began." The chemical and pharmaceutical giant IG Farben worked closely as a donor and contractor with the Nazi regime's war effort, including making the poison gas Zyklon B that killed well over one million Jews in death camp gas chambers.

28. Christgau, *"Enemies,"* 18; "Aliens: Robert Jackson's Busy Week," *Time*, May 19, 1941; "Alien Crackdown," *Newsweek*, May 19, 1941. See also Fox, *Unknown Internment*, 39.

29. Dingell to Roosevelt, August 18, 1941, Official File no. 197, FDRL. Dingell's exaggerated numbers reflected the common misidentification of aliens and citizens at the time.

30. *San Francisco Chronicle*, December 10, 1941; Welles to MacDougall, folder "Americans in Japan, 1941–42," box 89, SWPD, RG 59, NACP.

31. Biddle, *In Brief Authority*, 207; Stimson to Hull, February 5, 1942, Department of State File 740.00115 Pacific War/153, RG 59, NACP, quoted in Weglyn, *Years of Infamy*, 55–56; Knox to Roosevelt, August 16, 1943, President's Secretary File: War Department, FDRL; Knox to Hull, October 29, and Long to Strong, July 20, 1942, folder "Hawaii, 1942," box 186, SWPD, RG 59, NACP. Gullion, having no precise plans or places yet to house Japanese Americans, nonetheless felt it prudent to move all West Coast Japanese—aliens and citizens—to camps east of the Sierra Nevada mountains. Anything less, to use the common term of the day, would be "too little or too late." For context, see Daniels, *Prisoners without Trial*, chapter 2.

32. "Index of Japanese Organizations in the United States," WDC, Civil Affairs Division Research Branch, June 1944, HF, War Dept. #439A, PMG, box 20, RG 389, NACP.

33. "History of Japanese Program," PMG, Washington DC, Prepared by Japanese-American Branch, Presidio of San Francisco, Major Harbert, Commanding Officer, Edited by Captain Arnold, Executive Officer, January 20, 1943–September 1, 1945, HF, War Dept. #439A, PMG, box 20, RG 389, NACP.

34. "Totalitarian Doctrine, Organization, Propaganda Distribution and Intelligence Operations—Japanism," p. 1, E-73, SWPU, box 4, RG 60, NACP.

35. "Totalitarian Doctrine," 2–4. The ONI report remained classified until July 1994.

36. "Totalitarian Doctrine," 4–6, 9–12, 14–16.

37. Hoover to all SACS, June 15, 1940, box 129, SWPD, RG 59, NACP; Joseph Prendergast, "Memo for the Files," March 31, 1941, SWPU, box 9, RG 60, NACP; Hoover to Connelley, FBI, and SACS Re: Internal Security Custodial Detention List, April 30, 1941, FBI File #66-6200-100-33x, in Jacobs and Fallon, *World War Two*. Cards designated "Italian" were filed "Fascist." Cards designated "Nazi" were filed "German."

38. Prendergast, "Memo for the Files." The Voorhis Act required the registration of groups representing foreign governments, including those advocating the forcible overthrow of the government. Officials could then monitor their membership and activities.

39. "Many organizations voluntarily disbanded after Pearl Harbor. Others were destroyed by freezing their funds; by proceedings against their leaders—internment as alien enemies, revocation of naturalization followed by internment, or criminal prosecutions for espionage, sedition, or conspiracy." U.S. Department of State, *Report of the Delegation*, 14–15; memo for Smith, Re: Persons Being Considered for Possible Investigation for Alleged Activities, March 11, 1941, SWPU, "Interoffice #1," box 9, RG 60, NACP; Hoover to Connelley, FBI, and SACS, April 30, 1941, p. 1.

40. Hoover to Connelley, FBI, and SACS, April 30, 1941, 4–5.

41. U.S. Department of State, *Report of the Delegation*, 6–8. On May 22, 1940, FDR used the "startling sequence of international events" as the rationale for transferring the Immigration and Naturalization Service (INS) from the Labor to the Justice Department. On June 14, as German troops entered Paris, the president's Reorga-

nization Plan no. 5 did just that. INS functions included administering and investigating alleged violations of laws relating to the admission, exclusion, deportation, and naturalization of aliens..

42. Theoharis, *The Boss*, 156–57n, 185–87.

43. Mangione, *An Ethnic at Large*, 271. Mangione traveled the country for the Justice Department explaining relocation and internment policies to more than a million enemy aliens. This was no easy task, because "a good number of them, over and above the interned West Coast Japanese-Americans, were harassed, restricted, and even detained in custody for no proven crime except having German or Italian ancestry" (10). See especially chapter 13, "Concentration Camps—American Style."

44. U.S. Department of State, *Report of the Delegation*, 7; "Notice to Aliens of Enemy Nationalities," SWPU, folder "Instructions, Regulations, and Forms," box 9, RG 60, NACP; Rowe, "The Alien Enemy Program," 20. The INS reported 4,921,452 aliens registered beginning August 27, 1940. Roughly 20 percent were nationals of Germany, Italy, and Japan.

45. Testimony of James Rowe before the CWRIC, Washington DC, July 14, 1981, p. 48.

46. Andrew, *For the President's Eyes Only*, 86–87, 94–95; B. Smith, *The Shadow Warriors*. Smith notes the exaggerated fifth-column threat and found no trace of evidence that it existed in Britain, the United States, or elsewhere. FDR had long relied upon and trusted Donovan.

47. U.S. officials desired a liberal policy for aliens, resting upon reciprocity. Hull to American Legation, Bern, January 7, 1942, SDCF, 1910–49, Class 8, Internal Affairs of State, box 2819, RG 59, NACP; Fox, *America's Invisible Gulag*, 9, 315–16n36. German, Italian, and Japanese aliens became enemy aliens by definition when the United States entered the war.

48. Welles, Custody of Enemy Aliens in the U.S., October 31, 1941, box 98, SWPD, RG 59, NACP.

49. In July 1941, Canada placed all anti-Nazi refugees in refugee camps, "where there is more freedom." Davis to Smith, July 17, 1941, and Smith to Davis, July 21, 1941, "Interoffice #1," SWPU, box 9, RG 60, NACP.

50. Collins to Smith, Re: Proposed Plan of INS, June 26, 1941, Jackson to Patterson, May 29, 1941, and Patterson to Jackson, June 27, 1941, CLCF, folder "January–February 1942," box 5, RG 60, NACP.

51. Collins to Smith, SDU, Proposed Plan of INS re Alien Enemies, June 26, 1941, p. 1, CLCF, folder "January–February 1942," box 5, RG 60, NACP.

52. Dimock to the Attorney General, June 13, 1941, p. 1, CLCF, folder "January–February 1942," box 5, RG 60, NACP. Most recommendations came from those with "first-hand knowledge of the 1917 experience."

53. Collins to Smith, SDU, Re: Proposed Plan of INS re Alien Enemies, June 26, 1941, pp. 1–3, CLCF, folder "January–February 1942," box 5, RG 60, NACP.

54. Smith to Acting Attorney General, Re: Proposed Plan of INS for Alien Enemies, July 2, 1941, p. 2, CLCF, folder "January–February 1942," box 5, RG 60, NACP.

55. Schofield to Biddle, August 13, 1941, pp. 1–4, CLCF, folder "January–February 1942," box 5, RG 60, NACP.

56. Memo from Schofield to Biddle, August 13, 1941, pp. 3–12, Schofield to Biddle, Re: Male enemy aliens ordered interned for the duration, January 29, 1942, and memo from Schofield to Biddle, August 20, 1941, p. 1, CLCF, folder "January–February 1942," box 5, RG 60, NACP. The INS held internees longer than expected, as no more facilities would be ready until June.

57. Stimson to Biddle, February 1, 1942, CLCF, folder "February 1942," section 8, box 5, RG 60, NACP.

5. Pearl Harbor and the Home Front

1. Cantril, *Public Opinion*, 947; Dower, *War without Mercy*, 36.

2. DeWitt quoted in Okihiro, *Cane Fires*, 124.

3. *Honolulu Advertiser*, November 30, 1941; Marshall quoted in Patterson, *America in the Twentieth Century*, 268–69. Other papers had similar headline warnings; see the *Hilo Tribune Herald*, November 30, 1941. Occasional warnings spanned the entire year, from January 1941, when Ambassador Joseph Grew warned Washington of a Japanese surprise military attack on Pearl Harbor in the event "there was a break with the United States," to the many last-minute errors in judgment regarding radar blips of Japanese aircraft, Japanese midget submarines in the harbor itself, and partial intelligence decrypts along with the Western Union message conveyance.

4. Eleanor Roosevelt to Biddle, November 5, 1941, and Biddle to Eleanor Roosevelt, December 1, 1941, SWPU, "Interoffice #1," box 9, RG 60, NACP; poll numbers in Weber, "Japanese Camps in California," 45. Biddle also informed Mrs. Roosevelt that "to permit the naturalization of Japanese aliens would plainly require amendatory legislation."

5. LaGuardia quoted in *New York Times*, December 9, 1941; Allen, "Three Years of It."

6. LaGuardia to Conference of Mayors, December 20, 1941, folder "Civilian Enemy Aliens in U.S.," box 98, RG 59, NACP.

7. Lingeman, *Don't You Know*, 27; Stimson quoted in Andrew, *For the President's Eyes Only*, 119. The Allies' belief in Japanese inferiority lasted the entire war. Just after Pearl Harbor a poll showed that 48 percent believed Germany urged Japan to attack; two months later, 68.5 percent believed the attack was "part of German strategy." On Okinawa in April 1945 there were rumors that German experts had directed Japanese artillery fire—thought too accurate and beyond Japanese capabilities. Dower, *War without Mercy*, 37, 104–8, 324n10.

8. Rippley, *The German-Americans*, 217–31; O'Connor, *The German-Americans*, 437; Fulbrook, *German History since 1800*, 69–70; U.S. Department of Commerce, *Statistical History of the United States*, 56–57; U.S. Congress, House, *Report of the Select Committee*, 21–26; Fifteenth and Sixteenth Censuses of the United States: 1930 and 1940. There were 126,947 Japanese in the continental United States on April 1, 1940, of whom 47,305 were foreign born and therefore ineligible for citizenship.

9. Cantril, *Public Opinion*, 678, 947, 1067. Germany and Japan were primary enemies, Italy a reluctant belligerent. Continental defenses reached peak strength in late 1942, and only by June 1943 were ground defenses significantly reduced. In August

1945, both Defense Commands kept 17,000 on active duty. Most believed it "impossible to distinguish between loyal and disloyal Issei and Nisei," but one could among German and Italian aliens. McWilliams, "Japanese Out of California."

10. "Public Opinion Favors a Japan-First Strategy, 1942–1943," in Gallup, *The Gallup Poll*, 1:370; Perrett, *Days of Sadness*, 221–23; Grodzins, *Americans Betrayed*, chapter 7; Stoler and Gustafson, *Major Problems*, 171; Dower, *War without Mercy*, 114; U.S. Department of State, *Papers Relating to the Foreign Relations of the United States*, 793–94. Fears of invasion were pervasive as West Coast cities practiced blackouts well into 1942 and defenses ran the length of the entire continent's west coast. Between Pearl Harbor and FDR's issuance of Executive Order 9066, Biddle received 764 communications regarding evacuation, of which 671 (88 percent) called for control measures, including total evacuation, while only 93 (12 percent) advocated a liberal policy toward Japanese Americans.

11. Polenberg, *War and Society*, 40; Kennett, *For the Duration*, 20; "Public Opinion on Germany and Japan," *Fortune*, March 1942; Gallup, *The Gallup Poll*, 1:370; Cantril, "Opinion Trends in World War II"; Cantril, *Public Opinion*, 678, 947, 1067. On March 28, 1942, one poll showed that 62 percent felt the United States should fight Japan first, while 21 percent said Germany (17 percent were undecided). Another revealed that 67 percent favored all-out war against Japan, including its civilians. Only 23 percent thought the United States should attack Japanese military targets only. On June 17, 1942, two weeks after the Battle of Midway, 37 percent thought the United States should primarily fight Japan, while 46 percent now answered Germany. Despite the shift, in polls from February to October 1943, 53 percent felt Japan was the chief enemy, while 34 percent said Germany (13 percent had no opinion). "Racism there was," states Perrett, but the "racial element was only one factor among others." The West Coast Japanese became convenient scapegoats during a "run of Japanese victories" in early 1942. The evacuation was due most of all to that ancient phenomenon—the ritual sacrifice. Perrett, *Days of Sadness*, 221, 229–30.

12. "Nazis" and "Japs," Dower notes, "left space for the recognition of the 'good German,' but scant comparable place for 'good Japanese.'" *Time* magazine "frequently referred to 'the Jap' rather than 'Japs,' thereby denying the enemy even the merest semblance of pluralism." A popular saying noted, "The only good Jap is a dead Jap." Hatred of the Japanese was so commonplace that a March 1945 *Science Digest* short story titled "Why Americans Hate Japs More than Nazis" did not need to establish the veracity of the assertion, because "no one questioned such an observation." Dower, *War without Mercy*, 78–79. UVA Miller Center, Presidential Speeches, FDR Presidency, December 8, 1941: Address to Congress Requesting a Declaration of War.

13. *New York Times*, February 18, 1942; Kennett, *For the Duration*, 61; Perrett, *Days of Sadness*, 222.

14. "World War, THE PEOPLE: Smug, Slothful, Asleep?," *Time*, February 16, 1942; Buell, *Master of Seapower*, 531–33.

15. DeWitt to Gullion, December 26, 1941, quoted in Conn, Engleman, and Fairchild, *United States Army in World War II: Guarding*, 118n9.

16. "Pacific Coast Defense: How to Kill a Jap," *Life*, January 12, 1942, 70; Perrett, *Days of Sadness*, 205–6; Dower, *War without Mercy*, 114.

17. Biddle, *In Brief Authority*, 219.

18. Alien Information Bureau, "Enemy Aliens Apprehended in U.S. by FBI," PMG, box 1, RG 389, NACP; Hoover to Biddle, January 2, 1943, CLCF, folder "January 1943," box 6, RG 60, NACP; memos for General Gullion, December 9, 10, 12, 19, and 23, 1941, "Alien Enemies in Army Custody," Subject File 1942–'46, Entry 461, folder "Hawaii," box 2605, RG 389, NACP; Conn, Engleman, and Fairchild, *United States Army in World War II: Guarding*, 199. By December 9, 1941, the FBI had arrested 93 Germans out of 3,216, or 2.9 percent of the Hawaiian German population. A year later the FBI had arrested 5,467 Japanese (5,063 aliens and 404 citizens); 5,036 Germans (4,919 aliens and 117 citizens), and 2,295 Italians (2,270 aliens and 25 citizens). Hoover to Biddle, January 2, 1943.

19. The 1,875 relocated and interned Japanese were 1.2 percent of the Hawaiian Japanese; conversely, 98.8 percent of Hawaii's Japanese were neither relocated nor interned. Marshall and King argued that mass evacuation was "not feasible" in a July 3, 1942, memo to FDR. See Daniels, *Decision to Relocate*, 28, 70. Although FDR's Proclamation no. 2627 ended martial law on Hawaii on October 24, 1944, control of enemy aliens, including curfew, continued until the end of the war. Baker, *American and Japanese Relocation*, 199–200; Daniels, *Decision to Relocate*, 28, 70; Long to Strong, July 30, 1942, folder "Hawaii 1942," box 186, SWPD, RG 59, NACP. Hawaii's population was 423,330; the Japanese numbered 157,905 (37 percent), 37,353 aliens and 120,552 citizens.

20. DiStasi, *Una Storia Segreta*, 19. Perrett notes that roughly 7,000 Germans and Italians "living near sensitive facilities on the West Coast, were moved inland," while Fox states that 9,000–10,000 aliens expected to be relocated. Perrett, *Days of Sadness*, 218; Fox, *Unknown Internment*, 145.

21. U.S. Congress, House, *Report of the Select Committee*, 24–25. In 1934 the McCormack-Dickstein Committee recognized the need to retain the loyalty of the "twenty-odd-million Americans of German descent" and combat the Nazi's attempt to "enlist" them. See U.S. House, Special Committee on Un-American Activities, *Investigation of Nazi and Other Propaganda*.

22. U.S. Congress, House, *Report of the Select Committee*, 24–25. The committee was named after California Democratic congressman John H. Tolan and held hearings beginning on February 21, just two days after President Roosevelt signed Executive Order 9066; hearings lasted into March, 1942 for the purpose of determining the removal of enemy aliens and citizens, mainly Japanese Americans, from the West Coast. See the section "Tolan Committee" in chapter 6.

23. Corbett, *Quiet Passages*, 33.

24. Corbett, *Quiet Passages*, 33–34; *Final Act of the Third Meeting of Ministers of Foreign Affairs of the American Republics*, Rio de Janeiro, Brazil, January 15–28, 1942, State Department Bulletin, February 7, 1942, Publication 1696, pp. 19–20, box 124, RG 59, NACP.

25. G. S. Smith, "Japanese-Canadians and World War II," 102.

26. Barman, *The West beyond the West*, 265–69.

27. G. S. Smith, "Japanese-Canadians and World War II," 106–7. General DeWitt headed the WDC, while Major General Joyce was the commanding general of the Ninth Army Corps, Fort Lewis, Washington.

28. G. S. Smith, "Japanese-Canadians and World War II," 99, 105–7.

29. Weglyn, *Years of Infamy*, 57; Adolf Berle's influential February 1941 report, *The Pattern of Nazi Organizations and Their Activities in the Other American Republics*, led U.S. diplomats to believe that all Latin American Germans supported Nazi Germany. Adolf Berle, Memorandum to Chiefs of the Diplomatic Missions in the Other American Republics, *The Pattern of Nazi Organizations and Their Activities in the Other American Republics*, February 6, 1941, decimal file 862.20210/414A, 250/34/7/4, box 5505, RG 59, NACP. See also White to Lafoon, January 28, 1946, and White to Bingham, January 30, 1946, folder "Statistics," box 70, SWPD, RG 59, NACP; U.S. Department of State, *Report of the Delegation*, 13.

30. Alien Information Bureau, "Enemy Aliens Apprehended in U.S. by FBI," PMG, box 1, RG 389, NACP; Hoover to Biddle, November 3, 1943, CLCF, folder "August 1943," box 6, RG 60, NACP; "FBI Apprehensions" and "FBI Apprehensions of German Americans by State," December 7, 1941, to June 30, 1945, and Kelly to Vulliet, August 9, 1948, folder "Statistics," box 70, SWPD, RG 59, NACP; Alien Information Bureau, "Statistics," PMG, box 10, RG 389, NACP; "This Is War," *New York Times*, December 11, 1941; Corbett, *Quiet Passages*, 46; Fox, *Unknown Internment*, 156; Daniels, *Decision to Relocate*, chapter 2. The 16,062 arrests included 7,043 Germans, 5,428 Japanese, and 3,567 Italians. The 748 citizens arrested included 121 Germans, 598 Japanese, and 29 Italians. The FBI had taken into custody 1,301 German, 243 Italian, and 1,566 Japanese aliens by January 12, 1942.

6. Defeats, Rumors, and Reactions

1. Demands for the removal of enemy aliens, especially Japanese Americans, peaked from February 9 to February 15 and again from February 23 to March 1, 1942. See Grodzins, chapter 7, "Extent of the Regional Demand," and appendix 1, "The California Press"; Henry McLemore, "More about the Japs," *Los Angeles Times*, February 5, 1942, and "Why Treat the Japs Well Here?," *San Francisco Examiner*, January 19, 1942.

2. Lingeman, *Don't You Know*, 27–31; Kennett, *For the Duration*, 48–55.

3. Kennett, *For the Duration*, 51. General Stilwell, before heading off the China-Burma-India Theater in February 1942, had been in charge of forces at Fort Ord, California (just south of San Francisco), and like most military commanders stationed on the West Coast, he knew how woefully inadequate U.S. defenses were at the time.

4. Kennett, *For the Duration*, 52–68; Perrett, *Days of Sadness*, 205–6, 218–19; Pegler quoted in Daniels, *Concentration Camps USA*, 33; Henry McLemore, "More about the Japs," *Los Angeles Times*, February 5, 1942, and "The Japs Stay until Feb. 24!," *San Francisco Examiner*, February 5, 1942. See also the *Los Angeles Times*, the *San Luis Obispo Independent* (the first paper to ask for mass relocation), the *San Diego Union* (also vocal in demanding the evacuation of fifth columnists—any and all aliens and even citizens whose loyalty could not be "proven"), along with the *San Gabriel Sun*, *San Jose Mercury Herald*, and the *Los Angeles Examiner*, among many others. For West Coast newspaper headlines, stories, and analysis, see Grodzins, chapter 7, "Extent of the Regional Demand," and appendix 1, "The California

Press." Many dozens of headlines, including "Fifth Column Treachery Told," "Secretary of Navy Blames Fifth Column for the Raid," "The Home Front," and "Fifth Column Prepared Attack," were concerned with supposed fifth-column activities, while others warned of an imminent Japanese attack or invasion of the West Coast that would be abetted by fifth columnists. Many newspaper articles cited here and elsewhere were enclosed items sent by worried citizens to government officials and may be found (along with other articles) in folders "January 1942" and "January–February 1942," box 5, CLCF, RG 60, NACP.

5. Berge quoted in Grodzins, *Americans Betrayed*, 234.

6. "City Springs to Attention" and "Japanese Aliens' Roundup Starts," *Los Angeles Times*, December 8, 1941; "Hundreds of Japs Seized in L.A. Area," *Los Angeles Daily News*, December 8, 1941.

7. Special Agent Edward Poole to T. F. Fitch regarding obscene and insulting mail, February 4, 1942, "Objectionable mail," folder 3 of 3, box 109, RG 59, NACP.

8. "City Springs to Attention" and "Japanese Aliens' Roundup Starts," *Los Angeles Times*, December 8, 1941; "Hundreds of Japs Seized in L.A. Area," *Los Angeles Daily News*, December 8, 1941.

9. U.S. Department of State, *Report of the Delegation*, 7–10; Daniels, *Decision to Relocate*, 61–64; AP press release, July 28, 1942, CLCF, folder "August 1942," box 6, RG 60, NACP; Department of Justice, "Regulations Controlling Travel and Other Conduct of Aliens of Enemy Nationalitics" (Washington DC: GPO, 1942), folder "Enemy Aliens in U.S., General," box 129, SWPD, RG 59, NACP. Additional questions included whether the alien had "relatives living abroad or serving in the armed forces of a foreign country." U.S. Department of State, *Report of the Delegation*, 7. On Sunday, December 7, 1941, Roosevelt issued Presidential Proclamation 2525, followed the next day by proclamations 2526 and 2627. Together, they greatly empowered the federal government to take charge in handling the nation's Japanese, German, and Italian aliens.

10. U.S. Department of State, *Report of the Delegation*, 9; Department of Justice, "Regulations Controlling Travel and Other Conduct of Aliens." Biddle announced on Columbus Day that Italian aliens were no longer enemies and were exempt from regulations. FDR called the idea "a masterly stroke of international statesmanship and good politics." Fox, *Unknown Internment*, 136. Half of the 3,278 Italians interned remained in custody in 1944, and some until June 1945.

11. *San Francisco Chronicle*, December 16, December 23, 1941, and January 2, 1942, quoted in Fox, *Unknown Internment*, 42; Blum, *V Was for Victory*, 157; Perrett, *Days of Sadness*, 206; Dower, *War without Mercy*, 114; Conn, Engleman, and Fairchild, *United States Army in World War II: Guarding*, 87.

12. *Personal Justice Denied*, 55–56; Perrett, *Days of Sadness*, 217; "Fifth Column Treachery Told," *Los Angeles Examiner*, "Fifth Column Prepared Attack," *San Francisco Examiner*, and "Secretary of Navy Blames 5th Column for the Raid," *San Francisco Chronicle*, all from December 16, 1941. See also Grodzins, *Americans Betrayed*, appendix 1, "The California Press." The Knox report of the Pearl Harbor debacle was made public on December 16. Knox's request to remove Japanese from Oahu was impracticable, and FDR concluded that evacuating Hawaiian Japanese—whether

to Molokai or the States—was a bad idea for many reasons. News of the Japanese attack stunned Roosevelt and the nation. Unlike most Americans, the president knew where Pearl Harbor was, but like everybody else, he did not know the details of what had happened or how or why. To find out, Roosevelt dispatched Knox to Hawaii to ascertain what went wrong. Knox arrived on December 11 and just thirty-six hours later headed back to Washington.

13. Grodzins, *Americans Betrayed*, 399. The *Yellow Book* came from the muzzled *Yellow Paper*, Dies's unreleased August 1941 exposé of a massive (but nonexistent) Japanese spy ring comprising some 150,000 agents who had allegedly infiltrated West Coast power and water companies and were aiding a future invasion by sending valuable intelligence to the Japanese government. The much-publicized book was released to the press shortly after Executive Order 9066.

14. *Los Angeles Times*, December 10 and 13, 1941, and *Los Angeles Examiner*, December 13, 1941, cited in Grodzins, *Americans Betrayed*, 399. Reports told of "flashing lights" guiding Japanese planes to their targets.

15. Roberts Commission, January 23, 1942, quoted in Roberts Report, *Pearl Harbor Attack: Hearings before the Joint Committee on the Investigation of the Pearl Harbor Attack* (Washington DC, 1946), pt. 39, 1–21; *New York Times*, January 25, 1942, 1–5; U.S. Congress, House, *Report of the Select Committee*, 2; Grodzins, *Americans Betrayed*, 130. *Los Angeles Times* headlines "Suicide Reveals Spy Ring Here" and "What To Do in Case of Poison Gas Attacks" of December 19, 1941, along with "Japan Pictured as a Nation of Spies" of December 23, 1941, were typical.

16. Walter Lippmann, "Today and Tomorrow: The Fifth Column on the Coast," *Los Angeles Times*, February 13, 1942. See also Lippmann's articles in the *New York Herald Tribune* on February 5, 12, and 14, 1942. Lippmann, in his syndicated piece "The Fifth Column on the Coast," strongly supported the mass evacuation of all Japanese aliens and citizens from the West Coast (which he considered a "war zone"). Many reports reinforced fifth-column fears; see, for example, "Facing the Japanese Issue Here," *Los Angeles Times*, January 28, 1942; and "Mayor Tells Peril from Japs Here," *Los Angeles Examiner*, February 6, 1942. Walt Woodward, one of the few journalists who still cautioned against acting hysterically, nevertheless argued that all "Japanese people, whether citizens or aliens, must prepare themselves for what may seem to them unfair and unreasoning treatment" and prove their loyalty by removing themselves from the coast. Woodward, "More Plain Talk," *Bainbridge Island Review*, February 5, 1942.

17. Westbrook Pegler, "Fair Enough," *New York Times*, February 14, 1942, and "Fair Enough," *Washington Post*, February 15, 1942; Tom Treanor, "The Home Front," *Los Angeles Times*, January 29, 1942; Henry McLemore, "More about the Japs," *Los Angeles Times*, February 5, 1942. See also McLemore's "The Japs Stay until Feb. 24!," *San Francisco Examiner*, February 5, 1942. Pegler quoted Lippman's warnings in a February 16, 1942, "Fair Enough" story, adding even more ominous warnings of impending death and destruction from within and without.

18. Conference of sheriffs and district attorneys called by California Attorney General Warren, February 2, 1942, cited in Grodzins, *Americans Betrayed*, 95, 277; *San Francisco Chronicle*, February 9, 1942, quoted in Fox, *Unknown Internment*,

44; Western Defense Command and Fourth Army, *Final Report*. For a sampling of proposals of what to do with Japanese Americans (from the benign to the extreme) see "Solutions" in Grodzins, *Americans Betrayed*, 416–18. Policymakers knew there were over 1,000,000 German and Italian aliens compared to 47,000 Japanese aliens nationally (there were 85,000 German and Italian aliens along the West Coast), and in terms of American citizens of "enemy" heritage, the numbers looked, and were in fact, far worse. There were too many Germans and Italians to handle effectively (whether along the West Coast or nationally), as Roosevelt and others knew.

19. Kelly to Ennis, concerning the Theberath case, July 22, 1942, SWPD, RG 59, NACP.

20. Bruppacher to Kelly, April 20, 1944, Legation of Switzerland (Department of German Interests), SWPD, RG 59, NACP.

21. Hoover to Watson, December 10, 1941, folder "Stats," box 70, SWPD, RG 59, NACP; Alien Information Bureau, "Enemy Aliens Apprehended in U.S. by FBI," PMG, box 1, RG 389, NACP.

22. Testimonies of Eberhart Fuhr and Joseph Feilmeier, "World War II: The Internment of German American Civilians, Personal Stories," *The Freedom of Information Times*, https://www.foitimes.com/; Fiset, *Imprisoned Apart*, 3–25, 30–31. The FBI likely arrested Iwao because of his membership in Japanese organizations. As with German and Italian Americans, association with or membership in a suspect organization was all that was necessary for one's name to be placed on Hoover's ABC list. The FBI and ONI implicated more than 300 Japanese clubs and organizations in suspicious or subversive activities.

23. Hoover to SACs, September 5, 1936, cited in Theoharis, *Spying on Americans*, 70, and Theoharis, *The Boss*, 175; Hoover to Schofield, December 8, 1941, folder "INS, Individuals Considered for Custodial Detention," box 129, RG 59, NACP.

24. Conn, Engleman, and Fairchild, *United States Army in World War II: Guarding*, 117; "This Was the Worst Week," *Time*, February 23, 1942; Daniels, *Concentration Camps USA*, 34. *Time*'s cover had a drawing of hangman's nooses and Holocaust architect Reinhard Heydrich's profile with the caption "Heydrich: Gestapo Executioner, Can terror, hunger, propaganda rule 150,000,000 captives?" West Coast papers contained many predictions of Japanese attacks as disasters mounted in the Pacific. See, for example, "The Worst News," *Newsweek*, January 12, 1942. In the days following Pearl Harbor, Japan attacked U.S. bases in the Philippines, Guam, and Wake Island as well as British possessions in Malaya and Hong Kong. Over the next two months the Japanese military won a string of unprecedented victories, taking Manila on January 2 and Singapore (the "Gibraltar of the East" and the key to Southeast Asia) on February 15, and were poised to take the Philippines. By mid-March Japan's army had taken the Dutch East Indies while its navy destroyed a combined allied fleet at the Battle of the Java Sea.

25. Proclamation, "Executive Order 9066," *Federal Register* (February 25, 1942), vol. 7, no. 38, p. 1407; U.S. Congress, House, *Report of the Select Committee*; Daniels, *Prisoners without Trial*, 46; Robinson, *By Order of the President*, 122–24.

26. Stimson diary, February 10, 1942, cited in Dower, *War without Mercy*, 80; Stimson diary, February 11, 1942, cited in Conn, *Guarding the United States*, 132. Witnesses testifying before the Tolan Committee in late February and early March

reinforced the idea of the dangerous Nisei. The rationale was that "the aliens (Issei), being elderly and adjusted to their status as perpetual noncitizens in our land, constituted less a menace than the American-born (Nisei) who resented discriminatory treatment at the hands of fellow Americans." As to differentiating the "good" from the "bad" Japanese, the report added: "Most commonly it was said that homogeneity of racial and cultural traits made it impossible to distinguish between the loyal and disloyal." U.S. Congress, House, *Report of the Select Committee*, 14. The 1870 Naturalization Act barred Asian immigrants from citizenship.

27. Telephone conversation McCloy with Bendetsen, February 11, 1942, cited in Conn, Engleman, and Fairchild, *United States Army in World War II: Guarding*, 132. See also Daniels, *Prisoners without Trial*, 42–44; and Robinson, *By Order of the President*, 105–6. McCloy misrepresented the call to Bendetsen, for only Stimson talked to FDR.

28. *Congressional Record*, February 18, 1942, p. 1412; Grodzins, *Americans Betrayed*, 82.

29. *San Francisco Chronicle*, February 20, 1942; *Congressional Record*, February 18, 19, and 25, 1942, pp. 659–60, 1412, 1419–20; Grodzins, *Americans Betrayed*, 82–86, 326–30. There was a "complete absence of congressional criticism directed against the radical extension of executive (military) authority" (Grodzins, *Americans Betrayed*, 330).

30. *Congressional Record*, December 15, 1941, p. 9808, and February 19, 1942, pp. 1419–20. See also Grodzins, *Americans Betrayed*, 85–87; Daniels, *Concentration Camps USA*, 42–45; Weglyn, *Years of Infamy*, 54.

31. *Congressional Record*, February 19, 1942, pp. 1419–20; Grodzins, *Americans Betrayed*, 86. As Grodzins notes, numerous congressmen, including Bland of Virginia, Norrell of Arkansas, Randolph of West Virginia, and Coffee of Washington, "praised or corroborated" sections of Rankin's address.

32. *Congressional Record*, March 10, 1942, p. 931; Grodzins, *Americans Betrayed*, 328–29.

33. *Congressional Record*, February 26, 1942, pp. 1682–83; Grodzins, *Americans Betrayed*, 87.

34. "Seizure of All Japs in U.S. Demanded," *Washington Post*, April 23, 1943. Public Law 503 made it a federal crime for anyone to refuse to leave a designated military area, yet "no necessity existed for Public Law 503. Indeed, the law was not essential to the evacuation program at all." Grodzins, *Americans Betrayed*, 331–48.

35. U.S. Congress, House, *Report of the Select Committee*, 4; Grodzins, *Americans Betrayed*, 412–13; U.S. Office of War Information, *Pacific Coast Attitudes towards the Japanese Problem*, February 28, 1942, Report no. 7; U.S. Office of War Information, *West Coast Reactions to the Japanese Situation*, March 6, 1942, Report no. 6; U.S. Office of War Information, *The Japanese Problem*, April 21, 1942, Report no. 19. See also Perrett, *Days of Sadness*, 219; Daniels, *Prisoners without Trial*, 50. Opposing the evacuation would add to the disloyal stereotype. The crux of the Japanese American dilemma was proving their loyalty. For nearly all Nisei, this was demonstrated by submissiveness to authority. Daniels, *Concentration Camps USA*, 79–80.

36. U.S. Congress, House, *Report of the Select Committee*, 24–25; Blum, *V Was for Victory*, 150–51; Fox, *Unknown Internment*, 100; Leuchtenburg, *Roosevelt and the*

New Deal, 321; Lichtman and DeCell, *Thirteen Keys*, 269. There were 314,715 German and 695,363 Italian aliens out of 1,237,772 German and 1,623,579 Italian foreign-born. West Coast Japanese went to assembly centers, April to August 1942, and then to relocation centers, May to November 1942.

37. The INS did not give relocatees hearings; it did so only for Germans, Italians, and Japanese facing internment. Edward Ennis testified to this adding that his office decided whether an alien enemy should be "interned, paroled, or released." Testimony of Edward Ennis before the CWRIC, November 2, 1981, pp. 181–83, Records of the CWRIC, RG 220, NACP.

38. U.S. Congress, House, *Report of the Select Committee*, 23–25. For a brief overview of key developments along with differences in Japanese American evacuations from the West Coast versus Hawaii, the relationship between the War Department and the WRA, loyalty issues, and evacuee statistics, see *Report on Senate Resolution No. 166 Relating to Segregation of Loyal and Disloyal Japanese in Relocation Centers and Plans for Future Operations of Such Centers*, U.S. Senate, 78th Cong., 1st sess., Senate Document no. 96, September 14, 1943, p. 9, section 12, box 83, FBI HQ Files, RG 65, NACP.

39. FDR created the War Relocation Authority (WRA) by Executive Order 9102 on March 18, 1942. The Work Corps offered employment under federal sponsorship. The WRA and the Work Corps showed how thousands of German and Italian aliens and Japanese would support themselves outside restricted areas. U.S. Congress, House, *Report of the Select Committee*, 26.

40. U.S. Congress, House, *Report of the Select Committee*, 21. The Tolan Committee report provides a great deal of statistical information in three particular sections: "Statistics on Japanese," "Number and Distribution of German and Italian Aliens," and "Evacuation of Italian and German Aliens." It compares the three groups in the sections "Evacuation Policy," "Resettlement: Americanization or Deportation," and "Summary." See also "The Nature of the Evacuated Population," in *Report on Senate Resolution No. 166*, pp. 8–9.

41. Hearing boards never dealt with relocatees, but they heard all cases involving aliens arrested by the FBI or other agencies. U.S. Congress, House, *Report of the Select Committee*, 21–23. See also *Report on Senate Resolution No. 166*.

42. U.S. Congress, House, *Fourth Interim Report of the Select Committee*, 230–48. See also National Refugee Service, *Special Information Bulletin*, no. 18, May 29, 1942, CLCF, folder "May–June 1942," section 16, box 6, RG 60, NACP.

43. U.S. Congress, House, *Report of the Select Committee*, 24, and *Fourth Interim Report of the Select Committee*, 31. Biddle's press conference remarks of May 20 and Bendetsen's radio statement of May 26 are quoted in National Refugee Service, *Special Information Bulletin*. See also "Statement by the Attorney General on Evacuation of Alien Enemies from the East Coast," May 14, 1942, CLCF, folder "May 1942," section 14, box 5, RG 60, NACP. For more on Biddle's opposition to the evacuation of Japanese en masse and Germans and Italians more generally, see Grodzins, *Americans Betrayed*, 254–62, 271, 281. There were at the time fears of fifth-column activities by enemy aliens, especially German Americans, along the East Coast generally and cities like New York particularly. See, for example, "FBI Tightens Curb on 256,000

Aliens: Police Engaged in Check-up of Nationals of Enemy Countries Living in the City," *New York Times*, April 1, 1942. The article noted that New Yorkers were engaged in an "intensive watch" of their neighbors and that all families would be "visited" and "all activities noted" by police and FBI in the anti-fifth-column effort.

44. Steinbeck's close-knit Norwegian town was under Nazi occupation due to a local quisling (fifth columnist); "Six Ways to Invade the U.S.," *Life*, March 2, 1942; Pringle, "Don't Believe a Word of It!" *Collier's*, January 17, 1942.

45. "Sow mines" and "armed Japanese ready for Invasion" quoted in Blum, *V Was for Victory*, 158; "Olson Says War May Hit State," *Los Angeles Times*, January 26, 1942; Henry McLemore, "This Is War! Stop Worrying about Hurting Jap Feelings," *Los Angeles Times*, January 29, 1942. McLemore repeated these general sentiments in numerous subsequent articles, including "More about the Japs," *Los Angeles Times*, February 5, 1942, and "The Japs Stay until Feb. 24!," *San Francisco Examiner*, February 5, 1942. Similar headlines, themes, and quotations can be found in California's five major papers (the *Times* and *Examiner* of Los Angeles, the *Chronicle* and *Examiner* of San Francisco, and the *Bee* of Sacramento) and almost all West Coast papers in addition to many throughout the nation. See "Intern All Japs," *Wilmington Star*, February 19, 1942. The paper noted that "a Jap is a Jap" and hence citizens and non-citizens alike should be interned.

46. *San Francisco Chronicle*, January 31, 1942, quoted in Fox, *Unknown Internment*, 43–44.

47. "How to Tell Your Friends from the Japs," *Time*, December 22, 1941; High, "Japanese Saboteurs in Our Midst," 11–15. High wrote: "Japan is ready to hit us hard—from the inside. Japanese on the West Coast possess bases, equipment and disciplined personnel. The Japanese fishing fleet has 250 vessels. Perhaps 90 percent are Japanese Navy reservists. Not a single flying field on the entire West Coast does not have Japanese farmers nearby." Ehrenberg to Rowe, January 20, 1942, CLCF, folder "January 1942," box 5, RG 60, NACP; "California Is Japan's Sudetenland," *Time*, February 23, 1942.

48. Dower, *War without Mercy*, 124; "Why Are Japs Japs?," *Time*, August 7, 1944.

49. Lingeman, *Don't You Know*, 169, 335–36; Kennett, *For the Duration*, 74.

50. "Propaganda" and following quoted terms in A. H. Feller, "OWI on the Home Front," *Public Opinion Quarterly* 7 (Spring 1943): 57, cited in Polenberg, *War and Society*, 52; Blum, *V Was for Victory*, 31; Jeffries, *Wartime America*, 176–86; MacDonnell, *Insidious Foes*, 133–36; "I am perfectly willing" quoted in Kimball, *The Juggler*, 7. Americans went to theaters in unprecedented numbers and saw *Prelude to War*. Beginning in 1939, movie characters from Charlie Chan, Sherlock Homes, and Roy Rogers to the Invisible Man, Tarzan, and Superman fought Axis agents. In 1942 alone more than seventy films dealt with the fifth column. FDR often insisted that enemy agents were ready to wreak havoc. Roosevelt is quoting himself speaking to a special study group on Latin America, May 15, 1942 with Treasury Secretary and trusted adviser Henry Morgenthau. The president said: "You know I am a juggler, and I never let my right hand know what my left hand does. . . . I may have one policy for Europe and one diametrically opposite for North and South America. I may be entirely inconsistent, and furthermore, I am perfectly willing to mis-

lead and tell untruths if it will help win the war." Memo of conversation between Roosevelt and Morgenthau, May 15, 1942, Presidential Diary, p. 1092, Henry Morgenthau Papers, FDRL, and cited in Kimball, *The Juggler*, 7 and 203n1. *Prelude to War* won an Academy Award in 1942 for best documentary. The OWI also distributed short "Victory Films" shown in commercial theaters around the nation. See Lingeman, *Don't You Know*, 187–91.

51. "A tragedy" in *New York Times*, February 5, 1942, quoted in Girdner and Loftis, *Great Betrayal*, 21; Lingeman, *Don't You Know*, 223–33. Numerous radio reporters, especially Hughes, a Los Angeles news commentator for the Mutual Broadcasting Company, influenced public opinion through a barrage of statements accusing Japanese Americans of espionage and fifth-column activities and demanding their wholesale evacuation from the coast lest they help Japan achieve its master war plan. The Department of Justice itself acknowledged Hughes's many broadcasts as greatly "responsible for arousing public opinion and flooding the California Congressional Delegation with protests which had the tendency to push the government into hasty and ill-considered action." Ennis to Milton Eisenhower, WRA, March 29, 1942, quoted in Grodzins, *Americans Betrayed*, 386. See also *Personal Justice Denied*, 71, 377n124: "News and Views by John B. Hughes," radio transcripts, January 5–9, 15, 19–20, 1942, CWRIC, 8707-18.

52. Kennett, *For the Duration*, 6; Robert Leffingwell, "Little Joe: Give Till It Hurts?," cartoon, *Denver Post* and *Washington Post*, December 26, 1943. Batman, Spy Smasher, Wonder Woman, and the Green Hornet battled fifth columnists whose activities ranged from trying to blow up Congress to kidnapping Little Orphan Annie. Superman, addressing Congress, said, "I believe I can best serve the nation on the home front, battling our most insidious foes . . . the hidden maggots—the traitors, the Fifth Columnists." MacDonnell, *Insidious Foes*, 134. War posters assisted the military and persuaded Americans to help the war effort. Stark imagery (a merchant ship being torpedoed in "Loose Talk Can Cost Lives!") elicited powerful emotions and appealed to one's conscience, fears, and values. The posters called upon everyone—men, women, and children—to make personal sacrifices for the greater good and linked the home and military fronts. See American Merchant Marine website, http://www.usmm.net/postertalk2b.html.

53. "Great Improbabilities," *Time*, December 1, 1941; Aswell, "The Case of the Ten Spies"; Hoover, "War Begins at Home"; Farago, *German Psychological Warfare*; Shirer, "The Poison Pen."

54. Sayers and Kahn, *Sabotage!*, front cover. Kahn won national recognition for reporting German and Japanese conspiratorial activities in the Americas. The authors revealed Nazi sabotage techniques. In 1939, Albert E. Kahn became executive secretary of the American Council against Nazi Propaganda. As editor of *The Hour*, Kahn won nationwide recognition for his sensational reporting on German and Japanese conspiratorial activities in the Americas. In collaboration with Michael Sayers, Kahn wrote three books: *Sabotage! The Secret War against America*, one of the leading best-sellers of the war period; *The Plot against the Peace*, which achieved top sales in the immediate postwar period; and *The Great Conspiracy*.

55. Sayers and Kahn, *Sabotage!*, foreword, 21, 41–45, 53, 64–65, 254–55.

56. Lingeman, *Don't You Know*, 182–83; Carlson, *Under Cover*, 9, 412. The *New York Times* said of *Under Cover*: "This book is of sensational importance to everyone. Of the hundreds of persons he exposes, most are still free and carrying on their dirty work. Those who neglected to take them seriously enough in Europe are dead, in concentration camps, in hiding or in exile" (*Under Cover*, jacket).

57. "San Francisco Releases 6 Chinese Mistaken for Japanese," *New York Times*, January 9, 1942; Costigan, "The Plight of the Nisei"; Kennett, *For the Duration*, 82.

58. Conn, Engleman, and Fairchild, *United States Army in World War II: Guarding*, 118–19; Perrett, *Days of Sadness*, 221–22; Fox, *Unknown Internment*, 44.

59. "Japanese Spies and What They Did," *Liberty*, February 7, 1942; Chief of Naval Operations to Distribution List: Tripartite Alliance and the Japanese-American War, February 28, 1942, folder "E-70-73," SWPU, box 4, RG 60, NACP. The cover's bucktoothed Japanese octopus has tentacles grasping spy gadgets, radios, binoculars, a bag of cash, an eavesdropping Japanese waiter, and a scantily clad Japanese woman.

60. "Japanese Here Sent Vital Data to Tokyo," *Los Angeles Times*, February 6, 1942; "FBI Seizes Jap Uniforms in Raids on Coast," *Chicago Daily Times*, February 17, 1942; "Lincoln Would Intern Japs," *Los Angeles Times*, February 13, 1942. Bowron also stated: "Here is the hotbed, the nerve center. If an attack should start, plenty among our little brown brothers here would know the part to play for Japan. Measures taken so far are so ineffectual as to be ridiculous." "Mayor Tells Peril from Japs Here," *Los Angeles Examiner*, February 6, 1942.

61. W. H. Smith, "The Question of Japanese Americans," *Los Angeles Times*, February 2, 1942.

62. Borchert to Roosevelt, February 13, 1942, CLCF, folder "February 1942," box 5, RG 60, NACP. The overwhelming majority of letters written by citizens to Roosevelt (many of which included newspaper clippings of local, state, or regional fifth-column concerns) were sent to and answered by Edward Ennis's Alien Enemy Control Unit. The responding letter was slightly tailored to address particular concerns and letters were also modified over time in accordance to evolving United States policies, practices, orders, and actions regarding enemy aliens generally and Japanese Americans especially.

63. Wolff to Roosevelt, February 12, 1942, CLCF, folder "February 1942," box 5, RG 60, NACP.

64. Schilling to Roosevelt, February 16, 1942, CLCF, folder "February 1942," box 5, RG 60, NACP.

65. Miller to Roosevelt, February 16, 1942, CLCF, folder "February 1942," section 4, and Weddell to Roosevelt, February 19, 1942, CLCF, folder "February 1942," section 5, box 5, RG 60, NACP.

66. Lee to Roosevelt, February 11, 1942, CLCF, folder "February 1942," section 8, box 5, RG 60, NACP.

67. Margaret Utz to Roosevelt, February 12, 1942, CLCF, folder "February 1942," box 5, RG 60, NACP. George M. Heckel, a seventy-three-year-old "enemy alien," was "despondent over having to leave his home because of the prohibited alien area ruling." "Body of Alien Drifts Ashore in Santa Cruz," *Santa Cruz Sentinel*, February 12, 1942, CLCF, folder "February 1942," box 5, RG 60, NACP.

68. Putlitz, "Your German-American Neighbor," 322, 325, 328.

69. Offenheimer to Frankfurter, February 12, 1942, Frankfurter to Biddle, February 19, 1942, Biddle to Frankfurter, February 23, 1942, and Frankfurter to Biddle, February 24, 1942, CLCF, folder "February 1942," section 8, box 5, RG 60, NACP.

70. The Mayers' story is found in Chaim Shapiro to Biddle, February 9, 1942, and James Rowe to Chaim Shapiro, February 14, 1942, CLCF, folder "February 1942," box 5, RG 60, NACP. Some Jews, unfortunate victims of Hitler's persecution, also became unfortunate victims of the restricted and prohibited areas established by Stimson's recommendation. Biddle blamed Stimson for the evacuation, stating that "if Stimson had stood firm, had insisted that this wholesale evacuation was needless, the President would have followed." Quoted in Robinson, *By Order of the President*, 116. The Nuremberg Laws of 1935 established the legal framework for Jewish persecution and began the "Aryanization" process, including the confiscation of property and loss of Reich citizenship.

71. Liotta to Roosevelt, February 14, 1942, and Ennis to Liotta, March 24, 1942, CLCF, folder "February 1942," section 6, box 5, RG 60, NACP.

72. Mangione, *An Ethnic at Large*, 320n. Britain interned 27,200, mainly German and Austrian aliens; most were refugees. Tribunals examined 73,353 and interned 569, subjected 6,782 to special restrictions, and certified 64,254 as unquestionably loyal and freed them from all restrictions. U.S. Congress, House, *Report of the Select Committee*, 281; Charles Gordon, "Status of Enemy Nationals in the United States.," to Edward Ennis and the *National Lawyers Guild Review*, December 5, 1942, CLCF, box 6, RG 60, NACP; Gillman and Gillman, *"Collar the Lot!,"* 45, 222–25.

73. Biddle, *In Brief Authority*, 118; Albert Einstein et al., "Open Letter to President Roosevelt," quoted in M. M. Anderson, *Hitler's Exiles*, 251–52.

74. Hiller to Biddle, February 2, 1942, CLCF, folder "February 1942," box 5, RG 60, NACP. A July 1933 law deprived many of their German citizenship individually. Most, however, lost their citizenship with the Reich Citizenship Law of November 25, 1941. Friedlander, *Origins of Nazi Genocide*, 288.

75. Kimball to Biddle, September 24, 1942, CLCF, folder "September 1942," box 6, RG 60, NACP.

76. Ennis to Cooley, October 20, 1942, and Perry to Ennis, October 31, 1942, CLCF, folder "October 1942," box 6, RG 60, NACP.

7. Dual-Coast Relocation

1. Ford to Biddle, January 23, 1942, CLCF, folder "February 1942," box 5, RG 60, NACP; Rankin and Ford, December 15, 1941, *Congressional Record*, 77th Cong., 1st sess., pp. 9808–9; identical letters from Ford to Hoover, Knox, and Stimson, January 16, 1942, CLCF, folder "February 1942," box 5, RG 60, NACP. See also Dower, *War without Mercy*, 80; Conn, Engleman, and Fairchild, *United States Army in World War II: Guarding*, 122–23; Grodzins, *Americans Betrayed*, 64–67; Daniels, *Prisoners without Trial*, 35; Daniels, *Concentration Camps USA*, 42–46; Daniels, *Decision to Relocate*, 20–23. On January 20, Ford became the first person to speak for the necessity of mass evacuation on the House floor. Minus a February 5 speech by Bowron put into the *Congressional Record* on February 9, no further statement in Congress (House

or Senate) in favor of evacuation would be made until the February 18 debates. *Congressional Record*, p. 502 and appendix, pp. A457–59, cited in Grodzins, *Americans Betrayed*, 66 and 83. PDF files for the *Congressional Record* are available at https://www.govinfo.gov/app/collection/crecb/_crecb/Volume%20087%20(1941).

2. Ford to Hull, January 6, 1942, quoted in Grodzins, *Americans Betrayed*, 64; Daniels, *Concentration Camps USA*, 46-48; Ford, January 20, 1942, *Congressional Record*, 77th Cong., 2nd sess., 502; Ford speech on Blue Network (later Mutual Broadcasting System), February 9, 1942, *Congressional Record*, 77th Cong., 2nd sess., A661–62. Ford's call to place Japanese Americans in "concentration camps" appeared in the *Los Angeles Examiner* on January 20 and the *Los Angeles Times* and *San Francisco Examiner* on January 22, 1942. By the end of December 1941 the media gave voice to public and military pressures to search Japanese homes for contraband, which in turn fueled suspicion and fear. Ford and the California and Pacific Coast congressional delegations felt the hysteria and heat of public pressures to solve the "Japanese problem" immediately. Many stories "uncovered" intended fifth-column sabotage along the West Coast and throughout the nation. Grodzins notes that California's five major daily papers—the *Los Angeles Times* and *Examiner*, the *San Francisco Chronicle* and *Examiner*, and the *Sacramento Bee*—used the term "fifth column" so often that "the total effect was an assumption of sabotage guilt in every paper and almost every edition." Grodzins adds that even Walter Lippmann argued that the absence of sabotage was "a sign that the blow is well organized" and was being "held back until it can be struck with maximum effect." Grodzins, *Americans Betrayed*, 387, 399.

3. Ford to Biddle, January 23, 1942, Le Roy to Ford, January 20, 1942, and Ford to Biddle, January 23, 1942, CLCF, folder "February 1942," box 5, RG 60, NACP.

4. Biddle to Ford, January 24, 1942, CLCF, folder "February 1942," box 5, RG 60, NACP; Grodzins, *Americans Betrayed*, 64–67; Daniels, *Prisoners without Trial*, 35. Demands for evacuating the Japanese greatly intensified and within a few weeks peaked. Grodzins, *Americans Betrayed*, appendix 1, "The California Press." Calls for removing Germans and Italians were rare.

5. Palmer to Rowe, January 7, 1942, CLCF, folder "January 1942," box 5, RG 60, NACP; Warren quoted in Daniels, Taylor, and Kitano, *Japanese Americans*, xvi.

6. Stimson to Biddle, January 25, 1942, quoted in Conn, Engleman, and Fairchild, *United States Army in World War II: Guarding*, 120; Stimson to Ford, January 26, 1942, quoted in Daniels, *Decision to Relocate*, 22–23. See also Grodzins, *Americans Betrayed*, 64–65.

7. For context, see Grodzins, *Americans Betrayed*, 67–69, and Daniels, *Concentration Camps USA*, 52–55. That same day, top officials, including Stimson, Knox, Marshall, and Roberts, met at the White House to discuss what to do with Hawaii's substantial Japanese population. It is significant that at both meetings decision makers were beginning to realize the scope of numbers and the impact that any large movement of any group, however defined, might have on the nation's economy and its ability to wage and to win the war. California had 93,717 Japanese (33,569 aliens and 60,148 citizens) out of 112,353 Pacific Coast Japanese. California also had 100,910 Italian aliens out of 113,846 and 71,727 German aliens out of 97,080 on the Pacific Coast. Sixteenth Census, 1940: *Japanese Population of the United States* and *Foreign-*

Born Germans and Italians. For comparative purposes, see Sixteenth Census, 3-30233 and Fifteenth Census, 4:264–86.

8. Telephone conversation, DeWitt and Bendetsen, January 29, 1942, quoted in Daniels, *Concentration Camps USA*, 51. See also Conn, Engleman, and Fairchild, *United States Army in World War II: Guarding*, 122–23, and Grodzins, *Americans Betrayed*, 106–8, 274–77. DeWitt and Bendetsen also agreed that Japanese citizens should be evacuated along with all enemy aliens.

9. Telephone conversation, Bendetsen and DeWitt, January 30, 1942, quoted in Daniels, *Decision to Relocate*, 79–80; memo, Bendetsen to PMG Gullion, January 31, 1942, quoted in Conn, Engleman, and Fairchild, *United States Army in World War II: Guarding*, 122–23; California representative Clarence Lea to Stimson, January 30, 1942, Pacific Coast delegation summary recommendation quoted in Daniels, *Decision to Relocate*, 77–78; DeWitt's private thoughts of January 31, 1942, quoted in Conn, Engleman, and Fairchild, *United States Army in World War II: Guarding*, 123; DeWitt's multiple telephone conversations with Bendetsen and Gullion of January 31 and February 1, 1942, are quoted in Daniels, *Concentration Camps USA*, 54–55. See also the online resource Digital History, *Explorations: Japanese-American Internment*. For telephone conversation transcripts between DeWitt, Bendetsen, and Gullion as well as Lea's letter to Stimson, see Daniels, *Decision to Relocate*, documents 6–8, pp. 71–102, and for more context see Daniels, *Concentration Camps USA*, 44–55. Gullion was a central figure in the decision to relocate Japanese Americans. He believed, as did Army Intelligence and most Americans, that fifth columnists had enabled Hitler's European victories. Army G-2 and other intelligence sources reported that the United States was equally susceptible to fifth-column subterfuge.

10. Biddle, *In Brief Authority*, 216–17; the Gullion and McCloy statements from the February 1 meeting in Biddle's office are quoted in Daniels, *Concentration Camps USA*, 55–56. See also Daniels, *Prisoners without Trial*, 40–41.

11. Ford's February 18 telephone call to Biddle is quoted (minus the expletives) in Grodzins, *Americans Betrayed*, 81, and with expletives included in *Personal Justice Denied*, 84.

12. San Buenaventura City Council Resolution no. 1880, CLCF, folder "February 1942," box 5, RG 60, NACP.

13. "Public Opinion Favors Japan-First Strategy, 1942–43," quoted in Stoler and Gustafson, *Major Problems*, 174; Cantril's "Opinion Trends," *Public Opinion Quarterly*, cited in Perrett, *Days of Sadness*, 221–23. For an analysis of quantitative data regarding the extent and characteristics of the demand for mass evacuation, see Grodzins, *Americans Betrayed*, chapter 7, "Extent of the Regional Demand." Such trends continued, as Gallup polls conducted from February through October 1943 indicated that 53 percent felt Japan was the nation's chief enemy and 34 percent said Germany. As Americans fought and died in the Pacific and were doing neither in Europe, public pressures for revenge mounted. Fear and anger, not racism per se, influenced policymaking, and pragmatic economic, political, and military concerns directly affected waging the war and limiting actions taken against any one alien enemy group—whether the U.S. mainland, Hawaiian Islands, or Latin America.

14. "History of Japanese Program," Office of PMG, Washington DC, Prepared by Japanese-American Branch, Presidio of San Francisco, Major Clarence R. Harbert, CO, Edited by Capt. Stanley D. Arnold, EO, January 20, 1943–September 1, 1945; Historical Monograph of the Alien Employment Program, September 30, 1945, folder "Alien Employment Program," HF, War Dept. #439A, PMG, box 20, RG 389, NACP.

15. "Evacuation of Civilian Population, 1941," War Department under the Chief of Staff, U.S. Army, HF, War Dept. #439A, PMG, box 18, Vol. 3, Sect. 14, RG 389, NACP.

16. Daniels, *Decision to Relocate*, 36; Daniels, *Prisoners without Trial*, 41–42; Daniels, *Concentration Camps USA*, 70; Office of the Director, WRA, Strictly Confidential Memo for the Heads of Offices and Divisions, "Seven Confidential Memoranda on the Constitutional Power of the WRA to Detain Evacuees," June 15, 1942, box 81, FBI HQ Files, RG 65, NACP. The memorandum noted "considerable evidence of disloyal conduct of Japanese residents in East Asia and Central and South America, and evidence of active assistance by Japanese residents in the invasion and conquest of territory now overrun by the Japanese, through sabotage, aid to parachute troops, and active collaboration in military operations."

17. Blum to Roosevelt, January 28, 1942, and Lilah White to Biddle, February 9, 1942, CLCF, folder "February 1942," box 5, RG 60, NACP.

18. Arthur Caylor, "Behind the News," *San Francisco News*, March 2, 1942. See also "Internment of San Francisco Japanese," http://www.sfmuseum.org/war/evactxt.html.

19. Parts of Olson's and Bowron's speech are quoted in Grodzins, *Americans Betrayed*, 102–8, and Daniels, *Concentration Camps USA*, 60–62; Bowron, radio speech, February 5, 1942, *Congressional Record*, 77th Cong., 2nd sess., February 9, 1942, A457–59; Mrs. Ford to Biddle, (referred to and answered by Edward J. Ennis), February 10, 1942, CLCF, folder "February 1942," box 5, RG 60, NACP. Thousands copied, circulated, and sent this particular letter to Biddle in February 1942. Olson stated that while it would be possible, due in part to the Department of Justice's registration program, to separate loyal from disloyal German and Italian aliens, the same was not true for Japanese aliens and their citizen family members. Bowron also argued that one could not discern loyal from disloyal Japanese and said that it was "reasonably certain" that the "hotbed, the nerve center of the spy system" existed "right here in our own city." See also Bowron's statements in the *Los Angeles Examiner*, February 6, 1942.

20. Dr. Walters to Roosevelt, February 6, 1942, Albert Elliston to Roosevelt, February 5, 1942, "John Democrat" to Biddle, February 5, 1942, and Robert Duncan, Post Adjutant, Leland Bergesen Post No. 2658, to Roosevelt, February 3, 1942, CLCF, folder "February 1942," box 5, RG 60, NACP. An analysis of 267 letters to the Justice Department (three-fourths from California from January 26 to February 22, the peak of evacuation demands) reveals that 85 percent cited fear of sabotage, espionage, and fifth-column dangers posed by aliens, especially the Japanese. Grodzins, *Americans Betrayed*, chapter 7 and tables 11–13. Many letters to Biddle specifically or the Justice Department generally were referred to and answered by Edward J. Ennis.

21. State Department Memo: "Various American Agencies Holding Civilian Enemy Aliens and Participating in Their Control," June 19, 1942, folder "Enemy

Aliens in U.S.—General," box 129, SWPD, RG 59, NACP. Under the Justice, War, and State Departments, the INS, Border Patrol, WRA, and Wartime Civilian Control Administration (WCCA) handled enemy aliens and citizens.

22. Ennis to Shanafelt, March 12, 1942, and Rowe to Whitten, February 19, 1942, CLCF, folder "February 1942," box 5, RG 60, NACP. Few Americans knew that exclusion orders applied to Germans and Italians, aliens and citizens, along both coasts and throughout the nation and its territories based on military necessity under the authority of Executive Order 9066.

23. Fox, *Unknown Internment*, 88–99; Hoover to E. J. Connelley and SACs Re: Internal Security Custodial Detention List, April 30, 1941, FBI File #66-6200-100-33x, in Jacobs and Fallon, *World War Two*; Tolan Committee, *Hearings*, 31:11631–36, quoted in Fox, *Unknown Internment*, 116; Lingeman, *Don't You Know*, 336.

24. Fox, *Unknown Internment*, 42, 54–57; Polenberg, *War and Society*, 61; Grodzins, *Americans Betrayed*, 242, 274–76, 303; and Daniels, *Concentration Camps USA*, 50–58. Category A areas (prohibited to aliens) and Category B areas (restricted to aliens) were also referred to as Zones A and B and both category or zone areas were integrated into Military Area No. 1 with DeWitt's March 2 proclamation. See figure 7 in this volume for a map of relocation centers.

25. Baker, *American and Japanese Relocation*, 56. Following the directive of January 29, Biddle issued additional orders on January 31 and on February 2, 4, 7, and 24, 1942. Biddle agreed to the War Department's proposal as it only applied to aliens. He was not aware that DeWitt and Bendetsen had that very day agreed that Bendetsen should present their recommendation to the Pacific Coast delegation the next day that Japanese citizens be included with the removal of all enemy aliens in a coastal evacuation.

26. Polenberg, *War and Society*, 61–62.

27. Blum, *V Was for Victory*, 156.

28. Kelly to Vulliet, August 9, 1948, folder "Statistics," box 70, SWPD, RG 59, NACP; Daniels, *Concentration Camps USA*, 72–73, 104; Baker, *American and Japanese Relocation*, 12; Fox, *Unknown Internment*, 56, 129, 139. The government relocated 1,100 Japanese and interned 650 along with 230 voluntary internees and 383 Japanese renunciants from the Hawaiian Islands during the war. The sheer number of Japanese on the islands, as with Germans and Italians throughout the United States, meant that they were shielded from any sort of mass evacuation and detention.

29. Biddle, *In Brief Authority*, 217; Fox, *Unknown Internment*, 41. "From the start," Fox points out, "nearly everyone who had an opinion on the subject of alien restrictions wanted the Italian and German aliens treated exactly like the Japanese."

30. DeWitt, Olson, and Bowron quoted in Daniels, *Prisoners without Trial*, 39–43. See also Grodzins, *Americans Betrayed*, 100–108, 263–67.

31. See Conn, Engleman, and Fairchild, *United States Army in World War II: Guarding*, 16–44, for an overview of U.S. continental defense forces prior to the nation's entry into the war. In 1932 the War Department established four armies with specific territorial boundaries; by 1939 the commanders were taking an increasingly active role in war planning and internal security preparations.

32. "An Index of Japanese Organizations in the United States," WDC, Civil Affairs Division Research Branch, June 1944, HF, War Dept. #439A, PMG, box 20, RG 389, NACP.

33. U.S. Congress, House, *Report of the Select Committee*, 2n1; Biddle, *In Brief Authority*, 225; *Personal Justice Denied*, 55–58; DeWitt quoted in Lingeman, *Don't You Know*, 26.

34. Japanese submarine activity was worrisome. Nobody knew how many subs were operating or if attacks presaged an invasion. Kennett, *For the Duration*, 60; Conn, Engleman, and Fairchild, *United States Army in World War II: Guarding*, 86–87.

35. In response to FDR's request, "thousands raced to their local stores to purchase maps," resulting in stores selling their entire stocks within hours. The sixty-one million listeners were 80 percent of the nation's adult population. Goodwin, *No Ordinary Time*, 319–20; *New York Times*, February 24, 1942, quoted in Goodwin, *No Ordinary Time*, 320.

36. U.S. Congress, House, *Report of the Select Committee* and *Fourth Interim Report of the Select Committee*; Daniels, *Concentration Camps USA*, 74–81; FDR, Executive Order 9165, May 19, 1942, HF, War Dept. #439A, PMG, box 18, Vol. 3, Sect. 14, RG 389, NACP.

37. Gilfond to Ennis, January 28, 1942, CLCF, folder "January 1942," box 5, RG 60, NACP; United States Citizenship and Immigration Services, *This Month in Immigration History*, June 1940; Department of Justice, "Administrative History of the INS during World War II," INS General Research Unit, August 19, 1946. By early February nearly one million had reregistered, having answered additional questions such as "whether they had relatives living abroad or serving in the armed forces of a foreign country." U.S. Department of State, *Report of the Delegation*, 7–8. The text of the 1940 Alien Registration Act may be found at https://en.wikisource.org/wiki/Alien_Registration_Act_of_1940. Roosevelt's January 14, 1942, proclamation is discussed in chapter 6.

38. *New York Daily News*, June 29, 1942, cited in Gentry, *J. Edgar Hoover*, 291. By the end of 1942 some fifty-five agencies were working with the PMG's Internal Security Division. Col. George Engelhart, "Coordinating Wartime Internal-Security Programs," November 9, 1943, folder "Internal Security Program," HF, War Dept. #439A, PMG, box 17, Vol. 2, Sect. 7, RG 389, NACP; Memo of Conference with Counterintelligence Group, MID, Internal Security Division, PMG, July 7, 1942, folder "Counterintelligence Branch, MID," HF, War Dept. #439A, PMG, box 5, RG 389, NACP; Historical Monograph, "The War Department Internal Security Program and Its Integration with Other Related Programs," April 30, 1946, folder "War Department Internal Security Program," HF, War Dept. #439A, PMG, box 16, RG 389, NACP. For a detailed account of the capture, trial, and punishment of the Nazi saboteurs, see Louis Fisher's *Nazi Saboteurs on Trial*.

39. The admirals' quotations are in Daniels, *Decision to Relocate*, 20, and Conn, Engleman, and Fairchild, *United States Army in World War II: Guarding*, 119. For the impact on Germans and Italians, see Scherini, "When Italian Americans were 'Enemy Aliens,'" 19, and Fox, *Unknown Internment*, 145. Joyce, like DeWitt, believed

that fifth columnists had played a vital role at Pearl Harbor and was certain that "similar treacherous activity" would accompany a West Coast attack.

40. Daniels, *Concentration Camps USA*, 52. For more on the Hawaiian dilemma, see "The Question of Japanese Evacuation" in Conn, Engleman, and Fairchild, *United States Army in World War II: Guarding*, 206–14. Stimson pointed out that a mass confinement on the islands was "impractical." Robinson, *By Order of the President*, 146–58.

41. Stimson to McCormack, July 8, 1942, CWRIC 1:533–34, 529, quoted in Fox, *Unknown Internment*, 139. On March 2, DeWitt issued Public Proclamation No. 1, and so designated the Pacific Coast strip (Washington, Oregon, and California and including southern Arizona) as "Prohibited Zone A-1" and an adjacent strip in each state as "Restricted Zone B." Together the two zones (also known as Category A and Category B areas) were designated "Military Area No. 1." The entire remainder of the four states (roughly the eastern third of Washington, the eastern half of Oregon, and the eastern third or quarter of California along with the northern two-thirds to three-quarters of Arizona) was designated "Military Area No. 2." See Map 1, West Coast Military Zones, 1942–1945, in Daniels, *Prisoners without Trial*, 52. See figure 7 in this volume for a map of relocation centers.

42. FBI memorandum to the INS, April 29, 1941, Fort Missoula, RG 85, NA; Biddle, *In Brief Authority*, 167; Theoharis, *The Boss*, 194–96; Goodwin, *No Ordinary Time*, 172–76; Fox, *America's Invisible Gulag*, 313n23.

43. Francis Biddle, "Memo of Luncheon Conference with the President," February 7, 1942, box 2, Francis Biddle Papers, FDRL.

44. Rowe, "The Alien Enemy Program," 23; "Statement by the Attorney General on Evacuation of Alien Enemies from the East Coast," May 14, 1942, CLCF, folder "May 1942," section 14, box 5, RG 60, NACP.

45. DeLacy, Chairman, American Committee for Protection of Foreign Born, to Ennis, June 17, 1942, CLCF, folder "July–August 1942," box 6, RG 60, NACP.

46. The poster and the full text can be found in the North Carolina Digital Collections: Eastern Defense Command and First Army, Public Proclamation No. 1 (ncdcr .gov). See also U.S. Congress, House, *Fourth Interim Report of the Select Committee*; "Statement by the Attorney General on Evacuation of Alien Enemies from the East Coast," May 14, 1942, CLCF, folder "May 1942," section 14, box 5, and McCloy to Biddle, May 18, 1942, CLCF, folder "May 1942," section 13, box 5, RG 60, NACP. The poster with the full text of the proclamation also contained a map of the Eastern Military Area including Corps Areas I–IV.

47. Eastern Defense Command and First Army, Public Proclamation No. 1 (ncdcr .gov).

48. "Philadelphia Woman Defies Army Order That She Must Leave the Eastern Area," *New York Times*, May 8, 1943; "Forbids Exclusion from a Coast Area," *New York Times*, August 21, 1943. See also Fox, *America's Invisible Gulag*, 199. (Fox uses the spelling "Schuller" instead of "Schueller" and states that she was a thirty-eight-year resident rather than the *Times*'s report of thirty-two years. Whatever the actual spelling and number of years, Mrs. Schueller was a longtime resident and naturalized American citizen.) General Drum had publicly announced his intention to set

up military areas on April 26, 1942, followed by a written proclamation on April 27 and another on May 16, officially designating the Eastern Military Area, in accordance with War Department instructions.

49. *Japanese American Daily News*, February 7, 1942; Ohye to Biddle (referred to and answered by James Rowe Jr.), February 10, 1942, CLCF, folder "February 1942," section 4, box 5, RG 60, NACP.

50. B. Eiteneuer to James Rowe Jr., February 9, 1942, CLCF, folder "February 1942," box 5, RG 60, NACP.

51. Edwin J. Clapp, Department of Justice, to Edward J. Ennis, Re: Alien enemies who won't fight the Axis, October 15, 1942, CLCF, folder "October 1942," box 6, RG 60, NACP.

52. Conversation, Kennedy and Clapp, October 15, 1942, CLCF, folder "October 1942," box 6, RG 60, NACP.

53. Clapp to Ennis and Kennedy, November 19, 1942, CLCF, folder "November 1942," box 6, RG 60, NACP.

54. Niebuhr to Biddle, November 10, 1942, and Clapp to Ennis, November 19, 1942, CLCF, folder "November 1942," box 6, RG 60, NACP.

55. Clapp to Ennis, Re: Alien Enemies Who Refuse to Serve, December 31, 1942, CLCF, folder "December 1942," box 6, RG 60, NACP. Question 41 asked the alien to state whether or not he objected to service in the land or naval forces of the United States.

56. Hoover to Biddle and Ennis, Re: Japanese Alien Enemies State of Washington, October 5, 1942, pp. 1, 11–12, CLCF, folder "October 1942," box 6, RG 60, NACP. Suspicion of Japanese organizations thought to be under the "direct control of radical nationalistic elements in the Japanese Army, Navy, or government" applied to German and Italian organizations. The FBI arrested and urged internment for their members too.

57. Biddle to Cox and Hoover, July 16, 1943, CLCF, folder "July–August 1943," box 6, and Ennis to Biddle, Re: Review of Alien Enemy Cases, December 3, 1943, SWPU, folder "December 1943," box 7, RG 60, NACP; Theoharis, *The Boss*, 201; Theoharis, *Spying on Americans*, 43–44.

58. State Department, "Various American Agencies Holding Civilian Enemy Aliens," June 19, 1942, folder "Enemy Aliens in U.S.—General," box 129, SWPD, RG 59, NACP; Eleanor to Biddle, June 22, 1942, Biddle to Eleanor, June 24, 1942, and Cooley to Ennis, Re: Hoover Memo relating to alien enemy cases, June 15, 1942, CLCF, folder "June–July 1942," box 6, RG 60, NACP; "Some Useful 'Enemy Aliens,'" *New York Times*, May 11, 1942. Eleanor Roosevelt wrote: "It seems pretty hard to have people like this listed as enemy aliens."

8. Internment, Repatriation, and Exchange

1. "Policy of the U.S. Government in Regard to Repatriation of U.S. Nationals," 1944, "Exchanges of Civilian Nationals and Disabled POWs by Opposing Belligerents" [hereafter cited as "Exchanges by Belligerents"], Vol. 22, "Policy Books, 1939–1945," box 8, SWPD, RG 59, NACP. The number of Americans abroad dropped dramatically from January 1939 to January 1942. The Special Division was renamed the Special

War Problems Division (SWPD) on January 15, 1944, by Department Order 1218 following Undersecretary of State Edward R. Stettinius's reorganization efforts of the previous November. On October 3, 1945, another name change occurred and the SWPD became the Special Projects Division.

2. The Justice Department always asked arrested enemy aliens, "Whom do you want to win the war?" Even if swearing to fight against their birth nation, hearsay and bogus testimonials and "antagonistic," "arrogant," or "belligerent" alien attitudes often led hearing boards to opt for internment. The SWPD was responsible for Americans abroad. U.S. Department of State, *Report of the Delegation*, 13–14.

3. "Legacy of the Latin American Internees: A Few Facts and a Little Law," June 30, 1946, CLCF, folder "February–August 1946," box 7, RG 60, NACP; Summerlin to Fitch, July 3, 1941, and Woodward to Dunn, July 17, 1941, folder "Italian Dossier–Consular PR File," box 182, SWPD, RG 59, NACP.

4. *Final Act of the Third Meeting of Ministers of Foreign Affairs of the American Republics*, Rio de Janeiro, Brazil, January 15–28, 1942, State Department Bulletin, February 7, 1942, Publication 1696, pp. 19–20, box 124, SWPD, RG 59, NACP [hereafter cited as Department of State, *Final Act*]. Forty-seven officials from various U.S. government agencies plus representatives of the American Republics attended the meetings.

5. Corbett, *Quiet Passages*, 11–17; "Work of the Special Division," Brandt to Long, January 7, 1941, Vol. 69, folder "Miscellaneous," box 15; State Dept. Press Release, September 1, 1939, folder "Warnings to Americans," box 78; "Demand for Legislation to Repatriate Certain U.S. Nationals at Government Expense," Vol. 22, "Policy Books, 1939–1945," box 8; and "Exchanges by Belligerents," Vol. 22, "Policy Books, 1939–1945," box 8, all in SWPD, RG 59, NACP. See also Israel, *The War Diary of Breckinridge Long*. Thousands returned from Europe and the Far East on United States Lines ships—the *Orizaba*, *Shawnee*, *Iroquois*, *St. John*, and *Acadia*—while others took ships provided by neutrals. During the first half of 1940, as hostilities spread, officials utilized more vessels, including the SS *Manhattan*, *Roosevelt*, and *Washington* and the Army Transport *American Legion*.

6. Barnes to Secretary of State, March 10, 1941, Subject: Repatriation of Destitute and Needy American Citizens, Telegraphic Instruction no. 790, to Vichy, December 3, 1940, pp. 1–9, box 121; Department of State, untitled, Document no. 740.00115 European War, 1939, November 27, 1941, box 97; and Department of State, *Proposed Exchange between Germany and Great Britain*, September 30, 1941, 1–2, box 97, SWPD, RG 59, NACP. With the fall of France the FBI stepped up its efforts to obtain the names and addresses of dangerous and potentially dangerous individuals for detention. Hoover to all SACs, June 15, 1940, "To and from Justice Re: Enemy Aliens," box 129, SWPD; Hoover, "Memo for McGuire," August 21, 1940, in Jacobs and Fallon, *World War Two*.

7. "Exchanges by Belligerents," Vol. 22, "Policy Books, 1939–1945," box 8, SWPD, RG 59, NACP. Hospital ships, like Canada's *Letitia*, played an invaluable role in the exchanges, logging tens of thousands of miles across the oceans transporting civilians to and from the European and Asian theaters of war and the United States. Sev-

eral websites have information on the Swedish ships *Drottningholm* and *Gripsholm*. See http://www.salship.se/mercy.asp. For general archival information see boxes 69, 86, 97, 100, 101, 140, and 146, SWPD, RG 59, NACP.

8. Department of State, *Final Act*, 4, 19.

9. Department of State, *Final Act*, 20–21.

10. Department of State, *Final Act*, 21–26.

11. *Department of State Bulletin*, August 6, 1944, p. 146, cited in Weglyn, *Years of Infamy*, 58–59. The CPD yielded to State Department pressures to remove the perceived enemy (primarily German) threat by forcibly repatriating Axis nationals.

12. White to Lafoon, January 28, 1946, White to Bingham, January 30, 1946, and Kelly to Vulliet, August 9, 1948, folder "Statistics," box 70, SWPD, RG 59, NACP; Friedman, *Nazis and Good Neighbors*, 61–62. Within seventy-two hours of the Pearl Harbor attack the FBI had taken into custody nearly 4,000 enemy aliens, beginning a campaign that included the arrests of 15,607 persons (14,807 aliens and 717 citizens) by November 1943, and 16,062 aliens (7,043 Germans, 5,428 Japanese, and 3,567 Italians along with 11 Romanians, 12 Hungarians, and 1 Bulgarian) and 748 citizens (121 Germans, 598 Japanese, and 29 Italians) by war's end. Examining the arrests, one finds that the FBI never did single out the Japanese; rather, the FBI arrested nearly twice as many Germans and Italians as Japanese during the war. The FBI also arrested 121 German, 29 Italian, and 598 Japanese citizens along with 1 Bulgarian, 11 Romanian, and 12 Hungarian aliens. Italians were seen as reluctant belligerents and Italy as a possible ally—hence their low repatriation and internment numbers.

13. Selden Chapin to Melby, Wright, Woodward, and Bongal, April 29, 1942, folder "Japanese Exchange—South American Republics," box 189, SWPD, RG 59, NACP; LaFeber, *Inevitable Revolutions*, 84.

14. Artucio, *Nazi Underground in South America*, 12; Tejera, *Penetración Nazi en America Latina*; Giudici, *Hitler conquista América*.

15. "What Does Latin America Want?" and "Totalitarian Inroads in Latin America," along with other chapters from *The Coming Struggle for Latin America*, appeared in popular and scholarly articles. Gunther, *Inside Latin America*, 1–6, 159–60.

16. "Nazi Pipeline," *Newsweek*, July 22, 1940; Beals, *Dawn over the Amazon*; Earle, *Against This Torrent*, 20; Friedrich, "The Poison in Our System."

17. German businesses were "indispensable," and "virtually all" Germans in Latin America were "sincere supporters of [and] belong to the Nazi hierarchy." Adolf Berle, Memo to Chiefs of the Diplomatic Missions in the Other American Republics, *The Pattern of Nazi Organizations and Their Activities in the Other American Republics*, February 6, 1941, decimal file 862.20210/414A, 250/34/7/4, box 5505, SWPD, RG 59, NACP; Friedman, *Nazis and Good Neighbors*, 2, 106–9.

18. Corbett, *Quiet Passages*, 142–43. FDR had alerted U.S. officials in Latin America about German agents. In May 1940 he told Ambassador Claude Bowers in Chile that German agents were trying to topple American governments. Bowers, *Chile through Embassy Windows*, 60. Numerous reports sent from officials in Central and South America informed Washington policymakers that the local situation was sometimes desperate, though usually "potentially dangerous." See "Japanese

in Peru," Chapin to Melby, Wright, Woodward, and Bongal, April 29, 1942, folder "Japanese Exchange—South American Republics," box 189, SWPD, RG 59, NACP. Allied and Axis governments exchanged many diplomats and correspondents, most early in the war.

19. Hull, *Memoirs*, 1:602; Kimball, *The Juggler*, 219n4. Roosevelt's goal was "a Western Hemisphere with liberal institutions that looked to the United States for leadership" (Kimball, *The Juggler*, 120). With the Panama Declaration of October 1939, foreign ministers of twenty-one nations declared a "safety belt" up to one thousand miles around the hemisphere. With the Havana Act of July 1940, any violation of "the territory, sovereignty, or political independence of an American state by a non-American state" would be considered an act of aggression against all Latin American nations. On August 17, 1940, the United States joined Canada in creating a Permanent Joint Board on Defense.

20. The Rio conference produced the Emergency Advisory Committee for Political Defense.

21. Henry Wallace, "Price of Free World Victory Speech," May 8, 1942, Madison Square Garden. For the full text see Henry A. Wallace, "The Century of the Common Man," delivered May 8, 1942, americanrhetoric.com/speeches/henrywallacefreeworldassoc.htm.

22. FBI, *Bolivia Today*, p. 32, June 1942, "FBI Reports–Bolivia," box 141, Hopkins Papers, FDRL, quoted in Friedman, *Nazis and Good Neighbors*, 124.

23. Walker, *E. R. Stettinius, Jr.*, 333; Wood, *Making of the Good Neighbor Policy*, 119; Dwyre to Patterson, Lima, December 30, 1943, and Welch to Hull, Deportation of Germans from Peru, May 13, 1943, folder "Peru–Japanese," box 194, SWPD, RG 59, NACP. From Monroe's Doctrine and Roosevelt's Corollary to Pan-American Conferences in 1923 and 1933, the U.S. affirmed its right to intervene in Latin America. In December 1943, American vice consul Jack G. Dwyre, issued a secret report for Chargé d'Affaires Jefferson Patterson, Lima, warning that despite there being only 2,248 Germans there, "Nazis are effectively sabotaging our foreign policy towards Latin America, nullifying sincere goodwill and what benefits and security we may hope for in these markets."

24. "Official personnel" at times included diplomats and businessmen. Hull to American Legation, Bern, December 23, 1941, and American Legation, Bern, to Hull, January 15, 1942, "Exchanges by Belligerents," Vol. 22, "Policy Books, 1939–1945," box 8, SWPD, RG 59, NACP.

25. State Department Memos 42 and 58, January 6 and 16, 1942, Telegram 379, February 7, 1942, Memo 93, February 23, 1942, Memo of March 13, 1942, "Documents showing the development in the Japanese-American exchange agreement of a definite understanding on the inclusion of persons without regard to number or to their usefulness in prosecution of war," October 29, 1942, "Japanese Government Agreement," box 186, SWPD, RG 59, NACP [hereafter cited as State Department Memos].

26. Hull to American Legation, Bern, January 22, 1942, "Exchanges by Belligerents," Vol. 22, "Policy Books, 1939–1945," box 8, SWPD, RG 59, NACP; State Department Memos; Stimson to Hull, February 5, 1942, quoted in Weglyn, *Years of Infamy*, 55–56.

27. Frank Parker to Ennis, AECU, September 11, 1942, CLCF, folder "September 1942," box 6, RG 60, NACP; Leo J. Margolin, "Enemy Aliens Spit on Flag, Abuse Ellis Island Guards," *New York Times*, September 9, 1942, was enclosed with the personal letter from Parker to Ennis.

28. "Nazis Hold 14 U.S. Women," *New York Times*, January 22, 1943. Such stories often ran with those about government dealings with subversives and spies here, such as "2 German-born Men Held for Espionage: Plead Guilty to Aiding Convicted Spy" placed in an adjacent column in this case.

29. Alien Information Bureau, "Enemy Aliens Apprehended in U.S. by FBI," PMG, box 1, RG 389, NACP; "Repatriation of European Axis Nationals," Green to Long, April 13, 1942, folder "Exchange—Official Personnel," box 72, SWPD, RG 59, NACP; Corbett, *Quiet Passages*, 46; Fox, *Unknown Internment*, 156.

30. "Removal of Italian, Rumanian, and Bulgarian Diplomatic Staffs from Washington to White Sulphur Springs," January 13, 1942, folder "January 16, 1942," box 115, SWPD, RG 59, NACP; Hull and Welles to American Legation, Bern, February 10 and 25, 1942, "Exchanges by Belligerents," Vol. 22, "Policy Books, 1939–1945," box 8, SWPD, RG 59, NACP. Spain represented Japan's interests (in Hawaii it was Sweden) while the U.S. selected Switzerland. The Special Division dealt with the Pacific exchanges and the Atlantic exchanges via the Swiss.

31. State Department memo to Gullion, March 10, 1942, folder "March 1942," box 115, SWPD, RG 59, NACP; "112 Axis Nationals Here on U.S. Liner," *New York Times*, January 29, 1942. Of the 111 repatriates, according to the State Department document, there were 42 German officials and 56 German nationals along with 8 Italian officials and 5 Italian nationals. There is a one-person repatriate difference with what the *New York Times* reported; the *Times* also notes 52 diplomats, while the memo has 50.

32. "Memo: European Exchange," n.d., folder "*Drottningholm* to Lisbon, May 7, 1942," box 65, and Clattenburg to Chapin, May 9, 1942, folder "Exchanges of Official Personnel," box 72, SWPD, RG 59, NACP. See also telegrams, Hull to Ambassador R. Henry Norweb and Norweb to Hull, December 11, 1941, cited in Gardiner, *Pawns in a Triangle of Hate*. Gardiner covers the internment and repatriation of Japanese Peruvians, including United States policies with and intervention in Peru (169–74). Nearly all repatriates endured sickness, disease, and malnutrition in jails, prisons, and transit camps (including the U.S.-run Camp Empire in the Canal Zone) en route to the U.S. for internment. Friedman, *Nazis and Good Neighbors*, 116–17, 148–49.

33. "Recurring Statistics," May 11, June 6, 1942, HF, War Dept. #439A, PMG, box 10, folder "Monthly and Weekly Statistical Reports," RG 389, NACP. The Army held 1,094 Japanese, 735 Germans, 102 Italians, and 23 others. The Justice Department held 3,331 Japanese, 2,028 Germans, 1,255 Italians, and 91 others.

34. Long, Directives, Special Division, July 2, 1942, folder "Second *Drottningholm*," box 157; American Legation telegrams, March 28 and April 20, 1942, boxes 97–100 and 173–80; and Clattenburg to Keeley, December 10, 1943, folder "*Gripsholm* from Lisbon," box 67, all in SWPD, RG 59, NACP.

35. Britain objected to repatriating "dangerous" Germans, but the State Department noted: "It would be far more detrimental to the war effort to have these danger-

ous enemy aliens in the Western Hemisphere than to send them to their homelands." Green to Long, March 16, 1942, box 142, SWPD, RG 59, NACP.

36. "Memo: European Exchange," n.d., folder "*Drottningholm* to Lisbon, May 7, 1942," box 65, SWPD, RG 59, NACP; Keeley to Travers, December 15, 1942, "Memo regarding proposal to obtain release of Jews held by Axis in return for release by U.S. of German nationals held in U.S.," Vol. 22, "Policy Books, 1939–1945," box 8, SWPD, RG 59, NACP.

37. Bannerman to Fitch, "Diplomatic Exchange," July 30, 1942, box 112; "Americans in Japanese Custody," January 1945, box 76; Long to Green, June 15, 1942, Biddle to Hull, August 14, 1942, Hull to Roosevelt, August 27, 1942, folder "*Gripsholm*—Key File, 3 of 3," box 168; and Knox to Hull, "Importance of keeping Japanese repatriates from Hawaii from revealing military secrets to Japan," October 29, 1942, box 186, all in SWPD, RG 59, NACP; "Latin American Internees," June 30, 1946, CLCF, folder "February–August 1946," box 7, RG 60, NACP.

38. Roosevelt to Hull, August 15, 1942, folder "Japanese Exchanges," box 188; German Embassy to and from State Department via Legation of Switzerland, Bern, April 3, June 23, and July 7, 1943, "Exchanges by Belligerents," Vol. 22, "Policy Books, 1939–1945," box 8; Biddle to Roosevelt, August 20, 1943, folder "*Gripsholm* to Lisbon," box 67; Green to Long, July 6, 1942, "*Gripsholm II*," box 85; and Forrestal to Hull, August 5, 1942, and "Americans Returning from the Far East," August 22, 1942, folder "*Gripsholm*—1st Voyage from Africa," box 167, all in SWPD, RG 59, NACP; Corbett, *Quiet Passages*, 73–74. Frank Booth was among dozens of Americans returning home aboard the *Gripsholm* with potentially useful information.

39. Long to Green, June 15, 1942, Biddle to Hull, August 14, 19842, and Hull to Roosevelt, August 27, 1942, folder "*Gripsholm*—Key File, 3 of 3," box 168; Knox to Hull, "Importance of keeping Japanese repatriates from Hawaii from revealing military secrets to Japan," October 29, 1942, box 186; State Department letter, June 30, 1944, "Exchanges by Belligerents," Vol. 22, "Policy Books, 1939–1945," box 8; and U.S. Embassy, Mexico, to Hull, "Lists of Obnoxious Japanese for Possible Repatriation," October 23, 1945, box 193, all in SWPD, RG 59, NACP; Fox, *Unknown Internment*, 156. U.S. officials wanted returned those who could provide useful information but sought to keep repatriates from violating the conditions of the repatriation agreements as they continually sought to rid the hemisphere of "undesirables." The report to Hull mentioned "little direct evidence of any Japanese in Mexico having committed a specific act contrary to our interests." Yet U.S. officials offered a list of "obnoxious Japanese nationals who might be repatriated to the advantage of the United States and the Western Hemisphere."

40. State Department Memos; "Legacy of the Latin American Internees," June 30, 1946, CLCF, folder "February–August 1946," box 7, RG 60, NACP; Diggins, *Mussolini and Fascism*, 325. The 6,610 Latin American repatriates included 4,058 Germans, 288 Italians, and 2,264 Japanese.

41. "Fundamentals of the Japanese-American Exchange," March 1943, box 168, SWPD, RG 59, NACP.

42. Bannerman to Fitch, "Status of Japanese Exchange," January 30, 1943, box 170, SWPD, RG 59, NACP; U.S. Department of State, *Report of the Delegation*, 14. Throughout the war, the Departments of State and Justice did their best to "avoid the repatriation of dangerous or potentially useful Axis aliens to the countries of their origin" while simultaneously ensuring the safety and benevolent treatment of interned Americans. U.S. Department of State, *Report of the Delegation*, 14. The same desires and concerns held true for Germany and Japan. The major belligerent powers quickly discovered that indeterminately detaining individuals who might be useful to the enemy had its advantages, while expelling those who might actually be detrimental to the enemy, including criminals, the insane, and any considered "bottom of the barrel," would prove advantageous too.

43. Ennis to Biddle, Deportable Alien Enemies with Criminal Records, June 22, 1942, CLCF, folder "June–July 1942," box 6, RG 60, NACP.

44. Roosevelt to Hull, August 15, 1942, and Hull to Roosevelt, August 27, 1942, "Japanese Exchanges," box 188, SWPD, RG 59, NACP. See also "Department of State, July–December 1942," box 10, Official File 20, FDRL. Roosevelt sent a carbon copy of the letter to Hoover, which suggests "that it was the FBI director's complaints that had moved the president to action." Friedman, *Nazis and Good Neighbors*, 346. The United States had conducted two full wartime exchanges with Germany and one with Japan by the time Hull wrote Roosevelt. Hull may have been citing only the *Drottningholm* return voyages of May 22 and June 22, 1942.

45. "Conference to Discuss Certain Problems in Connection with Repatriation of Enemy Aliens," August 29, 1942, folder "*Gripsholm*—Key File, 3 of 3," box 168, and Long to Strong, July 30, 1942, folder "Hawaii 1942," box 186, SWPD, RG 59, NACP. The first exchange, the *Gripsholm*'s voyage from New York City to Lourenço Marques, included 1,500 persons exchanged for an equal number of Americans and allied nationals. "Departure of *Gripsholm*," June 18, 1942, folder "ss *Gripsholm*," box 113, SWPD, RG 59, NACP. Lourenço Marques is a former Portuguese port (now Maputo) in Southern Mozambique on the coast of southeast Africa. General Strong was U.S. Army Deputy Chief of Staff for Intelligence (G-2) from 1942 to 1944.

46. Keeley to Brandt, September 24, 1942, folder "Second Exchange, September–December 1942, 1 of 2," box 188, SWPD, RG 59, NACP.

47. Burling to Ennis, Re: Conference called by Commander Wharton, September 15, 1942, CLCF, folder "September 1942," box 6, RG 60; State Department Press Release, August 18, 1942, Document no. 416, box 113, RG 59, NACP.

48. Knox to Hull, "Importance of keeping Japanese repatriates from Hawaii from revealing military secrets to Japan," October 29, 1942, folder "Hawaii 1942," box 186, SWPD, RG 59, NACP. U.S. officials often complained about sending those who could "assist the enemy's war effort" while receiving persons of "not such benefit." Biddle to FDR, August 20, 1943, "*Gripsholm* to Lisbon, February 15, 1944," box 67, SWPD, RG 59, NACP. There was a great deal of speculation, including numerous reports by the American media, that Germany was sending spies and saboteurs among the legitimate repatriates. See, for example, "Diplomat Ship," "Infiltration Peril in Refugees Seen," "ss *Drottningholm* Passengers Report Trip Conditions Ideal for Subversive

Person's Entry into U.S.," and "Federal Agents Query Passengers," *New York Times*, June 2–3, 1942. Long, who orchestrated Special Division policy, was concerned that refugees, particularly Jews, were contaminating the nation and ruining his career. He listed his conspiratorial enemies as liberals, that is "communists, extreme radicals, Jewish professional agitators, and refugee enthusiasts." Corbett, *Quiet Passages*, 10. See also Fox, *America's Invisible Gulag*, 236.

49. "Americans Returning from the Far East on *Gripsholm*," August 22, 1942, folder "*Gripsholm*—1st Voyage from Africa," box 167, SWPD, RG 59, NACP.

50. "Exchange and Treatment of Prisoners of War," Remarks of Sen. Elbert D. Thomas, November 15, 1943, "Exchanges by Belligerents," Vol. 22, "Policy Books, 1939–1945," box 8, and "Activities of the United States government in removing from the American Republics dangerous subversive aliens," November 3, 1942, folder "Removal of Axis Aliens from other American Republics," box 180, SWPD, RG 59, NACP.

51. "Resolution concerning Detention and Expulsion of Dangerous Axis Nationals," Approved by the Committee May 21, 1943, and transmitted to the governments June 5, 1943, folder "Committee for Political Defense," box 86, and folder "Miscellaneous Reports," box 117, SWPD, RG 59, NACP.

52. "Resolution concerning Detention and Expulsion of Dangerous Axis Nationals." The committee and many U.S. officials felt that the Axis would "fight more violently the nearer it approaches its doom."

53. "Activities of the United States government in removing from the American Republics dangerous subversive aliens," November 3, 1942, folder "Removal of Axis Aliens from other American Republics," box 180, SWPD, RG 59, NACP.

54. Keeley to Travers, "Memo regarding proposal to obtain release of Jews held by Axis in return for release by U.S. of German nationals held in U.S.," December 15, 1942, "Exchanges by Belligerents," Vol. 22, "Policy Books, 1939-1945," box 8, SWPD, RG 59, NACP.

55. Smith to Keeley, "Notes on Proposal to Exchange Germans Interned in the United States for Jews in Germany and German-Occupied Territory," December 15, 1942, "Exchanges by Belligerents," Vol. 22, "Policy Books, 1939–1945," box 8, SWPD, RG 59, NACP. Smith added that "no suitable American vessels were available to effect the previous exchange of German and American nationals and this government was forced at great expense to charter a neutral Swedish vessel, the *Drottningholm*, to carry out the exchange. If such an exchange were considered desirable and feasible, it is probable that the *Drottningholm* or other neutral vessels could again be chartered."

56. "Exchange and Treatment of Prisoners of War," Remarks of Sen. Elbert D. Thomas, November 15, 1943, "Exchanges by Belligerents," Vol. 22, "Policy Books, 1939–1945," box 8, SWPD, RG 59, NACP.

57. Long to Green, June 15, 1942, Biddle to Hull, August 14, 1942, and Hull to Roosevelt, August 27, 1942, folder "*Gripsholm*—Key File, 3 of 3," box 168, SWPD, RG 59, NACP; U.S. Department of State, *Report of the Delegation*, 13–14. There were 3,058 Axis nationals repatriated on five European voyages in 1942. The U.S. sent 1,499 Japanese nationals to Japan in exchange for 1,451 persons. The U.S. received 3,299 persons (including 581 Latin nationals) on the first exchanges and repatriated 4,557 persons

to Germany and Japan. "Memo: European Exchange," n.d., folder "*Drottningholm* to Lisbon, May 7, 1942," box 65; "Departure of *Gripsholm*," June 18, 1942, folder "ss *Gripsholm*," box 113; and "Exchanges by Belligerents," Vol. 22, "Policy Books, 1939–1945," box 8, all in SWPD, RG 59, NACP.

58. U.S. Department of State, *Report of the Delegation*, 13–14; White to Lafoon and Bingham, January 28 and 30, 1946, "Statistics," box 70, SWPD, RG 59, NACP. Of the 837 voluntary repatriates, 812 were Japanese.

59. "Proper treatment" meant treatment standards "recognized by civilized nations." Hull to American Legation: American Interests—Japan, January 27, 1944, folder "Third Exchange with Japan," box 193, SWPD, RG 59, NACP.

60. Biddle to Roosevelt, August 20, 1943, folder "*Gripsholm* to Lisbon, February 15, 1944," box 67, SWPD, RG 59, NACP. When the exchanges resumed in September 1943 with Japan and in February 1944 with Germany they involved repatriating "inherently harmless" Axis nationals rather than "dangerous" ones. New exchanges would clear the nation's internment camps of "undesirables," including "obnoxious" and "bottom of the barrel" types along with those internees who had made it clear to camp authorities that they wanted to leave the United States. In addition, as James Keeley knew, even those who refused repatriation would be repatriated if "agencies of the government feel it desirable for certain individuals to leave the United States." C. K. Huston to Keeley, September 26, 1942, folder "Memo regarding Second Exchange, September–December 1942, 1 of 2," box 188, SWPD, RG 59, NACP.

61. Clattenburg to Col. George Dorroh, MID, December 24, 1942, folder "Military Intelligence Service, 1942," and Green to Spanish Embassy, July 6, 1942, folder "Memo for the files Regarding Japanese Exchanges," box 188; Bannerman to Fitch, Subject: Conference on the Diplomatic Exchange, September 2, 1942, folder "German Exchange," box 104, SWPD, RG 59, NACP.

62. Clattenburg to Bannerman, August 23, 1943, folder "*Gripsholm*—Key File, 1 of 3," box 168, SWPD, RG 59, NACP.

63. "American-German Exchange," June 30, 1943, folder "*Gripsholm* to Lisbon, February 15, 1944," box 67; Bannerman to Fitch, "Summary of Enemy Diplomatic Transfers," April 13, 1944, folder "Diplomatic Exchange—General, 1 of 2," box 170; and "Measures taken by the Department of State in behalf of American Nationals in Japanese custody: Treatment and Repatriation," January 1945, folder "January 1945," box 76, all in SWPD, RG 59, NACP. Some 2,000 additional tons of relief supplies arrived in Japan at the end of 1944 from a stockpile in Siberia.

64. Telegram "American Interests—Repatriation," American Legation, Bern to State Department, February 18, 1944, folder "*Gripsholm* to Lisbon, February 15, 1944," box 67; Clattenburg to Long, April 17, 1943, and Memo of Conversation between Clattenburg and Mr. Stauber, War Relocation Authority, March 17, 1943, box 186; and Long to Welles, April 2, 1943, folder "*Gripsholm* to Lisbon, February 15, 1944," box 67, all in SWPD, RG 59, NACP.

65. "*Gripsholm* Is in with 1,494 Back from Captivity" and "*Gripsholm* Docks with 1,494 from Japanese Captivity: Exchanged Internees Weep at Return to America, Tell of Privations," *New York Herald Tribune*, December 2, 1943; "*Gripsholm* from Mormugao," September 2, 1943, box 66, SWPD, RG 59, NACP.

66. As of May 23, 1944, the protecting powers and the International Red Cross reported that Japan held 19,919 POWs and 5,593 civilians (13,590 and 4,336, respectively, in the Philippines). *Report of the Subcommittee of the Committee on Foreign Affairs: Exchange of American Citizens Interned or Held Prisoners of War by the Japanese*, House of Representatives, 77th Cong., 2nd sess., 1944, box 8, SWPD, RG 59, NACP.

67. Secret Memorandum of Meeting: Post-war disposition of interned alien enemies received from the other American republics, August 31, 1944, folder "Removal of Enemy Aliens," box 181, SWPD, RG 59, NACP. Clattenburg and other officials realized the need to resolve the status of several thousand internees from Latin America.

68. U.S. Department of State, *Report of the Delegation*, Resolution XXIV, Concerning the exchange between the American nations and Germany, May 31, 1944, box 124, SWPD, RG 59, NACP. The CPD forcefully reminded Germany that Jews and others were under the Allies' protection. The threat of reciprocity was clear and helped shield the overwhelming majority of U.S. and Latin American nationals in Axis territory from harm or death.

69. Fitch to Seward, Ft. Stanton, New Mexico, December 30, 1944, folder "German Exchange Arrangements," box 100, SWPD, RG 59, NACP; "Wounded Yanks on *Gripsholm* Joke at Ordeals," *New York Herald Tribune*, March 17, 1944. Prior to one exchange, U.S. officials frisked all 853 Germans at Crystal City and strip-searched 127. Clattenburg to Fitch, March 3, 1944, folder "German Exchange Arrangements," box 177, SWPD, RG 59, NACP. While certain facets of the repatriation and exchange program remained beyond the public's purview, the State Department gave the press occasional statements and releases as papers covered the exchanges. See, for example, the following that appeared in the *New York Times*: "GRIPSHOLM OFF SATURDAY; Will Receive Americans From Reich Through Switzerland," January 5, 1945; "Foreign Exchange," January 31, 1945; "GRIPSHOLM DUE TODAY; Exchange Liner Bringing 1,206 Repatriates to United States," February 21, 1945; "Repatriated Civilians Quit Gripsholm Slowly," February 23, 1945; and "457 ON GRIPSHOLM CLEAR; 188 of Civilians Are Still Being Examined at Ellis Island," February 25, 1945. The FBI sometimes tracked suspected repatriates. See "GRIPSHOLM ARRIVAL IS ARRESTED BY FBI," May 26, 1945.

70. "Memo regarding U.S. government removing from American Republics dangerous subversive aliens," November 3, 1942, folder "Removal of Axis Aliens from American Republics," box 180, SWPD, RG 59, NACP. At local hearing boards, officials pressured or threatened internees with forced repatriation or deportation, which excluded the possibility of returning home. Voluntary repatriates knew they might be able to come back. The Schmitz family was among those who successfully fought repatriation.

71. Hall to Fitch, Departure of *Gripsholm* and *Letitia*, January 10, 1945, box 121; Bannerman to Fitch, German Exchange, January 7–February 21, March 15, 1945, box 160; Department of State, *List of Articles Which May or May Not Be Taken out of the United States by German Repatriates*, 1943, box 121; and Clattenburg to Nakanishi, August 19, 1943, folder "*Gripsholm*—Key File, 3 of 3," box 168, all in SWPD, RG 59, NACP.

72. Cabot to Costa Rican Foreign Minister, Wright, and Bonsal, November 15, 1943, Knapp to Wright, November 23, 143, and Cabot to the Division of the Ameri-

can Republics, November 24, 1943, box 31, SWPD, RG 59, NACP. Officials pressured internees and repatriates to behave, cooperate, and keep their experiences to themselves; otherwise they faced deportation or prospective employers learning of their "enemy" or "troublemaker" status.

73. Bannerman to Fitch, February 24, 1944, folder "German Exchange, February 1944," box 104, and Biddle to Roosevelt, August 20, 1943, folder "*Gripsholm* to Lisbon, February 15, 1944," box 67, SWPD, RG 59, NACP; Ennis to Biddle, Re: Deportable Alien Enemies with Criminal Records, June 22, 1942, CLCF, folder "June–July 1942," box 6, RG 60, NACP; Herman R. Landon, Acting Chief, Warrant and Deportation Branch, INS, to Ennis, December 19, 1942, CLCF, folder "December 1942," box 7, RG 60, NACP. Landon's memorandum referenced alien enemies deportable because of criminal records. U.S. officials developed code words by which they charged criminals—in this case, "renegade."

74. Wharton to Plitt, November 16, 1944, and Lafoon, Memo of conversation with Lt. Cmdr. Belin, ONI, "Clearance of German nationals for repatriation," November 16, 1944, both in folder "Correspondence with Security Agencies on Voyage of *Gripsholm* to Marseilles," box 69, SWPD, RG 59, NACP. Officials also used the code word "renegade" to charge and then deport even more alien enemies.

75. Hoover to Lafoon, Repatriation of German Nationals, December 14, 1944, and Military Intelligence Service to Plitt, "Confidential regarding German nationals requested by German government not cleared," December 8 and 11, 1944, folder "Correspondence with Security Agencies on Voyage of *Gripsholm* to Marseilles," box 69, SWPD, RG 59, NACP.

76. "Memo for Mr. Ennis," Harrison to Ennis, August 12, 1943, CLCF, folder "August 1943," box 6, RG 60, NACP. The Stewart Emotional Response Test was one of several batteries of tests used during World War II as part of Indian Personality, Education, and Administration Research: Hopi Study, 1942–1944.

77. "Memo for Harrison," Ennis to Harrison, August 22, 1943, CLCF, folder "August 1943," box 6, RG 60, NACP.

78. State Department: "Treatment of Americans in Japan," May 11, 1944, folder "Treatment of Americans in Japan, January–August 1944," box 89, SWPD, RG 59, NACP.

79. White to Lafoon, "Projects," July 23, 1946, folder "Statistics," box 70; White to Lafoon, January 28, 1946, and White to Bingham, January 30, 1946, folder "Statistics," box 70; Department of Justice, INS, Philadelphia, Detention Reports: Period Ending August 31, October 31, and December 31, 1945, and February 28, 1946, folder "Statistics," box 70; and "Confidential release for publication upon sailing of *S.S. Drottningholm* from Jersey City," May 6, 1942, No. 199, "*S.S. Drottningholm*, April–May 1942," folder "Axis Removal from U.S.-Diplomats," box 112, all in SWPD, RG 59, NACP. See also Weglyn, *Years of Infamy*, 59; Baker, *American and Japanese Relocation*, 12; and Christgau, *Enemies*, vii.

80. Ugo Carusi to all District Directors, Subject: Resumption of deportations to Europe and the Near East, August 23, 1945, Jacobs and Fallon, *World War Two*; Department of State, Bulletin 13, no. 332, November 4, 1945, 737–38, Jacobs and Fallon, *World War Two*; "Legacy of the Latin American Internees," June 30, 1946, CLCF,

folder "February–August 1946," box 7, RG 60, NACP; State Department Press Release no. 826, November 2, 1945, folder "German Nationals Deported by the Other American Republics via the United States," box 121, SWPD, RG 59, NACP.

81. "Legacy of the Latin American Internees," June 30, 1946, CLCF, folder "February–August 1946," box 7, RG 60, NACP; Kelly to District Directors, Subject: Repatriation, December 22, 1944, box 121, SWPD, RG 59, NACP.

82. Ugo Carusi to all District Directors, Subject: Resumption of deportations to Europe and the Near East, August 23, 1945, Jacobs and Fallon, *World War Two*; Department of State, Bulletin 13, no. 332, November 4, 1945, 737–38, Jacobs and Fallon, *World War Two*; Department of State, "Notice to the Internees from Latin America," January 4, 1946, folder "Japanese from Peru–Background," box 196, SWPD, RG 59, NACP.

83. Department of State, "Notice to the Internees from Latin America," January 4, 1946, folder "Japanese from Peru–Background," box 196, SWPD, RG 59, NACP; Ugo Carusi to all District Directors, Subject: Orders of the Attorney General directing the removal from the United States of alien enemies pursuant to Presidential Proclamation No. 2655 of July 14, 1945, June 4, 1946, Jacobs and Fallon, *World War Two*; U.S. Department of State, *Report of the Delegation*, 17.

9. Internment Camps and Relocation Centers

1. Charles Gordon, "Status of Enemy Nationals in the United States," to Edward Ennis and the *National Lawyers Guild Review*, December 5, 1942, CLCF, box 6, RG 60, NACP. The Army handled all male internees from July 1941 to May 1943, at which point the INS, already responsible for the temporary detention of all internees and the internment of females, took charge. Japanese, German, and Italian relocatees did not receive hearings, as DeWitt and others considered them too burdensome and time-consuming. Gordon added: "Human institutions frequently pursue the course of least resistance. With enemy nationals, this tendency has resulted in the creation of broad categories into which all have been cast. This segregation has imposed unjustified hardship on vast numbers of worthy persons, where sole offense was the accident of birth in a country which they had long since forsaken. Of course, we must provide measures to guard against enemies who are secreted among us, but those measures must be reasonably adjusted to the anticipated peril."

2. Testimony of Rowe and Ennis before the CWRIC, November 2, 1981, pp. 46–47 and 181–83, RG 220, NACP.

3. Ennis to Biddle, Re: Review of Alien Enemy Cases, December 3, 1943, folder "December 1943," SWPU, box 7, RG 60, NACP. Ennis reviewed 1,053 cases from July to November 1943 and found changes in 784.

4. Biddle, *In Brief Authority*, 207; Bailey, *The Home Front*, 25–27; Mangione, *An Ethnic at Large*, 320; Hull to Biddle, January 22, Stimson to Biddle, January 17, and Biddle to Stimson, January 30, 1942, CLCF, folder "January 1942," box 5, RG 60, NACP; Roosevelt to Stimson, May 5, 1942, quoted in Conn, Engleman, and Fairchild, *United States Army in World War II: Guarding*, 145. Stimson expressed the same concerns as Hull and Biddle, noting that under the Geneva Convention "confinement in jails and prisons is prohibited" and that the "Joint Committee agreed three months ago

that where the Department of Justice lacked suitable facilities for temporary detention, the Army would undertake to supply them." Stimson added that because "32 German, 5 Italian and 69 Japanese aliens, or a total of 106, are confined in city and county jails, the enemy governments may be expected to adopt retaliatory measures against our own nationals because of this fact." Stimson to Biddle, January 17, 1942.

5. National Refugee Service, *Special Information Bulletin*, no. 18, May 29, 1942, CLCF, "May-June 1942," section 16, box 6, RG 60, NACP.

6. The December 7 and 8 proclamations authorized the arrest and incarceration of alien enemies "deemed dangerous" to the "public peace or safety." The January 14 proclamation classified all subjects of Germany, Italy, and Japan living in the United States as "alien enemies" and required them to get certificates of identification. Department of Justice, "Regulations Controlling Travel and Other Conduct of Aliens of Enemy Nationalities" (Washington DC: GPO, 1942), folder "Enemy Aliens in U.S., General," box 129, SWPD, RG 59, NACP; AP release, July 28, 1942, CLCF, folder "August 1942," box 6, RG 60, NACP.

7. "Memo regarding activities of the United States government in removing from the other American Republics dangerous subversive aliens," November 3, 1942, folder "Removal of Axis Aliens from American Republics," box 180, SWPD, RG 59, NACP; La Macchia memo for Cooley, November 16, 1942, CLCF, folder "November 1942," box 6, RG 60, NACP.

8. Anonymous State Department official's notes titled "Legacy of the Latin American Internees: A Few Facts and a Little Law," June 30, 1946, CLCF, folder "February-August 1946," box 7, RG 60, NACP.

9. Japanese internee occupations, Fort Sill, Oklahoma, folder "Sill 1942," box 190, SWPD, RG 59, NACP; "FBI Apprehensions," "Apprehensions of German Americans, December 7, 1941, to June 30, 1945," and Kelly to Vulliet, August 9, 1948, folder "Statistics," box 70, SWPD, RG 59, NACP; Alien Information Bureau, "Enemy Aliens Apprehended in U.S. by FBI," PMG, box 1, RG 389, NACP; "Statistics," PMG, box 10, RG 389, NACP; Hoover to Biddle, November 3, 1943, CLCF, folder "August 1943," box 6, RG 60, NACP. Some "7,000 Germans and Italians living near sensitive facilities on the West Coast were moved inland." Perrett, *Days of Sadness*, 218. Another estimates "10,000 Italian aliens had to move from prohibited areas in California during February and March 1942." Scherini, "When Italian Americans were 'Enemy Aliens,'" 19. Daniels notes 1,100 Hawaiian Japanese relocatees. Daniels, *Concentration Camps USA*, 104.

10. INS, U.S. Department of Justice, 16 mm color/B&W film, *Alien Enemy Detention Facility*, Crystal City, Texas, with introduction ca. 1949, camp ca. 1944-45, Accession Number N3-85-86-1, NACP [hereafter cited as INS, *Alien Enemy Detention Facility*]; Baker, *American and Japanese Relocation*, 62; Mangione, *An Ethnic at Large*, 329.

11. "Memo to Harrison," Hoover to Harrison regarding a letter received from Hoey, October 21, 1942, Long to Biddle, October 26, 1942, and Hoover to Col. Bryan, Chief, Aliens Division, PMG, October 21, 1942, CLCF, folder "October 1942," box 6, RG 60, NACP. Economic hardship was widespread among internee families. Long wrote Biddle that the only solution for families who had endured many months of separation in distress was joint internment. Harrison told Hoover that wives and

children of internees were "frequently embittered" and had "extreme difficulty" finding "adequate relief facilities in their communities." Harrison to Hoover, October 14, 1942, CLCF, folder "October 1942," box 6, RG 60, NACP.

12. Christgau, *"Enemies,"* 7–47; Peters to Fraser and INS, September 22, 1942, CLCF, folder "September 1942," and Fraser to Ennis, October 3, 1942, CLCF, folder "October 1942," box 6, RG 60, NACP.

13. "Figures of Alien Detainees," January 7, 1942, folder "Number of Enemy Aliens in Custody—1942," box 190, SWPD, RG 59, NACP; untitled report from Col. Cowles to Col. Harloe, G-4, March 4, 1942, "Report of housing facilities for enemy aliens evacuated from West Coast," March 7, 1942, and "Report of the Eighth Corps Area Available Housing Facilities for Enemy Aliens," March 12, 1942, Subject File 1942–'46, Entry 461, folder "Second Report on Housing Facilities," box 2696, RG 389, NACP.

14. "Statistical Reports," June 1, 1942, and "Recurring Statistics," June 6, 1942, HF, War Dept. #439A, PMG, box 10, RG 389, NACP; Captain Edwards to Chief, Aliens Division, May 19, 1942, folder "Estimated Number of Internees at the end of 1942," Subject File 1942–'46, Entry 461, "Evacuation Reports from Corps Area Commanders on Housing Facilities," box 2589, RG 389, NACP; "Interned Enemy Aliens in Custody," July 20, 1942, folder "Detained List: Germans, Italians, Japanese," box 190, and White to Lafoon and Bingham, January 28 and 30, 1946, folder "Statistics," box 70, SWPD, RG 59, NACP; U.S. Department of State, *Report of the Delegation*, 13. Other Army internment camps included Angel Island, Fort Meade, Griffith Park, and Camps Forrest, Livingston, and McCoy.

15. INS detention facilities held alien enemies awaiting hearings. Immigration Stations were used before the United States entered the war, while the INS created Alien Detention Stations afterward. The INS ran several dozen camps and facilities. Miller to Bernard Gufler, November 5, 1942, folder "INS 1942," box 186, SWPD, RG 59, NACP.

16. The 31,275 figure includes those from abroad, volunteers who joined the "internee head of the family," or those pressured, threatened, or forced to "repatriate voluntarily." "FBI Apprehensions, December 7, 1941, to June 30, 1945," and Kelly to Vulliet, August 9, 1948, folder "Statistics," box 70, SWPD, RG 59, NACP.

17. INS, "Information concerning the INS Internment Camp at Crystal City, Texas," and "Historical Narrative of the Crystal City Internment Camp," September 11, 1945, folder "Crystal City," box 19, SWPD, RG 59, NACP; INS, *Alien Enemy Detention Facility*; Mangione, *An Ethnic at Large*, 331; Russell, *The Train to Crystal City*, 54–57. See also https://www.gaic.info/wp-content/uploads/2019/09/ORourke-C.C.-Narrative.smaller.pdf . As the Collear family arrived, a warm front arrived and afternoon temperatures in January rose into the mid-nineties. Collear's daughter Christine, much like the author's father, John (a child internee), remembered the heat and the rattlesnakes. O'Rourke was Dr. Amy Stannard's assistant at Seagoville before taking charge at Crystal City.

18. INS, "Historical Narrative of the Crystal City Internment Camp," 1–5; INS, *Alien Enemy Detention Facility*; Collaer to O'Rourke, January 19, 1945, folder "Crystal City," box 19, SWPD, RG 59, NACP.

19. INS, "Historical Narrative of the Crystal City Internment Camp," 6–10.

20. INS, "Historical Narrative of the Crystal City Internment Camp," 6–8; Department of Justice, INS, Detention Reports: August 31, October 31, December 31, 1945, and February 28, 1946, folder "Statistics," box 70, SWPD, RG 59, NACP; Detention Reports: June 30, September 30, November 30, 1945, and May 31, 1946, Alien Information Bureau, Alien Civilian Internees during WWII, 1941–1946, #466J, folder "Detention Reports," PMG, box 2, RG 389, NACP. Krammer mentions that 1,200 Japanese (presumably all from Crystal City) were repatriated to Japan on December 3, 1945 (*Undue Process*, 110). Most of the Japanese repatriates were renunciants who left Tule Lake for Japan during 1946.

21. Recollections of John A. Schmitz (the author's father), who was interned with his parents and siblings in Crystal City from July 1943 to July 1946; Mangione, *An Ethnic at Large*, 332–33.

22. "Crystal City Civilian Internment Camp," March 10, 1944, folder "Crystal City," box 19, SWPD, RG 59, NACP. Officials tried to prepare children for postwar life. For those parents who "contemplated remaining," the supervisor of education agreed to "an official school open to enrollment by any child who desired to continue or begin the American education" ("Crystal City"). Some were arrested, Mangione writes, because they had close ties with their native countries, were members of pro-Axis organizations, had not understood alien enemy regulations, or had opposed American intervention in the war (*An Ethnic at Large*, 321).

23. INS, "Historical Narrative of the Crystal City Internment Camp," 32–33.

24. Baker, *American and Japanese Relocation*, 93–94, 236; INS, "Historical Narrative of the Crystal City Internment Camp," 30–31.

25. INS, "History of the Santa Fe Internment Camp," 28–29, August 9, 1945, folder "Santa Fe," box 20, SWPD, RG 59, NACP; INS, "Historical Narrative of the Crystal City Internment Camp," 30–31.

26. INS, "History of the Santa Fe Internment Camp," 36.

27. INS, "Historical Narrative of the Crystal City Internment Camp," 4.

28. Proclamation, "Executive Order 9066," *Federal Register* (February 25, 1942) vol. 7, no. 38, p. 1407; Strictly Confidential: "Report on meeting with Governors and officials Regarding relocation of Japanese, Salt Lake City, Utah," April 7, 1942, folder "WRA, January–June 1942," box 19, SWPD, RG 59, NACP. See also Daniels, *Prisoners without Trial*, 65–87. Executive Order 9066 authorized the evacuation of all persons of Japanese ancestry from the West Coast, but the military had to find temporary assembly centers to house the evacuees until the completion of relocation centers. Beginning May 26, 1942, some 500 evacuees a day moved from the assembly to the relocation centers. Construction delays and the lack of supplies dragged on over a five-month period and transfers lasted until October 30, 1942. For regulations governing relocatee behavior, see Part 35 of the WCCA Operations Manual. See http://www.lib.washington.edu/exhibits/harmony/Documents/wcca.html.

29. Question 27 asked, "Are you willing to serve in the armed forces of the United States on combat duty, wherever ordered?" Question 28 asked, "Will you swear unqualified allegiance to the United States of American and faithfully defend the

United States form any or all attack by foreign or domestic forces, and foreswear any form of allegiance to the Japanese emperor, to any other foreign government, power, or organization?" Daniels, *Prisoners without Trial*, 68–70.

30. "WRA and Japanese Relocation Centers: Summary," August 2, 1946, box 84, FBI HQ Files, RG 65, NACP; FBI memo "WRA—Riots, Strikes, and Disturbances in Japanese Relocation Centers" (n.d., covers events through April 1943), section 9, box 83, FBI HQ Files, RG 65, NACP; letters and correspondences by Oroville residents are in "Postcards to President Roosevelt," June 1943, CLCF, folder "May–August 1943," box 6, RG 60, NACP; "Governor Warren Hits Release of Japs," *PM*, June 22, 1943; "200 Out of 110,000 West Coast Japs Now Released," *Washington Times-Herald*, December 19, 1942; Daniels, *Prisoners without Trial*, 74–75; "WRA Extremes in Coddling Nips Revealed," *Los Angeles Examiner*, June 21, 1943. Among dozens of well-publicized incidents, including riots and deaths (especially from the summer of 1942 to the summer of 1943), was the Manzanar uprising, which occurred on the first anniversary of Pearl Harbor. Ralph Ingersoll, former editor for the *New Yorker* (1925–30), *Fortune* (1930–35), and *Time* (1936–39), founded *PM* and first published it on June 18, 1940, as an alternative to the generally conservative New York newspapers. *PM* was anti-fascist and pro-Roosevelt.

31. Letters to President Roosevelt, December 1942, CLCF, "December 1942," box 6, RG 60, NACP.

32. James Chinn, "Jap Spies Released from Camps to Take Jobs in U.S., Dies Says: Among 1,000 Freed Each Week House Group Declares," *Evening Star* (Washington DC), May 29, 1943. The following day, the *Star* revealed to its readers that the Dies Committee charged "hundreds of Japs released had been trained in espionage at a school operated by the Imperialistic Black Dragon Society in Tokyo." "FBI Disclaims Blame for Release of Jap 'Spies' from Camps: Dies Committee Charges Many were Trained in Tokyo for Sabotage," *Evening Star*, May 30, 1943. "Majority Opinion at Jap Hearing—Keep Them Out after War: Many Testify at State Senate Committee Probe," *Watsonville Register*, July 9, 1943; "Release Not Advisable," *Palo Alto Times*, June 7, 1943. Newspapers nationwide echoed Dies Committee chief investigator Robert Stripling's warning that Japanese were released at "1,000 a week to run willy-nilly all over the country."

33. Elmer G. Still, City Clerk, City of Livermore, California, to FBI (referred to and answered by Hoover), November 2, 1943, SWPU, box 7, RG 60, NACP.

34. G. G. Orcutt to Hoover, November 19, 1943, section 11, box 83, FBI HQ Files, RG 65, NACP; "Jap Internees Cached Food for Invaders, Dies Group Told: Raised Own Ensign and Defied Guards in Poston Camp," *Washington Star*, June 11, 1943; Edna Deatrick to Hoover, November 18, 1943, and Edna Hesting to War Dept., December 1, 1943, section 11, box 83, FBI HQ Files, RG 65, NACP. Ordinary citizens wrote countless letters and postcards to various officials at all levels of government and many of these can be found in section 11 of box 83, FBI HQ Files, among other archival sources cited in the endnotes. Nearly all correspondences by citizens were handwritten, and some names are missing or illegible. The government replied to some of these persons, but for various reasons (not the least of which was the sheer

volume of mail from the West Coast and throughout the nation) could not and did not respond to so many who wrote.

35. Geo P. Porter, State Treasurer, Montana, to Tom Clark, Attorney General, December 20, 1945, CLCF, folder "November 1945–February 1946," box 7, RG 60, NACP. See Mangione, *An Ethnic at Large*, 337–42, for the incidents at the Santa Fe camp. Mangione met with many Japanese internees and noted that "there was anguish and anxiety in nearly every man" (339).

36. Internees Kaercher, Flor, and Maack to O'Rourke and O'Rourke to internees, April 10–11, 1945, folder "Crystal City," box 19; Hoyt to Fitch, repatriation of German internees at Fort Lincoln, January 13, 1945, box 100; Fitch to W. F. Kelly, November 17, 1944, and Fitch to Lee Seward, Ft. Stanton, December 30, 1944, folder "German Exchange Arrangements," box 100, all in SWPD, RG 59, NACP; Stout to Clark, August 13, 1945, CLCF, folder "May–August 1945," box 7, RG 60, NACP; "Memo for the Attorney General, Re: Italian Parolees," Wechsler to Biddle, May 26 and June 1, 1945, CLCF, folder "May–August 1945," box 7, RG 60, NACP. Most repatriates received a "light frisk" for "concealed contraband articles." Some, however, endured a "strip search."

37. Germany and Japan at times complained about the way the U.S. government had "exerted pressure" on Central and South American governments which then removed thousands from their homes, causing loss of property and the breakup of families. State Department Memo, "Treatment given American citizens in Japan," May 11, 1944, folder "Treatment of Americans in Japan, January–August 1944"; Memo of Conversation between Long and Spanish Ambassador Cardenas: "Complaints of Japanese interned in Camps Missoula and Bismarck," June 16, 1942; and Report: "Alleged Mistreatment of Nipponese Nationals Interned in the United States" to J. M. Wainwright, February 27, 1943, folder "Treatment of Americans in Japan, 1942–43," all in box 89, SWPD, RG 59, NACP.

38. State Department Memo: "Treatment given American citizens in Japan," May 11, 1944, folder "Treatment of Americans in Japan, January–August 1944"; Hull to Stimson, regarding alleged mistreatment of internees, November 27, 1942; Memo: "Japanese protests alleging mistreatment of Japanese subjects in United States and American protests regarding mistreatment of American nationals in Japan and Japanese-controlled territories" to Keeley, November 28, 1942; and "Alleged Mistreatment of Nipponese Interned in U.S.," February 27, 1943, folder "Treatment of Americans in Japan, 1942–43," all in box 89, SWPD, RG 59, NACP; Hull to American Legation, Bern, January 7, 1942, SDCF, 1910–49, Class 8, Internal Affairs of State, box 2819, RG 59, NACP. U.S. officials desired a liberal enemy alien policy and feared any abuse would prompt Axis retaliation against American nationals. Hull clearly articulated such sentiment shortly after the U.S. entered the war in a letter to the German government. (Hull to American Legation, Bern, January 7, 1942.) Hull indicated the same to Biddle and suggested avoiding using jails to confine civilian enemy aliens because once brought to the attention of enemy governments they would "seize the opportunity to apply retaliatory measures to American nationals." There are also numerous letters to this effect in boxes 15, 89, 168, 182, and 186, SWPD, RG 59, NACP. See also Fox, *America's Invisible Gulag*, 9, 315–16n36.

39. State Department to Mr. MacDougall, "P/W Americans in Japan, 1941–42," box 89, SWPD, RG 59, NACP. The exact date of the letter is unknown, though most likely early to mid-1942 given its location relative to other dated documents in the file. By the end of February 1942, Japan agreed to apply the terms of the Geneva Convention to civilians too.

40. Long to Bard, August 11, 1942, folder "Americans in Japan," box 89, SWPD, RG 59, NACP; Rising to State Department, February 24, and Long to Rising, February 26, 1942, folder "C/I W/W Individual Inquiries," box 99, SWPD, RG 59, NACP.

41. "Long Island Gets Alien Detention Pen: Concentration Camp Nearing Completion on Upton Grounds," *Brooklyn Daily Eagle*, October 18, 1941; Memo of phone conversation between Kelly and Clattenburg, Subject: Publicity Regarding Camp Upton, October 22, 1941, folder "Alien Legislation," box 98, SWPD, RG 59, NACP; Hull to American Legation, Bern, October 28, 1941, folder "Miscellaneous," box 15, SWPD, RG 59, NACP; Hull to American Legation, Bern, January 7, 1942, folder "Exchanges with Japanese," box 168, SWPD, RG 59, NACP; Hull to American Legation, Bern, January 7, 1942, SDCF, 1910–49, Class 8, Internal Affairs of State, box 2819, RG 59, NACP; and Hull to American Legation, Bern, January 27, 1944, folder "Third Exchange with Japanese," box 193, SWPD, RG 59, NACP. The last source contains a memorandum from Hull followed by a fairly detailed document titled "Outline of Negotiations for Exchange of American Civilians in Japanese Hands," covering the period from December 13, 1941, to March 3, 1944. On June 9, 1942, evidence of alleged "mental torture and physical violence" inflicted upon an American national, James Walker Brown, reached Breckinridge Long. The U.S. government emphatically protested the "cruel treatment" by the German government and "expected to be informed that the German government has taken prompt and adequate punitive measures against the guilty persons." Harrison to Long, January 25, 1943, and Tait to Hull, regarding "Protest treatment of James W. Brown," March 16, 1943, folder "Civilian Internees—Protests," box 9, and January 7, 1942, folder "Exchanges with Japanese," box 168, SWPD, RG 59, NACP.

42. "Enemy Aliens in U.S., General," Instruction No. 58, Schofield to INS concerning the treatment of alien enemy detainees, April 28, 1942, "To and from Justice," pp. 1–10, box 129, SWPD, RG 59, NACP [hereafter cited as "Enemy Aliens in U.S."].

43. "Enemy Aliens in U.S.," 5.

44. POW Manual CPC: "Regulations Governing Censorship and Disposition of Interned and Detained Civilian Mail," June 14, 1944, box 124 SWPD, RG 59, NACP; "Stamp collection of Tom Boden seized from his interned father, Carl Boden," Clark to Fitch, May 14, 1943, and Fitch to Franklin, State Department, regarding disposal of personal letters of Mr. Tamon Mayeda, former director of the Japan institute in New York, December 23, 1942, folder "Articles seized by Customs," box 170, SWPD, RG 59, NACP.

45. "Treatment of Enemy Alien Property," December 26, 1941, folder "Enemy Alien Property in the U.S.—August 1941–October 1942"; Crowley to Hull, March 9, 1943, folder "Enemy Alien Property in the U.S."; and State Department memo, "Treatment of Property Belonging to German Nationals," April 14, 1943, folder "Property of

Alien Enemies in U.S.," all in box 181, SWPD, RG 59, NACP; "Enemy Aliens in U.S.," 6–7. Enemy alien assets were frozen under the provisions of Executive Order 8389.

46. INS, "Historical Narrative of the Crystal City Internment Camp," 24; "Enemy Aliens in U.S.," 8–9; Baker, *American and Japanese Relocation*, 95.

47. "Ellis Island, New York," W. Ferrett, International Red Cross, to Philip Forman, Commander, Ellis Island Internment Facility, September 4, 1945, folder "To and from Justice, Re: Enemy Aliens," box 129, SWPD, RG 59, NACP.

48. "Down Memory Lane," *Crystal City Times*, January 2, 1946, folder "Crystal City," box 19, SWPD, RG 59, NACP.

49. "New Year's Eve," *The Latrine*, January 1, 1943, folder "Camp Forrest," box 27, SWPD, RG 59, NACP.

50. Kelly to Vulliet, August 9, 1948, folder "Statistics," box 70, SWPD, RG 59, NACP; Rothstein to Senator Lucas, May 8, 1947, CLCF, folder "August 1946–June 1947" box 7, RG 60, NACP; "Legacy of the Latin American Internees: A Few Facts and a Little Law," June 30, 1946, CLCF, folder "February–August 1946," box 7, RG 60, NACP; Neubacher to Kelly, November 26, 1945, CLCF, folder "November 1945–February 1946," box 7, RG 60, NACP.

51. Martin Hoisl to Senator Raymond E. Baldwin, January 20, 1947, folder "August 1946–June 1947," box 7, RG 60, NACP.

52. Elizabeth Guldemont to Senator Raymond E. Baldwin, January 17, 1947, folder "August 1946–June 1947," box 7, RG 60, NACP.

53. Shaughnessy to Rothstein, May 6, 1947, Rothstein to Lucas, May 8, 1947, Steiner to Cooley, March 6, 1947, Cooley to Steiner, March 19, 1947, and Lavery to Cooley, September 20, 1946, folder "August 1946–June 1947"; Solicitor to Attorney General, August 11, 1948, folder "August 1948"; Silverberg to Solicitor General, Re: German Alien Enemies, April 28, 1949, folder "June 1949"; and Rothstein to Hutchinson, June 29, 1949, CLCF, folder "June 1949," all in box 7, RG 60, NACP; INS, Detention Reports: August 1945–February 1946, folder "Statistics," box 70, SWPD, RG 59, NACP; Detention Reports: June 1945–May 1946, folder "Detention Reports," PMG, box 2, RG 389, NACP.

54. Masaoka to Clark and President Truman, March 20, 1947 (answered by Cooley, director, AECU), CLCF, folder "August 1946–June 1947," box 7, RG 60, NACP; INS, Detention Reports: Period Ending February 28, 1946, folder "Statistics," box 70, SWPD, RG 59, NACP; Memo for Hoover, Re: Release of Japanese by WRA, April 13, 1944, section 12, box 83, FBI HQ Files, RG 65, NACP; Daniels, *Prisoners without Trial*, 72, 86.

Conclusion

1. Cervantes, *Don Quixote*, 42.

BIBLIOGRAPHY

Archives and Manuscripts

Franklin Delano Roosevelt Library, Hyde Park NY
    Biddle, Francis. Papers.
Library of Congress, Manuscript Division, Washington DC
    Hull, Cordell. Papers.
    Long, Breckinridge. Papers.
National Archives, College Park MD
    RG 59, General Records of the Department of State
        Central Files, 1910–49
            Decimal Files, 1940-44, Civilian Prisoners
            Special War Problems Division, Subject Files, 1939–54
    RG 60, General Records of the Department of Justice
        Alien Enemy Control Unit-Closed Legal Case Files
        Alien Property Unit
        Special War Policies Unit
    RG 65, Records of the Federal Bureau of Investigation
    RG 80, General Records of the Department of the Navy
    RG 131, Records of the Office of Alien Property
    RG 210, Records of the War Relocation Authority
    RG 220, Records of Temporary Committees, Commissions, and Boards
        Records of the Commission on Wartime Relocation and Interment of Civilians
    RG 389, Records of the Office of the Provost Marshal General
        Records of the Information Branch, Alien Enemy Information Bureau
        Records of the Legal Office
National Archives, Washington DC
    RG 85, Records of the Immigration and Naturalization Service
    RG 107, Records of the Office of the Secretary of War

Government Documents

U.S. Commission on Wartime Relocation and Internment of Civilians. *Papers of the U.S. Commission on Wartime Relocation and Internment of Civilians.* Microfilm edition. Edited by Ralph Boehm. Frederick MD: University Publications of America, 1983.

U.S. Congress. House. *Fourth Interim Report of the Select Committee Investigating National Defense Migration.* 77th Cong., 2nd sess., House Report No. 2124, May 19, 1942.

———. *Report of the Select Committee Investigating National Defense Migration: Preliminary Report and Recommendations on Problems of Evacuation of Citizens and Aliens from Military Areas.* 77th Cong., 2nd sess., House Report No. 1911, March 19, 1942.

U.S. Congress. House. Special Committee on Un-American Activities. *Investigation of Nazi and Other Propaganda.* 74th Cong., 1st sess., House Report No. 878, February 15, 1935.

———. *Special Report on Subversive Activities Aimed at Destroying Our Representative Form of Government.* 77th Cong., 2nd sess. House Report No. 2748, January 2, 1943.

U.S. Congress. House. Special Committee to Investigate the National Security League. *Hearings.* 65th Cong., 3rd sess., 1919. Washington DC, 1918.

U.S. Department of Commerce. Bureau of the Census. *Fifteenth Census of the United States: 1930.*

———. *Sixteenth Census of the United States: 1940.*

———. *Statistical History of the United States from Colonial Times to the Present.*

U.S. Department of Defense. *The "Magic" Background of Pearl Harbor.* 8 vols. Washington DC, 1977.

U.S. Department of State. *Papers Relating to the Foreign Relations of the United States: Japan, 1931–1941.* Vol. 2. Washington DC, 1943.

U.S. Department of State. Emergency Advisory Committee for Political Defense. *Report of the Delegation of the Emergency Advisory Committee for Political Defense Which Made the Consultative Visit to the United States of America.* June 16, 1944.

U.S. Office of War Information. *The Japanese Problem.* Washington DC, 1942.

———. *Pacific Coast Attitudes toward the Japanese Problem.* Washington DC, 1942.

———. *West Coast Reactions to the Japanese Situation.* Washington DC, 1942.

Western Defense Command and Fourth Army. *Final Report: Japanese Evacuation from the West Coast, 1942.* Washington DC, 1943.

Published Sources

Allen, Frederick Lewis. "Three Years of It." *Harper's,* December 1944, 1–13.

Anderson, Mark M., ed. *Hitler's Exiles: Personal Stories of the Flight from Nazi Germany to America.* New York: The New Press, 1998.

Anderson, William E. "Guests for the Duration: World War II and the Crew of the S.S. Columbus. An Historical Archaeological Investigation of the Fort Stanton Enemy Alien Internment Camp (1941–1945)." Master's thesis, Eastern New Mexico University, 1993.

Andrew, Christopher. *For the President's Eyes Only: Secret Intelligence and the American Presidency from Washington to Bush.* New York: HarperCollins, 1995.

Armor, John, and Peter Wright. *Manzanar*. New York: Times Books, 1988.
Artucio, Hugo Fernández. *The Nazi Underground in South America*. New York: Farrar & Rinehart, 1942.
Aswell, Edward J. "The Case of the Ten Spies." *Harper's*, June 1941, 1–21.
Bailey, Ronald H. *The Home Front: U.S.A.* Alexandria VA: Time-Life Books, 1978.
Baker, Lillian. *American and Japanese Relocation in World War II; Fact, Fiction, and Fallacy*. Medford OR: Webb Research Group, 1990.
Barman, Jean. *The West beyond the West: A History of British Columbia*. Toronto: University of Toronto Press, 1991.
Barone, Michael. *Our Country: The Shaping of America from Roosevelt to Reagan*. New York: The Free Press, 1990.
Barth, Allan. "Financing the Fifth Column." *New Republic*, December 2, 1940, 745–47.
Beals, Carleton. *The Coming Struggle for Latin America*. Philadelphia: Lippincott, 1938.
———. *Dawn over the Amazon*. New York: Duell, Sloan and Pearce, 1943.
———. "Swastika over the Andes: German Penetration in Latin America." *Harper's*, July 1938, 176–86.
———. "Totalitarian Inroads in Latin America." *Foreign Affairs* 17 (October 1938): 78–89.
Beers, Burton F. "Protection of American Citizens Abroad." In *Encyclopedia of American Foreign Policy*, edited by Alexander DeConde, 3:838. New York: Scribner, 1978.
Bennett, David H. *The Party of Fear: The American Far Right from Nativism to the Militia Movement*. Rev. ed. New York: Vintage Books, 1995.
Ben-Zvi, Abraham. "American Preconceptions and Policies toward Japan, 1940–1941: A Case Study in Misperception." *International Studies Quarterly* 19 (June 1975): 228–48.
Bevege, Margaret. *Behind Barbed Wire: Internment in Australia during World War II*. Queensland: University of Queensland Press, 1993.
Biddle, Francis. "American-Aliens and the Registration Act of 1940." *State Government*, August 1940.
———. "Axis Aliens in America—Statement of Policy Issued December 19, 1941." *Survey Graphic*, January 1942.
———. "Identification of Alien Enemies: Let Us Not Persecute These People." *Vital Speeches of the Day*, February 15, 1942, 279–80.
———. *In Brief Authority*. Garden City NY: Doubleday, 1962.
Blankenship, Anne M. *Christianity, Social Justice, and the Japanese American Incarceration during World War II*. Chapel Hill: University of North Carolina Press, 2016.
Blum, John M. *V Was for Victory: Politics and American Culture during World War II*. New York: Harcourt Brace Jovanovich, 1976.
Bolino, August C. *The Ellis Island Source Book*. New York: Kensington Historical Press, 1985.
Bowers, Claude G. *Chile through Embassy Windows, 1939–1953*. New York: Simon & Schuster, 1958.
Breuer, William. *Hitler's Undercover War: The Nazi Espionage Invasion of the U.S.A.* New York: St. Martin's Press, 1989.

Brinkley, David. *Washington Goes to War*. New York: Knopf, 1988.
Britt, George. *The Fifth Column Is Here*. New York: Wilfred Funk, 1940.
Buell, Thomas B. *Master of Seapower: A Biography of Fleet Admiral Ernest J. King*. Boston: Little, Brown, 1980.
Buhite, Russell D., and David W. Levy, eds. *FDR's Fireside Chats*. Norman: University of Oklahoma Press, 1992.
Bullitt, William C. "America Is in Danger: Our Fate Depends on What Each One of Us Does Now." *Vital Speeches of the Day*, August 1940, 683–86.
Canedy, Susan. *America's Nazis: A Democratic Dilemma; A History of the German American Bund*. Menlo Park CA: Markgraf, 1990.
Cannistraro, Philip V. Introduction to *Italian Fascist Activities in the United States*, by Gaetano Salvemini, vii–xli. New York: Center for Migration Studies, 1977.
Cantril, Hadley. "Opinion Trends in World War II: Some Guides to Interpretation." *Public Opinion Quarterly* 12, no. 1 (Spring 1948): 30–44.
———, ed. *Public Opinion, 1935–1946*. Princeton: Princeton University Press, 1951.
Carlson, John Roy. *Under Cover: My Four Years in the Nazi Underworld of America—The Amazing Revelation of How Axis Agents and Our Enemies within Are Now Plotting to Destroy the United States*. New York: Dutton, 1943.
Cervantes, Miguel. *Don Quixote*. Translated by Walter Starkie. New York: Mentor Books, 1957.
Chan, Sucheng. *Asian Americans: An Interpretive History*. New York: Twayne, 1991.
Chang, Gordon H., ed. *Morning Glory, Evening Shadow: Yamato Ichihashi and His Internment Writings, 1942–1945*. Stanford CA: Stanford University Press, 1997.
Chopas, Mary Elizabeth Basile. *Searching for Subversives: The Story of Italian Internment in Wartime America*. Chapel Hill: University of North Carolina Press, 2017.
Christgau, John. *"Enemies": World War II Alien Internment*. Ames: Iowa State University Press, 1985.
Collins, Frederick L. *The FBI in Peace and War*. New York: Putnam, 1943.
Commission on Wartime Relocation and Internment of Civilians Act, July 1, 1980.
Conn, Stetson, Rose C. Engleman, and Byron Fairchild. *The United States Army in World War II, the Western Hemisphere: Guarding the United States and Its Outposts*. Washington DC: Office of the Chief of Military History, Department of the Army, 1964.
Conn, Stetson, and Byron Fairchild. *The United States Army in World War II, the Western Hemisphere: The Framework of Hemisphere Defense*. Washington DC: Office of the Chief of Military History, Department of the Army, 1960.
Corbett, P. Scott. *Quiet Passages: The Exchange of Civilians between the United States and Japan during the Second World War*. Kent OH: Kent State University Press, 1987.
Costigan, Howard "The Plight of the Nisei." *Nation*, February 14, 1942, 184–85.
Croog, Charles F. "FBI Political Surveillance, 1939–1941." *The Historian* 54 (Spring 1992): 441–58.
Culley, John Joel. "A Troublesome Presence: World War II Internment of German Sailors in New Mexico." *Prologue: Quarterly of the National Archives and Records Administration* 28 (1996): 279–95.

Cushman, Robert E. *The Impact of War on America: Six Lectures by Members of the Faculty of Cornell University.* Vol. 1, *The Impact of War on the Constitution.* Ithaca: Cornell University Press, 1942.

Daniels, Roger. *Concentration Camps USA: Japanese Americans and World War II.* New York: Holt, Rinehart and Winston, 1972.

———. *The Decision to Relocate the Japanese Americans.* Edited by Harold M. Hyman. New York: Lippincott, 1975.

———. *Prisoners without Trial: Japanese Americans in World War II.* New York: Hill and Wang, 1993.

Daniels, Roger, Sandra C. Taylor, and Harry H. L. Kitano, eds. *Japanese Americans: From Relocation to Redress.* Rev. ed. Seattle: University of Washington Press, 1991.

De Grand, Alexander. *Italian Fascism: Its Origins and Development.* 2nd ed. Lincoln: University of Nebraska Press, 1989.

Diamond, Sander A. *The Nazi Movement in the United States, 1924–1941.* Ithaca: Cornell University Press, 1974.

Dies, Martin. "The Real Issue Is Plain: We Have Succeeded Despite Handicaps." *Vital Speeches of the Day*, August 1938, 731–34.

———. *The Trojan Horse in America.* New York: Dodd, Mead, 1940.

Diggins, John P. *Mussolini and Fascism: The View from America.* Princeton: Princeton University Press, 1972.

DiStasi, Lawrence, ed. *Una Storia Segreta: The Secret History of Italian American Evacuation and Internment during World War II.* Berkeley: Heyday Books, 2001.

Dower, John W. *War without Mercy: Race and Power in the Pacific War.* New York: Pantheon, 1986.

Earle, Edward Meade. *Against This Torrent.* Princeton: Princeton University Press, 1941.

Ennis, Edward J. "Federal Control Measures for Enemy Aliens." *The Police Yearbook*, 1943, 31–37.

———. "Government Control of Alien Enemies." *State Government* 15 (May 1942): 99–100, 112–13.

Farago, Ladislas. *German Psychological Warfare.* New York: Putnam, 1941.

Feeley, Francis. *A Strategy of Dominance: The History of an American Concentration Camp; Pomona, California.* New York: Brandywine Press, 1995.

Feis, Herbert. *The Road to Pearl Harbor: The Coming of the War between the United States and Japan.* Princeton: Princeton University Press, 1950.

Feldman, Jay. *Manufacturing Hysteria: A History of Scapegoating, Surveillance, and Secrecy in Modern America.* New York: Pantheon Books, 2011.

Fenwick, Charles G. *International Law.* 4th ed. New York: Meredith, 1965.

Fiset, Louis. *Imprisoned Apart: The World War II Correspondence of an Issei Couple.* Foreword by Roger Daniels. Seattle: University of Washington Press, 1997.

Fisher, Louis. *Nazi Saboteurs on Trial: A Military Tribunal and American Law.* Lawrence: University Press of Kansas, 2003.

Fox, Stephen. *America's Invisible Gulag: A Biography of German American Internment and Exclusion in World War II.* New York: Peter Lang, 2000.

———. *Fear Itself: Inside the FBI Roundup of German Americans during World War II*. New York: iUniverse, 2005.

———. *Homeland Insecurity: Aliens, Citizens, and the Challenge to American Civil Liberties in World War II*. New York: iUniverse, 2009.

———. *The Unknown Internment: An Oral History of the Relocation of Italian Americans during World War II*. Boston: Twayne, 1990.

Friedlander, Henry. *The Origins of Nazi Genocide: From Euthanasia to the Final Solution*. Chapel Hill: University of North Carolina Press, 1995.

Friedlander, Saul. *Prelude to Downfall: Hitler and the United States, 1939–1941*. New York: Knopf, 1967.

Friedman, Max Paul. *Nazis and Good Neighbors: The United States Campaign against the Germans of Latin America in World War II*. Cambridge: Cambridge University Press, 2003.

Friedrich, Carl J. "Foreign Language Radio and the War." *Common Ground* 3 (Autumn 1942): 65–72.

———. "The Poison in Our System." *Atlantic*, June 1941.

Frye, Alton. *Nazi Germany and the American Hemisphere, 1933–1941*. New Haven: Yale University Press, 1967.

Fulbrook, Mary, ed. *German History since 1800*. London: Arnold, Hodder Headline Group, 1997.

Fussell, Paul. *Wartime: Understanding and Behavior in the Second World War*. Oxford: Oxford University Press, 1989.

Gallup, George H., ed. *The Gallup Poll: Public Opinion, 1935–1971*. 3 vols. New York: Random House, 1972.

Gardiner, C. Harvey. *Pawns in a Triangle of Hate: The Peruvian Japanese and the United States*. Seattle: University of Washington Press, 1981.

Gellately, Robert. "The Gestapo and German Society: Political Denunciation in the Gestapo Case Files." *Journal of Modern History* 60 (December 1988): 654–94.

Gentry, Curt. *J. Edgar Hoover: The Man and the Secrets*. New York: Norton, 1991.

The German Reich and Americans of German Origin. New York: Oxford University Press, 1938.

Gilkey, Langdon. *Shantung Compound*. New York: Harper & Row, 1966.

Gillman, Peter, and Leni Gillman. *"Collar the Lot!" How Britain Interned and Expelled Its Wartime Refugees*. London: Quartet Books, 1980.

Girdner, Audrie, and Anne Loftis. *The Great Betrayal: The Evacuation of the Japanese Americans during World War II*. London: Macmillan, 1969.

Giudici, Ernesto. *Hitler conquista América*. Buenos Aires: Editorial Acento, 1938.

Goodwin, Doris Kearns. *No Ordinary Time—Franklin and Eleanor Roosevelt: The Home Front in World War II*. New York: Simon and Schuster, 1994.

Grodzins, Morton. *Americans Betrayed: Politics and Japanese Evacuation*. 1949. Chicago: University of Chicago Press, 1974.

Grzesinski, Albert. "Hitler's Branch Offices, U.S.A.: How Nazi Agents Are Plotting against the U.S. under U.S. Protection." *Reader's Digest*, December 1940, 28–32.

Gunther, John. *Inside Latin America*. New York: Harper & Brothers, 1941.

Haglund, David G. *Latin America and the Transformation of U.S. Strategic Thought, 1936–1940*. Albuquerque: University of New Mexico Press, 1984.
Hall, Melvin, and Walter Peck. "Wings for the Trojan Horse; German and Italian Airplanes over South America." *Foreign Affairs* 19 (January 1941): 347–69.
Hansen, Arthur A., ed. *Japanese American World War II Evacuation Oral History Project*, Part 1: Internees, Part 2: Administrators, Part 3: Analysts, Part 4: Resisters, Part 5: Guards and Townspeople. London: Meckler, 1991.
Harrison, Earl G. "Axis Aliens in an Emergency." *Survey Graphic* 30 (September 1941): 465–68.
———. "Civilian Internment–American Way." *Survey Graphic* 33 (May 1944): 229–33, 270.
———. "How State and Local Officials Can Assist in the Alien Registration Program." *State Government*, October 1940, 204–5.
Hart, Bradley. *Hitler's American Friends: The Third Reich's Supporters in the United States*. New York: St. Martin's Press, 2018.
Hatfield, Dianna. "Internment of Germans and German Americans during World War II: The Untold Story." *Society for German-American Studies Newsletter* 13, no. 3 (June 1993).
Hawgood, John A. *The Tragedy of German-America*. New York: Putnam, 1940.
Hershey, Amos S. *The Essentials of International Public Law and Organization*. Rev. ed. New York: Macmillan, 1927.
High, Stanley. "Japanese Saboteurs in Our Midst." *Reader's Digest*, January 1942, 11–15.
Hilton, Stanley E. *Hitler's Secret War in South America, 1939–1945: German Military Espionage and Allied Counterespionage in Brazil*. Baton Rouge: Louisiana State University Press, 1981.
Hitler, Adolf. *Mein Kampf*. Munich: Franz Eher, 1934.
Holian, Timothy J. *The German-Americans and World War II: An Ethnic Experience*. New York: Peter Lang, 1996.
Hoover, J. Edgar. "Alien Enemy Control." *Iowa Law Review* 29 (March 1944): 396–408.
———. "War Begins at Home." *American Magazine*, September 1941.
Houston, J. W. *Farewell to Manzanar*. New York: Houghton Mifflin, 1973.
Howard, John. *Concentration Camps on the Home Front: Japanese Americans in the House of Jim Crow*. Chicago: University of Chicago Press, 2008.
Hull, Cordell. *The Memoirs of Cordell Hull*. 2 vols. New York: Macmillan, 1948.
Humphreys, R. A. *Latin America and the Second World War*. Vol. 1, *1939–1942*. London: Athlone/Humanities Press, 1982.
Hunt, Michael H. *The Making of a Special Relationship: The United States and China to 1914*. New York: Columbia University Press, 1983.
An Intelligence Officer [Kenneth D. Ringle]. "The Japanese in America: The Problem and the Solution." *Harper's*, October 1942.
Iorizzo, Luciano J., and Salvatore Mondello. *The Italian Americans*. Boston: Twayne, 1980.
Iriye, Akira. *Power and Culture: The Japanese-American War, 1941–1945*. Cambridge: Harvard University Press, 1981.

Irons, Peter. *Justice at War: The Story of the Japanese American Internment Cases.* Oxford: Oxford University Press, 1983.

Israel, Fred L., ed. *The War Diary of Breckinridge Long: Selections from the Years 1939-1944.* Lincoln: University of Nebraska Press, 1966.

Jacobs, Arthur D. *The Prison Called Hohenasperg: An American Boy Betrayed by His Government during World War II.* Universal Publishers/uPUBLISH.com, 1999.

Jacobs, Arthur D., and Joseph E. Fallon. *The World War Two Experience.* Vol. 4 of *German-Americans in the World Wars,* edited by Don Heinrich Tolzmann. Munich: K. G. Saur, 1995.

Jeffries, John W. *Wartime America: The World War II Home Front.* Chicago: Ivan R. Dee, 1996.

Katz, Friedrich. *The Secret War in Mexico.* Chicago: University of Chicago Press, 1981.

Kempner, Robert M. W. "The Enemy Alien Problem in the Present War." *American Journal of International Law* 34 (July 1940): 443-58.

Kennedy, David M. *The American People in World War II. Part Two, Freedom from Fear.* Oxford: Oxford University Press, 1999.

———. *Over Here: The First World War and American Society.* Oxford: Oxford University Press, 1980.

Kennett, Lee. *For the Duration . . . The United States Goes to War: Pearl Harbor-1942.* New York: Scribner, 1985.

Kimball, Warren F. *The Juggler: Franklin Roosevelt as Wartime Statesman.* Princeton: Princeton University Press, 1991.

Kirchwey, Freda. "The Fifth Column." *Nation,* April 27, 1940, 529-30.

Krammer, Arnold. *Undue Process: The Untold Story of America's German Alien Internees.* New York: Rowman & Littlefield, 1997.

Kraut, Alan M. *The Huddled Masses: The Immigrant in American Society, 1880-1921.* Arlington Heights IL: Harlan Davidson, 1982.

Kuhn, Fritz. *Awake and Act! Aims and Purposes of the German American Bund: An Appeal to all Americans of German Stock.* New York: Deutscher Weckruf und Beobachter, 1936.

Kumamoto, Bob. "The Search for Spies: American Counterintelligence and the Japanese American Community, 1931-1942." *Amerasia Journal* 6 (1979): 45-75.

LaFeber, Walter *Inevitable Revolutions: The United States in Central America.* New York: Norton, 1993.

Lamm, Hans. "I Am an Enemy Alien." *Common Ground* 2 (Summer 1942): 15-18.

Landau, Henry. *The Enemy Within: The Inside Story of German Sabotage in America.* New York: Putnam, 1937.

Lasker, Loula D. "Friends or Enemies?" *Survey Graphic,* June 1942.

Lea, Homer. *The Valor of Ignorance.* New York: Harper, 1909.

Lee, James Ward, ed. *1941: Texas Goes to War.* Denton: University of North Texas Press, 1991.

Lees, Lorraine. "National Security and Ethnicity: Contrasting Views during World War II." *Diplomatic History* 11 (Spring 1987): 113-25.

Leigh, Michael. *Mobilizing Consent: Public Opinion and American Foreign Policy, 1937–1947*. Westport: Greenwood Press, 1976.
Lengyel, Emil. "Germany's Fifth Column." *Nation*, October 14, 1939, 404–6.
Leuchtenburg, William E. *Franklin D. Roosevelt and the New Deal, 1932–1940*. New York: Harper and Row, 1963.
Lewis, Frederick. "Japanese Spies and What They Did." *Liberty*, February 7, 1942, 12–15.
Lichtman, Allan J., and Ken DeCell. *The Thirteen Keys to the Presidency*. New York: Madison Books, 1990.
Lingeman, Richard R. *Don't You Know There's a War On? The American Home Front, 1941–1945*. New York: Putnam, 1970.
Lotchin, Roger W. *Japanese American Relocation in World War II: A Reconsideration*. Cambridge: Cambridge University Press, 2018.
Luebke, Frederick C. *Bonds of Loyalty: German-Americans and World War I*. DeKalb: Northern Illinois University Press, 1974.
MacDonnell, Francis. *Insidious Foes: The Axis Fifth Column and the American Home Front*. New York: Oxford University Press, 1995.
Mangione, Jerre. *An Ethnic at Large: A Memoir of America in the Thirties and Forties*. New York: Putnam, 1978.
McWilliams, Carey. "Japanese Out of California." *New Republic*, April 6, 1942.
———. "Moving the West Coast Japanese." *Harper's*, September 1942, 359–69.
Meissner, Carlos. "A Resilient Elite: German Costa Ricans and the Second World War." PhD diss., University of York, 2010.
Miyamoto, Shotaro Frank. "Social Solidarity among the Japanese in Seattle." *University of Washington Publications in the Social Sciences* 11, no. 2 (December 1939): 57–130.
Moss, Norman. *Nineteen Weeks: America, Britain, and the Fateful Summer of 1940*. New York: Houghton Mifflin, 2003.
Muller, Eric L. *American Inquisition: The Hunt for Japanese American Disloyalty in World War II*. Chapel Hill: University of North Carolina Press, 2007.
Nagler, Jörg. "Internment of German Enemy Aliens in the United States during the First and Second World Wars." In *Alien Justice: Wartime Internment in Australia and North America*, edited by Kay and Roger Daniels, 66–79. Queensland: University of Queensland Press, 2000.
Newton, Ronald C. *The "Nazi Menace" in Argentina, 1931–1947*. Stanford: Stanford University Press, 1992.
———. "The United States, the German-Argentines, and the Myth of the Fourth Reich, 1943–47." *Hispanic American Historical Review* 64 (February 1984): 81–103.
Nishimoto, Richard S. *Inside an American Concentration Camp: Japanese American Resistance at Poston, Arizona*. Edited by Lane Ryo Hirabayashi. Tucson: University of Arizona Press, 1995.
O'Connor, Richard. *The German-Americans: An Informal History*. Boston: Little, Brown, 1968.
Offner, Arnold A. *American Appeasement: United States Foreign Policy and Germany, 1933–1938*. Cambridge: Harvard University Press, 1969.

Ogden, August Raymond. *The Dies Committee: A Study of the Special House Committee for the Investigation of Un-American Activities, 1938–1944*. Washington DC: Catholic University of America Press, 1945.

O'Higgins, Harvey. *The German Whisper*. Washington DC: Committee on Public Information, 1918.

Okihiro, Gary Y. *Cane Fires: The Anti-Japanese Movement in Hawaii, 1865–1945*. Philadelphia: Temple University Press, 1991.

———. *Margins and Mainstreams: Asians in American History and Culture*. 2nd ed. Seattle: University of Washington Press, 1996.

———. *Whispered Silences: Japanese Americans and World War II*. Seattle: University of Washington Press, 1996.

Patterson, James T. *America in the Twentieth Century: A History*. 4th ed. Fort Worth: Harcourt Brace, 1994.

Perrett, Geoffrey. *Days of Sadness, Years of Triumph: The American People 1939–1945*. Baltimore: Penguin, 1973.

Personal Justice Denied. Report of the U.S. Commission on Wartime Relocation and Internment of Civilians (CWRIC). Seattle: University of Washington Press, 1997.

Polenberg, Richard. *War and Society: The United States, 1941–1945*. New York: Lippincott, 1972.

Pringle, Henry F. "Don't Believe a Word of It!" *Collier's*, January 17, 1942, 19.

Putlitz, Wolfgang zu. "Your German-American Neighbor and the Fifth Column." *Harper's*, February 1942, 322–28.

Rauschning, Hermann. *The Voice of Destruction*. New York: Putnam, 1940.

Riess, Curt. *Total Espionage*. New York: Putnam, 1941.

Riley, Karen Lea. "Schools behind Barbed Wire: A History of Schooling in the United States Department of Justice Internment Camp at Crystal City, Texas, during World War II, 1942–1946." PhD diss., University of Texas at Austin, 1996.

Rippley, La Vern J. "Ameliorated Americanization: The Effect of World War I on German-Americans in the 1920s." In *America and the Germans: An Assessment of a Three-Hundred-Year History*, edited by Frank Trommler and Joseph McVeigh, 2:217–31. Philadelphia: Philadelphia University Press, 1985.

———. *The German-Americans*. Boston: Twayne, 1976.

Robinson, Greg. *By Order of the President: FDR and the Internment of Japanese Americans*. Cambridge: Harvard University Press, 2001.

Rostow, Eugene V. "The Japanese American Cases—A Disaster." *Yale Law Journal* 54 (June 1945): 489–533.

———. "Our Worst Wartime Mistake." *Harper's*, September 1945, 193–201.

Rowe, James H., Jr. "The Alien Enemy Program—So Far." *Common Ground* 2 (Summer 1942): 19–24.

Russell, Jan Jarboe. *The Train to Crystal City: FDR's Secret Prisoner Exchange Program and America's Only Family Internment Camp during World War II*. New York: Scribner, 2015.

Salvemini, Gaetano. *Italian Fascist Activities in the United States*. Edited with an introduction by Philip V. Cannistraro. New York: Center for Migration Studies, 1977.

Saunders, Kay, and Roger Daniels, eds. *Alien Justice: Wartime Internment in Australia and North America*. Queensland: University of Queensland Press, 2000.
Sayers, Michael, and Albert E. Kahn. *Sabotage! The Secret War against America*. New York: Harper & Brothers, 1942.
Scherini, Rose D. "When Italian Americans Were 'Enemy Aliens.'" In *Una Storia Segreta: The Secret History of Italian American Evacuation and Internment during World War II*, edited by Lawrence DiStasi, 280–306. Berkeley: Heyday Books, 2001.
Scherman, David E., ed. *Life Goes to War: A Picture History of World War II*. New York: Time-Life Films, 1977.
Schmidt, Margaret [pseud.]. "I Married a Nazi." *Reader's Digest*, March 1940, 89–90.
Schmitz, David F. *The United States and Fascist Italy, 1922–1940*. Chapel Hill: University of North Carolina Press, 1988.
Schmitz, John E. "Democracy under Stress: The Internment of German-Americans in World War II." Master's thesis, North Carolina State University at Raleigh, 1993.
Schwarzenberger, Georg. *A Manual of International Law*. 5th ed. New York: Frederick A. Praeger, 1967.
Sheridan, Peter B. "The Internment of German and Italian Aliens Compared with the Internment of Japanese Aliens in the United States during World War II: A Brief History and Analysis." Staff Paper, Congressional Research Service, Library of Congress, November 24, 1980.
Shirer, William L. "The Poison Pen." *Atlantic*, May 1942, 548–52.
Smith, Arthur L. *The Deutschtum of Nazi Germany and the United States*. International Scholars Forum, No. 15. The Hague: M. Nijhoff, 1965.
Smith, Bradley. *The Shadow Warriors: O.S.S. and the Origins of the C.I.A.* New York: Basic Books, 1983.
Smith, Geoffrey S. "The Japanese-Canadians and World War II." In *Alien Justice: Wartime Internment in Australia and North America*, edited by Kay and Roger Daniels, 93–113. Queensland: University of Queensland Press, 2000.
Smith, Page. *Democracy on Trial: The Japanese American Evacuation and Relocation in World War II*. New York: Simon & Schuster, 1995.
Sondern, Frederic. "Hitler Looks to South America." *Reader's Digest*, August 1940, 47–50.
Sorrentino, Frank M. *Ideological Warfare: The FBI's Path toward Power*. Port Washington NY: Associated Faculty Press, 1985.
Sperry, Earl. *The Tentacles of the German Octopus in America*. New York: National Security League, 1918.
Spicer, Edward H., Asael T. Hansen, Katherine Luomala, and Marvin K. Opler. *Impounded People: Japanese-Americans in the Relocation Centers*. New York: University of Arizona Press, 1969.
Stent, Ronald. *A Bespattered Page: The Internment of His Majesty's "Most Loyal Enemy Aliens."* London: Andrew Deutsch, 1980.
Stokesbury, James L. *A Short History of World War I*. New York: William Morrow, 1981.
———. *A Short History of World War II*. New York: William Morrow, 1980.

Stoler, Mark A., and Melanie S. Gustafson, eds. *Major Problems in the History of World War II*. Boston: Houghton Mifflin, 2003.
Tateishi, John. *And Justice for All: An Oral History of the Japanese American Detention Camps*. With a Foreword by Roger Daniels. New York: Random House, 1984; Seattle: University of Washington Press, 1999.
Tejera, Adolfo. *Penetración Nazi en America Latina*. Montevideo: Editorial Nueva América, 1938.
tenBroek, Jacobus, Edward N. Barnhart, and Floyd W. Matson. *Prejudice, War and the Constitution: Causes and Consequences of the Evacuation of the Japanese Americans in World War II*. Berkeley: University of California Press, 1954.
Theoharis, Athan G. *The Boss: J. Edgar Hoover and the Great American Inquisition*. Philadelphia: Temple University Press, 1988.
———. *From the Secret Files of J. Edgar Hoover*. Chicago: Ivan R. Dee, 1991.
———. *Spying on Americans: Political Surveillance from Hoover to the Houston Plan*. New York: Temple University Press, 1978.
Thompson, Dorothy. "Nazi Foreign Missions: German Propaganda in the United States and the World." *Vital Speeches of the Day*, September 1937, 712–17.
Thompson, John A. "The Exaggeration of American Invulnerability: The Anatomy of a Tradition." *Diplomatic History* 16, no. 1 (Winter 1992): 23–43.
Thompson, Richard Austin. *The Yellow Peril, 1890–1924*. New York: Arno Press, 1978.
Tindall, George Brown, and David E. Shi. *America: A Narrative History*. Vol. 1. 4th ed. New York: Norton, 1996.
Trommler, Frank, and Joseph McVeigh, eds. *America and the Germans: An Assessment of a Three-Hundred-Year History*. Philadelphia: University of Philadelphia Press, 1985.
Tunney, Thomas J. *Throttled! The Detection of the German and Anarchist Bomb Plotters*. Boston: Small, Maynard, 1919.
Turkel, Studs. *"The Good War": An Oral History of World War II*. New York: Ballantine Books, 1984.
Turrou, Leon G. *Nazi Spies in America*. New York: Random House, 1939.
Uchida, Yoshiko. *Desert Exile: The Uprooting of a Japanese-American Family*. 3rd ed. Seattle: University of Washington Press, 1991.
Uno, Edison. "Crystal City Internment." *Outlook: Japanese-American Citizens League*, June 1975, 1–3.
Valtin, Jan. *Out of the Night*. Edinburgh: AK Press, 2004.
Von Rintelen, Franz. *The Dark Invader: Wartime Reminiscences of a German Naval Intelligence Officer*. New York: Penguin, 1933.
Walker, Richard. *E. R. Stettinius, Jr.* New York: Cooper Square, 1965.
Wattenberg, Ben J. *Statistical History of the United States: From Colonial Times to the Present*. New York: Basic Books, 1976.
Weber, Mark. "The Japanese Camps in California." *Journal of Historical Review* 2 (Spring 1981): 45–58.
Weglyn, Michi. *Years of Infamy: The Untold Story of America's Concentration Camps*. New York: Morrow Quill, 1976.

Weinberg, Gerhard L. *The Foreign Policy of Hitler's Germany: Diplomatic Revolution in Europe, 1933–1936*. Atlantic Highlands NJ: Humanities Press, 1994.

———. *The Foreign Policy of Hitler's Germany: Starting World War II, 1937–1939*. Atlantic Highlands NJ: Humanities Press, 1994.

———. *Germany, Hitler, and World War II: Essays in Modern German and World History*. Cambridge: Cambridge University Press, 1995.

———. *A World at Arms: A Global History of World War II*. Cambridge: Cambridge University Press, 1994.

Wilson, Theodore A., ed. *World War II: Readings on Critical Issues*. New York: Scribner, 1974.

Wilson, Woodrow. *The Public Papers of Woodrow Wilson*. Edited by Ray Stannard Baker and William E. Dodd. 6 vols. New York: Harper & Brothers, 1925–27.

Winkler, Alan M. *Home Front U.S.A.: America during World War II*. 2nd ed. Wheeling IL: Harlan Davidson, 2000.

———. *The Politics of Propaganda: The Office of War Information, 1942–1945*. New Haven: Yale University Press, 1978.

Wolfe, Henry C. "Hitler's 'Fifth Columns.'" *New Republic*, June 29, 1938, 206.

Wood, Bryce. *Dismantling the Good Neighbor Policy*. Austin: University of Texas Press, 1985.

———. *The Making of the Good Neighbor Policy*. New York: Columbia University Press, 1961.

INDEX

ABC list, 71, 315n22
Acadia, 220, 299n25, 329n5
Alaska, 33, 191, 267
Alien and Sedition Act (1918), *fig. 1*, 26
Alien and Sedition Acts (1798), 21
Alien Detention Stations, 341n15. *See also* immigration stations
Alien Employment Program (AEP), 177
alien enemies. *See* enemy aliens
Alien Enemy Act (1798), 21, 133
Alien Enemy Control Unit (AECU), Department of Justice, xxiii, 139, 201, 203, 207, 243, 286, 303n25, 320n62
Alien Enemy Detention Facility (INS Crystal City film documentary), 262
"alien enemy problem," xx, 80–81, 108, 110
alien enemy program, xxii, 201, 232, 308n44
Alien Property Custodian (APC), 280
alien registration, *fig. 3*, *fig. 4*, xx, xxi, xxiv, 78, 105, 107, 113, 157, 172, 242
Alien Registration (Smith) Act (1940), *fig. 4*, xx, 78, 106–8, 133, 192, 214, 326n37
Alien Registration Division, 78, 163, 166, 251
aliens: arrests of, xxii, xxiii, 1, 8, 32; and CDI, xviii, xx, 72; citizens informing FBI about, 59, 71; classification of, 107; Congress and, 64–65, 95–96, 97; definition of, 21; as disloyal, 30, 31, 33–35, 79; early treatment of, 16–17, 19–20, 108–9; FBI investigations of, xix, xx, 64–65, 71–73, 79–81; fear of, 25, 27, 54–55, 64, 90, 102; identification of, xx; internment preparation for, xxi, 16–17, 81, 108–9, 110–12; legislation against, 64–66; loyalty of, 27, 30, 58, 65, 78, 105, 118; media depiction of, 84, 96–97; reclassification as alien enemies or enemy aliens, xxii–xxiii, 293n1; registration of, *fig. 3*, *fig. 4*, xx, xxi, xxiv, 7, 105, 107, 113; state actions against, 67; as threat, 64, 71, 79, 81, 82, 87, 90, 105, 115; violence against, 77; WWI and, 19–21, 23, 32–33, 67. *See also* Biddle, Francis; Federal Bureau of Investigation (FBI); Great Britain; Hoover, J. Edgar; Immigration and Naturalization Service (INS)
American citizens: aiding and abetting Axis powers, 84, 190; arrests of, xxii, 128, 254, 311n18, 330n12; assistance to, and repatriation of, 48, 82, 97, 206, 208–9, 217, 226, 231, 233–34; Chinese and Japanese as, 15; and court challenge to evacuation, 198; and EO 9066, 3, 197; evacuation (removal) and, 175, 177, 187, 194, 196; as fifth columnists, 44, 46, 59, 60, 84, 190; Germans and Italians as, 148, 166; internment of, 260; investigations of, 73, 80, 203; Japanese as, 143, 266; and nativist or patriotic organizations, 15, 17, 25, 26, 29, 57, 81, 145, 182, 295n12, 296n27, 303n23; Nazi agents masquerading as, 42; reciprocity and treatment of, 109, 117, 231, 233–34, 236, 274–78
American Legion, 29, 57, 81, 145
American Nazis: deportations urged for, 42, 52; headlines about, 42, 51, 53, 299n21, 299n30, 299–300n31, 305–6n119; investigations of, xvii, xviii, xix, 10, 40–41, 44–47, 52, 54, 56–63, 71, 302n16; refugees against, 109, 148, 164; and sabotage, 155. *See also* Federal Bureau of Investigation (FBI); German American Bund; Hoover, J. Edgar; House Un-American Activities Committee (HUAC); Kuhn, Fritz Julius; McCormack-Dickstein Committee; Nazi Party

Angel Island, 75, 112, 341n14
anti-Asian movement: and Chinese, 15; and Japanese, 14–17
anti-fascists, 36, 38, 40, 53, 58, 204
anti-immigrant legislation and sentiment, 13, 16, 294n2
anti-Nazi refugees, 109, 148, 164
anti-Semitism. *See* Jews
Argentina, 88, 89, 126, 211, 214, 215
Army, U.S.: anticipating attack on East Coast, 130; and facilities (camps), 108, 109, 235, 258–59, 341n14; and G-2 (Intelligence), 9, 41, 87, 323n9; Hawaii and, 123, 189; and internment, xxii, 108–9, 123, 172, 200–202, 220–21, 249, 253, 339n1; and military necessity argument, 130, 149, 175; quartering male internees, 109; and removal (evacuation), 9, 147, 268–69; and restricted areas, 98, 172, 217; and West Coast, 9, 87, 98, 108–9, 130, 147, 149, 172, 175, 188, 217, 268–69, 339n1
"Arsenal of Democracy" speech, xxi, 77, 84, 90–91. *See also* fireside chats
assembly centers, *fig. 6*, xxvi, 259, 267, 317n36, 342n28. *See also* War Relocation Centers
assimilation (Americanization), 13, 33; of Germans, 18, 19, 22, 23, 25–26, 28–29, 34, 134, 148, 184–85; of Italians, 19, 35, 134, 148, 184; of Japanese, 124, 183, 185; racism and, 13, 14, 18, 27, 45, 60, 120, 127, 141, 185, 299n23
Auslandsorganisation (AO), xvii, 51, 58, 60
Australia, *fig. 3*, 20, 121, 236

Bannerman, R. L., 224, 234
barbed-wire disease, *fig. 12*, 254, 255
Bard, Ralph, 276
Battle of Britain, 119
Beals, Carleton, 212, 213
Belgium, invasion of, xx, 77, 208
Bendetsen, Karl R., 141, 149, 172–75, 177–78, 187–88, 251, 267, 323n9
Berle, Adolf A., 71, 83, 88, 117, 208, 214, 312n29
Biddle, Francis: and alien registration (identification), *fig. 4*, xxiv, 192; and alien regulations, 133, 134, 184; as attorney general, 78; concern for aliens and refugees, 113, 164–66, 250, 253, 257, 274, 313n10; criticism of, 142, 159, 175, 180–81, 272–73; and departmental cooperation, 175, 186; and FDR, 122, 164; fifth-column views, 54–55, 64; and Germans and Italians, 184, 195; and Hoover, xxvii, 79, 82, 203–4; and INS, 109–10; and internment, 171; and mass evacuation, 149, 317n43, 321n70, 325n25; Pearl Harbor and, 117, 189; and repatriation and exchange, 222–23, 224, 232, 233, 242; and Stimson, 149, 171; and West Coast versus East Coast policies, 195–96
Bismarck ND. *See* Fort Lincoln ND
Black Dragon society, 156, 270, 343n32
Black Tom, 24, 31, 296n23
Bohle, Ernst, 60
Bolivia, 88, 215, 216, 220
books, 105; best-selling, 154, 156–57; comic books (and characters), 153, 318n50, 319n52; textbooks, 102
Border Patrol, 182, 239, 261, 325n21
"bottom of the barrel," 9, 128, 223, 225, 242, 334n42, 336n60
Bowron, Fletcher, 131, 137, 144, 158, 180, 184, 188, 320n60, 321–22n1, 324n19
Brandt, George, 226
Brandt, Willie, 201
Brazil, 88–90, 93, 126, 213–15, 306n20
British Columbia, 126, 127
Britt, George, 53
Brown, James Walker, 345n41
Bullitt, William, 87–88
Bureau of Investigation, xviii, 16, 17, 23, 32, 38, 55. *See also* Federal Bureau of Investigation (FBI)
Burling, John, 226

Cabot, J. M., 240–41
California: alien control measures in, 126–27, 185, 249; camps in, 112, 260; demands for action in, 142, 168, 169–70, 172, 175, 178; EO 9066 and, 142, 183; Germans in, 147, 254, 340n9; Italians in, 34–35, 147, 340n9; Japanese in, 102, 125, 138, 142, 153, 157, 191, 269, 271, 294n3, 322n7; as military area, *fig. 6, fig. 7*, xxv, 327n41; military threats to, and attacks on, xxiii, 17, 94, 128, 130, 169, 190; and Pearl Harbor references, xxiv, 156, 171, 179, 188; press coverage of, 132, 134, 137, 150–51, 318n45, 319n51, 322n2; racism in, 15, 17–18, 198

Camp Crystal City. *See* Crystal City
Camp Empire, Panama Canal Zone, 332n32
Camp Forrest TN, 138, 261, 282
Camp Kenedy TX, 254, 260, 263
Camp Liebenau, Germany, 218–19
Camp Siegfried, Long Island NY, 305
Camp Upton, Long Island NY, 220, 277
Canada: border of, 95; cooperation with U.S., 109, 237, 331n19; and evacuation, 126–27; and fifth-column fears, 126; Germans and refugees in, 300n45, 308n49; Japanese in, 125, 126–27; Pearl Harbor and, 125–27; repatriates of, 222, 239; WWI internment, 67; WWII relocation and interment, 127
Canaris, Wilhelm Franz, 43
Capra, Frank, 152
Carillo, Leo, 169
Carlson, John Roy, 156–57
Carter, John Franklin, 91, 93; and Carter's Report, 91, 94
Carusi, Ugo, 244, 246, 257
Category A and B areas, 184, 325n24, 327n41. *See also* zones
Certificate of Identification, *fig. 4*, xxiii, xxiv, 133, 165, 192, 231, 251, 340n6
Cervantes, Miguel, 290
China: Americans in, xxii, 48, 235; camps in, 235; Japan and, 98, 101, 126, 209; and *Panay* incident, 49, 299n27
Chinese: compared with Japanese, 132, 151, 157; and Exclusion Act (1882), 16; and immigration, 16; movement against, 15; racism and, 15, 33
Christianity, 49, 142–43, 294n4
Churchill, Winston, 86, 108, 115, 118, 154
Citizen Isolation Camps, *fig. 6*, 250, 260
Citizen's Protective League et al. v. Tom C. Clark, 246–47
Civil Affairs Division (CAD) of the WCCA, 267
civil defense program(s), 67, 130
Civilian Conservation Corps (CCC), 76, 104, 174, 258, 260
Civilian Exclusion Order No. 1, xxvi, 144
civil liberties: British example of, 70; and citizenship, 142; and Japanese Americans, 8, 142, 179, 185; and Justice Department, 183; national security and, 65, 70
Clapp, Edwin, 200–201, 202, 253

Clark, Tom, 144, 246, 273
classification system (of aliens and "dangerous" persons), 203, 237, 253
Clattenburg, Albert, 221, 232, 234, 236, 277, 337n67
Collaer, Nicholas, 261, 262
Collier's, 150
Collins, Patricia, 111–12
Colombia, 88, 92, 219, 220, 305n18
Columbus, ss, 75–76, 77, 112, 302n19
Columbus Day, 166, 257, 313n10
comic books (and characters), 153, 318n50, 319n52
The Coming Struggle for Latin America (Beals), 212, 330n15
Commission on Wartime Internment and Relocation of Civilians (CWRIC), 22–23
Committee for Political Defense (CPD). *See* Emergency Advisory Committee for Political Defense (CPD)
Committee on Public Information (CPI), 24, 25, 27–28
communism, 39, 61, 299n26
communists: FBI investigations of, 55, 57–58, 74, 79–80, 89, 103; FDR and, 57; media warnings about, 39; other investigations of, xvii, 8, 38, 39, 47, 49, 99
Confessions of a Nazi Spy, 150
Congress, U.S.: concerns of, and investigations by, 39, 40–41, 46, 59, 106; delegations of, xxiv, 168, 173, 178, 185, 319n51; FDR addressing, xx, 49; and German Americans, xxi, 26, 65; and Japanese Americans, xxiv, 65, 322n2; and Wilson, 30. *See also specific acts and resolutions*
congressional delegations: California, 168, 185, 319n51; Pacific (West) Coast, 172–73, 178, 322n2
Constitution, U.S.: citizens and patriotic groups references to, 36, 39, 43, 45, 159; Ennis and, 183; FDR and, 122–23; McCloy and, 175; protection of (the document), 130; relocation and interment and, 122–23, 167, 175. *See also* constitutional rights
constitutional rights, 21, 45, 54, 66, 137, 159, 167, 183
Cooley, Thomas, 166, 204–5, 252, 286
Costa Rica, 240–41, 263

INDEX   363

Costello, John, 142
Coughlin, Charles, 49
courts: alien enemies and, 249; anti-alien legislation in, 66; appellate, xxviii, 246–47, 286; district, xxviii, 286; FDR and, 123; German American citizen challenge in, 198; hearing boards and, 249; Japanese American use of, 270; relocation of Japanese Americans and, xxvii, 178; traditional access to, 20; upholding Naturalization Act, 303n25; U.S. Supreme Court, xxvii, 26, 28, 79; WRA view of, 178
CPD. *See* Emergency Advisory Committee for Political Defense (CPD)
Creel, George, 24, 25
criminals: aliens not, 160, 285; code words for, 338n73; FBI investigating, 38, 54, 106; internees feeling like, 264; repatriating (expelling), 128, 225, 334n42, 338n73; states treating aliens as, 64
Crystal City: background and location of, *fig. 9*, 112, 260; births in, 263; censorship of internees, 279; children in, *fig. 14*, *fig. 15*, *fig. 16*, 264, 265; closure of, 263, 286; Collaer and, 261; daily life in, 264–67; deaths in, 263, 281; demographics of, 263; facilities, *fig. 10*, 262; film about, 262; Geneva Convention and, 266–67; Germans in, xxviii, 261, 262, 263, 286; hospital and medical care in, 255, 280–81; housing, 261; humane treatment of internees in, 279; Instruction No. 58 and, 278–79; internee arrivals at, 261; internee departures from, 239, 337n69; internee morale at, *fig. 12*, 264, 282; internee numbers at, *fig. 9*, 261, 263; internee views of war, 265, 266; Italians in, 263, 274; Jacobs and, 282; Japanese in, 262, 263, 286, 287; Latin Americans in, 260, 263; Mangione and, 261, 264; music, *fig. 12*, *fig. 13*, 262; organizational structure of, 267; O'Rourke and, 261, 262, 263, 264; personnel, 262; recreation and leisure, *fig. 12*, *fig. 15*, 262, 264; Schmitz family and, *fig. 14*, *fig. 15*, *fig. 16*, xi, xiii, xiv, 342n21; schools and education, *fig. 14*, *fig. 15*, *fig. 16*, 262, 264; security, 255, 261; voluntary internment in, 265; worship and religious services, 264

Crystal City Times, 282
curfew, xxiv, 183, 311n19
Custodial Detention Index (CDI), xviii, xix, 8, 65, 72–74, 78–79, 110, 140, 203, 302n16. *See also* Federal Bureau of Investigation (FBI); Hoover, J. Edgar; "suspect list"

dangerousness, xxvii, 201, 207, 229, 253, 301–2n12
Davis, Elmer, 152
Dawn over the Amazon (Beals), 213
denaturalization, 81
Denaturalization Act (1944), 245
deportations: and Alien Enemy Act, 21; alien registration equated with, 78; CPD and, xxiv, 126, 207, 209, 232; for crimes, 224, 338n73; of dangerous aliens, xxiv, 2, 81, 207, 211, 221, 237; through Ellis Island, 200, 239, 281, 284; through error, 236, 237; for exchange purposes, xxiv, 126, 207, 209, 211, 244–45; and family separation, 281; forced, 221, 223, 233, 239, 245, 282, 285; hearings and, 224, 246, 285, 337n70; Justice Department and, 107, 192, 207, 246; from Latin America to Europe and Asia, 2, 211, 233; from Latin America to U.S., 2, 126, 207, 209, 211, 220, 223, 236, 254; legal issues concerning, 107, 245, 246; orchestrated by U.S., 2, 211, 241; preparations for, 81, 113; reasons for, 242, 244–45; reporting of, 96; resisting, 239, 244, 245; State Department and, 207; threats of, 338n72; urging of, for Japanese, 138, 168, 272; urging of, for Nazis, 42, 52; voluntary, 232, 239, 245; WWI and, 291
Deutschtum (Germanness), 27, 42, 48, 63, 298n11
DeWitt, John: background of, 188; and Bendetsen, 173, 187; and enemy alien program, xxiii, 126, 128, 184; and EO 9066, xxv, 187, 196; exclusion orders of, xxvi, 144, 250, 325n22; and faulty intelligence, 193–94; and FDR, 128, 184; fifth-column views, 87, 128, 173, 180, 188, 326–27n39; and Japanese, xxvii, 114, 121, 128, 137, 171, 173, 174, 184, 188, 190, 191, 195, 323n8; and mass removals, xxvi, 122, 124, 128, 137, 145, 146, 149, 174, 184, 187, 194; and military control of Hawaii, 16, 115; and Pearl Harbor, 115,

121, 128, 173, 187, 190, 194; proclamations issued by, xxv, xxvi, 144, 325n24, 327n41; and public gatherings, 131; and relocatee hearings, 339n1; and sabotage, 128, 131, 173; security responsibilities of, 7–8, 184, 187, 188, 189, 267, 325n31; and superiors, 137, 149, 177–78, 184; and Tolan Committee, 144, 146; and WCCA, 267. *See also* Western Defense Command (WDC)

Dickstein, Samuel, xvii, xviii, 45–46, 59, 62

Dies, Martin: and Bund, 59, 61, 300n50; and HUAC, 59, 95, 96; and subversives, xviii, 95, 97, 153; and *Yellow Book*, 135, 142

Dies Committee, xix, 59, 61, 63, 270, 299n22, 343n32

Dimock, Marshall, 23, 110

Dingell, John, 97, 307n29

Donovan, William, 87, 88, 107–8, 194, 308n46

Don Quixote, 212, 290

Drottningholm, SS, 222, 329–30n7, 334n44, 335n55

Drum, Hugh, xxvi, xxvii, 188, 197, 198, 327n48

Duck Soup, 50

East Coast: attack on, as possibility, 130, 144, 152, 187; Biddle and, 149, 195–96; Black Tom and, 24, 31, 296n23; compared to West Coast, 119, 144, 148–49, 195–96, 251; DeWitt and, 149, 196; Drum and, xxvi, xxvii, 188; EDC and, 196; EO 9066 applied to, xxvi, 196; FDR and, 196, 251; fear of fifth-column activities along, 136, 317–18n43; and German saboteurs, 129, 192–93; Germans and Italians returning to, 187; hearing boards and, 148; and mass evacuation, xxvi, 149, 251; and mass removal, 147, 149, 187, 196; Navy and, 32, 130, 235; relocation and removals from, 3, 76, 136, 197, 199; selective relocation and internment from, 147, 197, 199; Stimson and, xxvi, 149, 196. *See also* internment; relocation and removal; West Coast

Eastern Defense Command (EDC), xxvi, 196–97

Eastern Military Area, xxvi, xxvii, 149, 197, 327–28n48

Ecuador, 220, 242

Einstein, Albert, 164, 165

Eiteneuer, B., 199–200

Ellis Island (detention camp or "regular immigration station"), 75, 112; conversion to camp, 258; as "country-club," 218; deportations through, 200, 239, 281, 284; German and Italian sailors interned at, xxii, 75, 76, 112; Germans interned at, xxviii, 263, 281, 285, 286; hearings at, 202, 218; internee population of, 76, 281, 285, 286; Kurt Peters and, 256; Latin Americans interned at, 219–20, 281; postwar, 244, 263, 281, 284, 285, 286

Emergency Advisory Committee for Political Defense (CPD): bargaining power of, 229; cooperation within, 126, 209, 210–11, 232; deportations and, xxiv, 126, 207, 209, 232; and fifth-column hemispheric threats, 228–29; and Germany, 237–38, 337n68; hemispheric security and, xxiv, 126, 207, 209; information gathered by, 210; internment policies, 208, 210, 229; Justice Department and, 231, 232; measures against aliens, 210, 231; nations of, 126, 209, 211, 231–32; and obstructionists, 210; Pearl Harbor and, 126; protection of non-dangerous aliens, 210; purpose of, 126, 209–10, 231; and reciprocity, 237–38, 337n68; repatriation and exchange, xxiv, 126, 207, 208, 210–11, 229, 231–32, 237–38; reports of, 228–29, 231; in Rio de Janeiro, 126, 207, 209, 215, 331n20; State Department and, 211, 228, 330n11; U.S. involvement with, 211–12, 231–32, 241; in Washington DC, 208, 231

enemy aliens: British internment of, xx, 20, 69, 301n10, 321n72; calls for action against, 119, 186; Canadian actions against, 125–27; as civilian matter, 250; classification of, xxiii, 133, 140, 146, 150, 163; consistency of treatment, 7, 121–24, 128, 136, 146, 167, 174, 187, 195, 323n13; defined, xxii–xxiii, 21, 293n1; demands for removal (evacuation) of, 3, 116, 119, 121, 136, 168–79, 181–82, 184, 187; as deportable, 224–25; domestic control of, xxiii, 125–26, 134; on East Coast, 3, 121, 149, 195–97; FBI arrests of, 123, 125, 128, 131, 138, 140, 182, 195–96, 211, 250;

enemy aliens (*cont.*)
fear of, 120, 136, 179, 183; hearing boards, xxi, xxv, 147, 148, 182, 249–50; hemispheric control of, 207; justification of actions against, 130; Latin America and, 125, 127, 209–11, 212, 215–16, 225, 228, 231, 232–33, 244; media reports of, 132–33, 136–37, 151, 153, 158; Mexican actions against, 125–27; as military matter, 128, 147, 164, 174, 195, 250; numbers of, 118, 121–24, 145, 147, 149, 325n28; politics of, 23, 24, 31; public opinion and, 159–60, 179–82; registration of, 133, 163, 192; removal of, 3, 8, 9, 121–22, 127, 187; restrictions on, xxiii, 184–85, 250–51; as scapegoats, 35, 165–66; shielded, 145–47, 165–66, 177, 325n28; and stigma, 163, 165–66; support for, 160; treatment of, 108–9, 121, 131; on West Coast, 3, 121, 122, 149, 168–79, 184, 193, 195. *See also* Alien Enemy Control Unit (AECU), Department of Justice; alien enemy program; Certificate of Identification; exchanges; German Americans; internees; internment; Italian Americans; Japanese Americans; relocation (removal); repatriation and exchange

Ennis, Edward J., 107, 303n25; and alien enemy hearings, 250, 303n25, 317n37; as director of AECU, 139, 303n25; and FBI methods, 203; and Japanese Americans, 183; leniency toward German and Italian Americans, 166, 204, 339n3; response to citizens' concerns, 164, 183, 202; and Stewart Test, 243; and West Coast measures, 172, 175

Espionage Act (1917), 26

Ethiopia, 37, 54

Etolin, 220

evacuation. *See* relocation (removal)

exchanges: advantages of, 128, 217, 225, 229, 333n29, 336n60; benevolent reciprocity ensured by, 9, 97–98, 207, 248; cooperation for and coordination of, 208–9, 219, 221, 227–28, 235, 333n39, 334n42; CPD and, xxiv, 126, 207, 208, 210–11, 229, 231–32, 237–38; of dangerous Axis nationals, xxiv, 9, 217, 221, 223; deportations for, xxiv, 126, 207, 209, 211, 244–45; disadvantages of, 222, 225, 227; *Drottningholm* and, 222, 329–30n7, 334n44, 335n55; European, 207, 208, 216, 221; first series ending, 222, 223; France and, 208; with Germany, xxvi, xxvii, 207, 216–17, 219, 222–23, 234–38, 273; global, 9, 187, 207, 209, 215, 222, 232; *Gripsholm* and, 222, 234–35, 238, 242, 263, 334n45, 334–35n48, 335–36n57; hemispheric, 9, 187, 207, 215, 216, 221, 238; of inherently harmless Axis nationals, xxvii, 223, 228, 233; internment and, 8–9, 207, 248; with Japan, xxvii, 123, 207, 216–17, 219, 222–23, 227, 234–35, 263; Justice Department and, 9; *Letitia* and, 329n7; logistics of, 217, 219, 221; Long and, 123; media coverage of, 220, 337n69; negotiations of U.S. and Germany for, 207, 225, 230–31; negotiations of U.S. and Japan for, xxiii, 207, 223–24, 226; through New York, 219–20, 235, 263; of objectionable persons, 217; of officials (diplomats), 82, 207, 211, 216, 219, 222, 331n18; pause in, 230–31; policy shift of, xxvii, 223, 229, 231, 233; of POWs, 82, 207, 227, 232, 233, 235, 238–39; purpose of, 2, 223–24, 229, 231–34, 289, 292, 333n39, 334n42, 336n60; resumption of, 233–38; safe conduct and, 218, 222, 228, 230, 232; *Santa Lucia* and, xxiv, 219; secrecy about, 238–39, 242, 273; Spain and, 216; State Department and, 207; success of, 9, 216, 289; Switzerland and, 216, 219, 235, 238, 240, 332n30; of undesirable persons, 128, 222, 225, 228; U.S. leading role with, 207, 211, 216, 221, 232, 245; of women and children, 2, 217. *See also* internees; repatriates; repatriation and exchange

exclusion orders, xxvi, xxvii, 144, 198, 250, 287, 325n22

exclusion zones, 124, 196

Executive Order (EO) 9066, 141; California political reaction to, 142, 316n29; Constitution and, 183; DeWitt and, xxv, 193–94, 196; Drum carrying out, xxvi, 197; and East Coast, 196–97; FDR and, xxv, 3, 127, 141, 196, 267; German and Italian Americans affected by, 3, 141, 193, 197–98, 250–51, 325n22; and Hawaii, 141; Japanese Americans affected by, 3, 141, 193; legal challenge to, 198; racism and, 141; Supreme Court

and, xxvii; and West Coast, xxv, 3, 141–42, 183, 187, 193–94, 250–51, 267, 325n22, 342n28
Executive Order (EO) 9102, xxv, 259, 317n39
Executive Orders, other: EO 8389, 346n45; EO 8757, xxii; EO 8771, 76; EO 9095, 280; EO 9106, xxvi; EO 9165, xxvii, 191; EO 9562, xxvii
expropriation, 214

Fama, Charles, 36
fascism: challenges and reactions to, 38–42; *Duck Soup* and, 50; flirtations with, 37–38; investigations of, 56–58; warnings about, 36–37, 300n32
FBI. *See* Federal Bureau of Investigation (FBI)
Federal Bureau of Investigation (FBI): American Legion and, 57, 81; arresting aliens, xxii, xxiii, 1, 8; arresting aliens (as Bureau of Investigation) during WWI, 32; arresting citizens, xxii, 128, 254, 311n18, 330n12; arresting enemy aliens, 123, 125, 128, 131, 138, 140, 182, 195–96, 211, 250, 254; arresting German and Italian sailors, 74–75, 76; arresting German correspondents, 97; Biddle and, 203, 253; *Bolivia Today* report, 216; as central clearinghouse, 64–65, 71–72, 80, 112, 131; criticisms of, 57, 105–6, 174, 203, 253, 272, 303n28; determining internee outcomes, 235; DeWitt and, 174; directed to investigate subversive actions, xix, 7, 43, 54–57, 79; Ennis and, 203; expansion of power, 57, 58, 71–74, 79–82; and fascist threat, 39, 55, 56–58, 89; FDR and, xix, 7, 43, 54–57, 64–65, 71, 79, 80; and fifth-column consensus, 9, 87, 153; and fifth-column threat, 8, 62, 79–82, 87, 89, 91, 106, 115; initial investigations by, 56–58; internment planning and preparation, 66, 71–74, 79–82, 109–10, 187, 249; investigating aliens, xix, xx, 64–65, 71–73, 79–81; investigating American Nazis, xviii, 54, 56–59; investigating citizens, 73, 80, 203; investigating communists, 55, 57–58, 74, 79–80, 89, 103; investigating criminals, 38, 54, 106; investigating German American Bund, 103, 104–5; investigating German organizations, 103–5; investigating Japanese organizations, 99; jailing

enemy aliens, 182–83; in Latin America, 55, 187, 211, 213–14, 259; letters and memos sent to, 59, 71; and map of Axis threat to South America, 93; master index (custodial detention) card classification scheme, 103–5, 107, 302n16; McGuire and, 80; McKellar and, 57, 105–6; Norris and, 106; number of agents, 58; ONI assisting, 71, 105, 242, 315n22; as part of IIC, xix, 70–71; refugees considered threat by, 82, 304n33; and repatriates, 239, 242; sabotage investigations of, xix, xx, 65, 71, 72, 90, 177; spot searches by, xxiv, 157, 172, 202; student records provided to, 73; and War Department cooperation, 109, 187, 207, 221, 226, 235. *See also* Bureau of Investigation; Custodial Detention Index (CDI); Hoover, J. Edgar; "suspect list"
fifth column and fifth columnists: Americans' belief in, 70, 84, 110, 118, 129, 290, 291; Biddle's views of, 54–55, 64; British fears of, 69, 85, 95, 308n46; Canadian fears of, 126; collapse of France caused by, 85, 89, 95, 189; comic book depictions of, 153, 319n52; and CPD, 228–29; DeWitt's fears of, 87, 128, 173, 180, 188, 326–27n39; Dies and, xviii, 95, 97, 153; Dies Committee and, xix, 59, 61, 63, 270, 299n22, 343n32; and East Coast, 136, 317–18n43; and Eleanor Roosevelt, 83; and FBI, 8, 62, 79–82, 87, 89, 91, 106, 115; FDR's fears of, xx, xxii, 49–50, 65, 87–88, 90–94, 121, 164, 167, 186; fear of, 1, 3, 7, 8, 44, 62, 80, 110, 120, 129, 147, 189, 289, 304nn7–8, 324n20; fireside chats and, xx, xxii, 50, 84, 90–91, 92; German American, 3, 42, 53, 63, 87, 95, 118, 122, 161, 176, 317–18n43; Germany's (Hitler's and Nazi) use of, in Europe, xx, 49, 50, 85, 89, 95, 134, 162, 189, 323n9; global threat posed by, 62, 88–89, 93; Gullion's belief in, 178, 323n9; headlines on, 42, 51–52, 53, 96, 305n14, 305–6n19, 317–18n43, 322n2; and Hoover, 38, 55, 80, 82, 89, 105, 187; and HUAC, 62, 95, 153; Hughes and, 153, 319n51; Hull's belief in, 87; Italian American, 87, 122; Japanese American, xxiv, 3, 81, 87, 94–95, 99–103, 116, 118, 122, 131–37, 142, 150–51, 153, 156–58, 167, 170–73, 178, 180,

fifth column and fifth columnists (cont.) 188, 251, 312–13n4, 314nn14–16, 318n45, 319n51, 323n9; Japanese in the Philippines as, 151, 179; Knox's belief in, 87, 93; in Latin America, 88–90, 92–93, 118, 212–16, 259; Long's fears of, 82–82, 87; Los Angeles fears of, 137, 150–51, 153, 156, 158, 180, 188, 314nn14–16, 318n45, 319n51; magazine stories of, 48, 52, 84, 89–90, 92, 96, 150, 151, 154, 158, 213; McCormack-Dickstein Committee investigating, xvii, xviii, xix, 46, 50–51, 58, 311n21; movies about, 50, 53, 150, 152, 156, 318n50; municipal efforts to stymie, 88; New York City and, 37, 42, 317–18n43; in Norway, 85, 134, 162, 189; novels about, 53, 96, 150, 154–57, 212–13, 318n44; ONI concerns about, 87, 99–103, 115, 213, 315n22; origins of, xviii, 3, 8, 24, 27, 31, 42, 44, 85; and Pearl Harbor, xxiii, 9, 93, 116, 118, 122, 129, 134–36, 150, 291, 305n19, 313–14n12, 327n39; posters about, 153–54; press coverage of, 51–53, 96, 132–33, 135, 136–37, 150–52, 158, 305n14, 305–6n19, 312–13n4, 313–14n12, 314n16, 317–18n43, 322n2; public opinion and, 158–60, 182; and radio broadcasts, 153, 319n51; refugees (including Jews) as, 31, 69, 85, 96, 137, 151, 195, 213, 304n33; Roberts Commission and, xxiv, 136, 157, 173; rumors about, 85, 87, 126, 136; sabotage and, xxii, 95, 215, 322n2; and San Francisco, 102, 140, 153, 180, 191; scholarly articles about, 48, 151–52, 213; state actions taken against, 67; Stimson's concerns about, 55, 87, 93, 94, 164; Wallace's concerns about, 214, 215–16; and War Department, 81, 87, 171, 188

fifth-column consensus, 9, 70, 87, 88, 110, 153, 186

films. *See* movies

fireside chats: "Arsenal of Democracy," xxi, 77, 84, 90–91; on fifth-column threat, xx, xxii, 50, 84, 90–91, 92, 305n18; galvanizing support for war, xxi, 49; on new kind of war, xxv, 120, 190–91; popularity of, 89, 91, 120; on war for world domination, 91–92, 305n17. *See also* Roosevelt, Franklin Delano

first papers, 19, 34, 51, 73, 137, 161, 205, 295n14

Fish, Hamilton, 38–39, 40

Fitch, T. F., 238, 273

Ford, Leland: contact with Biddle, 170, 175; on internment as humanitarian, 169; and Japanese Americans, 168–69, 170, 322n2; and Mexico, 125; and removal of West Coast Japanese, 171, 321n1; Stimson responds to, 171–72

Foreign Agents Registration Act (FARA) (1938), xix, 73, 74, 302n17

Fort Douglas UT, *fig. 2*, 33

Fort Lincoln ND, *fig. 11*, xxii, 75, 76, 112–13, 239, 256, 257, 258, 287

Fort Missoula MT, xxii, 75, 76, 112–13, 140, 256, 268

Fort Oglethorpe GA, 33, 138

Fort Sam Houston TX, 258

Fort Stanton NM, xxi, xxii, 75, 76–77, 112–13, 239, 258

Fortune, 84, 85, 119

Fox, Stephen, 6, 24–35, 306n27, 311n20, 325n29

France: Americans in, 208; and exchanges, 208; FBI and, 329n6; fifth column and, 85, 89, 95, 189; Germany's defeat of, xx, 67, 69, 77, 164; and refugees, 68, 82, 162; and WWI, 20

Frankfurter, Felix, 59, 161–62

Fraser, Bert, 256–58

Friends of New Germany, xviii, 41, 47

Friends of the New Germany, 29, 41, 45–46, 51, 58–59

G-2. *See* Military Intelligence Division (G-2 or MID)

Gau-USA, 29, 41

Geneva Convention (1929): and civilians and POWs, 82, 207, 275–76; and Germany, 274; and jails and prisons, 339–40n4; and Japan, 274, 276, 345n39; posted in camps, 278–79; public unawareness of, 267; reciprocity (retaliation) and, 274, 275–76, 277, 278; Special Division Internee Branch and, 82; spirit and letter of, 243, 278; Stewart Test and, 243; and U.S., 233, 234, 266, 278

Geneva Prisoners of War Convention (1929), 207

German American Alliance, 26, 27, 296n31

German American Bund: activities and backlash, 34, 37, 41–42, 50, 51, 53; background of, 29, 34, 41, 51; congressional investigations of, 58, 59, 63, 300–301n50; FBI investigations of, 103, 104–5; media coverage of, 51, 61–62, 84, 150, 305–6n19;

membership of, 63; Naturalization Act and, xxi, 303n25; as threat, 58, 62; ties with Nazi Germany, 45–46, 51, 63; Vooros and, 59. *See also* American Nazis; Nazi Party

German American Bundists, xxi, 22, 51, 59, 61, 63, 66, 105, 150

German Americans: assimilation (Americanization) of, 18, 19, 22, 23–24, 25–26, 34, 134, 184–85; Biddle and, 184, 195; Bureau of Investigation arrests of, 32–33; in California, 147, 254, 340n9; compared with Japanese Americans, 7, 10, 19, 65, 93–94, 115, 121, 122, 123–25, 145, 160, 186, 311n18, 322n7, 323n13, 325n28; and Congress, xxi, 26, 65; Constitution and relocation and internment of, 122–23, 167; in Crystal City, xxviii, 261, 262, 263, 286; DeWitt on, 124, 137, 146, 149, 174, 194; East Coast mass relocation of, arguments for/against 144, 149, 187, 195–97, 199; Ennis and, 166, 204, 339n3; and EO 9066, 3, 141, 193, 250–51, 325n22; equality of citizenship arguments for, 148, 166; factors shielding from mass relocation, 147–49; FBI arrests of (citizens), xxii, 128, 254, 311n18, 330n12; FBI arrests of (enemy aliens), 123, 125, 128, 138, 140, 182, 195–96, 211, 250, 254; FDR and, 19, 31, 77, 83, 95, 122, 134, 149, 150, 164, 178, 186, 195, 250–51; as fifth columnists, 3, 42, 53, 63, 81, 87, 95, 118, 122, 161, 171, 176, 188, 317–18n43; hearings (Tolan Committee) for, xxv, 124, 144, 311n22, 315–16n26; interned at Ellis Island, xxviii, 263, 281, 285, 286; internment of (WWI), 20, 33; jailed (enemy aliens), 182–83; leniency toward, 166, 204, 339n3; loyalty of, 18–19, 27, 28–29, 30, 42, 51, 58–59, 87, 118, 145, 160–66, 183–84, 196, 311n21, 324n19; and mass removal, 124, 129, 145, 146–47; New York City's fears of, 42, 317–18n43; numbers of (compared with Italian and Japanese Americans) determining treatment, 124, 129, 145, 146–49, 177; organizations of, investigated, 103–5; "patriotic murders" of, 28, 296n30; Pearl Harbor effect on, 116–17, 122, 127, 133; population of, 14, 18–19, 63, 118, 121, 147, 149, 177, 186–87, 196, 197, 254, 322n7; *Preliminary Report* (Tolan Committee) and, 129, 144–48; relocation (removal) of, as a military matter, xxv, 146, 164, 325n22; relocation from East Coast, 3, 197; removal from vital areas along East Coast, 199; returning to homes along East Coast, 187; and sabotage, 22, 31, 33; statistical information about, 146–49, 317n40; Stimson and, 164, 177–78, 250; surveillance of, 31, 56–57, 302n16; Tolan Committee and, 124, 144, 147–49; treatment of, 148, 166; War Department handling of, compared with Japanese Americans, 167, 177, 178, 195, 250; West Coast mass relocation of, arguments for/against, 124, 137, 144, 146, 149, 174, 178, 194, 250; witness testimony (Tolan Committee) about, 144, 189; and WWI, *fig. 1*, 18, 19, 22, 23, 24, 25–26, 27, 28, 30, 31, 296n30. *See also* hearing boards and hearings; internees; internment; repatriation and exchange

The German Reich and Americans of German Origin, 59–61, 299n23, 300n45

German sailors, *fig. 11*, xxi, xxii, 20, 74–76, 77, 112, 256

Germany: British concerns about fifth columnists from, 69, 85, 95, 308n46; CPD and, 237–38, 337n68; defeat of France, xx, 67, 69, 77, 164; and Deutschtum, 27, 42, 48, 63; espionage in Mexico, 82; and exchanges with U.S., xxvi, xxvii, 207, 216–17, 219, 222–23, 225, 230–31, 234–38, 273; fifth-column use of, in Europe, xx, 49, 50, 85, 89, 95, 134, 162, 189, 323n9; and Geneva Convention, 274; German American Bund's ties with, 45–46, 51, 63; immigration from, 14, 18, 23; influencing public opinion, 43, 298n15; and Italy, xix, xxi, xxiii, 37–38, 80, 100–101; and Japan, 100–101; and nationals in/from Latin America, 3, 9, 41, 127–28, 141, 187, 217, 221, 248, 254, 279, 284, 300n45; and occupation of Norway, 77, 85; and Pearl Harbor attack, 117, 195, 309n7; polls about, 84–85, 116, 117, 119, 176, 309n7, 309n9, 310n11, 323n13; public opinion against, 309–10n9, 310n11, 318–19n50, 323n13; reciprocity with Latin American nationals, 237–38, 337n68; relations with U.S., xviii, 22–23, 38, 42, 51, 58–59, 63, 80, 219, 298n13; reports of mistreatment of Jews in, 41, 45; saboteurs from, on East Coast, 129, 192–93. *See also* Hitler, Adolf

Gibson, Raleigh, 125

Goebbels, Joseph, xvii, 41, 42–43, 51. *See also* Propaganda Ministry (PROMI)
Good Neighbor policy, 211, 215, 216, 241
Gorer, Geoffrey, 151–52
Great Britain: coordination with U.S. officials about internment policies, 69–70; encouraging aliens to leave, 68; and FDR, 107–8; and fifth-column fears, 69, 85, 95, 308n46; and Home Office, 67–68, 69, 88, 301n6; intelligence, 76, 91, 95, 108, 221; interning enemy aliens, xx, 20, 69, 301n10, 321n72; internment preparations, 67–68; internment program of, as example for U.S., 70, 88, 107–8, 111, 164, 237, 305n11; Jews interned in, 69; refugees and, 67–68, 69; relations with U.S., 72, 78, 95; repatriation and exchange, 48, 208, 236, 332–33n35; rethinking interment policies, 67, 69, 301n10; and tribunals, 69, 321n72; WWI internment, 20, 67, 209
Greenbrier Hotel, 219, 220
Gripsholm, SS: American passengers on, 222, 227, 235, 240, 333nn38–39, 337n69; exchanges by, 222, 234–35, 238, 242, 263, 334n45, 334–35n48, 335–36n57; and relief supplies, 222, 234–35; voyages, 239–40, 245
Grodzins, Morton, 5, 135
Grotius, Hugo, 19
Gulf Coast, xxvi, 122, 130, 197
Gullion, Allen: and Alien Employment Program (AEP), 177; belief in fifth column, 178, 323n9; discussing removal of Japanese and all aliens, 174; and mass evacuation of Japanese, 98, 140, 178, 307n31; meetings with senior officials, 175, 177–78; nationwide military area proposal, 196; urging evacuation of all Japanese and "dangerous" persons, 178
Gunther, John, 154, 212–13

habeas corpus, 137, 140, 171, 175
Harper's, 84, 154, 161
Harrison, Earl G., 78, 243, 261, 264, 303n25, 340n11
Havana Act (1940), 331n19
Hawaii: Army and, 123, 189; DeWitt and military control of, 16, 115; EO 9066 and, 141; FDR and Japanese on/from, 47–48, 123, 194, 313–14n12; German Americans compared with Japanese on, 7, 10, 19, 65, 93–94, 115, 121, 123–25, 145, 186, 311n18, 322n7, 323n13, 325n28; Issei on, 7; Italian Americans compared with Japanese on, 7, 10, 19, 65, 93–94, 115, 121, 123–25, 145, 186, 311n18, 322n7, 323n13, 325n28; Japanese as numerous and influential on, 19, 65, 121, 123–25, 145, 186; Japanese as percentage of island population, 7, 123, 311n19; Japanese internees on/from, 7, 65, 121, 123–25, 141, 145, 186, 254; Japanese population of, 7, 121, 123, 186, 194–95, 254, 311n19, 322n7; Japanese remaining free on, 123–25, 186, 194–95, 254, 311n19, 332n7; Japan's exchanges with U.S. of Japanese on/from, 123, 226; Knox and Japanese on, 194, 313–14n12, 322n7; mainland (West Coast) Japanese compared with Japanese on/from, 10, 19, 33, 48, 65, 94, 101, 102, 121, 124–25, 141, 143, 317n38; Navy and, xxiii, 47, 223, 227; Nisei on, 7; Pearl Harbor attack and Japanese on, xxiii, 135, 143; repatriation and exchange of Japanese from, 98, 123, 225–26, 227; Stimson and Japanese on/from, 194–95, 322n7, 327n40; War Department plans to intern enemy aliens on, 17, 115; White House recommendations for/against mass relocation of Japanese on, 134–35, 194, 196, 313–14n12, 322n7. *See also* Japanese Hawaiians
hearing boards and hearings, xxi, xxv, 111, 112, 121, 146–48, 200, 202–5, 218, 224, 246, 248–50, 273, 317n37, 317n41, 329n2, 337n70, 339n1, 341n15
Hemingway, Ernest, 53
hemispheric security: CPD coordination of, xxiv, 126, 207, 209; Declaration of Panama and, 214; Havana Act and, 331n19; internment and, 229; U.S. taking charge of, 211, 212; zone for, 214, 331n19
Hiller, Gerhard, 165
Hitler, Adolf: and Deutschtum, 27, 42, 48, 298n11; envisioning Reich in Western Hemisphere, 88, 92, 306n20; and fascist challenge to U.S., 41–43; FDR warning about, xxii, 92; and fifth column in Europe, xx, 49, 50, 85, 89, 95, 134, 162, 189, 323n9; and fifth column in U.S., 107; and

Holocaust, 321n70; ideas of race and racism, 27, 45, 47, 60, 237, 298n11, 299n23; internee support for, 265; media warnings about, 51–53, 61–62, 85–86, 89–90, 92, 150–51, 154, 155–57, 212; *Mein Kampf*, 46, 158, 299n23; and National Socialist German Worker's Party (NSDAP), 29, 45, 46, 60, 299n21; polls about, 85; and propaganda in the U.S., 45–47; and radio, 49; and reciprocity, 277; rise to power, xvii, 39, 58. *See also* Auslandsorganisation (AO); Germany
"Hitler Looks to South America" (Sondern), 89, 92
Hoey, Jane, 255
Hokoku Seinen Dan, 266
Hollywood, 152, 167
Holocaust, 306n27, 315n24
Hoover, J. Edgar: appointment as director, 55; arresting aliens, xxii, xxiii, 1, 8; arresting citizens, xxii, 128, 254, 311n18, 330n12; arresting enemy aliens, 123, 125, 128, 131, 138, 140, 182, 196, 211, 250, 254; arresting German and Italian sailors, 74–75, 76; arresting German correspondents, 97; avoiding written records, 79; and Biddle, xxvii, 79, 82, 203; criticisms of, 57, 79, 95, 105–6, 174, 203–4, 253, 272, 303n28; and Eleanor Roosevelt, 58; and FBI as secret police force, 71; and FDR, 55, 56, 64–65, 71, 80, 302n16; and fifth column and fifth columnists, 38, 55, 65, 80, 82, 89, 105, 187; and fifth-column consensus, 9, 55, 87; and Fish, 38; Ford writing to, 168, 169; General Intelligence Division, 65; increasing FBI's authority and power, 57, 65, 71–74, 79–82; information accuracy and sources, 79–80; initial investigations by, 56–58; internment planning and preparation, xx, xxi, 55, 66, 71–74, 79–82, 109–10, 187, 249; investigating aliens, xix, xx, 64–65, 71–73, 79–81; investigating American Nazis, xviii, 54, 56–59; investigating citizens, 80; investigating communists, 55, 57–58, 74, 79–80, 89, 103; investigating criminals, 38, 54, 106; investigating German American Bund, 103, 104–5; investigating German organizations, 103–5; investigating Japanese organizations, 99; investigating subversive actions, xix, 7, 43, 54–57, 79; jailing enemy aliens, 182–83; and Latin America, 55, 187, 211; McKellar opposition to, 57, 105–6; misusing FARA, 73–74; National Academy (FBI) speech, 80; and patriotic citizens groups, 81; and Pearl Harbor, 128; surveilling subversives, 56; views of Issei, 203; "War Begins at Home," 154; War Department and FBI cooperation, 109, 187, 207, 221, 226, 235; White House meetings, 56, 57. *See also* Bureau of Investigation; Custodial Detention Index (CDI); Federal Bureau of Investigation (FBI)
Hopkins, Harry, 87
House Resolution (HR) 198, xvii, 46, 52
House Resolution (HR) 220, xvii
House Resolution (HR) 282, xix, 59, 299n22
House Un-American Activities Committee (HUAC), xix, 59, 299n22; and fifth-column threat, 62, 95, 153; Krebs' influence on, 96; *Special Report*, xxvii, 62; *Yellow Book*, 135
Hughes, John B., 153, 319n51
Hull, Cordell: and Americans abroad, 108, 208, 233, 277; belief in fifth-column menace, 87; and evacuation and internment (U.S.), 186, 196; with FDR and Hoover, 56, 57; and Ford, 169, 170; and interned Americans, 98; and internee reciprocity issues and policies, 108, 217–18, 250, 274, 275, 344n38; and Latin America, 93, 214, 305n18; and Mexico, 125, 333n39; and Nazi activities, 44, 58–59; and repatriation and exchange, 206, 216–17, 219, 222, 225

Ickes, Harold, 87
Immigration (Johnson-Reed) Act (1924), 27, 75, 113, 185
Immigration and Naturalization Service (INS), 301n2; *Alien Enemy Detention Facility*, 262; and "alien enemy problem," 109–10; and Biddle, 109–10, 192; camp regulations, 274, 278, 279–80; camps and other facilities, *fig. 8*, *fig. 9*, *fig. 10*, *fig. 11*, 112–13, 259, 260, 281, 287, 339n1, 341n15; and Carusi, 244, 246, 257; and Crystal City, 260–61; determining internee outcomes, 235; diplomats held by, 219–20; and enemy alien program, 110–12; and Ennis, 139, 250, 303n25, 317n37; and FBI, 109–10,

Immigration and Naturalization Service (INS) *(cont.)*
182, 249; first internees, 75; functions and responsibilities of, xx, 107, 308n41; Geneva Convention and, 274; and Harrison, 78, 243, 261, 264, 303n25, 340n11; hearings and hearing boards, 111, 112, 146–48, 200, 202, 204–5, 218, 224, 246, 248–50, 317n37, 341n15; humane treatment of internees, 278–80; Instruction No. 58, 278; interning women, xxii, 109, 339n1, 340–41n11; internment as distinct from relocation, 248, 339n1; internment plans and preparations, xx, xxi, 104, 109, 110; investigations by, xx, 56; Kurt Peters and, 257; move from Labor to Justice Department, 65, 107, 110, 307n41; number of persons held by, 112–13, 221, 244, 281, 287; and parolees, 249; Peter Theberath and, 139; reciprocity concerns, 109, 250, 278; registration of aliens, xx–xxi, 78, 192, 308n44; regular immigration stations, 112; repatriation of internees, 235, 245–46; report of American Nazi Party, 44; Stewart Test and, 243; taking charge of Army internees, 109, 259, 260, 339n1; treatment of internees, 279–80; and War Department, 110. *See also* Harrison, Earl G.; Justice Department; *and specific camps*
immigration stations, *fig. 8*, 112–13, 341n15
Inside Latin America (Gunther), 154, 212–13
Instruction No. 58, 278
intelligence services: British (SIS or MI6), 95, 108; Japanese, 102; U.S. (Military Intelligence Division or Service), 204, 242
Interdepartmental Intelligence Committee (IIC), xix, 70–71
internees: Americans abroad, 97–98, 274–78; as "bottom of the barrel," 9, 128, 223, 225, 242, 334n42, 336n60; censorship of, 279; children, *fig. 14*, *fig. 15*, *fig. 16*, 2, 217, 223, 225, 228, 235, 242, 245, 246, 262, 264–65, 293n1, 340–41n11, 342n22; Crystal City, *fig. 9*, *fig. 10*, *fig. 14*, *fig. 15*, *fig. 16*, 239, 255, 260–67, 278–79, 280–82, 286; daily life for, 264–67; deaths of, 263, 281; deportable and non-deportable, 224, 245, 338n73; at Ellis Island, xxii, xxviii, 75, 76, 112, 219–20, 256, 263, 281, 285, 286; as "exchange bait," 235, 245; feeling like criminals, 264; Geneva Convention and, 266–67; German, xxviii, 261, 262, 263, 281, 285, 286; German and Italian sailor, xxii, 75, 76, 112; and *Gripsholm* voyages, 222, 227, 234–35, 238, 240, 242, 263, 333nn38–39, 334n45, 334–35n48, 335–36n57, 337n69; hearings and hearing boards and, xxi, xxv, 111, 112, 121, 146–48, 200, 202–5, 218, 224, 246, 248–50, 273, 317n37, 317n41, 329n2, 337n70, 339n1, 341n15; hospital and medical care for, 255, 280–81; housing for, 261; Hull and, 98, 108, 217–18, 274, 275, 344n38; humane treatment of, 278–80; and immigration stations, *fig. 8*, 112–13, 341n15; as inherently harmless, 223, 228, 231, 233, 252, 336n60; Instruction No. 58 and, 278–79; Italian, 263, 274; Jacobs family, 282; Japanese, 262, 263, 286, 287; Japanese Hawaiian, 7, 65, 121, 123–25, 141, 145, 186, 254; Jewish (in Great Britain), 69, 301n10; Kurt Peters, 256–58; from Latin America, 219–20, 260, 263, 281; from Mexico, 238, 239; morale of, *fig. 12*, 264, 282; and music, *fig. 12*, *fig. 13*, 262; Nisei, 7; numbers of, 112–13, 221, 244, 281, 284, 287; O'Rourke and, 261, 262, 263, 264; POWs equality of treatment with, 207, 249, 275, 277; reciprocity and, 97–98, 108–9, 217–18, 250, 274–78, 344n38; recreation and leisure, *fig. 12*, *fig. 15*, 262, 264; Red Cross and, 279, 282; repatriation of, 235, 245–46; rumors of mistreatment of, 243, 274, 275; Schmitz family, *fig. 14*, *fig. 15*, *fig. 16*, xi, xiii, xiv, 342n21; schools and education for, *fig. 10*, *fig. 14*, *fig. 15*, *fig. 16*, 254, 262, 264, 268, 342n22; selection criteria for, 252; support for Axis, 265–66; treatment of, 254–56, 262–67, 278–81, 286; views of war, 265, 266; women, xxii, 2, 69, 109, 217, 218–19, 223, 225, 228, 242, 260, 265, 281, 339n1, 340–41n11. *See also* Federal Bureau of Investigation (FBI); fifth column and fifth columnists; Immigration and Naturalization Service (INS); internment; Justice Department; repatriation and exchange
internment: *Alien Enemy Detention Facility*, 262; of American citizens, 260; of Amer-

icans abroad, 98, 274–75; Army and, xxii, 108–9, 123, 172, 200–202, 220–21, 249, 253, 339n1; benevolent reciprocity and, 9, 146, 231, 237, 248, 289; Biddle and, 171; of "bottom of the barrel," 9, 128, 223, 225, 242, 334n42, 336n60; British, xx, 20, 67–70, 88, 107–8, 111, 164, 237, 301n10, 305n11, 321n72; camp organizational structure, 267; Canadian, 127; CPD policies, 208, 210, 229; and daily life, 264–67; deaths during, 263, 281; of diplomats and officials, 214, 219, 220; as distinct from relocation, 248, 268, 276–77, 317n37, 317n41, 339n1; exchanges and, 8–9, 207, 248; facilities, *fig. 10*, 262; FBI planning and preparation for, 66, 71–74, 79–82, 109–10, 187, 249; Ford and, 169; Geneva Convention and, 266–67; of German Americans (WWI), 20, 33; of German and Italian Americans (East Coast), 147, 197, 199; of German and Italian sailors, xxii, 75, 76, 112; hearings and hearing boards, xxi, xxv, 111, 112, 121, 146–48, 200, 202–5, 218, 224, 246, 248–50, 273, 317n37, 317n41, 329n2, 337n70, 339n1, 341n15; and hemispheric security, 229; historians on reasons for, 4–8; Hoover's planning and preparation for, xx, xxi, 55, 66, 71–74, 79–82, 109–10, 187, 249; Hull and, 186, 196, 250, 274, 275, 344n38; as humanitarian, 169; of inherently harmless aliens, 223, 228, 231, 233, 252, 336n60; INS and, xx, xxi, 75, 104, 108–13, 146–48, 200, 202, 204–5, 218, 221, 224, 244, 246, 248–50, 279–81, 287, 317n37; Instruction No. 58 and, 278–79; international legal justification for, 19–21; of Jews, 69; Latin American policies, 208, 210, 229, 253; Mangione and, 261, 264; by Mexico, 125; military necessity for, 125; and parolees, 112, 249, 274; personnel, 262; plans and preparations for, xx, xxi, 16–17, 81, 108–13, 115, 140; pragmatism of, 7, 65, 123, 125, 128, 289, 323n13; public opinion and, 70; race and racism and, 4–8, 87; reasons for, 4–10, 87, 177, 186–87, 194–95, 218, 254, 322n7; reciprocity and, 97–98, 108–9, 217–18, 250, 274–78, 344n38; Red Cross and, 279, 282; of refugees (in Great Britain), 67–68, 69, 321n72; and repatriation and exchange, 8–9, 207, 221, 229, 232, 248; of Schmitz family, xi, xiii, xiv, 342n21; schools, *fig. 10*, *fig. 14*, *fig. 15*, *fig. 16*, 254, 262, 264, 268, 342n22; security, 255, 261; selection criteria for, 252; U.S. coordination with Great Britain, 69–70; U.S. legal basis for, 21–22; voluntary, 265; War Department and, xx, xxii, 17, 115, 140, 235, 274–75; WWI, 3, 19–23, 33, 67, 153, 209, 291. *See also* Federal Bureau of Investigation (FBI); Immigration and Naturalization Service (INS); internees; Justice Department; Latin America; repatriation and exchange; *and specific camps and forts*

Issei: camp rallies of, 265–66; compared with Nisei, 293–94n1, 316n26; distrust of, 141, 203; in Hawaii, 7; Hoover's views of, 203; ineligibility for naturalization (citizenship), 185, 293–94n1; loyalty of, 141, 176, 179, 310n9, 316n26; relocation of, compared with Germans and Italians, 248. *See also* Japanese Americans; Japanese Hawaiians; Nisei

Italian Americans: assimilation (Americanization) of, 19, 35, 134, 184; Biddle and, 184, 195; in California, 34–35, 147, 340n9; compared with Japanese Hawaiians, 7, 10, 19, 65, 93–94, 115, 121, 123–25, 145, 186, 311n18, 322n7, 323n13, 325n28; consequences of removing en masse, 124, 129, 145, 146–47; Constitution and relocation and interment of, 122–23, 167; in Crystal City, 263, 274; DeWitt and possibility of mass West Coast removal of, 124, 137, 146, 149, 174, 194; East Coast mass relocation of, arguments for/against, 144, 147, 149, 187, 195–97, 199; Ennis and, 166, 204, 339n3; EO 9066 and, 3, 141, 193, 250–51, 325n22; equality of citizenship arguments for, 148, 166; evacuation hardships, 167, 177; factors shielding from mass relocation, 147–49; FBI arrests of (citizens), xxii, 128, 254, 311n18, 330n12; FBI arrests of (enemy aliens), 123, 125, 128, 138, 140, 182, 195–96, 211, 250, 254; FDR and, 19, 77, 122, 134, 149, 150, 164, 178, 186, 195, 250–51; as fifth columnists, 87, 122; hearings (Tolan Committee) for, xxv, 124, 144, 311n22, 315–16n26;

Italian Americans (*cont.*)
jailed (enemy aliens), 182–83; leniency toward, 166, 204, 339n3; loyalty of, 134, 145, 160–66, 330n12; as minor threat, 122, 160; and Mussolini, 48, 120, 150; nationwide military area proposed for, 196; numbers of, along East Coast, 196; numbers of (compared with German and Japanese Americans), determining treatment, 124, 129, 145, 146–49, 177; population of, 14, 18–19, 118, 121, 147, 149, 177, 186–87, 196, 197, 254, 322n7; *Preliminary Report* (Tolan Committee) and, 129, 144–48; relocation (removal) of, as military matter, xxv, 146, 164, 325n22; relocation from East Coast, 3, 197; removal of, from vital areas along East Coast, 199; returning to homes along East Coast, 187; statistical information about, 146–49, 317n40; Stimson and, 164, 177–78, 250; Tolan Committee and, 124, 144, 147–49; treatment of, 148, 166; War Department handling of, compared with Japanese Americans, 167, 177, 178, 195, 250; West Coast mass relocation of, arguments for/against, 124, 137, 144, 146, 149, 174, 178, 194, 250; witness testimony (Tolan Committee) about, 144, 189. *See also* hearing boards and hearings; internees; internment; repatriation and exchange

Italian sailors, *fig. 11*, xxii, 75, 76, 112, 113

Italy: American views of, 37–38, 39–41, 47, 48–49, 53–54, 66; and Ethiopia, 37, 54; FDR and, 90–91; and Germany, xix, xxi, xxiii, 37–38, 80, 100–101; immigration from, 14, 18; and Japan, 100–101; and nationals in/from Latin America, 141, 254, 259, 284, 289; and Order of the Sons of Italy, 37, 39–40, 297n3; polls about, 38, 309n9; relations with U.S., 37–38, 44–45, 54, 80, 90–91, 219

It Can't Happen Here (Lewis), 53

Jackson, Robert, 78–79, 88, 96, 104, 109, 110, 285

Jacobs, Arthur D., 240, 282

Japan: and China, 98, 101, 126, 209; and exchanges with U.S., xxvii, 123, 207, 216–17, 219, 222–24, 226, 227, 234–35, 263; and Geneva Convention, 274, 276, 345n39; and Germany and Italy, 100–101; and nationals in/from Latin America, 9, 127–28, 141, 187, 217, 221, 254, 259, 284; and Pearl Harbor, 115; and Philippines, 98, 117, 217, 315n24; polls about, 116, 118, 119, 176, 309n9, 310n11, 323n13; and Red Cross, 274; relations with U.S., 48, 80, 102–3; rumors of military activity by, 115, 116, 122, 129, 134, 136; as threat to white race, 17, 98, 101, 121, 180, 217; and treatment of U.S. POWs, 97, 236, 272

Japanese American Citizens League (JACL), 144, 145, 287

Japanese Americans: and anti-Asian sentiment, 14–17; anti-Japanese sentiment, 14–18; assimilation of, 124, 183, 185; Bowron and, 144, 158, 180, 184, 188, 320n60, 321–22n1, 324n19; in California, 102, 125, 138, 142, 153, 157, 191, 269, 271, 294n3, 322n7; civil liberties and, 8, 142, 179, 185; compared with Chinese, 132, 151, 157; concern about well-being of, 168, 183, 286; and Congress, xxiv, 65, 322n2; Constitution and relocation and interment of, 122–23, 167, 175; courts and, xxvii, 178, 270; in Crystal City, 262, 263, 286, 287; decision for removal of, from West Coast, 140, 178; demands for actions against or harm to, 138, 158–60, 168–69, 179–80, 181–82; demands for immediate and total removal of, from West Coast, 98, 137, 171, 173, 174, 178, 307n31, 321n1, 323n8; deportations urged for, 138, 168, 272; DeWitt and, xxv, xxvi, xxvii, 87, 121, 128, 131, 137, 145, 171, 173–74, 180, 184, 187–88, 195, 323n8, 326–27n39; EO 9066 and, 3, 141, 193; evacuations of, xxvi, 121, 177; exclusion orders for, xxvi, xxvii, 144, 287; FBI arrests of (citizens), xxii, 128, 254, 311n18, 330n12; FBI arrests of (enemy aliens), 123, 125, 128, 131–32, 138, 140, 171, 182, 188, 211, 250, 254; FDR and, 41, 47, 115, 122, 133, 141, 167, 178, 195, 250–51, 294n4; FDR deferring to military for West Coast removal of, xxiv, 178, 184, 187, 250; fear of, 102, 140, 147, 153, 180, 191; as fifth columnists, xxiv, 3, 81, 87, 94–95, 99–103, 116, 118, 122, 128, 131–37, 142, 150–51, 153, 156–58, 167, 170–73, 178, 180, 188, 251, 312–13n4, 314nn14–16, 318n45, 319n51, 323n9, 326–27n39; Ford and, 168, 168–70, 171, 321n1, 322n2; Geneva Convention applied to, 233; as greater threat than German Americans, 122, 160; Gullion and, 98, 140, 174, 178, 196, 307n31, 323n9;

hearings (Tolan Committee) for, xxv, 124, 144, 311n22, 315–16n26; Immigration Act (1924) and, 185; jailed (enemy aliens), 182–83; lack of assimilation, 124, 183, 185; language schools and, 102, 140; and Los Angeles, xxvi, 99, 102, 121, 132–33, 137–38, 150–51, 153, 156, 158, 179–82, 188, 314nn14–16, 318n45, 319n51; loyalty of, 98–99, 121, 184, 188; mainland (West Coast) compared with Japanese Hawaiians, 10, 19, 33, 48, 65, 94, 101, 102, 121, 124–25, 141, 143, 317n38; mass removal (West Coast) as precedent for mass removal of Germans and Italians, 124, 137, 146, 149, 174, 194; nationwide military area proposed for, 196; numbers of, along East Coast, 196; numbers of (compared with German and Italian Americans), determining treatment, 124, 129, 145, 146–49, 177, 186–87; Olson and, 144, 150, 173, 180, 183–84, 187, 324n19; and ONI, 33, 47, 87, 99–103; organizations investigated by FBI, 99; and Pearl Harbor, 115; as perceived threat, 33, 47, 87, 99–103; polls about, 116; population of, 14, 19, 100, 118, 124, 147, 149, 188–89, 194–95, 294n3, 322n7; *Preliminary Report* (Tolan Committee) and, 129, 144–48; pressures to remove, from West Coast, 122, 128, 130–38, 168–77, 322n2; prewar American views of, 22; public opinion against, 144, 173, 309–10n9, 310nn10–11, 318–19n50, 319n51, 323n13; race/racism and, 15, 17, 120, 141, 143, 151, 184, 294n4; relocation of, from East Coast, 76, 177; relocation (removal) of, as military matter, xxv, 146, 164, 178, 325n22; relocation of, from West Coast, xxv–xxvi, 2–3, 7, 8–9, 121, 145, 184–85, 186–87, 193–95, 268–69; removal of, as military necessity, 173, 176–77, 268; renouncing citizenship, 266; rumors about sinister activities of, 129, 135, 136, 140, 152; as saboteurs, 128, 131, 135, 150–51, 152, 153, 156, 159, 173, 178, 188–89, 190, 271, 314n15, 322n2, 324n20, 324n16; and San Francisco, 102, 140, 153, 180, 191; statistical information about, 146–49, 317n40; Stimson and, 141, 143, 177–78, 184, 250; suspicious activities of, 99, 102, 132, 137, 153, 170; Tolan Committee and, 124, 144, 148–49, 315–16n26; as unassimilable, 15, 17, 120, 141, 143, 151, 184, 294n4; War Department handling of, compared with German and Italian Americans, 167, 177, 178, 195, 250; War Department taking charge of West Coast mass removal of, 175, 178, 184, 250, 317n38; Warren and, xxiv, 131, 171, 173, 183–84, 189, 191, 270; WDC and, xxiv, xxviii, 98–99, 172, 188–89; witness testimony (Tolan Committee) about, 144, 189, 191, 315–16n26. *See also* Hawaii; internees; internment; Issei; Japanese Hawaiians; Nisei; Pearl Harbor; repatriation and exchange; West Coast; yellow peril

Japanese Hawaiians: arrests of, 123, 311n18; Black Dragon Society and, 156; Carter's report and, 93–94; compared with German and Italian Americans, 7, 10, 19, 65, 93–94, 115, 121, 123–25, 145, 186, 311n18, 322n7, 323n13, 325n28; compared with West Coast (mainland) Japanese, 10, 19, 33, 48, 65, 94, 101, 102, 121, 124–25, 141, 143, 317n38; demands for action against, 143, 151, 179, 194; DeWitt on, 16, 115; and economy (island/nation), 123, 194–95, 254, 332n7; EO 9066 and, 141; FDR and, 47–48, 123, 194, 313–14n12; as fifth columnists or threat, xxiii, 33, 102, 134–35, 137, 143, 151, 189–90; internment discussions and plans for, 17, 97, 115; Japan working with, 101; Knox's report about, 134–35; movie about, 152; no mass relocation or internment of, 7, 65, 121, 123–25, 141, 145, 186, 254; numbers of, sent to relocation or internment camps, 123, 311n19; as numerous and influential, 19, 65, 121, 123–25, 145, 186; and Pearl Harbor attack, xxiii, 135, 143; population of, 7, 121, 123, 186, 194–95, 254, 311n19, 322n7; reasons for remaining free, 123–25, 186, 194–95, 254, 311n19, 332n7; repatriation of nationals from, 98, 123, 225–26, 227; selective action against, 194; subject to martial law and restrictions, 115, 123, 311n19; surveillance of, 41; as threat to island way of life, 16; White House recommendations for/against mass relocation of, 134–35, 194, 196, 313–14n12, 322n7. *See also* Hawaii; internees; internment; Issei; Japanese Americans; Nisei; Pearl Harbor; repatriation and exchange; West Coast; yellow peril

Jersey City NJ, 239
Jews: and anti-Semitism in the U.S., 27, 28, 29, 49, 301n10, 335n48; Arthur and Margarethe Mayer, 162–63; *Bolivia Today* report and, 216; CPD's protection of, 337n68; as dangerous refugees, 69, 82–83, 195, 301n10, 335n48; failed efforts to rescue, 230–31; FDR views on, 69, 301n10; fleeing Hitler's Reich, 68; Gerhard Hiller, 165–66; German Americans and, 61, 86; Holocaust and, 306n27, 321n70; internment of, in Great Britain, 69, 301n10; internment of, in U.S., 162–63, 321n70; and Nuremberg Laws, 321n70; petition by, to deport Nazi propagandists, 52; reports of mistreatment in Germany, 41, 45
Johnson, Hiram, 178
Joyce, Kenyon, 126, 186, 194, 312n28, 326n39
Justice Department: and alien enemies, xxii, 78, 107–8, 183–84, 192, 197, 199, 219–20, 246–47, 329n2; and civil liberties, 183; and CPD, 231, 232; and deportations, 107, 192, 207, 246; and exchanges, 9; and FBI, xix, 110, 202–3, 251; INS moving to, 65, 107, 110, 307n41; and internee outcomes, 235; and internment, *fig. 8*, xxvii, 9, 75–76, 107–10, 207, 244, 254, 258–59, 280; investigating subversives, xxi, 104, 140; and Japanese Americans, xxv, 183–84, 324n20; and Latin America, 231, 232; and Mangione, 106–7, 164, 308n43; and State Department, 81–82, 108–9, 153, 211, 242, 246, 269; and Voorhis Act, 104; and War Department, xx, xxii, 108–10, 149, 153, 157, 172, 184, 235, 250, 258, 269. *See also* Alien Enemy Control Unit (AECU), Department of Justice; Alien Registration Division; Biddle, Francis; Ennis, Edward J.; Immigration and Naturalization Service (INS); Neutrality Laws Unit (NLU), Department of Justice; Special Defense Unit (SDU), Department of Justice; Special War Policies Unit (SWPU), Department of Justice

Kearney, Dennis, 15
Keeley, James, Jr., 226, 230–31, 232, 336n60
Kelly, W. F., 139, 245, 277
Kibei, 294n1
King, Ernest, 121, 123, 311n19

King, Mackenzie, 126, 127
Knapp, Laurence, 240, 241, 337–38n72
Knox, Frank: and evacuation and internment, 186, 194; and fifth column, 87, 88, 93, 134–36; and Ford, 168, 169, 170; and Hawaiian Japanese, 194, 313–14n12, 322n7; and interned Americans, 98; and Latin America, 93; and Pearl Harbor, 134–36, 313–14n12; and repatriation and exchange, 98, 227
Korematsu v. United States, xxvii
Krebs, Richard, 96, 306n27
Kuhn, Fritz Julius, xviii, 41–42, 51, 59, 61–63, 242–43, 300–301n50. *See also* German American Bund

Lafoon, Sidney, 242
LaGuardia, Fiorello, 88, 116, 117
La Stampa Libera, 39, 40
Latin America: "Arsenal of Democracy" and threat to, 77, 84, 90–91; bargaining power of, 229; Beals on, 212, 213; bilateral agreements with U.S., 215; cooperation within, 126, 209, 210–11, 232, 331n19; coups in, 88; CPD nations of, 126, 209, 211, 231–32; CPD reports about, 228–29, 231; Crystal City aliens from, 260, 263; defenses of, as inadequate, 130; deportations back to, 232; deportations to Europe and Asia, 2, 211, 232, 233; deportations to U.S., xxiv, 2, 126, 207, 209, 211, 220, 223, 236, 254; Ellis Island aliens from, 219–20, 281; and enemy aliens, 125, 127–28, 209–11, 212, 215–16, 225, 228, 231, 232–33, 244; FBI involvement in, 55, 187, 211, 213–14, 259; FDR's views of, 42, 88, 92–93, 127–28, 214, 219, 233, 234, 330n18, 331n19; fears of seditious activities in, 127–28, 211, 221, 232, 259; fifth column in, 88–90, 92–93, 118, 212–16; fifth-column threats to, 84–85, 118, 127–28, 228–29; fireside chats about, xxii, 50, 84, 89, 90–92, 305nn17–18; Germans in/from, 3, 9, 41, 127–28, 141, 187, 217, 221, 248, 254, 279, 284, 300n45; Germany and reciprocity and, 237–38, 337n68; Goebbels's plans for, xvii, 41, 42–43, 51; Gunther on, 154, 212–13; hemispheric security of, xxiv, 126, 207, 209, 214, 331n19; Hoover and, 55, 187, 211; internee totals from, 284; internment pol-

icies, 208, 210, 229, 253; Italians in/from, 141, 254, 259, 284, 289; Japanese in/from, 9, 127–28, 141, 187, 217, 221, 254, 259, 284; Justice Department and, 231, 232; Long on removing all enemy aliens from, 225; magazine stories about, 84, 89, 92, 154, 212–13; measures taken against aliens, 127–28, 210, 229, 231; mutual defense in, 126, 209–10, 331n19; nations from, in Rio de Janeiro, 126, 207, 209, 215, 331n20; nations from, in Washington DC, 208, 231; Nazi interest in, xvii, 41–43, 88, 298n15; novels about, 89, 96, 154–55, 212–13; Pearl Harbor and, 125–27; polls about German conquest of, 84–85; press coverage of, 89, 92, 212; PROMI and, xvii, 41–43, 51; protection of nondangerous aliens, 210; refugees (including Jews) as threats to, 69, 195; registration and control of aliens in, 210; repatriation and exchange of nationals from, xxiv, 126, 128, 207, 208, 210–11, 215–18, 220–23, 227–29, 231–33, 236–38, 244–46, 248, 333n39; reports about aliens in, 127–28, 221, 232, 253, 259; sabotage expected in, 155, 210, 216, 228; scholarly articles about, 212, 213–14; Sondern and, 89–90, 92; State Department and, 28, 127, 330n11; Stimson and, 93; surveillance of Axis nationals in, 210; U.S. concerns about, 2, 3, 42, 88–89, 91–92, 93, 125, 127–28, 206, 212, 306n20; U.S. fears of Nazi-inspired coups in, 43, 88, 93, 95, 306nn20–21; U.S. intervention in, 2, 3, 93, 207–8, 211–12, 215–16, 231–32, 241, 331n23; U.S. taking charge of security matters in/for, 127–28, 207–8, 211–12, 216, 306n20, 331n19, 331n23; U.S. treatment of Axis nationals in, 254; Wallace and, 214, 215–16; War Department study on, 54. *See also* Emergency Advisory Committee for Political Defense (CPD); Western Hemisphere

The Latrine, 282–83

Lea, Homer, 17

Letitia, 329n7

Lewis, Sinclair, 53

Liberty Magazine, 158

Life, 25, 49, 68, 84, 85, 122, 150, 299n26, 305n19

Liotta, Albert, 163–64

Lippmann, Walter, 136, 187, 314n16, 322n2

"little brown men," 14, 133, 320n60

Long, Breckinridge: and Americans abroad, 208; anti-Semitism of, 301n10, 335n48; and Eleanor Roosevelt, 83; and FDR, 82, 83, 208; fifth-column fears, 82–82, 87; and Latin American, 225; reciprocity, 225–26, 276–77; and refugees, 82–83, 301n10, 335n48; on relocation and internment differences, 276–77; and repatriates, 98, 222, 232; and repatriation and exchange, 123, 225–26, 235

Los Angeles: "Battle of Los Angeles," 120–21, 191; and concern for Japanese, 183, 286; and demand for actions against Japanese, 138, 158–60, 179–80, 181–82; dummy aircraft plants near, 131; Eleanor Roosevelt and LaGuardia visit to, 116; fifth-column fears, 137, 150–51, 153, 156, 158, 180, 188, 314nn14–16, 318n45, 319n51; first large-scale Japanese evacuation from, 121; reports in, after Pearl Harbor, 132–33, 135, 137, 150–51, 158; sabotage fears in, 135, 150–51, 156, 188, 314n15; suspicion of Germans and Italians in, 137; suspicion of Japanese activities in, 99, 102, 132, 137, 153; as target, 116, 190; Tolan Committee and, 144, 148. *See also* Bowron, Fletcher; *Los Angeles Daily News*; *Los Angeles Examiner*; *Los Angeles Times*; Terminal Island

Los Angeles Daily News, 133

Los Angeles Examiner, 150, 169, 312n4, 322n2

Los Angeles Times, 132, 135, 150, 158, 169, 312n4, 314nn15–16, 318n45, 322n2

MacArthur, Douglas, 98, 117, 118–19, 217, 236

Manchuria and Korea, 123, 226

Mangione, Jerre, 106, 164, 255, 261, 264, 308n43, 342n22, 344n35

Manzanar CA, xxvi, 255, 343n30

Marshall, George, 93, 115, 123, 177, 191, 194, 311n19

Marx Brothers, 50

Masaoka, Mike, 5, 145, 287

Matsushita, Iwao and Hanaye, 139–40, 315n22

Maverick, Maury, 88

INDEX 377

Mayer, Arthur and Margarethe, 162–63, 321n70
McCloy, John J., 141, 144, 149, 175, 177–78, 196
McCormack, John W., xvii, 46, 195
McCormack-Dickstein Committee, xvii, xviii, xix, 46, 50–51, 58, 311n21
McGuire, Matthew, 80
McKellar, Kenneth, 57, 105–6
McLemore, Henry, 137, 150–51, 182, 318n45
Mein Kampf (Hitler), 46, 158, 299n23
Menzies, Stewart, 108
Messersmith, George, 71, 82, 208
Mexico: as example for U.S., 125, 127; German espionage in, 82; internees from, 238, 239; internment by, 125; Japanese in, 125, 333n39; Japanese intrigues in, 102, 333n39; Nazi agents in, 89, 92; Pearl Harbor and, 125–27; relations with Germany, 32; relations with U.S., 122, 125, 126, 216
Mexico City, 31, 252
MID. *See* Military Intelligence Division (G-2 or MID)
Military Area No. 1 and No. 2, xxvi, 195, 325n24, 327n41
military areas: Biddle and, 149; defined, 268; DeWitt's Proclamation No. 1 and, xxv; East Coast, xxvi; EO 9066 and, xxv, xxvi, 141; evacuation of, 268; proposed extension of, 196; Public Law 503 and, xxvi, 144, 316n34; voluntary and forced movement from, xxvi, 145; WRA relocating aliens from, 267–68. *See also* Eastern Military Area; West Coast (Pacific) military area
Military Intelligence Division (G-2 or MID), xix, 9, 71, 81, 87, 188, 193, 207, 323n9
military necessity: Army and, 149, 173, 175, 268; DeWitt and, 187–89; EO 9066 and, 250–51, 325n22; FDR and, 141–42; German and Italian relocation and, 164, 325n22; internal threat and, 191–93; internment and, 128; JACL and, 145; Japanese relocation and, 173, 176–77, 268; as main reason for relocation, 125; perceived, 125; West Coast and, 189–91
Monroe Doctrine, 331n23
The Moon Is Down (Steinbeck), 150
Morgenthau, Henry, 56, 87, 318n50

movies, 32, 50, 153, 156; characters in, 318n50; documentary films, 150, 262, 298n14; and movie stars, 169
Murphy, Frank, 72
Mussolini, Benito: admiration and support of, 37, 41, 53; FDR condemning, 303n24; internee support of, 265; Italian Americans and, 48, 120, 150; plans of, 76; Salvemini and, 40; warnings about, 36, 37, 40, 53
Myer, Dillon, 268, 271–72

Nation, 84, 85, 305n19, 306n27
National Defense Tax Bill, 77
National Security League (NSL), 18, 26, 295n12
National Socialism/Socialists, 42, 45, 46, 51, 59–60
National Socialist German Worker's Party (NSDAP), 29, 45, 46, 60, 299n21
National Socialist Teutonia Association, 29, 41, 44
nativism and intolerance, 15–17, 23–24, 25–26, 28, 29, 33
naturalization, 19, 30, 107, 148, 185, 247; Nationality (Naturalization) Act (1940) and, xxi, 78, 303n25; Naturalization Act (1870) and, 16, 316n26
Navy, U.S., xxiii, 32, 47, 48, 75, 119, 130, 177, 189, 223, 227
Nazi Party: connections to proxy groups and Germany, 58, 85, 216; guises of, 41; Hoover investigation of, xviii, 54, 56–59; influence in New York City, 37, 42, 317–18n43; INS report on, 44. *See also* American Nazis; Federal Bureau of Investigation (FBI); Friends of New Germany; Friends of the New Germany; Gau-USA; German American Bund; Hoover, J. Edgar; House Un-American Activities Committee (HUAC); McCormack–Dickstein Committee
Neutrality Laws Unit (NLU), Department of Justice, xix, xxii, 71, 80–81. *See also* Smith, Lawrence; Special Defense Unit (SDU), Department of Justice; Special War Policies Unit (SWPU), Department of Justice
New Orleans, 91, 220, 252
New Republic, 25, 33, 52, 85, 306n27

Newsweek, 84, 85, 86, 96–97, 213, 315n24
New York City: Bundists in, 63; exchanges through, 219–20, 235, 263; fascist and Nazi influence in, 37, 42, 317–18n43; fears of fifth columnists in, 317–18n43; Japanese resettling in, 269; mayor LaGuardia, 88
New York Times: on arrests of Nazi sailors, 96; on Bund membership, 63; and Eleanor Roosevelt, 204; on enemy aliens, 218; on exchanges, 220; fifth-column headlines, 42, 51–52, 53, 96, 305n14, 305–6n19, 317–18n43, 322n2; on fireside chat, 191; *Gripsholm* headlines, 337n69; on interned American women, 218–19; on Nazi agents in U.S., 42, 51, 53; Nazi headlines, 51, 299n21, 299n30, 299–300n31, 305–6n19; and Schueller case, 198
Niebuhr, Reinhold, 202
Nisei: camp rallies of, 265–66; combat unit of, 269; compared with Issei, 293–94n1, 316n26; demographics of, 147–48; distrust of, 141, 315–16n26; in Hawaii, 7; loyalty of, 141, 176, 179, 310n9, 316n26; racism and, 141; relocation of, compared with Germans and Italians, 248; as unassimilable, 141; views of, after Pearl Harbor, 134; and West Coast removal, 173. *See also* Issei; Japanese Americans; Japanese Hawaiians
Norris, George, 106
Norway, 91; fifth column in, 85, 134, 162, 189; German occupation of, 77, 85; and pressure to deport American women, 218–19
Nyassa, 222

Oahu, *fig.* 8, 16, 48, 135, 194, 313–14n12
Offenheimer, Mrs. Ernst, 161–62
Office of Civilian Defense, xxii, xxvii, 67; and civilian defenses, 171, 305n17
Office of Facts and Figures, 27
Office of Naval Intelligence (ONI): assisting FBI, 71, 105, 242, 315n22; and FDR, 31–32; fifth-column concerns, 9, 87, 99–103, 115, 213, 315n22; and German Americans, 32; and Japanese as threat, 33, 47, 87; as part of IIC, xix, 71, 204, 207, 213; warning about Pearl Harbor, 47; and West Coast vulnerabilities, 100
Office of Strategic Services (OSS), 82, 87, 115, 304n33

Office of War Information (OWI), 152–53, 156, 320n50
Olson, Culbert, 144, 150, 173, 180, 183–84, 187, 324n19
Order of the Sons of Italy, 37, 39–40, 297n3
O'Rourke, Joseph, 261–64, 341n17
Out of the Night (Valtin), 96, 306n27

Pacific (West) Coast Congressional delegation, xxiv, 172–73, 178, 322n2
Panama: Declaration of, 214, 331n19; Japanese focus of, 211; U.S. bases in, 215
Panama Canal (and Zone), 75, 92, 101, 115, 130, 213, 214
patriotic and nativist organizations, 15, 17, 25, 26, 29, 57, 81, 145, 182, 295n12, 296n27, 303n23
The Pattern of Nazi Organizations and Their Activities in the Other American Republics (Berle), 214, 312n29, 330n17
Pearl Harbor: arrests before and after, 8, 97, 128, 140, 330n12; attack on, xxii, 114, 116, 118; Biddle and, 117, 189; Canada and, 125–27; CPD and, 126; DeWitt and, 115, 121, 128, 173, 187, 190, 194; effect of, on Germans, 116–17, 122, 127, 133; effect of, on Japanese, 2, 116–17, 119–20, 122, 127, 133; FDR and, 117, 313–14n12; and fear of Japanese invasion, 122, 127, 179; fifth-column work at, xxiii, 93, 116, 129, 134, 291, 305n19, 327n39; and Germany, 117, 195, 309n7; and hatred of Japanese, 119, 121, 179, 198; Hollywood reaction to, 152, 167; information about Japan's plans to attack, 115; Knox findings (report) on fifth columnists and, 134–36, 313–14n12; Latin America and, 125–27; literary impact of, 154; media reaction to, 97, 133, 135, 150–51, 305n19, 315n24; Mexico and, 125–27; ONI warning of Japanese activities near, 47; political reaction to, 143–44, 150, 153, 169–72, 180, 185, 188, 270; polling after, 116, 119, 176, 309n7; pop-culture responses to, 153–54; public reactions to, 116, 169–70, 179–82; reinforcing fifth-column fears, 9, 93, 118, 122, 129, 150; revenge for, 114, 119, 143–44, 179; Roberts Commission report on, xxiv, 136, 157, 173; and sabotage, 115, 135, 136, 189; U.S. reaction to, 2, 114, 116, 117, 127; War Department expectations prior to, 115; and West Coast fears of repeat attack, xxiv, 127

INDEX 379

Pegler, Westbrook, 131, 137, 180, 314n17
Perrett, Geoffrey, 35, 310n11, 311n20
Perry, Donald, 105, 166
Personal Justice Denied, 22, 323n11
Peru, 211, 214, 220, 332n32
Peters, Kurt Heinrich Rudolf, 256–58
Phelan, James, 15
Philippines: Japanese attacks on, xxiii, 117, 315n24; Japanese fifth columnists and, 151, 179; Japanese occupation of, 98, 217; U.S. civilians (nationals) in, 98, 217–18, 231, 236, 337n66
Pine Island, Cuba, *fig. 8*, 254
polls (Gallup and others), 38, 77, 84–85, 116–19, 176, 309n7, 310n11, 323n13
posters, *fig. 5*; popular slogans on, 153–54; proclamations on, xxvi, 107, 197, 246, 278–79, 327n46; war, 319n52
Prager, Robert, 28, 296n30
Prendergast, Joseph, 103
"The Price of Free World Victory" (Wallace), 215–16
Princeton, 86
prisoners of war (POWs): aid to, 234; Axis-held, 220, 273, 337n66; Canada helping U.S. with, 109; exchanges of, 82, 207, 227, 232, 233, 235, 238–39; Geneva Convention and, 82, 207, 275–76; internee equality of treatment with, 207, 249, 275, 277; Japan's treatment of U.S., 97, 236, 272; reciprocity, 97, 274, 276–77; reports about, 276; Special Division and, 82; U.S. receiving, 113, 259; U.S. treatment of Japanese, 97, 275; WWI and, *fig. 2*, 209
Proclamation No. 1: DeWitt's, xxv, 327n41; Drum's, xxvi, 197, 327n46
prohibited zones, 194
Propaganda Ministry (PROMI), xvii, 41, 42, 51. *See also* Goebbels, Joseph
protecting (neutral) powers (Spain, Sweden, and Switzerland), 82, 219, 236, 243, 278, 304n33, 337n66
protective agencies (AECU, FBI, MID [G-2], ONI), 207, 221, 224, 226, 230
Public Law 503, xxvi, 144, 316n34
public opinion: and FARA, xix, 302n17; German attempts to influence, 43, 298n15; against Germany, 309–10n9, 310n11, 318–19n50, 323n13; and internment, 70; against Italy, 37; against Japanese, 144, 173, 309–10n9, 310nn10–11, 318–19n50, 319n51, 323n13; and Japanese evacuation, 116, 122; and Nazi movement, 62, 273–74; and Roberts report, 136; West Coast and, 179–82; and Zimmerman telegram, 32
Puget Sound, 99, 102, 126
Putlitz, Wolfgang Zu, 161

Quarantine Speech (1937), xviii, 49, 88
Quisling, 85, 318n44

race and racism: anti-Semitism in the U.S., 27, 28, 29, 49, 301n10; and assimilation (Americanization), 13, 14, 18, 27, 45, 60, 120, 127, 141, 185, 299n23; and Christian Right, 49; creating climate for relocation and internment, 8, 87; EO 9066 and, xxv, 141, 314n13; Hitler's ideas of, 27, 45, 47, 60, 237, 298n11, 299n23; and Japanese Americans, 15, 17, 98, 101, 120, 121, 141, 143, 151, 180, 184, 185, 217, 294n4; and nativism and intolerance, 15–17, 23–24, 25–26, 28, 29, 33; and notions of superiority, 14, 17, 127; and relocation and internment argument, 4–8; and stereotypes, 22, 27, 33, 88, 153, 316n35; and yellow peril, 17, 33, 34, 120, 127, 191, 272, 304n8
race and space, doctrines of, 41
Rankin, John, 142–43, 168, 184
Reader's Digest, 85, 86, 89, 92, 151
Red Cross (American and International or ICRC): and internees, 279, 282; and Japan, 274; relief and repatriation efforts of, 82, 208, 218, 222; reports of, 220, 265, 274, 275–76, 278, 337n66; representatives (personnel) of, 217, 278, 281
Red Scare, 27, 28, 38, 119
refugees: advocates for, and advocacy by, 83, 165–66; as anti-fascist and anti-Nazi, 109, 146, 148, 164–65; in Bolivia, 216; British handling and internment of, 67, 68, 69, 321n72; in Canada, 308n49; FDR and, 69, 164–65, 301n10; fears of Jews among, 69, 82, 301n10; as fifth columnists, 31, 85, 96, 137, 151, 213; Long and, 82–83, 301n10, 335n48; numbers of, 166, 195; support of, and sympathy for, 148–49, 160, 164, 230; as

threat, 82, 228, 301n10, 304n33, 335n48; as victims of Nazis, 157, 161–62; WWI and, 31
relocation (removal): of American citizens, 175, 177, 187, 194, 196; Army and, 9, 147, 268–69; Axis military victories and, 8–9, 93, 110, 129–30, 176, 292, 305–6n19; Canada and, 127; Constitution and, 122–23, 167, 175; courts regarding Japanese American, xxvii, 178; demands for enemy alien, 3, 116, 119, 121, 136, 168–79, 181–82, 184, 187; DeWitt and en masse West Coast German and Italian, 124, 137, 146, 149, 174, 194; as distinct from internment, 248, 268, 276–77, 317n37, 317n41, 339n1; of enemy aliens, 3, 8, 9, 121–22, 127, 187; EO 9066 and, xxv, 141, 314n13; factors shielding German and Italian Americans from en masse, 147–49; FDR defers to military for West Coast Japanese, xxiv, 178, 184, 187, 250; Ford and, 169–71, 321n1, 322n2; of German and Italian Americans en masse from East Coast, arguments for/against, 76, 144, 147, 149, 187, 195–97, 199; of German and Italian Americans en masse from West Coast, arguments for/against, 124, 137, 144, 146, 149, 174, 178, 194, 250; of German and Italian Americans selectively from East and West Coasts, 3, 9, 76, 121, 122, 145, 197, 199; Gullion and, 98, 140, 174–75, 177–78, 196, 307n31; hearings rejected for those impacted by en masse, 339n1; historians on reasons for, 4–8; of internee sailors and others from East Coast, 76, 136; of Japanese Americans en masse from West Coast, xxv–xxvi, 2–3, 7, 8–9, 121, 145, 184–85, 186–87, 193–95, 268–69; of Japanese Americans from East Coast, 76, 277; of Japanese Hawaiians selectively, 7, 65, 121, 123–25, 141, 145, 186, 254; of Jews, 321n70; Long and, 276–77; as military matter, xxv, 146, 164, 178, 325n22; news about, 269–72; peak demands for, 119, 125–26, 129, 151, 180, 186, 312n1, 322n4, 324n20; pragmatism of, 7, 65, 121, 123, 125, 137, 194, 289, 323n13; pressures against West Coast Japanese Americans, 122, 128, 130–38, 168–77, 184, 187, 322n2; race and racism creating climate for, 8, 87; reasons involving, 4–9, 121–22, 125, 136, 145, 186–87, 194–95, 254, 322n7; Tolan Committee and, xxv, 124, 129, 144–49, 317n40; War Department and, 142, 172, 175, 177–78, 184, 195, 250, 317n38; White House recommendations for/against Japanese Hawaiians en masse, 134–35, 194, 196, 313–14n12, 322n7; WRA and, 267–68; and WWI precedents, 3, 19, 20, 22, 33, 67, 153, 291. See also DeWitt, John; East Coast; War Relocation Authority (WRA); War Relocation Centers; West Coast; Western Defense Command (WDC)

removal. See relocation (removal)

repatriates: aiding the enemy, 98; Biddle and, 222, 232; as "bottom of the barrel," 9, 128, 223, 225, 242, 334n42, 336n60; Canadian, 222, 238; classification of, 236–37; criminals desired as, 225; as dangerous, xxiv, 9, 19, 217, 221, 223, 231; as destitute or imperiled Americans, 82, 206, 208–9; FBI and, 239, 242; inherently harmless, xxvii, 223, 228, 231, 233; numbers of, 222; objections to, 217, 221, 223–24, 226–27, 234, 242–43, 332–33n35; from Peru, 220, 332n32; qualities and desirability of, 225–30; selected through error, 236; U.S. officials disappointed by, 222, 232

repatriation and exchange: advantages of, 128, 217, 225, 228, 229, 333n39, 336n60; background of, 213–14; bargaining power of American republics for, 228, 229; Biddle and, 222–23, 224, 232, 233, 242; of "bottom of the barrel," 9, 128, 223, 225, 242, 334n42, 336n60; complexities of, 239–40; comprehensive policy for, 227–28, 333n39, 334n42; CPD and, xxiv, 126, 207, 208, 210–11, 229, 231–32, 237–38; of dangerous Axis nationals, xxiv, 9, 217, 221, 223; deportations for, xxiv, 126, 207, 209, 211, 244–45; dilemma and shift in, 223–25; duration of, 206–7; ethics of, 240–42; European, 20–29; FDR and, 217, 222, 225; first voyages, 219–23; forced, 207, 220, 221, 232–33, 235, 245–46, 282, 290, 337n70; Great Britain and, 48, 208, 236, 332–33n35; hearing boards and, 337n70; Hull and, 206, 216–17, 219, 222, 225; inaccurate information and repatriation and exchange (cont.) outright duplicity of, 232; of inherently harmless Axis nationals, xxvii, 223, 228, 233; internment and, 8–9, 207, 221, 229, 232, 248; of Japanese Hawaiians, 123, 226; Knox and, 98, 227; Latin American nationals and, xxiv, 126, 128, 207, 208, 210–11, 215–18, 220–23, 227–29, 231–33, 236–38, 244–46, 248, 333n39; Long and, 123, 225–26, 235; media coverage of, 220, 337n69; military and national-security context of, 98, 222–23, 227–28, 229, 231–32, 290; overview of, 206–8; pause in, 230–31; of persons of certain qualities and desirability, 225–30; planning of, 209–11; policy shift (from dangerous to inherently harmless aliens), xxvii, 223, 229, 231, 233; postwar, 246; pragmatism of (including internment), 7, 65, 123, 125, 128, 289, 323n13; protective agencies (AECU, FBI, MID [G-2], ONI) and, 207, 221, 224, 226–27, 230; purpose of, 2, 128, 206, 223–24, 229, 231–33, 289, 292, 333n39, 334n42, 336n60; resistance to, 239, 245; results of, 244–45; resumption of, 233–38; *Santa Lucia* and, xxiv, 219; secrecy of, 238–39, 242, 273; Special Division and, 82, 206, 208, 221, 226, 332n30; State Department and, 206, 227–28; of undesirables, 128, 222, 225, 228; U.S. leading role with, 2, 207, 211, 215–16, 221, 232, 240–42, 245; U.S. taking charge of, 215–16; voluntary, 207, 232–33, 245. *See also* exchanges; internees; internment; repatriates

restricted areas, xxiii, xxiv, 98, 146, 172, 217, 251, 317n39

restricted zones, 134, 183, 184; Restricted Zone B, 327n41

Reynolds, Robert, 95

Ringle, Kenneth, 94

Rio de Janeiro, inter-American conference in, 126, 207, 209, 215, 331n20

Roberts, Owen, 135, 322n7

Roberts Commission, report of, xxiv, 136, 157, 170, 173, 184; testimony to, 189

Roosevelt, Eleanor: and Biddle, 116, 204, 309n4, 328n58; and fifth-column threat, 83; Hoover investigating, 58; and LaGuardia, 116; and Long, 83

Roosevelt, Franklin Delano: addresses to Congress, xx, 49; belief in saboteurs and subversives, 31, 95, 120, 128, 133, 318n50; and Biddle, 122, 164; and Churchill, 115, 118; and Constitution, 122–23; declaration of "unlimited national emergency," xxii, 74, 91–92, 305n17; deferring to military for West Coast Japanese removal, xxiv, 178, 184, 187, 250; and DeWitt, 128, 184; distrust of Germans during WWI, 31, 83, 95; and Donovan, 107; elections of, 77, 145, 185–86; and FBI, xix, 7, 43, 54–57, 64–65, 71, 79, 80; and fifth-column consensus, 9, 88; fifth-column fears, xx, xxii, 49–50, 65, 87–88, 90–94, 121, 164, 167, 186; and German and Italian Americans, 19, 77, 122, 134, 149, 150, 164, 178, 186, 195, 250–51; and Great Britain, 107–8; and Hawaiian Japanese, 47–48, 123, 194, 313–14n12; and Hoover, 55, 64–65, 71, 80, 302n16; and IIC, xix, 71; and Japanese Americans, 41, 47, 115, 122, 133, 141, 167, 178, 195, 250–51, 294n4; and Latin America, 42, 88, 92–93, 127–28, 214, 219, 233, 234, 330n18, 331n19; and Long, 82, 83, 208; measures against aliens, xxii, 65, 116; mobilizing for war, 72, 77, 93, 106; and Nazi hemispheric menace, xxii, 92–93, 120; and new global war, xxv, 49, 50, 91; and Pearl Harbor, 117, 313–14n12; proclamations of, xxii, xxiii, xxvii, 66, 74, 91–92, 133, 192, 214, 305n17, 311n19, 313n9; and Public Law 503, 144; radio addresses, 49, 50, 91, 120; refugees writing to, 164–65; repatriation and exchange, 217, 222, 225; speeches of, xviii, 77, 88, 93; and Stimson, 141, 149, 250; as suspicious of refugees, including Jews, 69, 301n10; winning the war as top priority, 122, 124, 133, 153, 191. *See also* Executive Order (EO) 9066; fireside chats

Roosevelt, Theodore, 13

Roosevelt corollary, 331n23

Rowe, James, 107, 172, 175, 183, 188, 249

rumors (tales): of accidents and diseases during WWI, 25; of arrows, 135, 140, 152; along East Coast, 152; of fifth-column activity, 85, 87, 126, 136; about Germans during WWI, 22, 25, 27; of internee atrocities or mistreatment, 243, 274, 275; of Japanese American sinister activities, 129, 135, 136, 140, 152; of Japanese military activity, 115, 116, 122, 129, 134, 136; of sabotage and espionage, 22, 25, 33; along West Coast, 116, 122, 129

sabotage: absence of, as ominous, 127, 128, 137, 189, 193, 322n2; actions countering, 131, 133; Atlantic and Gulf Coast and, 197, 271; Biddle and, 192; in books, 96; Carter's report of, 94; citizens' fears of, 159, 324n20; DeWitt's fears of, 173, 175; EO 9066 and, 267; EO 9165 protecting against, xxvii, 191; in Europe, 95, 155, 228; and FBI, xix, xx, 65, 71, 72, 95, 103; and FDR, 92, 128; fifth column and, xxii, 95, 215, 322n2; German Americans and, 22, 31, 33; IIC and, 71; as imminent, 135, 146, 154, 173; Japanese Americans and, 135, 150–51, 152, 153, 156, 159, 178, 188–89, 190, 271, 314n15, 322n2, 324n20, 324n16; Japanese invasion and, 146, 271; lack of evidence of, 90, 136–37, 152, 177, 189, 193, 196, 291; in Latin America, 155, 210, 216, 228; magazine stories about, 33, 150, 151, 318n47; movies and, 156; Nazis and, 155; as part of warfare, 131, 155; Pearl Harbor and, 115, 135, 136, 189; press reports of, 22, 96, 133, 135, 152; reassuring public about, 133, 192; Roberts report of, 136–37; state delegates discussing, 67; Tolan Committee and, 189; Wallace predicting, 215–16; War Department and, 54, 191; West Coast and, 156, 173, 181, 190; widespread assumptions of, 135, 322n2; WWI and, 31, 33
Sabotage! The Secret War against America (Sayers and Kahn), 154-56, 319n54
Salvemini, Gaetano, 40
San Antonio, 88, 260
San Francisco: fears in, after Pearl Harbor, 190; INS immigration station in, 112; internees arriving in, 220; Japanese fifth column (disloyals) in, 102, 140, 153, 180, 191; labor movement in, 15; Nazi diplomatic pipeline from, 213; PMG Office in, 141; Presidio in, 188; reactions to German sailor internees in, 75; report of attack on, 116; as target of Japanese military, 116, 153; Tolan Committee in, xxv, 144

San Francisco Chronicle, 14, 17, 97, 134, 151, 294n8, 322n2
Santa Fe NM, 244, 260, 266, 267, 272, 287, 344n35
Santa Lucia, xxiv, 219
Saturday Evening Post, 18, 85
Sayers, Michael and Albert Kahn, 154, 319n54
Schenck v. United States, 28
Schmitz, John A., *fig. 16*, 341n17, 342n21
Schofield, Lemuel B., 113, 278
schools: closing, 130; for espionage and sabotage studies, 270, 271, 343n32; internment camp, *fig. 10, fig. 14, fig. 15, fig. 16*, 254, 262, 264, 268, 342n22; interwar era, 66; Japanese language, 102, 126, 140; Japanese men in, 294n8; student records provided to FBI, 73; WWI and, 23, 25, 26
Schueller, Olga, 198, 327n48
Seagoville TX, 239, 260, 263, 265, 284
Security Index, xxvii, 204, 302n16. *See also* Custodial Detention Index (CDI)
Sedition Act (1798), 21
Selective Service Act (1940), 77, 201; and Boards, 197
Serpa Pinto, 222
Seward, Lee, 238
Shawnee, 220, 299n25, 329n5
Sheean, Vincent, 150
Sheppard, Harry, 142
Shirer, William, 154
Silver Shirt Legion, 46, 47, 104
Singapore, fall of, 127, 141, 159, 189, 315n24
Smith, D. W., 230, 335n55
Smith, Lawrence, 8, 71, 112, 231
Smith Act. *See* Alien Registration (Smith) Act (1940)
Sondern, Frederick, 89–90, 92
Spain: legation of, and exchanges, 216; as protecting (neutral) power, 219, 236, 332n30
Spanish Civil War (1936–39), xviii, 85, 298n13
Special Defense Unit (SDU), Department of Justice, xxii, 8, 69, 71, 80–81, 109, 111. *See also* Neutrality Laws Unit (NLU), Department of Justice; Smith, Lawrence; Special War Policies Unit (SWPU), Department of Justice

Special Division (SD), State Department, xix, xxii, 82–83, 206, 208, 226, 328–29n1, 332n30, 335n48. *See also* Long, Breckinridge; Special War Problems Division (SWPD)
Special Report on Subversive Activities (HUAC), xxvii, 62
Special War Policies Unit (SWPU), Department of Justice, 71, 231. *See also* Neutrality Laws Unit (NLU), Department of Justice; Smith, Lawrence; Special Defense Unit (SDU), Department of Justice
Special War Problems Division (SWPD), State Department, 82, 276, 328–29n1, 329n2. *See also* Long, Breckinridge; Special Division (SD), State Department
Sperry, Earl, 26
Stannard, Amy, 265, 341n17
State Department: and Americans abroad, 48, 54, 82, 108–9, 208–9, 275, 277; and Auslandsorganisation and Hitler, 58–59; and CPD, 211, 228, 330n11; determining internee outcomes, 235; and exchanges, 207; and FARA, 73; fascism concerns, 40, 58–59, 100; fifth-column concerns, 83; and forced deportations of Latin Americans (Axis nationals), 207; and Germany and Italy, 38; and *Gripsholm*, 239–40; and halt in exchanges, 230–31; and Justice Department, 81–82, 108–9, 211, 242, 246; and Latin America, 127–28, 211, 216–17, 219–23, 225–30, 236–38, 240–42, 282; and media, 238, 337n69; and new exchanges, 233–36; postwar forced deportation/expatriation, 246–47; prioritizing exchanging official personnel, 216–17; and reciprocity, 108–9, 275–78; and repatriates, 225–30; and repatriation and exchange, 82–83, 206–7, 208–9, 216–17; repatriation and exchange policies, 223–30, 332–33n35; and Stewart Test, 243; and War Department, 81–82, 108–9, 235, 250. *See also* Hull, Cordell; Long, Breckinridge; Special Division (SD), State Department; Special War Problems Division (SWPD), State Department
Statue of Liberty, 281, 285, 296n23
Steinbeck, John, 150, 318n44
Stettinius, Edward, 216, 328–29n1

Stewart, Tom, 142, 143
Stewart Emotional Response Test, 243, 338n76
Stimson, Henry: and alien enemy investigations, xx, 81, 108; and American internees, 98; and Biddle, 149, 164, 171, 321n70; and Drum, 197; and East Coast, 196–97; and EO 9066, xxv; and FDR, 141, 149, 250; fifth-column concerns, 55, 87, 93, 94, 164; and Ford, 168, 169, 171–72; and German and Italian Americans, 164, 177–78, 250; and *The German Reich*, 59–61; and Hawaiian Japanese, 194–95, 322n7, 327n40; and Hull, 217–18; and Italian fascism, 38, 40; and Japanese Americans, 141, 143, 177–78, 184, 250; and Knox, 135; and Latin America, 93; and mass evacuation of West Coast Japanese, xxiv, 141; and Nisei combat unit, 269; and racism, 98, 117, 141, 217, 309n7; and reciprocity, 98, 113, 218, 243, 275, 339–40n4. *See also* War Department
Stone, Harlan Fiske, 55
Stout, Rex, 273
Stringtown OK, 258
"suspect list": as basis of investigations and actions, 81, 82, 104, 108, 110, 303n29; creation of, xviii, 56; as forerunner of CDI, xviii, 72, 302n16; persons on, xxi, 72
Sweden, 219, 232, 304n33, 332n30
Switzerland, 232, 238, 304n33; and exchanges, 216, 219, 235, 238, 240, 332n30; Legation of, 1, 138, 216, 233, 235; reports by, 236, 276; representatives of, 240, 265

Tamm, Edward, 80
Tate, Robert, *fig. 16*
Terminal Island, 113, 121, 137
Theberath, Peter and Marie, 1, 138–39
Time, xxv, 61, 85, 96, 121, 141, 151, 152, 154, 303n23, 310n12
Tolan, John, 124, 144, 311n22
Tolan Committee: and DeWitt, 124; and EO 9066, xxv, 144; follow-up (*Fourth Interim*) report, 148–49; and Germans and Italians, 124, 129, 144, 145, 146–49; hearings (duration and locations), xxv, 124, 144, 311n22, 315–16n26; hearing testimony, 144, 189, 191, 315–16n26; and Japanese, 124, 144, 148–49, 315–16n26; *Preliminary*

Report, 129, 144–48; and refugees, 148–49, 164; statistical information about Germans, Italians, and Japanese, 146–49, 317n40; Warren's testimony, 189, 191; and West Coast, 144–49; West Coast compared to East Coast, 148–49; witnesses, 144, 315–16n26
total war, *fig. 3*, 2, 20, 93, 291
Trojan Horse, 50, 59, 84, 87, 92, 305n19
Truman, Harry, xxvii, 244
Tule Lake, California, *fig. 6*, 244, 255, 259, 268, 269, 271, 287, 342n20

Under Cover: My Four Years in the Nazi Underworld of America (Carlson), 156–57, 320n56
U.S. Army. *See* Army, U.S.
U.S. Coast Guard, 76, 199, 220
U.S. Congress. *See* Congress, U.S.
U.S. Constitution. *See* Constitution, U.S.
U.S. Navy. *See* Navy, U.S.

Valenti, Girolamo, 39–40
The Valor of Ignorance (Lea), 17
Valtin, Jan (Richard Krebs), 96, 306n27
Vattel, Emerich von, 19
Victory Huts, *fig. 10*, 260, 261
Voorhis, Jerry: and Voorhis Act (1940), 104

Wallace, Henry, 87, 155, 214, 215
War Department: and American internees, 274–75; and Biddle, 149, 175, 325n25; determining internee outcomes, 235; downplaying evacuation hardships, 167, 177; and FBI, 109, 187, 207, 221, 226, 235; and FDR, 178, 250; and fifth-column consensus, 9, 87; and fifth-column threat, 81, 87, 171, 188; handling of Germans and Italians compared with Japanese, 178, 195, 250; hesitancy to relocate citizens, 177; improving domestic military readiness, 188, 325n31; and Japanese sabotage at Pearl Harbor, 115; and Justice Department, xx, xxii, 108–9, 110, 184, 235, 250; and Latin America, 54; lifting exclusion orders, xxvii, 287; and mass relocation of Germans and Italians, 178, 250; overruling DeWitt, 149, 177–78; Pacific Coast delegation and, 172–74; as part of IIC, 70–71; plans to intern Hawaiian enemy aliens, 17, 115; and *Prelude to War*, 152; reciprocity, 274–75; and State Department, 108–9, 235, 250; and Tolan Committee, 144; West Coast mass removal of Japanese, 175, 178, 184, 250, 317n38; West Coast removal recommendations of, 142; and *Why We Fight* series, 152; WWI camps, 33. *See also* McCloy, John J.; Military Intelligence Division (G-2 or MID); Stimson, Henry
War Relocation Authority (WRA), *fig. 6, fig. 7, fig. 8*, xxv, xxviii, 3, 9, 178–79, 219, 244, 248, 259, 267–69, 272, 281, 287, 317nn38–39. *See also* Myer, Dillon; War Relocation Centers
War Relocation Centers, *fig. 6, fig. 7*; closure, xxviii, 268, 287; conditions of, 268; courts and, 178; draft crisis and, 269; EO 9102 and, xxv, 259, 317n39; establishment of, xxv, 268; five-point program of, 268; Japanese Americans moved (from assembly centers) to, xxvi, 268–69, 317n36, 342n28; life in, 268–69; location of, 259, 267–68; medical care and, 281; news about relocatees, 269–72; purpose of, 3, 259, 267–68; release from, 269–72; relocation as distinct from internment, 248, 268, 276–77, 317n37, 317n41, 339n1. *See also* assembly centers; relocation (removal); War Relocation Authority (WRA)
Warren, Earl, xxiv, 131, 171, 173, 183–84, 189, 191, 270
Wartime Civil Control Administration (WCCA), *fig. 6, fig. 8*, xxv, 259, 267, 325n21, 342n28
Washington DC, 24, 47, 130, 152, 168, 208, 219, 231
Washington Post, 28, 296n30
Welles, Sumner, 83, 87, 97, 108, 208, 219, 235, 301n10
Wells, H. G., 33
West Coast: Army and, 9, 87, 98, 108–9, 130, 147, 149, 172, 175, 188, 217, 268–69, 339n1; attack on, believed imminent, 114, 128, 173, 190, 191; Biddle and, 195–96; Category A and B areas, 184, 325n24, 327n41; compared to East Coast, 119, 144, 148–49, 195–96, 251; demands for removal of all Japanese from, 98, 136–38, 171, 173, 174,

West Coast (*cont.*)
178, 307n31, 321n1, 323n8; enemy aliens, 3, 121, 122, 149, 168–79, 184, 193, 195; EO 9066 and, xxv, 3, 141–42, 183, 187, 193–94, 250–51, 267, 325n22, 342n28; exclusion orders, xxvi, 144, 250, 287, 325n22; FDR defers to military for removal of Japanese Americans from, xxiv, 178, 184, 187, 250; and fifth column, 87, 128, 173, 180, 188, 326–27n39; Ford and, 171, 321n1; Gullion and, 98, 140, 174–75, 177–78, 196, 307n31, 323n9; Japanese Americans on, compared with Japanese Hawaiians, 10, 19, 33, 48, 65, 94, 101, 102, 121, 124–25, 141, 143, 317n38; mass relocation arguments for/against German Americans on, 124, 137, 144, 146, 149, 174, 178, 194, 250; mass relocation arguments for/against Italian Americans on, 124, 137, 144, 146, 149, 174, 178, 194, 250; Navy and, xxiii, 47, 118–19, 130, 141, 276; Nisei, 147–48, 173; numbers of Japanese Americans (compared with German and Italian Americans) on, determining treatment, 124, 129, 145, 146–49, 177, 186–87; pressures to remove Japanese Americans from, 122, 128, 130–38, 168–77, 184, 187, 322n2; prewar fears of Japanese attack/invasion of, 32, 33, 34; proclamations concerning, xxii–xxiii, xxv, xxvi, 144, 313n9, 325n24, 327n41; public gatherings postponed, 131; public opinion against Japanese Americans on, 144, 173, 179–82, 309–10n9, 310nn10–11, 318–19n50, 319n51, 323n13; relocation (removal) of Japanese Americans, xxv–xxvi, 2–3, 7, 8–9, 121, 145, 184–85, 186–87, 193–95, 268–69; relocation (removal) of Japanese Americans as military matter, xxv, 146, 164, 178, 325n22; removal of Japanese completed from, xxvii, 195; sabotage expected on, 128, 131, 173; threats to, 129–30; Tolan Committee and, 144–49; vigorous enemy alien program urged for, xxiii, 126, 128, 184, 196; as vulnerable to Japanese attack, 121, 188, 194; as "war zone," 314n16. *See also* DeWitt, John; internment; relocation and removal

West Coast (Pacific) military area, xxv, xxvi, 3, 145, 164, 268, 276

Western Defense Command (WDC): and "Battle of Los Angeles," 120–21; and DeWitt, 188; enemy aliens registering with, xxiv, 172; and Japanese, xxviii, 98–99, 188–89; Research Branch of, 98–99; security responsibility of, 188, 190. *See also* DeWitt, John

western defensive zone, *fig. 6*, 259

Western Hemisphere, 10; CPD and, 209, 238; dangerous persons residing throughout, 69, 195, 206, 229–30; FDR and, 305n17, 331n19; Germany and, xvii, 41, 43, 88, 217, 298n15, 300n45, 304n33; U.S. and, 2, 305n17, 331n19, 332–33n35, 333n39. *See also* Latin America

White Sulphur Springs, 219, 220

Why We Fight (Capra), 152

Wilson, Woodrow, *fig. 1*, 23, 24, 25, 30, 32, 34

World War I: anti-German sentiment, 18, 25–26; Australian registration of aliens, *fig. 3*; Bureau of Investigation arrests during, 32–33; European internment numbers, 20; and German Americans, *fig. 1*, 19, 23–26, 28, 30, 34, 296n30; and German immigration, 14, 18, 23; internment during, 19–21, 20, 33; and Italian immigration, 14, 18; nativism and intolerance during and after, 17, 23–24, 25–26, 28, 29, 33; parallels with WWII, 22–23; and "patriotic murders," 28, 296n30; and POWs, *fig. 2*, 209; relocation and internment precedents set during, 3, 19, 20, 22, 33, 67, 153, 291; U.S. legal basis for internment, 21–22. *See also* Black Tom; Committee on Public Information (CPI); Prager, Robert; Wilson, Woodrow; Zimmerman telegram

xenophobia, 25, 27, 179

Yellow Book (HUAC), 135, 142, 314n13

yellow peril, 17, 33, 34, 120, 127, 191, 272, 304n8

Yellow Peril (movie), 152

Zimmerman telegram, 32

zones: danger (strategic), 48, 132, 158–59, 180; exclusion (military), *fig. 6*, 124, 196; hemispheric, 214; prohibited, 194; restricted, 134, 183, 184; West Coast as "war zone," 314n16; Zones A and B, 325n24. *See also* Category A and B areas; Military Area No. 1 and No. 2; military areas; Panama Canal (and Zone); restricted areas; western defensive zone

www.ingramcontent.com/pod-product-compliance
Lightning Source LLC
Chambersburg PA
CBHW030345240426
43661CB00052B/1753